Judy & Ruth

Best neighbours
in the world.

Very best wishes

Danny

The Speaker's Chaplain
&The Master's Daughter

The Speaker's Chaplain & The Master's Daughter

A GEORGIAN FAMILY & FRIENDS

Barry Shurlock

~Scholarly Sources~

WINCHESTER

Text of this volume and transcripts of the Letters hosted at
www.winchestercollege.org/archives Barry Shurlock © 2015

barryshurlock@gmail.com

First published in 2015 by Scholarly Sources, 21 Marston Gate,
Winchester, SO23 7DS, UK

A catalogue record for this book is available from the British Library

ISBN 978 0 903330 28 2

Set in Garamond, Printed & bound in Great Britain by Berforts
Information Press, Stevenage, Hertfordshire

Contents

Illustrations & Letters in Text

[19] William Stanley Goddard, an immensely philanthropic successor to Joseph Warton and a protégé of Sarah Williams's father, Thomas Collins.

[20] A 1008-page set of proofs of the ill-fated edition of the works of the Greek historian Polybius that Philip Williams worked on for 37 years.

[21] A long note by Philip Williams, revealing the fear that he and many others had of the 'dangerous turbulence of Democracy'.

[22, 23] Two very different caricatures by James Sayers of Charles Wolfran Cornwall, Philip Williams's patron, and Speaker of the House of Commons: doing business in the House, and 'Gulliver casting a damper upon the royal fireworks at Lilliput'.

[24] Folliott Herbert Walker Cornewall [sic], second cousin of the Speaker of the House of Commons, Charles Wolfran Cornwall and his chaplain before Philip Williams, a portrait of 1813 by William Owen.

[25] Privy Garden, alongside the Palace of Whitehall, where chaplains lodged in the official residence of the Speaker.

[26] The politician Charles Jenkinson, 1st baron Hawkesbury (later the 1st earl of Liverpool), for whom Philip Williams was at one time a private chaplain (an engraving of 1791 by Charles Warren, after Charles Benazech).

[27] The country seat of Charles Jenkinson, Addiscombe House, Croydon, then in Surrey, a frequent haunt of Philip Williams.

[28-31] Some of many people Philip Williams knew in London and elsewhere: Harry Peckham in about 1762, later recorder of Chichester (by Joseph Wright of Derby); Michael Wodhull, minor poet and book collector; Jonathan Shipley, bishop of St Asaph; and Beilby Porteus, bishop of London, and an anti-slaver (mezzotint ca 1800, from portrait by John Hoppner).

[32] The Square, Winchester, 1827, by George Shepherd.

[33] A spoof race card, lampooning Winchester worthies including the grandee Sir Henry Paulet St John Milday, Henry Penton MP, surgeon Joseph Barker, one of 'the tribe' of Earles, attorney John Ridding, draper John Silver, grocer and soap-boiler RH Lloyd and upholder John Crabb.

[34] The theatre opened in Jewry Street (then called Gaol Street), Winchester, in 1785, a print of 1803 by T. Woodfall Villers.

[35] No 11, The Close, Winchester, the prebendal residence allocated to Philip Williams in 1797, when he resigned a stall at Canterbury for one closer to home, though he never occupied the house.

[36] The namesake elder son of Philip and Sarah Williams, who had a successful career as a lawyer, including a spell as the Vinerian Professor of English Law at Oxford (a sketch by George Woodley).

[37] The stern gaze of Charles Williams, the younger son of Philip and Sarah Williams, who pursued a quieter path than his brother, as tutor to the Stanhope family (earls of Chesterfield) and rector of Gedling, Nottinghamshire.

[38] Compton village, near Winchester, in 1735, still with medieval strip farming, a detail from a map by William Burgess of Sir William Heathcote's estate, showing the church and rectory facing each other on opposite sides of Carman's Lane, still so named.

[39] The church of All Saints, Compton, near Winchester, which Philip Williams served as rector for 50 years.

[40] A native of Winchester, George Isaac Huntingford, once a curate at Compton, where he is buried, a warden of Winchester College and successively bishop of Hereford and Gloucester.

[41] Lydiard Park, Lydiard Tregoze, Wiltshire, once the seat of the St John family, an engraving of 1808 by F[rederick] Nash.

[42] A memorial in All Saints church, Compton, near Winchester, to Sarah Williams, who died in child-bed aged 30.

[43] The hatchment of Charlotte Viscountess Bolingbroke (née Collins) in the church of St Mary, Lydiard Tregoze, Wiltshire, who died aged 44 in 1804, estranged from her husband.

[44] The 3rd viscount Bolingbroke, George Richard St John, who married Charlotte Collins, sister of Sarah Williams, and gave her a title, but did little to make her happy. A portrait by John Hoppner.

Original letters in the text

p. 66: Lovelace Bigg (later Bigg-Wither) writing on 23 February 1765 to his friend, Philip Williams, curate of Adderbury, Oxfordshire (Letter 4).

p. 84: The master's daughter, Sarah Williams, writing in early March 1781 to her husband at the Somerset Coffee House in the Strand (Letter 35).

p. 127: The Speaker's chaplain, Philip Williams, writing on 23 July 1785 to his wife, Sarah ('Sally), in Kingsgate Street, Winchester (Letter 110).

p. 145: Mrs Molly Strong, a much-loved maid, writing in June 1803 to Philip and Sarah Williams's daughters, Charlotte and Elizabeth (W197).

p. 162: The Lincoln canon, Dr John Gordon, writing on 31 December 1780 to his stepson, Philip Williams, at Winchester, congratulating him on the birth of his namesake son (Letter 28).

p. 186: Dr John Gordon, writing from Lincoln on 22 September 1787 to his stepson, Phillip Williams, sending his condolences on the death in childbed of his wife Sarah three days earlier (Letter 128)

The Williams Family

PW(I): Revd Philip Williams (1658-1719) - Clergyman, son of the Revd Rice Williams (1617-1671), an Oxford graduate. Educated at St John's College, Cambridge. Married Elizabeth Nalson. Rector of Doddington, Cambridgeshire, in succession to his father-in-law.

PW(II): Dr Philip Williams (1694-1749) - Son of PW(I), who like his father went up to St John's College, Cambridge, where he became President (senior fellow) and Public Orator of the University. In 1729 he was presented to the rectorship of Starston, Norfolk, which he ceded in 1747, having been instituted to Barrow, Suffolk, in 1740. He married Anne Dighton, daughter of Dr John Dighton, rector of Newmarket.

PW(III): Revd Philip Williams (1742-1830) - Son of PW(II) and the principal object of this study, born in 1742 at Starston, Norfolk. Married Sarah Collins, the daughter of the second master at Winchester College, and after her death Helen Ward Fagg, the daughter of a titled Kent clergyman. Fellow of Winchester College, served as Speaker's chaplain and held multiple cathedral and parochial benefices.

PW(IV): Professor Philip Williams KC (1780-1843) - Son of PW(III), a prominent lawyer, King's Counsel, Vinerian Professor of Common Law at Oxford 1824-1843, JP and recorder of Winchester. He married Jane Blachford from a family long-established on the Isle of Wight.

PW(V): Philip Williams (1824-1899) - Nephew of PW(IV), son of the younger son of PW(III) and his wife Sarah, Charles Williams (1784-1866), who married Charlotte Roberts, daughter of a master at Eton College.

PW(VI): Philip Williams (1852-1939) - Son of PW(V), a master at Eton College, 1878-1911, and father of Mrs Edwyn Jervoise (née Lettice Williams).

PW(VII): Philip Williams (1884-1928) - Son of PW(VI), and the end of the dynasty.

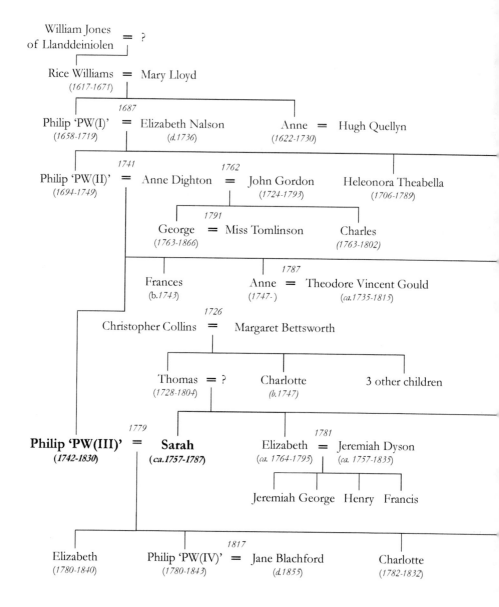

Sarah and Philip Williams
A family tree over nine generations

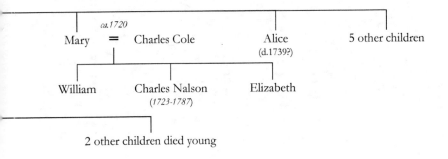

Mary   **=**   Charles Cole *ca.1720*   Alice (d.1739?)   5 other children

William   Charles Nalson *(1723-1787)*   Elizabeth

2 other children died young

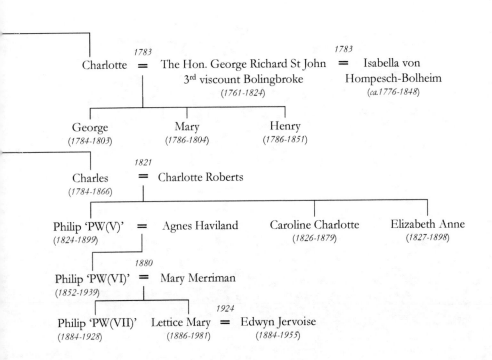

Charlotte **=** *1783* The Hon. George Richard St John 3rd viscount Bolingbroke *(1761-1824)* **=** *1783* Isabella von Hompesch-Bolheim *(ca.1776-1848)*

George *(1784-1803)*   Mary *(1786-1804)*   Henry *(1786-1851)*

Charles *(1784-1866)* **=** *1821* Charlotte Roberts

Philip 'PW(V)' *(1824-1899)* **=** Agnes Haviland   Caroline Charlotte *(1826-1879)*   Elizabeth Anne *(1827-1898)*

Philip 'PW(VI)' *(1852-1939)* **=** *1880* Mary Merriman

Philip 'PW(VII)' *(1884-1928)*   Lettice Mary *(1886-1981)* **=** *1924* Edwyn Jervoise *(1884-1955)*

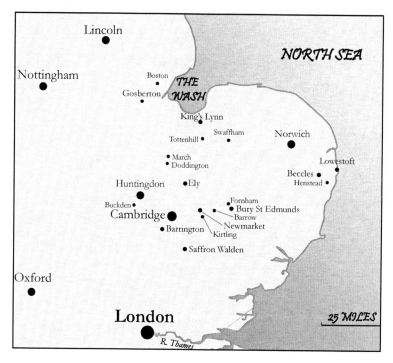

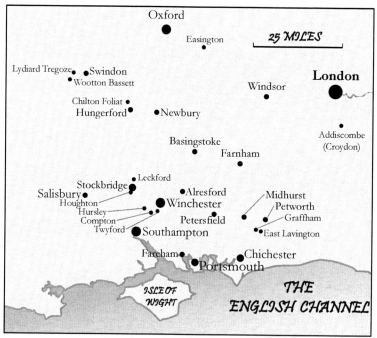

Introduction

THIS VOLUME is based on a collection of letters and related papers on the Revd Philip Williams (1742-1830), his first wife Sarah (ca 1757-1787) and others (*see* pp. ix-xi and Chapter 17). It focuses mainly on 133 letters written between 1760 and 1790, most of them between husband and wife, in the period 1780 to 1787. He was sometime chaplain to the Speaker of the House of Commons, and much more. She was a daughter of a second master of Winchester College, the English public school, founded more than 600 years ago. Until about 50 years ago, the papers passed from member to member of a family that had known seven generations of an eldest son called Philip (*see* p. ix). Subsequently, they were donated to, and now form part of the archives of the College (classmark WCA/M/PW). It is with the permission of the Warden and Fellows, and the huge support of the College Archivist, Suzanne Foster, that I have been able to work on the papers and publish my findings.

I first came across the Williams Papers in a cryptic footnote to a paper by G.H. Blore published privately in the late 1950s (HRO/12M73/Z62). He had taught history at the school and recognised the value of the material, especially the letters to Philip Williams from Sarah. He intended to use them in a larger study of Winchester and its environs in the eighteenth century, but never completed the work. My interests are similar, and so this volume presents the first study of a tranche of the Williams Letters, both in their own right and as an historical source for studies of the mid-Georgian period. Although Philip Williams was not a person of great consequence, he was well educated, well connected, well informed and well travelled. He had a footprint that included London, Oxford, Cambridge and more generally his native East Anglia, as well as his home city of Winchester and many other places. Sarah was an intelligent woman in her own right.

Personal letters are arguably one of the richest forms of historical evidence. Written generally not to be read by others, they often reveal the inner thoughts and feelings of the writer, and incidently give colour and substance to events more baldly recorded elsewhere. The letters of Philip and Sarah Williams, especially hers, are certainly of this kind. In particular they provide intimate insights into the lives of the middling sort of people, the professional class – churchfolk like themselves, academics, lawyers, doctors, minor landowners and the like. As a class they were certainly not poor, but money was always an issue, marriage had to be carefully considered and relationships with anyone who might be able to provide advancement were crucial.

Philip Williams was trying to build a career based on patronage and preferment, which ultimately involved long absences at Westminster. His wife was trying to bring up a family of four in Winchester, coping with her own neurotic tendencies, networking with local acquaintances, as well as keeping face within the walls of Winchester College, where her father – a sensitive soul – struggled to hold his own. They might have been characters in an Austenesque novel, especially as the daughters of one of Philip Williams's closest friends, the lush-named Lovelace Bigg-Wither, were intimates of the novelist-to-be and are a footnote in her letters. In fact, with hindsight, the lives of Philip and Sarah lend themselves to a more believable story than the rather statuesque plots of Jane Austen, and they certainly applied to a larger slice of Georgian England.

The Speaker's Chaplain covers the period from 1760, when Philip Williams was an undergraduate at Oxford, and his first wife was a tiny girl, to 1789, two years after her death. Others letters in the Williams Papers, written between 1797 and 1828, are not covered here in detail, since they relate to a later phase of his life, when he had remarried and was writing to his two spinster daughters. This volume therefore gives a detailed account of his earlier life, and provides background information on several generations of his family, the institutions they served, the localities they occupied and the period in which they lived. This book has been written in the belief that the story it tells impinged on the lives of thousands of the middling sort in Georgian England. The Letters on which it is based have been transcribed and annotated and placed online on the Winchester College Archives website (www.winchestercollege.org/archives).

Sources of this kind for this period have a particular value. Whilst the antics of the *bon ton* and the struggles of the working class have been well studied, the middle classes have received less attention. It is suggested, therefore, that *The Speaker's Chaplain* will be a useful source for social historians and others who wish to cover a broad class spectrum in the late eighteenth century. Janeites (as lovers of the works of Jane Austen are called) may also find much of interest. This volume complements other much quoted sources, such as the letters of Edmond Pyle (Hartshorne,

1905) and John Mulso (Holt-White, 1907), and especially the diaries of Parson James Woodforde published by the eponymous society devoted to him (Winstanley and Jameson, 17 volumes), in which Philip Williams frequently featured during his time at New College, Oxford – not always in a favourable light! His and his wife's letters are rich in worldly detail and, therefore, virtually the antithesis of Woodforde's extensive but every-day scribblings: although they were exact contemporaries at Winchester and Oxford, the parson never married, he lived all his adult life in a small village and he scarcely travelled.

One of the challenges of working on these letters has been the enormous range of people and topics they cover. Tolerance is therefore asked of those with specialist knowledge. Nearly a thousand individuals have been identified who in one way or another, directly or indirectly, came under the quills of Philip and Sarah Williams. It was an acquaintanceship that came from the diaspora of the Church of England and the close networks of Winchester College, the Universities and the West End of London. Mostly it was expressed in social activity, as Philip Williams was by nature as much a 'corporate affairs executive' as a 'finance director'. Even so, his rewards were, by the standards of the day, relatively modest. In many ways, Sarah was more ambitious than he and given the opportunity might have been able to use her undoubted neurotic energy to better ends, as some of her near-contemporaries did, such as Jane Warton, Melesina Trench and Georgiana Hare Naylor (née Shipley).

Major sources which have been especially useful in background research include, for the Universities, Sutherland and Mitchell's *The Eighteenth Century* in the multivolume *History of Oxford University* and Gascoigne's *Cambridge in the Age of Enlightenment*; for the church, Sykes's monumental *Church and State in the XVIIIth Century* and Walsh, Taylor and Haydon's *The Church of England, c.1689–c.1833*; for the Classics, Stray's chapter in Eliot's recent *History of Oxford University Press*; for Winchester College, a succession of works by Kirby, Leach, Adams, de Firth and others, as well as Custance's sixth-centenary commemorative volume; and, for New College, Oxford, Buxton and Williams's authoritative history. The account of the marriage of Charlotte Collins to the Hon. G.R. St John (later the 3rd viscount Bolingbroke) would have been much more sketchy without the articles of Brian Carne and others in the *Reports of the Friends of Lydiard Tregoz*, whilst the lives of Lovelace Bigg-wither and family would probably have slipped into even more obscurity without R.F. Bigg-Wither's *Materials for a History of the Wither Family*, published more than a century ago. As well as these, many other sources have contributed to the story told in this volume, as listed in the Bibliography. Although most have been cited in detail, there are some major ones which have generally been used silently, including the online version of the *Oxford Dictionary of National Biography*, Foster's and Venn and Venn's alumni for Oxford and Cambridge, respectively, the *Oxford English Dictionary,* the Church of England Clergy Database (www.theclergy database.org.uk), British History Online (www.british-history.ac.uk) and the History of Parliament (www.historyofparliamentonline.org). Researching many of the individuals and topics mentioned in the Letters would scarcely have been possible before the advent of the internet. To guard against the pitfalls of electronic media, the information gleaned has, where possible, been traced to source and/or checked against printed authorities.

Finally, for anyone thinking of researching any cache of letters, be warned that it is a task that may at times seem so elephantine that one's whole existence is being taken over. That certainly would be the view of my long-suffering, but immensely supportive wife, Liz! Yet there is probably no better way of entering the lives of people from other periods. For our own lives such sources will not be available, unless a technical and legal framework for reading past emails and other electronic communications is devised and legitimised.

Acknowledgements

I AM IMMENSELY grateful to the many people who have helped me to bring this work to a conclusion, but none more than Suzanne Foster, the Winchester College Archivist, who enthusiastically embraced my first thoughts of working on the William Papers, generously provided me with copies of all the letters and many other documents, helped me to understand the Wiccamical world, commented on various drafts and helped to research the illustrations. In the course of working on the eclectic collection of the Eccles and Fellows' Library at Winchester College, the librarian, Dr Geoffrey Day, discovered that the hand of Philip Williams was still in evidence there and fed me several useful leads. Chief amongst these was a bound copy of the page proofs of Williams's edition of the works of Polybius that ran to more than a thousand pages, but never got to print.

I was first helped to locate the Williams Papers by John Hardacre, then Winchester Cathedral Librarian, who showed me the transcripts made in about 1939 by the local historian John Summers Drew. Many other professionals and expert historians have helped in various ways, including the staff of the Hampshire Record office, especially Sarah Lewin in the early days; Fiona Ainsworth, Royal Botanical Gardens, Kew; Caroline Allington, formerly Collections Manager, Lydiard Tregoze House, Lydiard Tregoze, Wiltshire; Jo Asquith, New College School, Oxford; Anne Buchanan, Local Studies Librarian, Bath; Canon Brian Carne, whose extensive studies of the St John family were invaluable, and Sonia St John, a descendant, who gave some perceptive insights; Fiona Colbert, Archivist, St John's College, Cambridge; R. Cosgrave, Lambeth Palace Library; Will Fenton, Archives Assistant, Cambridgeshire City Council; Amanda Goode, Archivist, Emmanuel College, Cambridge; Alison McCann, Assistant County Archivist, West Sussex; Dr Mary South, who has made a study of smallpox in Winchester and elsewhere in the eighteenth century; Dr Christopher Stray, Honorary Research Fellow, Department of Classics, Swansea University, for advance sight of his contribution on the Classics in the *History of Oxford University Press* (Simon, 2013: vol. II, Chapter 10); Jennifer Thorp, Archivist, New College, Oxford; and Winchester theatre historian Phil Yates. I am also grateful for assistance in finding illustrations to Elaine Arthurs from Lydiard House & Park, Elizabeth Taylor from the National Portrait Gallery and David Rymill from the Hampshire Record Office. Where necessary, copyright is acknowledged in the captions.

As usual, my IT-savvy son, Jon, has employed his skills to solve the layout problems: without him I would have struggled. Over the years my friends Pamela Johnston, Peter Finn and Tony Dowland, have fuelled my interest in the past. And above all, without the support of my wife, Liz, who read many drafts and gave me the benefit of her wisdom, several years of 'Just Williams' would have led nowhere.

BCS, Winchester, September 2014

A Note on the Williams Papers

THE WILLIAMS PAPERS are kept in Winchester College Archives under classmark WCA/M/PW. A detailed account of them, aimed at archivists and researchers, is provided in Chapter 17. The key papers are 130 original letters (plus three from other sources), transcripts of which are all available online at www.winchestercollege.org/archives. They are referred to in this volume as Letter 1, 2 etc, arranged chronologically. All references here to other letters and many other items in the Williams Papers use a truncated citation, so, for example, W395 is an abbreviation for WCA/M/PW/395, where 395 is the piece number in the typescript catalogue of the papers.

As its name suggests, the Concordance of Letters & Piece Numbers of Williams Papers in Appendix I (p. 323) is provided to facilitate cross-reference between the Letter numbers used in this volume and the relevant piece numbers of the Winchester College Catalogue of the Williams Papers.

1. *Welsh Roots, English Foundations*

LIKE SO MANY other families, the Williamses, who originated from North Wales, rose from humble origins to middle-ranking comfort in England. Their rise started in the early seventeenth century, when North Wales had been under English rule since 1284 (11Barrow, 1956), though total English governance throughout the principality was not in place until the late seventeenth century. One much-travelled corridor of achievement led from the Welsh countryside to the Universities. A casual examination of alumni records shows that it was relatively common for men from small Welsh communities to go up to Oxford and Cambridge, often receiving financial support and bed and board as sizars or servitors. Thereafter, advancement might come from academic promotion or a church living, both laced with a hefty dose of politics and patronage. Until 1920, the established church in Wales was the Church of England.

The main correspondent of these letters, Philip Williams (1742-1830), was probably aware of the struggles of his Welsh ancestors, though he had become wholly imbued with advancement English-style at a time when the Enlightenment had not got hold of many minds and Reform was a vague and disturbing idea. Although, like his father, he was well educated, his life had less of an academic tenor and leaned more on the church and preferment. His son was even more involved in worldly affairs and became a successful lawyer. Hereafter, the seven men called Philip Williams will generally be distinguished as indicated on Page ix, though plain 'Philip Williams' is to be taken to mean, Philip Williams (1742-1830).

The Williams family can be traced back in North Wales to the early seventeenth century. It was a link that had practical implications for at least 200 years. When in 1832 PW(IV) declared his landed interests to qualify for a place on the Hampshire Commission of the Peace he included, amongst his holdings, land at Llanwnda, a village about 4 miles south of Caernarfon in the county of Gywnedd (W336; HRO/Q27/3/313). It was from this part of Wales in 1634, from the village of Llanddeiniolen, midway between Bangor and Caenarfon, that Rice (or 'Riese') Williams (1617-1671), son of William Jones, a 'plebeian',

1

set out on the long journey to Christ Church College, Oxford, where he matriculated as a servitor. According to the Williams Papers (W401), after graduating he returned to Wales, to the Isle of Anglesey, where he married Mary Lloyd, a daughter of the Revd Robert Lloyd, rector of Llanfachraeth, together with the nearby villages of Llanyghenedi and Llanfigael. It seems that at first he had a living elsewhere, as in 1660 he was collated to his father-in-law's living. No trace of the church buildings he would have known survive. That at Llanfachraeth is Victorian, that at Llanfigael is thought to date from the eighteenth century and nothing remains at Llanfigael, where the first church had probably been built in the early seventh century (about 50 years before Winchester became a capital and *cathedra* of Wessex, in succession to Dorchester-on-Thames) – and a Victorian church has been removed in its entirety and attached to a church elsewhere! For the last three years of his life Rice Williams held the living of Llandwrog, a village five miles south of Caenarfon.

The Welsh roots of the family intrigued PW(VI) when, at the turn of the nineteenth century, and comfortably installed as a master at Eton College, at the very heart of English privilege, he started to take an interest in his ancestors. It was via an Eton contact, Colonel Henry Howard, that he engaged in a long correspondence with the Lord Lieutenant of Flintshire, H.R. Hughes of Kimnel Park, Abergele, North Wales, whose knowledge of Welsh genealogy was profound. He gently directed his correspondent towards the right sources, navigated him round the complexities of Welsh customs, and untangled for him the many parishes whose name began with 'Llan'. It was he who traced the family back to William Jones, of humble origin, whose son Rice founded a dynasty of academics, clerics and professional men that lasted well into the 20th century.

It was Hughes who also raised the idea that the son of Rice Williams, PW(I), had been spurred by an awareness of the career of John Williams (1582-1650), archbishop of York and much else, whose portrait hung in the hall of St John's College, Cambridge. He was an ambitious and successful Welshman of noble birth, seated at the houses of Cochwillan and Penrhyrn, near Bangor, who had risen to great heights (before falling!). It was quite likely, suggested Hughes, that it was from him that the Williams family, with no formal justification, had taken the custom of bearing the arms of Ednyfed Vychan, a celebrated Welsh warrior and seneschal to the Kingdom of Gwynned, from whom Owen Tudor and the Tudor royal dynasty descended. The coat-of arms which is at the head of the memorials to Philip Williams and his wife in the church at Compton, Hampshire, bears three heads, which are said to represent those of the

English nobles that Ednyfed Vychan claimed in one battle (Bezzant Lowe, 1912, p. 355). A similar motif was used as a bookplate and surmounts the tomb of his aunt Heleonora Theabella Williams in Ely cathedral (W309, 414).

Hughes wrote (W272/1):

> Philip the 1st [1668-1719], finding himself with a good education, holding English preferment, and in a better social position than his father, might have desired a coat of arm[s] – either for a Seal, or a Bookplate, or to impale with those of the Lady he married. ...

No family of the day liked to lose its perceived right to bear arms, but as the correspondence wore on, PW(VI) was persuaded to do so. In a later letter, Hughes wrote (W286):

> I admire your resolution to abandon the Coat of Arms which has been born[e] by several generations of your family unless you can provide your right to it. Few people would have the courage to do this!

Referring to 'our friend Colonel Howard', he added coyly:

> Between ourselves, he is one of those persons who bear arms which he is not entitled to. His ancestor was a joiner in the town of Conway; but he bears the well known arms of Howard!

***

THE REVEREND Rice Williams's son, PW(I), followed a similar path to his father, except that left Wales to go up to Cambridge, as a sizar at St John's College, where he graduated MA in 1681. He advanced his position by becoming curate to a prominent author and polemicist of the day, Dr John Nalson (ca 1637-1686), also a St John's alumnus, who held the living of Doddington, Cambridgeshire. In 1668, Nalson had married Alice Peyton and succeeded her father, the Revd Algernon Peyton, as rector of Doddington, in the same way that PW(I) was to succeed him. At various times, the men of the Peyton family served as Members of Parliament for Cambridgeshire. The link with the Williams family continued for some years, as shown by a letter of 1725 from Florence written to PW(II) by Thomas Peyton (W1). Until 1856, when it was split into seven rectories, Doddington was the largest parish in England and, with the draining of the Fens, became 'the best benefice in the diocese of Ely, being well worth £600 per annum' (Thoresby Society, 1912, vol 21, p 92).

Nalson was ambitious for preferment and would have been a model for the Williams family to follow. His ODNB entry, written by R. C. Richardson, portrays him as exemplifying 'the ecclesiastical rivalries of his day, the deeply ingrained prejudices against nonconformists and Roman Catholics, the inseparable connections between religion and politics in the age of party, and the enduring legacy of the civil wars.' He notes that modern historians have variously depicted Nalson as 'almost a caricature of the frenzied Tory clergyman of Charles II', 'one of the original and noisiest defenders of Charles's reputation', but nonetheless 'an authority'. He was a prolific author: when the Williams Papers were given to Winchester College, they were accompanied by *The Countermine* (London, 4 ed., 1684), a book by Nalson on 'the dangerous principles, and secret practices of the dissenting party… shewing that religion is pretended, but rebellion in intended'. A major work was his two-volume *An Impartial Collection of Great Affairs of State* (1682-3), which was probably aimed at helping him into high office in the church. Richardson comments:

> Nalson exemplifies many of the characteristics of the Anglican church of his day, not least the way its structure was underpinned by patronage and place-seeking, clerical dynasties, and extended networks.

These were characteristics that were to be wholeheartedly embraced by the men of the Williams family. But Nalson exemplified the fact that the gifts of such practices were not easily gained: for him, the only preferment, a prebend at Ely, was not acquired until two years before his death at Doddington on 24 March 1686, at the young age of 49.

During the last few years of Nalson's life PW(I) was his curate (W238) and in 1685, just before his death, was presented to Doddington by the minor patron and nephew of Nalson's wife, Sir Sewster Peyton (with his guardian Henry Oxborough). Within 18 months, PW(I) had married one of Nalson's daughters, Elizabeth (W251). They had twelve children, of which only five survived, and only one of then a son (Clanchy, 1970, W238). PW(I) served the parish until his death in 1719, making registers that were, apparently, 'orderly kept and beautifully written'. His hand is exemplified in the Williams Papers by love letters to Elizabeth of 1687, and a book of prayers in a miniature script (W349-352A, 416-417). One letter he wrote to her starts (W351; Clanchy, 1970):

My heart could not suffer the messenger to return from hence without commissioning my Pen to tell you how eagerly it flies every moment to its dear treasure, and could it speak without me it would prevent my Pen & you might hear it softly whisper into your ears some of those grateful resentments which y[ou]r Pity and compassionate goodness has inspired it with.

Other items that have survived are copies of PW(I)'s will (dated 19 October 1715, probate 22 September 1719; W219) and his wife's (dated 29 March 1733, probate 1 April 1736; W220). A black marble tablet in the south aisle of the choir of Ely cathedral carries an inscription to Elizabeth Nalson and her daughter Alice , who died three years after her in 1739, and was 'Possessed of the amiable Virtues of her most excellent Parents' (Bentham, 1812, appendix, p. 49; W310). The inscription says of the couple, Philip Williams's grandparents:

They lived thirty years together,
Constantly employed in works of Piety,
Charity, and Hospitality.

Whatever else PW(I) did, he laid the ground rules for his descendants, probably apeing his father-in-law. Like so many others, it became a family in which preferment, nepotism, the old boy network and favouritism all flourished and allowed it to enjoy a relatively comfortable and secure status. The Welsh Williams had learned that the way to advancement for a man without aristocratic advantages was an Oxbridge education, a prudent marriage, and good connections with those who might be minded to recommend preferment. A tory tilt, rather than the perceived waywardness of whiggism also did no harm. And significantly, such security did not depend in any way whatsoever on what hindsight knows to be the growing motor of the times – no members of the Williams family were ever scientists, engineers, or entrepreneurs. Nor were they artists, writers, explorers, or epic travellers - excepting perhaps Philip Williams's tour of the Highlands (*see* Chapter 3)!

***

AFTER SCHOOL in Huntingdon, PW(II), like his father, went up to St John's College, Cambridge, in 1710 on a 'county grant', as the Platt Scholar for Cambridgeshire. It was a college favoured by the well-born with generous stipends for fellows (Gascoigne, 1989, pp. 16, 22). Here he followed a college career that showed that the Williams family had firmly established itself in the English establishment. As an undergraduate and young fellow, he would have known a college that was arch-tory in its politics, supporting nonjurors and the divine rights of kings, against attempts of a post-Revolution government to remove fellows with such views from the college. On which side of the debate he stood is not known, but from about 1727 he might have experienced a change, as St John's underwent a transition towards whig politics (Beales, 2011, pp.177-92).

For a church living he turned in 1729 to Sir Rowland Hill Bt, who had purchased the advowson of Starston, Norfolk, about 20 miles east of Thetford, from the duke of Norfolk, but was tied to appoint a fellow of St John's (Blomefield, 1808, pp 344-51). Although the family link is not obvious, it was evidently quite close, as Sir Rowland was a sponsor of the baptism of PW(II)'s son, Philip, in 1742. Even though PW(III) was to go up to Oxford, he must always have been aware of his father's achievements at Cambridge and the roots the family had put down in that part of the country. His letters are certainly laced with Fenland news!

PW(II) was sometime president – or senior fellow – of St John's and in 1730, the year in which he graduated Doctor of Divinity, was appointed public orator of Cambridge University. The post, which dates from 1522 and still exists, was meagrely rewarded, but held a not-inconsiderable status, according to Tanner (1917, p. 47):

> The Orator was to have precedence of all other Masters of Arts, and, as a mark of honour, to walk in processions and sit in public acts separate from the rest; but the stipend attached to this dignified office was only forty shillings a year.

The letters that all public orators wrote, in Latin, up to 1867, have been transcribed and preserved in the Cambridge University Registry in three volumes entitled *Epistolae Academicae* (Tanner, ibid). The post required holders to act as a sort of master of ceremonies and intellectual policeman. Former orators included the poet George Herbert, who served between 1618 and 1628 (*George Herbert Journal* 2003/4;27:53-66). The OED defines the post as:

> ...an officer of the Universities of Oxford and Cambridge, whose functions are to speak in the name of the University on State occasions; to go in person, when required, to plead the cause of

the University; to write suitable addresses, letters of congratulation or condolence; to introduce candidates for honorary degrees, and to perform other like duties.

Thus, PW(II) contested William Broome, a poet and translator, on his authorship of a sermon, and he demanded that Conyers Middleton, a clergyman and the Woodwardian Professor of Geology at Cambridge, recant his attack on a Dr Waterland, a respected Anglican (ODNB). PW(II) had hoped to follow Dr Robert Lambert as Master of St John's in 1735, but failed to be elected, though he was 'generally esteemed to be a very worthy, upright man, and seemed as much calculated for the post he aimed at, and deserved, as he that attained it' (Nichols, 1812, 1, p 553). His opponent was John Newcome, the Lady Margaret Professor of Divinity (founded by Lady Margaret Beaufort, mother of the first Tudor monarch, Henry VII, and foundress at Cambridge of the colleges of St John's and Christ's). The antiquary Cole noted:

> The votes being much upon a par, and neither party willing to yield, the *flying squadron*, as it was then called, managed matters...

It appears that six crucial votes swung towards Newcome and PW(II) was therefore defeated (Baker, 1869, p. 1033). It is likely that he suffered because of his tory leanings: even before the pious whig champion Thomas Holles, duke of Newcastle, became chancellor in 1748, Cambridge in general, and St John's in particular, were becoming strongholds of whig politics. Also, although the University ethos incurred a strong belief in the power of mathematics, about 60 per cent of alumni took holy orders and the divinity chair of Newcome was therefore a powerful force (Gascoigne, 1989, pp. 17, 21).

In 1740 PW(II) was instituted to the rectorship of Barrow, Suffolk, and in the following year he did what so many academically disappointed dons did, he resigned his college post and married; the marriage articles, dated 25 May 1741, still survive (W221). It was a lucrative living (rated at more than £23 in the King's Books of 1535) and by a bequest of an ancestor of the previous incumbent, Henry Boughton, was destined for the 'senior divine' of the college, though this led to some controversy (Torry, 1888, pp. 61, 79). His bride was Anne Dighton, a woman 30 years his junior, a daughter of Dr John Dighton (ca 1680-1752), vicar of Wood Ditton, Cambridgeshire, and rector of St Mary's church, Newmarket, Suffolk, and his wife Elizabeth (née Janes). Not unexpectedly, contemporary opinion regarded it 'as rather a disproportionate match in point of age' (Nichols, 1812, 1, p. 553).

Barrow was only a few miles from the home of his bride-to-be, Newmarket, though the couple seem to have started their married life at Starston, in distant Norfolk, where he had held the living since 1729. They lived there for at least two years, as witnessed by the birth of Philip Williams in 1742, though his sister, Frances, came into the world the next year at Barrow. There were two more children, but only Anne survived. The delay in moving from Starston was no doubt due to the building of a new parsonage house at Barrow, which several sources report to have cost the new rector £1000 of his own money. He may have then have come under pressure from his college to relinquish Starston, but held on until 1746 when, after unsuccessfully canvassing the earl of Suffolk for the mastership of Magdalen College, Cambridge (W322), he drew on his late father's connections with the Peytons of Doddington. Thus in 1746 he resigned Starston and was presented to the living of Sutton St Mary, Long Sutton, Lincolnshire, about 10 miles west of King Lynn, by Bridget Peyton (acting with the consent of her trustees, Richard Dashwood and John Lambert), which he held *in absentia* until his death in 1749 (pers. comm. Fiona Colbert, St John's College). This was a throwback to the time of his father, who had been patronised by the Peyton family. He seems to have harked back to the days of his youth, as he made a bequest to the poor of March, held with the living of Doddington, as recorded in a inscription in the chapel there, according to the antiquary Cole (W237)

***

PHILIP WILLIAMS must have known his father and recalled the obvious anxiety that surrounded his early death and his mother's widowhood, but it is unlikely that a disappointed don turned parson, aged 56 when he died, would have had a close relationship with a young boy of 7. PW(II) probably died from cancer, described by Cole as 'an ulcer in his kidney, [which]…was opened to see what his complaint was and [then he was] buried in his church at Barrow…' (BL Add MSS 5883, cited in W321). A memorial inscription on the south wall of the church at Barrow records what must have been regarded as his greatest attributes (BL, Add MSS 19,166, cited in the Biographical Archive of St John's College, typescript):

> He was a distinguished tutor of St John's College [,] Public Orator of the University of Cambridge and an admired preacher. An exemplary follower of those doctrines which it was the uniform

study of his life to illustrate and explain. ... he left 3 children Philip Franc[e]s and Ann to deplore the loss of an excellent parent.

During the young boy's early years the most important person in his life must have been his mother, still in her mid-20s when widowed. With her husband in the grave at Barrow, his living was soon in the hands of a new rector, Dr John Green, the senior divine at St John's College (John Gascoigne, 'John Green', ODNB), who later became bishop of Lincoln. Mrs Anne Williams (who was to marry a future chaplain of Green's, John Gordon) was left with the task of bring up Philip and two sisters, Frances (or 'Fanny'), aged 6, and Anne (or 'Nanny'), aged 2. How she managed it and where she lived in the years immediately after the death of her husband is not clear. Did she perhaps return to the fold of the Dighton family in Newmarket, or, as sources suggest, take lodgings in Cambridge? Whatever happened, she benefitted from the terms of the marriage settlement with her first husband and his will, under which she received rents from small Fenland estates, which had once belonged to her father, Dr John Dighton (Letter 10). She might have done better, but a house of his in Newmarket had had to be mortgaged under a decree in chancery to pay the 'fortunes' of her sister-in-law, Miss Heleonora Theabella Williams ('Aunt Bell'). Even so, the estate rents apparently yielded sufficient for her to give Philip an allowance, though it was not all plain sailing. The problems of rent collecting surfaced in a letter she wrote to her son in 1760, two years before she remarried (Letter 1):

> I was in great hopes to have sent you your quarter's allowance the instant it was due, but have met with such unexpected disappointments from my tenants as has made me incapable of doing it, which has fretted me very much; but hope a very few days will produce the cash, and then you may depend upon hearing from me the minute I receive it.

She also made clear in the letter that she had not entirely made up her mind about her second husband-to-be, John Gordon. In 1758 he had been instituted to a living at Henstead, Suffolk, southeast of Beccles and a few miles from the coast. Like Philip Williams's father, he had presumably decided it was time to pitch his ambitions outside the University and get some family life. She was about to pay a visit to his parish and was obviously inclined to accept his solicitations:

You know I hinted this to you when you was home, I hope if I do it will be for the mutual happinesse – of us all, as I think we shall be able to live very confortably on our join[t] incomes, keep a post chaise, a couple of men, and appear genteelly, which I think will be far preferable to the way of life I am at present in, and as to you, and your sisters, I give you my word and honour, it is a match {which} will not ~~at all strai~~ in the least alter or straighten your circumstances, and I believe you know so much of the generosity of Mr Gordon's disposition, that was I bad enough to desire to injure my children, he would not suffer it, and as to your sisters I think it will be better for them, than continuing at Cambridge.

Two years later, in June 1762, the knot was tied in Cambridge. Despite the bustle of a marriage ceremony, she found the time to scribble a note to her son (Letter 2), assuring him that 'the change of name can never make the least change of affection in me to my Dearest Phil, who I am convinced will still continue that same duty and affection to his old Parent with a proper quantity to his new one, who from his great honour and generosity of behaviour, I may justly say has the strictest claim to it both and the whole family.'

The sentiments were buttressed by his new-found stepfather, who was clearly overwhelmed by the event, but managed to add a note to the same letter, which he admitted was the 16th he had written that day:

We're in a devilish hurry that's the truth on't – so no more from thy aged PARENT as thy pious mother stiles me, but that I would have thee look upon me in the same light thou hast hitherto done – thine as before.

2. *Wykeham's Twin Gifts*

BY THE MID-EIGHTEENTH century the Williams family had migrated from North Wales into England, with the Church of England as the means and the Universities as staging posts, at first Oxford and then, more deeply, Cambridge. When the time came to set the stage for young Philip Williams, then living with his widowed mother in Cambridge, it was to Winchester College that he was propelled, and then on to New College, Oxford. This set the track that he was to follow for the rest of his life: it shaped his mentality, prescribed his close friends, gave him his magnum opus (*see* Chapter 4) and ushered him into mid-Hampshire. Narrow though this world was, he was fortunate in having family and friends in Cambridge and the Fens, London and elsewhere, as well as having an obvious love of travel and an involvement with college, cathedral and parish, and even parliament. As with some of the more fortunate of his contemporaries, this multifaceted experience probably gave him a relaxed attitude to life and the ability to move easily in all ranks of society.

In 1755, at the age of 13, Philip Williams was elected a scholar of Winchester College, situated in the city of that name, the capital of the county of Hampshire (then called the county of Southampton). The importance of this event cannot be overemphasised. How he came to be elected is a puzzle, but the nature of the ancient institution he entered was to determine almost every aspect of his life and to become the 'comfort bubble' within which he moved until he died. The school, which has the longest continuous history of any in England, was founded in 1382 by William of Wykeham, bishop of Winchester and chancellor to Edward III and Richard II. Despite his name, he lived as a boy not in the Hampshire village of Wickham, but in nearby Bishop's Waltham, where the bishop of Winchester had a palace. Winchester College was designed as a feeder school for New College, Oxford, founded three years earlier, and as such set a pattern for later schools: until modern times, it was the custom of many Oxbridge colleges, in a non-formulaic way, to forge links with schools and take their most able pupils. Many of these schools are not well known, unlike Eton College, the British institution, which aped Winchester College and became a feeder school for King's College, Cambridge. Founded at the behest of Henry VI, it used Wykeham's statutes and even took some Winchester scholars and the head master of the school at the time, William Waynflete, to set up the new institution.

Once at Winchester, Philip Williams would have entered a world where tradition was paramount and where for nearly 400 years young boys had been educated, mainly in the Classics. For those with the means, education had always involved a choice between being taught by a private tutor 'at home' or attending a school in the company of others of like age, generally selected for intellectual promise. In England, before the advent of state-funded education, such establishments came to be called public schools (a term that might better have been reserved for schools funded from the public purse!). Those schools with the greatest reputations drew their pupils from throughout the kingdom and therefore had to offer boarding facilities. The carefully worded charter that William of Wykeham drew up at the time of the school's foundation was subsequently treated as 'gospel' and followed like a 'management manual'.

The main purpose of Wykeham's foundations at Oxford and Winchester was to provide a steady stream of well-educated young men fit to enter the church – which then encompassed many of the functions which might today be the preserve of parliamentarians or civil servants. Its statutes laid down in immense detail a constitution and the way in which it should be governed. Thus, the establishment of Winchester College was to consist of a warden and ten fellows, two masters, three chaplains, two lay clerks, sixteen choristers (or quiristers) and seventy scholars. Admission was moderated by means of a cursory viva voce undertaken in the Election Chamber by senior members of both the school and New College. T. A. Trollope, brother of the novelist, recalled the process (1887, vol 1, p. 97, quoted by Clarke, 1912, p. 175):

> Examiner: Well, boy, can you sing?
> Candidate: Yes, sir.
> Examiner: Let us hear you.
> Candidate (*singing*): All people that on earth do dwell…
> Examiner: Very well, boy. That will do!

This process was echoed by Sarah Williams, who recorded the plight of 'young Bowers' (Letter 66):

... I am afraid [he was] very stupid, as he could say nothing for his task but two lines out of the accidence [the rudiments of Latin grammar]; he is designed for the sea so it does not much signify.

However, her assessment of the boy was wide of the mark: Henry Bower (1773-1840) was admitted a scholar to Winchester, went on to Queen's College, Oxford, and became vicar of Taunton and chaplain to the earl of Rosebery (www.kittybrewster.com/bower/ bower.htm). The reality was, as Firth concluded (1961, p. 33):

By the eighteenth century, that golden age of private patronage, the examination [for a Winchester scholarship] had become a pure form, and nomination on private grounds the reality.

The charade was part of Election Week, when each year at the end of the summer term the warden of New College, Oxford, assisted by 'posers' or examiners, came down to Winchester College to admit boys as scholars to the school, as well as choosing 'probationary fellows' for New College, from a roll of senior pupils regarded as ready to go up. Priority for both institutions was given to 'founder's kin', that is, those who could prove descent from William of Wykeham. Next in line for a place at the school were those who lived in localities where it held properties, then, in order, from the diocese of Winchester, from counties in the south and south-east of England, plus Cambridgeshire, and finally from the rest of the country (Aylmer: In Custance, p. 287). In practice 'this rule, [which was] completely superseded after the Reformation by the rapidly developing system of simple patronage, was at no time strictly enforced...' (Firth, p. 31). In addition to scholars, the masters could take on 'commoners', who paid fees and shared some of the teaching and mentoring given to scholars. They lived outside the hub of the college, in 'houses' made available by the masters, notably in buildings called Old Commoners, and later New Commoners. In the eighteenth century they rarely outnumbered the scholars, but by the nineteenth century and beyond, the system mushroomed —essentially for financial reasons — so that the original complement of 70 scholars became dwarfed by a huge number of commoners, living in houses scattered around the old school. Today it has almost 700 pupils.

In 1755, Philip Williams was 12th on the roll of 14 scholars elected, including two founder's kin (Kirby, 1888, pp. 252-253). The election total was close to the average in the eighteenth century of about 16 scholars each year (ibid, p. xvii). The electors from New College were the warden

John Purnell and two posers, Banks and Pye, and from Winchester, warden John Coxed, vice-warden Thomas Cheyney and head master John Burton. First on the election list was Benjamin Bathurst, admitted as founder's kin – though now known to be based on a false pedigree (Squibb, 1972) – who left after three years. Then Charles Fanshaw, also founder's kin, who went up to New College and graduated MA. Of the twelve other scholars, five went up to New College, which was close to the average annual number of six (Alymer, In: Custance, p. 283), and five to other Oxford colleges. One left the school after three years and another after the same period was superannuated (i.e. reached an age when he *had* to leave), as he had been admitted late and reached his eighteenth year. All those who went up to Oxford graduated, and two went on to a doctorate. Of the twelve scholars, two became clergymen and two fellows of Winchester College, including Philip Williams who fell into both of these categories.

Presumably Philip Williams made the long journey from Cambridge to Winchester for the election and then again for the start of term. He might have recognised the scene sketched by a future warden of New College, Philip Shuttleworth (quoted in Locke, 1912, p.171):

> Now gives Mama her last caressing,
> And fond Papa bestows his blessing.
> These sweet endearments scarcely o'er,
> The chaise drives rattling to the door.

Mrs Anne Williams, her first husband long dead, may have been relieved to see her boy going off to a reputable establishment, but in fact Winchester at the time was way behind its rivals, Eton and Westminster. One historian has suggested that its 'slow growth and relative unimportance' compared with Eton 'was surely due in part at least to the absence of Founder's Kin' at the latter (Aylmer; In Custance, p. 282). One harsh assessment is that 'for 300 years after the Reformation Winchester as a school really has no history to relate of any public significance...' (Firth, 1961, p.56, quoted by Aylmer, ibid, p. 281). As late as 1853, a Wykehamist wrote of being 'plunged straight into the Middle Ages' when he entered the school (Fearon, 1924, p.2).

Young Williams would quickly have been subject to the attentions of Dr John Burton as head master and Dr Joseph Warton as second master. He would have entered into a routine recalled by many Wykehamists: thus he would have worn a Scholar's gown, eaten in Hall, been taught in the seventeenth-century building called School, except in the summer when he might have taken the air and lessons in the Cloisters (barred to boys after 1780) or in the 'children's airing ground' in College Meads, trooped up to 'Hills' (St Catherine's Hill), drunk water from the Logie stream, prayed in Chapel, and slept in a room off Chamber Court. And he would have mastered 'notions', the slang and jargon by which members of the school described the physical elements of the buildings and grounds and the strict patterns of domestic life, work and play that were followed (Stevens, 1998, London). For example, 'Toytime' was prep or homework, 'Scob' a chest or desk, and 'Div', a class or form. He would also have known the fagging system, as depicted much later in *Tom Brown's Schooldays*, based on Rugby School and published in 1857, whereby junior boys acted as 'valets' for seniors. There was a complex system of command at Winchester, which had a total of 18 prefects in College (that is, that part of the school and its life involving scholars, but not commoners), headed by 'Aul: Prae:' , an abbreviation for Aulae Praefectus, or Prefect of Hall, who was the head boy of the school. Philip Williams obviously mastered the system well, as he ended his schooldays in 1759 as Aul: Prae.

Like all masters before them, Burton and Warton took advantage of a provision of the statutes which allowed them to take, for fees and at their discretion, boys who were not subjected to examination. These were the commoners (*commensales*), of which ten could be noblemen (*extranei*). They lodged outside the main school site, either with Warton in a part of the extramural campus called Old Commoners, or, in the case of young aristocrats in college, under the same roof as Burton. When Burton and his young men visited Chilbolton, in the Test valley, in 1731 their host, The Hon. Mrs Sarah Osborn, wrote to her brother about it (Osborn, 1890, p. 45, quoted by Leach, 1899, p. 375):

> ...we had Dr. Burton, the Master of Winchester School, and his ten young noblemen's sons that live with him, for which he has £200 a year for each, and is as a private governour to them, and they also have the advantage of a publick school at the same time, which surely must be a fine way of educating them.

One of the noblemen, David Lord Elcho, who spent twelve to sixteen days travelling down from his ancestral home, Wemyss Castle, in the county of Fife, did not share her optimism. He wrote (Ewald, 1904; Charteris, 1907, quoted by Clarke, 1912, pp. 168-70):

We did not learn Latin and Greek as well as we should have done had we been placed with a private tutor, but we were taught how to live as men of the world which, if cultivated, could be very useful to us in after life.

Only ten years before Philip Williams entered Winchester, the same Lord Elcho had lent Prince Charlie £1000 (never repaid) and joined the '45 rebellion, for which he was attainted. In fact, the reputation of the school in the first half of the century had been tarnished by Jacobitism and pitched battles between Jacobites and 'Georgites' were common. Burton was apparently a Jacobite and the second master in the time of Elcho, Christopher Eyre, a Hanoverian. Political leanings continued to be reflected in the fate of masters, as in the case of Samuel Speed – a very active second master – who was forced to resign for being too whiggish, thereby providing an opportunity for Joseph Warton, who arrived in December 1755 with his wife and family. It was not an easy job and politics was rarely far away. In the early 1760's, for example, he faced the tricky problem of looking after two sons of John Stuart, 3rd earl of Bute, tutor to George III, who had sent them to the school as commoners. Bute was a close relative of the Pretender and a deeply unpopular, if shortlived prime minister; in 1762 the controversial libertarian, John Wilkes is reported to have harangued – even bullied – one of the boys in a 'bookseller's shop' in Winchester (Cash, 2006, p. 75) – it could have been P.& G. Wells, which was established by the 1750s (pers. comm. Crispin Drummond) and still stands a short walk from Winchester College.

Warton was probably the person who more than anyone had day-to-day contact with Philip Williams during the years 1755-60, when he was a pupil. A twentieth century history master at the school, G.H. Blore, gave a loving portrait of the second master, to whom he dedicated his *Some Wykehamists of the Eighteenth Century*, published in 1944:

> As a schoolmaster he had his weaknesses. He had blind spots in Greek and Latin grammar, and was even corrected in class. In the exercise of discipline he was hissed by unruly pupils. But his early poems still have charm, his notes on Virgil and his criticisms of Pope are still of value, and by his revival of interest in Spenser and the romantic poets he showed himself ahead of his generation. His Winchester pupils and his Oxford friends continued to love him throughout his life.

When young Williams entered the school it was not in great shape. One assessment is that: 'In the eighteenth century Winchester School attained the height of glory and the depths of depressions' (Leach, 1899, p.367). As Burton himself put it in 1763, reciting the names of former wardens:

> In Warden Dobson's time [1724-30] we were in the height of glory. In Bigg's time [1731-40], a very different man, we just supported ourselves. In Coxed's time [1740-57], we sunk to nothing. In the late Warden Golding's time [1757-63], we began to rise…

As mentioned above, Winchester was probably hindered by its insistence on founder's kin, generally referred to as C.F., or *Consanguineus Fundatoris*. At any one time at each of both Winchester and New College, the statutes allowed for eighteen 'poore, pious and hopeful' kinsmen, although in 1651 this was extended – in principle, but not in fact - to twenty (Squibb, 1972, p. 42). An authoritative list of known founder's kin at Winchester covers more than five pages (ibid., pp. 188-194). Amongst these are members of several families that in fact should never had received the privilege, including the Bathursts, who 'profited from…[a] false pedigree of 1729', namely, Robert in 1742, Allen in 1744, Benjamin in 1755, Henry in 1756, Charles William in 1767, another Robert in 1769, another Henry in 1793, another Benjamin in 1797, and finally Robert Andrew in 1827.

Evidence on founder's kin given to a Royal Commission in 1852 was scathing (Squibb, 1972, p. 115):

> It is notorious that the Founder's Kin at Winchester have been the least distinguished boys in the school… [as] indicated by the common Winchester proverb, "as thick as a Founder"…

This was not, of course, always the case; Martin Wall, for example, who was elected to Winchester as founder's kin in 1760, went on to become a distinguished physician at Oxford, holding the Lichfield professorship of clinical medicine for thirty-nine years. And Henry Bathurst, elected in 1756 – the year after Philip Williams – became bishop of Norwich. And detailed analysis of the entries in the ODNB has shown that, in practice, the system may not have been as bad as the Victorians thought (Custance, 1982.

It was not only Wykeham's foundations that bowed to founder's kin; the practice was widespread (Squibb, 1972, p. 3):

That a substantial proportion or even a majority of the members of a college or school might owe their positions to the accident of family connections was accepted with little question as a fact of academic life for half a millennium. Although questioning began in the eighteenth century, it was not until the nineteenth that it became insistent enough to lead to action.'

The privileges of Wykeham's kin to a scholarship at Winchester, and priority on the roll of leavers seeking a place at New College, Oxford, were abolished by parliament in 1857 and 1854, respectively.

Long before the eighteenth century the wardenship and fellowships of Winchester, and associated church livings, had become well remunerated positions open only to ordained ex-pupils (Wykehamists), and were often more avidly sought than similar positions at the universities. Indeed, from the end of the seventeenth century, until 1757, when the pattern was broken, the warden of New College automatically assumed the wardenship of Winchester when it became available. A newly appointed Winchester prebendary, Edmund Pyle, explained the scenario at the time to his correspondent, Dr Samuel Kerrich (Hartshorne, 1905, p. 302):

> ...the Heads of New College has [sic] not studied or cared for, anything, for many years, but making, & keeping up an interest in their fellows; in order to be, by them, elected to the Headship [he means the Wardenship] of Winton, in case of a vacancy. So that learning has been got, or not, just as young men were of themselves inclined; all discipline is lost, & sometimes there has not been so much as a tutor in the college [i.e. New College], to instruct those, who, after two years were to be Fellows of it.

In interpreting this passage, it should be noted that 'fellows' were senior undergraduates. The laxness at Oxford sketched by Pyle, and the treatment of Winchester as a convenient 'cash cow' had implications for the sort of education that Philip Williams knew, at least in his early years. The fact is that involvement of the Warden and fellows in the day-to-day activities of the school was virtually zero; the real work was done by a head master and the second master, as the charter stipulated. The governing body of the school, which had weathered the storm of the Reformation, was therefore semi-monastic in constitution, without any of the disadvantages of a cloistered life. This issue was, of course, in essence, the theme of *The Warden* published in 1855 by Anthony Trollope (a Wykehamist, and one with extremely unhappy memories), with the difference that the corrupt institution he had in mind was the Hospital of St Cross, Winchester, or its equivalent elsewhere. In the same letter, Pyle outlined the set-up that Philip Williams experienced:

> ... Winchester College (where the Warden of New College is visitor, to all intents & purposes, of the school [formally, the visitor was the bishop of Winchester]), the Warden and ten fellows, have swallowed up so much of the revenue, that an education of that foundation, designed by W. of Wykeham to be almost without charge, is become so expensive, that few persons of very good fortunes can afford to send a son thither.

Philip Williams was to achieve a deep knowledge of 'the revenue' many years later, when he acted as a bursar, and thereby supported – tacitly or otherwise – a system of governance that was systemically corrupt. As Bell remarks (In Custance, 1982, p. 353):

> The evidence against the warden and fellows for appropriating to themselves a disproportionate amount of the collegiate revenue, thus feathering their nest with nearly half the income and leaving the educational side of the school scandalously under-provided, is overwhelming.

When the Public Schools Commission looked into the matter in the early 1860s they decided that fellows who did not reside in the school did nothing of benefit for it, yet took home a large part of the income and could be dispensed with without being 'injurious' to its interests (Anon, 1861, *Report of the Public Schools Commission*, III, 327; quoted by Custance: In Custance, 1982,. p. 347). In 1868, these old practices were swept away by the Public Schools Act.

In retrospect, therefore, the lot of masters Burton and Warton was not a happy one: they had no reliable salary, were burdened with founder's kin and short-changed by the warden and fellows. However, it is doubtful that they ever thought of themselves like this – it was, after all, the norm at Winchester and was not very different at many other schools. Although the masters crammed in the essentials of a gentleman's education, especially the Classics, their real passion was English literature, especially poetry, and it has even been suggested that Winchester at this time presaged the Romantics. It fostered poets such as Robert Lowth (professor of poetry at Oxford), poet laureate William Whitehead, and Williams Collins of Chichester, although only Collins (whose verse was once recited on the Winchester stage; Viveash & Lefroy, 2009, pp.106-113) is likely to be found in modern anthologies Whitehead recalled his time at the school:

> …the Muses revel'd most,
> When Bigg presided and when Burton taught.

Joseph Warton was the son and brother of professors of poetry at Oxford (which still appoints a Thomas Warton Professor of English Literature) and a poet and literary critic in his own right. He had been ordained, but took to schoolmastering as he lacked patronage. His style, rather light and whimsical, is apparent in *Ode to a Lady who Loves the Town better than the Country*, in which, incidentally, he mentions Edmond Hoyle (1672-1769), a barrister by profession and the first writer on the rules of whist and other card games, which was a very serious matter in the eighteenth century (Warton, 1747):

> 'Insipid Pleasures these! you cry,
> Must I from dear Assemblies fly,
> To see rude peasants toil?
> For Opera's listen to a bird?
> Shall SYDNEY's fables be preferr'd
> To my sagacious HOYLE?'

> O falsly fond of what seems great,
> Of purple pomp and robes of state,
> And all life's tinsel glare!
> Rather with humble violets bind,
> Or give to wanton in the wind
> Your length of sable hair.

The year before Philip Williams's election Warton had published a four-volume translation of Virgil. And the year after *An Essay on the Writings and Genius of Pope*, which is still recognised as a lasting contribution to the canon. His literary 'other life' often took him to London, where he mixed with writers, actors and painters of the day. Boswell included a letter of 1758 from Dr Johnson to the Greek scholar Bennet Langton which reported (Womersely, p. 175):

The two Wartons [Joseph and Thomas] just looked into town, and were taken to see Cleone, where, David [Garrick] says, they were starved for want of company to keep them warm.

The two brothers both became members of Johnson's Literary Club, in the company of other Winchester literati, such as bishop Jonathan Shipley of Twyford and his son-in-law, the orientalist Sir William Jones (Womersley, p. 252; Franklin, 2011). Joseph Warton often contributed to Johnson's literary projects, though the two fell out, as recorded in Wooll's *Biographical Memoirs of the Late Revd Joseph Warton D.D*, published in 1806 (p. 98, quoted by Leach, p. 391):

Johnson: Sir, I am not used to being contradicted.

Warton: Better for yourself and friends, Sir, if you were. Our admiration for you could not be increased, but our love might.

This shows Dr Johnson at his bombastic best, but he had once been humbly grateful to Joseph Warton's brother, Thomas, for favours done, as Boswell recorded (Womersley, pp.146-150). In the final stages of compiling his famous *Dictionary*, Johnson wanted to have the title-page graced by the initials MA after his name. As an undergraduate he had only spent a year at Oxford, at Pembroke College, having been obliged by the poverty of his father to leave without a degree. In 1754 he revisited the town for the first time since leaving and there he met Thomas Warton, then a fellow of Trinity College, the younger son of the vicar of Basingstoke, and later poet laureate and the Camden professor of history. His name is still remembered in an annual lecture on English poetry sponsored by the British Academy, and his ODNB biographer has even suggested that the 'Age of Johnson' should be called the 'Age of Warton'. Together with Francis Wise, the Radclivian librarian, he ensured that Johnson was recommended for the degree of Master of Arts 'by diploma' for, amongst other things, 'a series of essays, excellently calculated to form the manners of the people'. Job done and worth a fee, which Johnson offered in a letter to Warton written in December 1754 (Womersley, 2008, p.150):

Be pleased to let me know what money I shall send you for bearing the expense of the affair; and I will take care that you have it ready at your hand.

Although, as outlined above, Winchester College in the 1760s was not at its best, the state of the school that Philip Williams entered should not be talked down too much: at a time when few received any education at all, it provided large doses of the three R's and gave pupils a sound Classical education, with small helpings of such subjects as French, drawing and dancing. The acid test of the success of the school, which could always find its complement of scholars and quiristers, was the number of commoners it could attract. This fell from 93 in 1737, to 8 in 1751, and only rose again to 20 in 1756. When in 1766 Burton aged 74 resigned, after forty-four years as head, he was succeeded by Warton, whose hopes were expressed in his *Verses on the Death of Dr Burton* :

> May Wykeham's much-loved walls
> Be still with Science, Fame and Virtue blest…

What is especially interesting in this quote is its mention of 'Science', a subject which had not yet, at least formally, entered the curriculum, but is being used in the sense of 'knowledge, as opposed to opinion'. But science in the modern sense was also in the air: Boswell noted: 'I observed an apparatus for chymical experiments, of which Johnson was all his life very fond' (Womersely, p. 230).

One of the puzzle's of Philip Williams's career is how he came to go to Winchester College. At the age of seven, living in the new-built rectory at Barrow, Suffolk, he had lost his father at the relatively young age of 56. Six years later, in 1775, he was 12th on a list of 14 scholars elected to the school. Winchester, like many other schools at the time, was in relative decline, but obviously it had a reputation in Cambridge circles (others were no doubt Eton and Westminster) and there were adult minds at work on behalf of someone who was probably showing signs of being a very clever young boy. A more straightforward choice might have been The Perse School, Cambridge, founded in 1615 by a local don, though it was not in the same league as Winchester and was in any case in steep decline itself. The Williams family had strong links, father and grandfather, with Cambridge, and in particular with St John's College. His mother was the daughter of a man with roots in Newmarket and Ely. Wykeham's statutes did include Cambridge (or Cambridgeshire) as one of its favoured counties, but these priorities had long ceased to be important and in practice all entrants were nominated by someone who had some connection with Winchester or New College. Thus in 1778, doing a favour for a member of his Literary Club, Boswell records (Womersely, p. 722):

Dr Johnson not only wrote to Dr Joseph Warton in favour of Dr [Charles] Burney's youngest son, who was to be placed in the college of Winchester, but accompanied him when he went thither.

Ten years later Philip Williams was doing the same for another (Letter 123):

> I have had a letter from the Warden of New College [Oxford], whom I wrote to about a nomination for young May, in which he promises to visit us at Compton after the [Winchester College] election.

It is interesting to note that, as well than Philip Williams and his sons, there are about 40 scholars with the Williams surname listed in Kirby's *Winchester Scholars* (1888), including several founder's kin, from the family of Daniel Williams, a scholar of Llanpythid (or Llanspyddid), near Brecon (now in Powys), admitted in 1763. Perhaps there were family links with these members of the Williams diaspora and their patrons, but without further evidence the young boy's entry to Winchester must remain something of a mystery.

A possible candidate for nominating the young boy to the college is the Cambridge divine Thomas Balguy (1717-1795), who in 1757 was collated to a prebend at Winchester under the patronage of Benjamin Hoadly, and three years later moved to the city as archdeacon (Blore, 1951). Like Philip Williams's father, though 20 years later, Balguy had been a don at St John's College, Cambridge. He also served as a deputy to James Tunstall, PW(II)'s successor as the university's public orator (ODNB). He would no doubt, therefore, have been aware that the young son of a former orator was being brought up by his widowed mother in difficult circumstances and may have put a word into the ear of Hoadly, who as bishop was the ultimate visitor to Winchester College. There is certainly evidence from that Philip and Sarah were close to Dr Balguy and his wife (*see* Letters 19 and 73, and p.218).

However it came about, Philip Williams's entry to Winchester was undoubtedly a defining moment in his life and career. Long after he had left he kept in close touch with fellow pupils, mainly through informal contacts and often when he was in London. In addition, the regular meetings of the Wykehamist Society provided an opportunity for him to survey the scene. In his day it was a relatively new thing, having only been established in 1758, initially to meet monthly at the Crown and Anchor in the Strand, but soon settling into annual 'anniversary meetings' (WCA/G8/1/1-2). The event was advertised in *The Times*, and perhaps elsewhere; it was the job of stewards, who varied year on year, to encourage Wykehamists to buy elaborately decorated tickets, at 5s. each. The stewards, in equal measures, had to make good any shortfall in funds. It seems that Philip Williams first attended in 1772 and three years later was elected a steward, which cost him £2 17s. 6d.; his name was last on the list of stewards (others were The Rt Hon Lord Bruce, Ambrose Goddard Esq, Thomas Estcourt Esq, Timothy Caswall Esq, George Pitt Junr Esq, Chas Fanshaw Esq, and the Revd Henry Bathurst). He is also shown attending in 1776, 1779 and 1785 (Letter 88). He may have attended more frequently, though it impossible to be sure if 'Mr Williams' was him or his namesake, the Revd Daniel Williams.

The list of names in 1785, which may have reflected 'table order', shows him in what looks like a Winchester City clique of clerics: he was next to Thomas Heathcote (a son of Sir William Heathcote of Hursley Park), in whose coach he had come, and then John Brereton, A. Milton, Wm Hayes, Henry Stephens (rector of St Thomas's, Winchester), Lascelles Iremonger (Winchester prebendary), George Huddesford, Charles Bathurst etc. Although he calls the meeting 'thin' there were in fact 64 members present, plus seven stewards. The 'thinnest year ever known, owing to the negligence of the stewards' was 1787, when a total of only 57 attended.

The record of Wykehamists who attended each anniversary meeting was arranged in order of rank. Some names appear regularly, but this opportunity to rub shoulders with other old boys, some of them in positions of power, was, as the letter reveals, not cherished by Philip Williams, suggesting that he was not obsessive in the pursuit of patronage and favours (Letter 88). Each year the toasts drunk were listed, the total number reducing slightly with time; in 1782, for example, the list was headed by the king, followed by the queen, the prince of Wales and others in the royal family, then '*Omnibus Wykehamicis*'; 'the two universitys; Prosperity to the two St Marys Winton colleges [Winchester and New College]; Success to the 3 great seminarys Westminster, Eton and Winchester; the Stewards elect [for the next year, all named]; Success to the next Anniversary Meeting', and finally 'The Health of the senior Wykehamist present, the Revd Dr Yates.' The word 'seminary' was commonly used for schools and similar institutions, often though not always with a religious purpose.

AS OUTLINED above, New College, Oxford, was founded by William of Wykeham as a destination college for pupils educated at Winchester College. Its constitution was very similar: it provided for a warden and seventy scholars, ten chaplains, three lay clerks and sixteen choristers. Of course, the scholars at New College were at least five or six years older – but more importantly, membership there could extend for long periods – up to thirteen years for holders of a Bachelor of Arts degree, longer for others. Each year the masters of Winchester College prepared a list, called the *ad Oxon* roll, of founder's kin and the best of other pupils whom they considered ready to proceed to New College. During Election Week at the school the successful entrants were chosen from the roll by the warden and 'posers' of New College, according to the number of vacancies, which was, in turn, determined by the number of members who had left in the year – either because they had married, taken a living or died. The scene in 1784 is depicted by Sarah Williams (Letter 66):

> Worsley is sent upon [the] Roll, which will half kill his father with joy, as he has another year to stay, and it is hard if he does not get to New College; our little friend Wetherell I understand made the best figure in the election chamber; there was a very good appearance of candidates, 18 in number, about ten of them admitted…

One of the boys mentioned was a son of Nathan Wetherell, sometime master of University College, Oxford, and vice-chancellor of the university. Philip Williams ranked very high on the 'long roll', in 3rd place and only behind two boys who were Founder's Kin, and thereby entitled to upstage allcomers. He matriculated (i.e. formally entered New College) on 5 March 1760, one of 197 who did so in the whole University in the year (Anon, 1900, *The Historical Register of the University of Oxford*). It was a well-worn track for Wykehamists as New College, according to its statutes, could only take students from the school. Even those who were not at first selected for New College, and had to matriculate at another Oxford college, might later be able to migrate and thereby join their Wiccamical friends.

The shortcomings of Winchester College outlined above, especially the privileges extended to founder's kin, fed through to New College, which 'produced few men of distinction' in the eighteenth century (Buxton and Williams, 1979, pp. 64-5). Two years after going up, scholars (the term undergraduate was not then generally used) were elected to a junior fellowship – even before graduation – which granted them certain privileges, including being able to vote for the wardens of both institutions. It was therefore no particular mark of distinction to be a fellow – six of the twelve scholars elected to Winchester in the same year as Philip Williams went on to become fellows of New College. In practice, the main virtue of being a fellow was the membership of a *de facto* Anglican seminary, 'a base, from which he could hold curacies, and as a source of patronage, which would ultimately supply him with a permanent living. Life was a matter largely of filling in the time and deciding by vote upon the disposal of offices in the gift of the college,' including church livings (*ibid.*, pp. 64-5). Fellows usually only resigned if they inherited an estate, or wanted to marry and earn a living.

It took a very long time for this cosy situation to be reformed. Many Enlightenment thinkers ridiculed the path taken by Wykehamists and many others at the time, including Joseph Priestley, who is now remembered as a scientist but was even more a theologian. He wrote (Porter, 2000, p. 398):

> I bless God that I was born a Dissenter, not manacled by the chains of so debasing a system as that of the Church of England, and that I was not educated at Oxford or Cambridge.

At the time in Britain, it was Scotland that led the way in university education. And it was not until the setting up of the first University Commission in 1850 that the privileged position of Winchester with regard to New College gradually began to be reduced. Thereafter, the rights of founder's kin were abolished and undergraduate admission and the fellowship were opened to competition. 'By 1866 open scholarships had been created: this was both for the sake of keeping Wykehamists up to scratch, and in order to induce non-Wykehamists to come to New College as commoners' (A. Ryan, In: Buxton and Williams, 1979, p. 84).

Nonetheless, Philip Williams seemed to get off to a very good start. Following the death of George II, duke of Brunswick-Lüneburg, in 1761, the university set to work to produce, at lightning speed, a valedictory volume of poems, some in Latin, others in English and Italian. Entitled *Pietas universitatis Oxoniensis in obitum serenissimi regis Georgii II. et gratulatio in augustissimi regis Georgii III in augurationem*, it was edited by Thomas Warton, professor of poetry and brother of the second master of Winchester College, where a copy is still kept in the Fellows' Library (Bk 7426). Both Philip Williams and his friend Lovelace Bigg-Wither (then plain Bigg) contributed, in English and Italian, respectively. Not unexpectedly,

Philip's 17-stanza poem is a patriotic, jingoistic, toadying piece, decorated with Classical learning and strong on the greatness of George II, who at the battle of Dettingen was the last British monarch to lead his soldiers into action. An Anglo-Hanoverian force of 40,000 defeated a French army of 60,000, driving many of them into the river Main. The relevant verses run:

> What Time the Blood-besprinkled *Mayne* convey'd
> The swift-retreating *Gaul* from GEORGE's Ire,
> What Time at *Dettingen*, with Plumes display'd,
> Triumphant Vict'ry crown'd the Monarch's Fire:
>
> Thrice did the Foe with hostile Rage advance,
> In vain; no Freedom warm'd their Slave-born Hearts;
> Thrice did they sink beneath the *British* Lance,
> Such Ardour Liberty's bold Zeal imparts.

Such praises were to be mocked by Thackeray a century later, who in an article in the *Cornhill Magazine* aimed his barbs at churchman Beilby Porteus, who had written an elegy to George II (A. Robinson, 'Beilby Porteus', ODNB). Philip Williams might therefore have felt himself amongst like-minded people when he later got to know the great preacher as master of St Cross Hospital. In fact, under George II Oxford had not been regarded with favour in royal circles, though its fate was to change under George III (Mitchell, L.G. In: Sutherland and Mitchell, 1986, p.4). At the time a volume of poetry might have been noticed at court, so Wykehamists worked hard at the craft, as did Philip Williams, with such ripe purple verses as:

> Heav'n view'd with ravish'd Eye the Godlike Man,
> Admir'd him rip'ning from his early Birth,
> Mark'd out the Course which He so nobly ran,
> Then snatch'd the Hero from th'afflicted Earth.

His 17 stanzas for royal consumption were commissioned by Thomas Warton, probably with the support of his schoolmaster brother, Joseph, who extolled the *Pietas* (Wooll, 1806, pp. 279-80). It is hardly surprising that Wykehamists were involved in literary pursuits of the day. A modern assessment of the sort of education that the school offered concluded (Blakiston and Glynn, 1971):

Winchester [College] can boast in the eighteenth century a Poet Laureate, two Professors of Poetry at Oxford and in ... *Night Thoughts* [by Edward Young, born at Upham, Hampshire] the most successful poem of the age; and for once it is legitimate to see a direct correlation between writers and their schooling. These men are in a real sense 'produced' by the formal teaching of the Classics and by the informal encouragement of literary pursuits which was almost part of the system...

However, in the case of Philip Williams such encouragement did not bear fruit in the long term. The only other poetry he is known to have written was, by comparison, tame stuff for family amusement, like a piece about a spider and his young daughter Charlotte (W246):

> Up flew her petticoats
> Down-slipt her hose
> This way her garters fled
> Another way her hose;

> What's ye matter, Charlotte cries,
> Meaning to deride her;
> 'Laugh not, for I have catch'd a prize,'
> And out she pulled a – spider.

Yet, on occasions his advice on verse was sought (Letter 80):

I have been pestered with a miserable copy of verses addressed to the Speaker and intended to be printed in the papers, from your father's old schoolfellow Dan. Chaunler – however as he submitted it to my judgement, I have roundly told him the verses would reflect no credit upon the poet, or the subject of his panegyric and advised him to suppress them. He sent me a lampoon upon the Dutchess of Devonshire, the publication of which I am quite indifferent to as well as an epigram upon Lord North – Dan's muse takes fire at the Dutchess, and he exclaims, "who would not gladly seize, that more than paradise within her <u>stays</u>["]. I was afraid of affronting him or else I should have suggested <u>knees</u> to him as a better rhyme, and [a] less vulgar word than stays.

Sarah Williams, too, took an interest in verse and in one letter commented on *The Mine, A Dramatic Poem*, first published in 1785 by parliamentarian John Sargent, a friend of her father's.

In Sutherland and Mitchell's standard work on Oxford University in the eighteenth century, Philip Williams is only mentioned twice, once for his contribution to the *Pietas* for George II, mentioned above, and once, in the same year, for binge drinking. That fly on the wall and fellow Wykehamist, James Woodforde, recorded in his diary (cited from Hargreaves-Mawdsley, 1969, p.41, in Sutherland and Mitchell, 1986, p. 338):

> On 4 November 1761 Dyer of New College bet Mr Williams 2s 6d that he would drink three pints of wine in three hours and write out six verses from the Bible correctly, but he was so 'immensely drunk' that he 'could not write for his life'.

Nothing odd in this: poets and undergraduates often run off the rails for a while!

The sense of fellowship that Philip Williams must have felt living at New College with young men he had known at Winchester must have been immense. His letters are peppered with the names of the boys he had known, some of whom clung to New College for long periods – Charles Fanshaw held his fellowship for 20 years; William Henry Reynell for 28, before taking livings in Essex and Cornwall; and John Ballard stayed on for 14 years, before taking a fellowship at Winchester. His closest friend at Winchester, however, was Lovelace Bigg (to become Bigg-Wither), who had deep roots in Wykeham's foundations (his uncle Henry Bigg had been warden at New College 1725-30, then 1730-40 at Winchester College), but was clearly a man of the world. Before gaining his BA he entered the Middle Temple and started to study for the bar (Bigg-Wither, 1907, p. 48), gaining his first briefs after two years (Letter 4):

> Twice have I wore an ample wig, twice have I paid twenty pounds, and now am fully qualified to assist at ruining any client who is fool enough to go to Law and employ me.

He told his friend that fellow Wykehamist, William Henry Reynell, was following a similar path, at Clement's Inn, but had in fact come to London 'at the end of term ... to hear the debates in the House of Commons'. Bigg's efforts at the law were scarcely more earnest, as he knew he would succeed to a fortune, and had already married. His bride was Rachel Clitherow, who died in childbed less than a year later. She was the sister-in-law of his cousin, the celebrated jurist William Blackstone, and died in the same year that he commenced publication of his *Commentaries on the Laws of England*. In a matter-of-fact letter to Bigg, he wrote: 'Providence has happily ordered it, that violent sensations are not lasting' (Bigg-Wither, 1907, p. 48). It is difficult to imagine how Philip Williams, aged only 23, felt when he opened his friend's letter with the distressing details (Letter 5):

> The poor creature lay for upwards of five days in inexpressible torments, and she was at length delivered in a most violent manner by two man-midwives... . She at last sunk away, within two hours after her delivery, and died I believe without a groan. Her death we attribute to the wrong position of the child, and some other causes which detained it beyond its time. The infant was a boy, and born alive; but the head having received some injury, on cool recollection its loss (were it the only one) is I think a happiness.

Recent estimates suggest that about 7 per cent of women died in childbed during their years of fertility, approximately the same proportion as those who died in an accident or from infectious diseases. Between the ages of twenty-five and thirty-four, perinatal complications accounted for one in five deaths of women (Vickery, 1998, pp.97-8).

As already mentioned, two years after Philip Williams went up to Oxford his mother married and settled down in Cambridge with a man who in future years was able to help his stepson on the ladder to preferment. This was the Revd Dr John Gordon, to whom within a year she had given a son, and a year later another, so that when Philip Williams graduated BA in 1764 he had four siblings – two sisters on the way to adulthood and two baby step-brothers. A few months after the marriage he seems to be living in Cambridge, or at least paying a visit, which elicited some sarcasm from Lovelace Bigg-Wither (Letter 3):

By the by are all your Cambridge people asleep? No bon mots from the Westminster & Eton wits at Trinity and King's? No remains of good-fellowship (beating a Proctor or the like) from any of the more solid Colleges? No capital strokes in the Newmarket way?

The letter, dated only four days after the warden of Winchester, Christopher Golding, had collapsed and died in Chamber Court (Kirby, 1892, p. 399), urged him to attend the election at New College. The 'country parson', James Woodforde, records in his *Diary*, on 5 December 1763, that for the same event he had received seven letters canvassing his vote (Beresford, 1924). It was eight years since Philip had entered Wykeham's world and as a fellow of New College he was qualified to cast a vote. His friend wrote:

> ...I must now bid adieu to smartness, and condole with you on the melancholy event at Winchester college; melancholy enough indeed in itself and more especially so to you at the time, as you had not the consolation of communicating the earliest intelligence of it to your friends. [William Henry] Reynell's letter [(]which I enclose to save myself trouble,) mentions that your attendance will be required at the election; I don't know why, but it may be so you shall hear again from me when I arrive at the field of action, and that will probably be next week. In the mean while I am not a little elated with my imaginary importance...

The election of a new warden was held in New College chapel on 10 December. The three candidates were George Sale, Thomas Hayward and Harry Lee, who was elected, much to the chagrin of the Winchester head master, Dr Burton.

Four years later, Philip Williams had another opportunity to vote, this time for the wardenship of New College. Thomas Hayward had only held the job for four years and 'did the College [great service], by increasing its Revenues, and putting the Estates on a better establishment', according to Nichols (*Literary Anecdotes*, vol 9, p. 256). He also sought to restrict the freedoms of fellows with regard to college livings and other matters (see, for example, 9 April 1767, NCA 9793). He had the misfortune to fall from his horse at a New College estate, probably whilst on a progress cum visitation. He was succeeded by John Oglander, a man only five years older than Philip Williams, from a family seated since the Conquest at Nunwell on the Isle of Wight. His portrait in pastel by John Smart shows him to have been a fashionable man. He was warden for 26 years and New College stills owns the celestial and terrestrial globes he donated, but otherwise he has left little trace.

Long after Philip Williams had resigned his fellowship at New College he, like others with an MA degree, was summoned from time to time to vote on appointments. Thus in April 1785 he was asked to support the candidature of the physician Martin Wall five years his junior for the Lichfield chair of clinical medicine, as his wife informed him (Letter 87):

> There is a great contest at Oxford it seems for the professorship and as you are a Wykehamist, it is expected that you influence as many of your friends as you can for Dr Wall.

His reply was characteristically curt and negative (Letter 88):

> I am happy in having no vote for Oxford; pestered every day about it; as Wall has a family, I wish him success.

Others were more supportive and in fact the election was extremely close, as his wife Sarah reported (Letter 91):

> ... Mr [William Stanley] Goddard [the second master of Winchester] was obliged to go to Oxford, to vote for Dr Wall, and by way of going as expeditiously as possible he took Mrs G in a whisky with him... I am glad Goddard went, as otherwise the votes would have been exactly even, for though there was a majority of two for Dr Wall, one of them was objected to, and has been since found to have been no vote.

Wall held the appointment until his death in 1824, after which an obituary extolled his attributes, 'his capacity for exhilarating conversation and his hilarity of temper, lively anecdotes, and urbanity, as well as his free treatment of poor patients' (N. Moore rev. J. Loudon, 'Wall, Martin', ODNB) – rather like Philip Williams, except perhaps for the last item.

After graduating BA, Philip Williams was ordained deacon at Christ Church and two years later priest. Soon after being ordained deacon he served as curate to Adderbury with Milton, near Banbury, where the rector John Cox was obviously near the end of his life; he died two years later and Henry Blackstone, a brother of the jurist, got the living. No matter, Philip had by this time been presented to Easington, about 12 miles southeast of Oxford, by John Green, bishop of Lincoln (although the institution in February 1767 was by the bishop of Oxford, John Hume). The hand of his stepfather, John Gordon, who had been chaplain to Green, and in 1766 appointed archdeacon of Buckinghamshire, can be glimpsed at work. The outgoing incumbent, Dr Timothy Neve, was not giving up much; he had three other livings of Lincoln – notably a valuable one at Geddington, Northamptonshire – and was eventually set for high places, including in 1783 the Lady Margaret Professorship of Divinity at Oxford. When Philip took hold of Easington, Neve had just published *Animadversions upon Mr. Phillips's History of the Life of Cardinal Pole,* 'a vindication of the doctrine and character of the reformers from the attacks made by the Roman Catholic priest Thomas Phillips' (W. P. Courtney and E. Major, 'Timothy Neve', ODNB). The argument between the two clerics was, in short, a re-run of the Council of Trent of 1545, when the Catholic church eventually got round to condemning what it considered the heresies of Protestants, following Luther's declarations of 1517.

After four hundred years, Wykeham's plan was obviously still working. Educated young men were willing and able to serve churches in the most out-of-way places, in small villages devoted to farming (Easington also had alum mines), where few could read or write and knowledge of the outside world was minimal. Clergymen at the time were a sort of ecclesiastical broadband. Admittedly, they were often not resident: in the case of Easington, Philip Williams needed a curate like Mr Macock, probably Henry Macock, who had held the fort since Neve ceded the living. He was a young man from Queen's College, Oxford, ordained priest in December 1767, and several years later was given two Oxfordshire vicarages, at Marston and Harwell.

Philip Williams was also receiving a good deal of practical, businesslike support from his stepfather, who, within a few months of his institution to Easington, was advising him on the tricky question of dilapidations – the costs chargeable to the departed incumbent Neve for repairs to the parsonage house (Letter 6):

> As to the article of Dilapidations – they seem disposed to trifle with you, and to hum you as we call it – which woud make me more earnest in procuring my just right. I shoud therefor be for

talking in a more firm tone. As to Macock you have nothing to do with him – Dr Neve must look to what bargain may have subsisted between them. You shoud however if you prosecute this point (which in prudence, I think you ought) make Macock a proper compensation for what assistance he gave you in taking care of your church during the vacancy. It is all a joke about not claiming Dilapidations sooner – you may claim them, I believe (I have not time at present to consult my books) any time during your incumbency – the only remedy they can have, is to shew what part of the dilapidations may reasonably be supposed to have happend since your occupancy. However as you want only to be secure against future demands, I shoud think the matter might easily be adjusted by Dr Neve's giving a bond to pay such a sum, as upon fair appraisement to be settled by workmen on both sides, may seem to be due during the late incumbent's time. If there had been any force in their plea about your not making this claim sooner, you have obviated it by settling an appraiser to work within a month or two of your getting possession. I{f} any present help however is necessary to keep the buildings standing, this bond wont do. It must be ready cash. Old buildings however have a faculty of standing much longer for your comfort, than one coud well suppose … I had more to say about Dilapidations but I cannot recollect it at present – and I think the best way will be for you to come over at Christmas, and then we can deliberate more fully upon these subjects.

In the same letter, John Gordon set his mind to advising him whether or not to take on the task of preparing a new edition of the works of the Greek historian Polybius, a task which was to occupy him for 37 years and makes a long story in its own right (*see* Chapter 4). He was also concerned with his step-son's obligations to a 'young gentleman', Samuel Isted (ca 1750-1827), who had matriculated at New College in November 1768, aged 18, and was later to accompany him on a tour of Scotland (*see* Chapter 3). It is clear from an admonitory letter from his stepfather written in December 1768 that being a tutor, probably for the first time, had rather gone to Philip Williams's head (Letter 10):

What occasion, at least for the present, can you have my Dear Lad, for a servant and horses? I woud make it a point not to let this new peice of preferment [as rector of Easington] make any alteration in my way of living, till it had produced me some profit.

You will live I take it for granted in Coll[ege] with your new Pupil chiefly for this next year. And for that time at least I shoud think need make no change in your system. If you are to ride about with your young man, the Father ought to provide you a horse, or otherwise he will not comply with the conditions proposed of your travelling at his expense. You cannot, I am positive, keep a man and two horses, exclusive of the first price of the cattle [chattel] and the loss you will be continually liable to by them, for less than [£]70 a year. If that therefor be a condition your Pupil brings with him, you will be no great gainer out of the [£]100 stipend allowd for his tuition. And as to a servant, Mr Isted will of course, I imagine keep one, who ought to be at your service – and it will be a kindness to employ – as there is not anyone circumstance that spoils so many servants, as the having nothing to do – the effects of which are most thoroughly seen in almost all the servants kept in College; who are in general the most worthless of the whole tribe.

Philip Williams was following an established path: tutoring young men was undertaken by many young fellows in order to supplement their meagre income from college stipends, together with an annual share of the profits, mainly from estate rents.

Comparison of Philip Williams's progress at New College, with other fellows shows that he was probably well up in the pack. For example, Francis Wykeham Swanton (1746-1823), five years junior to him, served as a curate in the Itchen valley, near Winchester, a few months after ordination as deacon, but had to wait seven years before gaining a living, at Stratton St Michel in 1778, and then only in distant Norfolk – in fact, confusion of exactly which parish was intended meant that he was instituted twice, the second time to 'Stratton Long alias Long Stratton' (Shurlock, 2008). Thereafter, he gained no further preferment until 1808, when he was presented to the tiny parish of Hellington, near Stratton St Michel.

Greater insight is available in the case of the Revd James Woodforde (1740-1803), three years senior to Philip Williams, from his *Diary of the Country Parson* (Beresford, 4 vols, 1924-31, Oxford). As he reached the age to leave Winchester College he was only seventh on the *ad Oxon* roll and did not make New College, but instead went first to Oriel, only migrating to the alma mater after 'a little judicious bribery' by his father (R. L. Winstanley, ODNB). After graduating BA in 1763 and proceeding to ordination he left Oxford and served as a curate at several parishes in the vicinity of his native, Ansford, Somerset, where his father – a third-generation cleric – was the rector, as well as being vicar of nearby Castle Cary. When he took his MA in 1767, along with Philip Williams, he had taken over as curate at Castle Cary.

The 'mass production' of young churchmen recorded in Woodforde's *Diary* was standard practice. When examined for his deacon's orders in May 1763 – suffering from a wound to the head, for reasons that will be clear – he was questioned for 'quite half an hour' and 'asked... a good many hard and deep questions'. He 'had not one question that Yes or No would answer.' These might have included exercises in Greek and Latin, which were standard practice in the examination of candidates for ordination (Sykes, 1934, pp 106-7). Six days later, he was ordained, together with 25 other new deacons and 13 priests, and after another six days was appointed curate of Newton Purcell, Buckinghamshire, where he delivered his first sermon. Like many new ordinands, he was for a while a jobbing curate. In September, for example, he served at Drayton, near Abingdon, for 'half a guinea, a dinner, and stabling for my horse'. More to his liking was a curacy at Thurloxton, close to his home, where he says he was taken in by the local squire, 'likewise my horse'. He had just come down from Oxford, where he attended a party with much drunkenness. Chastened by a blow to the head that he had suffered just before his ordination, he wrote:

> I was very sober, as I had made a resolution never to get drunk again ...[regretting the time] in April last, when I fell down and cut my Occiput [back of the head] very bad indeed.

Woodforde took his MA in 1767 in the company of Philip Williams, as recorded in an unabridged edition of his diary, *The Ansford Diary of James Woodforde*, (Winstanley, 1986). As well as his initiation as a curate at Newton Purcell, he had by this time also served as a curate at several places in Somerset, including Thurloxton, Babcary and Castle Cary, where his father was the vicar. The process of obtaining his MA required no arduous study, and as he no longer had rooms at his college he bedded down where he could. After sleeping in William Milton's rooms, he paid 12s. for a Master of Arts silk Hood from Whitmore (probably Edward Whitmore, a Winchester scholar who was, amongst other things, Master of New College School between 1758 and 1763). Then, he migrated to William Reynell's rooms, where he was waited upon by the bedmaker Brazier and his boy, to whom he gave 6d. for his trouble. The next day, 8

May 1767, he breakfasted in 'Williams Senr. Rooms… and after[wards] disputed together as we are to go up in the Schools to Morrow to do Austins, for our M.A…..' The epithet 'senior' was necessary to distinguish Philip Williams from Daniel Williams, who was two years his junior (Kirby, 1888, p. 253). 'Austins' was an examination – originally set by an Augustinian monk holding an MA – in which in its original form the student swore that he had read certain books, his tutors testified to his abilities, and he was then asked to argue on an academic subject. By this time, it had become a nugatory ritual. The following day the *Diary* records:

> I went up into Schools at one o'clock with Williams Senr. of our House, and did Austins under one Wintol of Pem: Coll: Mag, Schol: I was respondent Williams Opp: we each gave Wintol 0 –5 – 0 We were in the schools from one till three – there were six Sets – We afterwards dined and spent the Afternoon in the Chequer, & for Wine there we each paid 0 – 0 – 9 .

Then on 20 May, he performed *quodlibets* (L. 'what it pleases'), that is, an exercise in theological or philosophical disputation' (OED):

> …I did Quodlibets this morning in the Schools under [Charles] Fanshawe, and Williams Senr. did the same also – I gave to the Man of the Schools for the use of a Hood – 0 – 6 I responded to 3. Questions and was up about 2. Minutes…

A day later he recorded:

> There was a meeting of the House this morning to give away the Livings of Pawlesperry and little Sandford in Essex – the first was given to Dr. [Henry] Blackstone, the latter to Peter Goodwin – After a good deal of Trouble I at last got a meeting of the thirteen to be examined and was examined by Cotton Senr. with Williams Senr. – Watkins was examined by the same for his Batchelors Degree – We had also our Graces past – I took up of Hook the Bursar this Afternoon for my M.A. degree, for which I gave him my Note of the Sum of 10 – 0 – 0. I shall take my Degree now I believe next Saturday … Mr. Goodwin treated both the Common Rooms this Afternoon with Wine as usual on having been presented to a Living…

In fact, the handout of livings was more complex, and suggestive of a certain amount of horsetrading, or perhaps administrative convenience, to prevent the advowson from lapsing. Blackstone had already been instituted to Paulerspury, a small parish between Brackley and Northampton, in the January, but in October ceded it to Goodwin. Meanwhile, Goodwin was instituted to Little Sampford, 10 miles northeast of Braintree, in June and ceded it to William Downes 16 months later.

On 22 May, 1767, Woodforde took another step towards graduation, by declaring adherence to the Thirty-Nine Articles. This took place in The Chequers, an Oxford pub a short walk from New College (still in business, in a small cul-de-sac off the High Street) prior to being presented on the following day for his MA in Convocation House, then the venue for the university's governing body, and still used to enthrone the chancellor:

> ... I read the 39. Articles to [Edward] Whitmore this afternoon in the Chequer he being to present me to Morrow in the Convocation House...

Finally, there was the usual drinking to celebrate the occasion, as noted on 26 May, 1767:

> ...I paid Williams Senr. this Evening the Bowle of Wine that [I] lost with him concerning Blackstone & Goodwin in the M C R [Masters Common Room] for which I paid Will: Bignel our Com: Room Man 0 – 1 – 6. I had some more of my Rum made into Punch this Evening and carried into the Senior Com: Room pro bon public – I sent a Letter to my Father to let him know that I purpose to set out for Ansford next Tuesday...

By comparison with Philip Williams, James Woodforde was not doing very well. He had hoped to gain his father's living after his death in 1771, but failed to do so. He had meanwhile made a 'cautiously guarded proposal' to a relative by marriage, Betsy White, and in 1773, in order to secure an income, made an unsuccessful bid for the mastership of Bedford School, which was in the gift of New College. In the event, it went to John Hooke, a year his junior but founder's kin. In the following year he therefore returned to Oxford to try to better his luck and in December was voted to the living of Weston Longville in Norfolk, far from his roots. He was up against Hooke again, but this time he won, by 21 to 15 votes. He wrote in his diary (Hargreaves-Mawdsley, 1967, pp.265-7):

Many learned & warm arguments started & disputed – and after 2.
Hours Debate the House divided and it was put to the Vote.

However, in a world of hard knocks, Betsy had not waited for him, but
had married a far richer man.

The quasi-parliamentary process that had given Woodforde his benefice
was used for many other similar matters – sealing leases, setting an annuity
for a steward who had resigned, choosing a successor, debating whether
the ex-steward should retain his fellowship etc. Major decisions – such as
the appointment of bursars, deans (of civil law, canon law and arts) and
posers were, however, made by the Warden and Thirteen, that is, the
warden, sub-warden and thirteen senior fellows. It was a very inward-
looking, self-contained society – in all but name a monastic house that had
escaped dissolution. Until 1834, students were put up to the Oxford
Congregation to be awarded degrees by the college itself, without
reference to any kind of university examination (Buxton & Williams,
1979, p. 67).

Although Woodforde has become a symbol of the eighteenth century
cleric, he was a very ordinary product of Winchester New College, even by
the standards of the time. His biographer in his entry in the ODNB, R. L.
Winstanley, notes: 'He read little, and his exclusively classical education
left only the faintest impression on his mind.' It is clear that, like him,
Philip Williams and many of his friends were in no way serious scholars.
They treated their time at Oxford as something to be got through in order
to enjoy the fruits of a secure profession – rather like someone might
study, say, quantity surveying today. As none could be married whilst a
fellow, the degree of sexual repression is not hard to imagine, though the
spectrum of celibacy, prostitution and homosexuality is unfathomable.
The subject scarcely ever surfaces; Lovelace Bigg-Wither got closest, when
he wrote in November 1763 about the London stage (Letter 3):

> Now I can only recollect the passage in which the Fairy-queen of
> about 8 mentions with singular archness the pleasures of bed &
> board. The only piece of Indecorum remaining in the farce is
> when Bottom, though without his ass's head, takes the fairy in his
> arms, lays himself on a bank or couch, and her with him. …Must I
> add anything more on the cursed Squire of Alsatia it is too low to
> keep up the laugh that at first is easily raised. For the morality of
> it, the most amiable personage in the comedy, has a child by one
> woman, debauches a second, and marries a third.

At least one of Philip Williams's friends fathered a child illegitimately. This was the lawyer Harry Peckham, who held a New College fellowship until his death: the matter stayed secret until his will came to light, when it was seen that the principal beneficiary was a daughter, Sarah, born mid-way through his 26 years as fellow. He also provided an annuity for a widow, Sarah Thompson, 'for an injury which many years since I attempted to do her' (Brayne, 2008).

In October 1768 the order book of John Oglander, fresh to the wardenship of New College, shows that Philip Williams was one of the governing body, the Warden and Thirteen, and one of the two deans of arts (NCA 960). It was a post he had held for at least two years (NCA 940). As he looked around the table at his fellows, he might have wondered where his future lay. Charles Fanshaw, founder's kin, was destined to remain a fellow for another 10 years. Harry Peckham, mentioned above, was about to go on a tour on the Continent, to become a successful lawyer and to be one of those who codified the rules of cricket, ultimately dying in a lingering way after breaking his neck in a hunting accident (Brayne, 2008). William Master, baptised in Broughton, Hampshire, was eight years off being given the living of Paulerspury, Northamptonshire. William Henry Reynell had a similar future, but 20 years on and in Essex and Cornwall. John Hooke was to find his vocation as a school master, first as head in succession of two tiny schools, namely, Thame Grammar School and Bedford School. Edward Loggin died a young man in 1772, still at New College. John Lucas, the other dean of arts, had to wait seven years before being elected a fellow of Winchester, gaining the rectorship of Milborne Port, Somerset, three years later (a living also held by PhilipWilliams, in 1780).

With his fellowship, his MA, his living in Easington and his contract to work on Polybius for the Oxford press, Philip Williams might have stayed at New College for a very long time and subsequently taken one or other of these tracks. But instead, he went back to Winchester. His motivation is unknown: perhaps he wanted to get on with life, rather than slumber at New College (though he did not marry for ten years); perhaps he saw better chances of patronage in the Winchester orbit, where he did indeed tap into Charles Jenkinson and his relatives; perhaps he just felt more comfortable in a place where personal relationships were easier, where ambition was less heightened and where, after all, fourteen years earlier he had come from a widow's home and prospered.

3. 'Bear Leader' & Bigg-Wither's Best Friend

THE HUGE DIFFERENCE today between a school – even the best – and an English university was very much less marked in the eighteenth century. They were both embedded in the Anglican diaspora, with the universities focused on Divinity and the Classics, which were reckoned to offer the sort of finishing education required by young priests, and were therefore the most influential faculties. Difficult though it is to credit, young men who were fellows of an Oxbridge college vigorously contested elections to a fellowship of a public school, especially Winchester and Eton. The reasons were essentially economic: most fellows at a university college treated their time as a period for seeking patronage to set themselves up for life. There were, of course, exceptions – some young men became lawyers, some doctors of medicine, others were placemen at Westminster, or inherited a fortune. Science, Modern Languages and History were, however, mainly the preserve of amateurs and eccentrics. At Cambridge especially, where Newton was revered, Mathematics was also treated seriously. Philip Williams must have been acutely aware that it was at his father's and his grandfather's alma mater, St John's College, that in 1765 the first university examination in the country was set, with Mathematics and Classics in the rubric.

But, notwithstanding all the intellectual and social changes that, as we now know, were going on, and given the choices that were open to a young man in the third quarter of the eighteenth century, Philip Williams, who had been raised in the conservative environment of Wykeham's two foundations, chose the safe-soft option of a fellowship at Winchester. His decision exhibits a certain shrewdness, since he had no powerful patrons at Oxford and he avoided the long wait that many other New College fellows had to endure before gaining any sort of benefice, and often then an unattractive one. At least he avoided the entombment at Weston Longville of a Parson Woodforde and the plural curacy and distant benefice in Norfolk of a Francis Wykeham Swanton (Shurlock, 2008). In any event, there were lucrative livings to be had from Winchester College, such as those at Portsea, Wymering (combined with Widley), Andover and Portsmouth, all in Hampshire, and others at Milborn Port, Somerset, and

Bradford Peverell, Dorset (WCA/C8/1/f.4). There were also two desirable Winchester livings in Wiltshire, at Bradley and Downton, both with a 'good house', an asset that also accompanied another lucrative living at Ash, Surrey. There were a few others that yielded only very small incomes, like 'Hound with Hamble Chapel' in Hampshire and 'Buddeston alias Bidston' (today spelt Biddestone), in Wiltshire; for the latter the college only seemed to exercise its right of presentation when two small parishes at Biddestone had been joined with nearby Slaughterford.

Philip Williams did not come from a distinguished family, his father had died when he was young and all his relatives had links with only one major centre, Cambridge. Fortunately for him, however, he managed to inhabit a much larger world, perhaps because he seems to have had the knack of making friends easily, a trait which served him well at Winchester and New College. Even allowing for hyperbole, the memorial in the church at Compton, Hampshire, where he was rector for 50 years, is probably close to the truth:

> An easy urbanity of manners, and social disposition of mind render'd him a general favourite in the intercourse of society at large; and his various classical attainments and character as a scholar and divine commanded the esteem and regard of his equals and superiors alike...

These attributes came into play early in his life, when he managed to acquire a fellowship of Winchester College. His chances of such a near-sinecure in the late 1760s rested on a strong friendship with his lifelong friend Lovelace Bigg-Wither, whose father Walter Bigg had been a fellow since 1730 and whose uncle Henry Bigg had been in succession warden of New College and Winchester.

In origin, the fellows of Winchester College were not fellows in the modern sense of the word, i.e. scholars of distinction attached to university colleges, but were part of a 'college of priests', though the description had become meaningless by the eighteenth century. Each year fellows were elected to the posts of sub-warden (Philip Williams served as such for a year from December 1772; WCA/C8/1/f.19) and sacrist, and two others were elected bursars, but the task of 'the society' was as much to assure the godliness of the college as to run it as an institution. As time went by, and particularly after the Reformation, the religious role of the society became less important. By the time Philip Williams was admitted on 25 January 1769, a fellowship at Winchester had long been little more than a source of income for a Wiccamical cleric, without the inconvenience of a parish and a church. Involvement of the governing body in the day-to-day activities of the school was virtually zero, the main work being done by a head master and second master, as its foundation charter stipulated.

Wykeham's statutes provided for 10 fellows, who had to be ordained priests and were appointed for life, unlike the schoolmasters and chaplains, who could be dismissed. After a vacancy occurred, either by death or resignation, the warden and the remaining fellows were required to meet in the college chapel and elect a successor, who had to be a Wykehamist. As with the election of scholars, priority for a fellowship was, according to the statutes, given to natives of the diocese of Winchester, then to the natives of various counties, in order, but this seems not to have been strictly adhered to. Amongst other things, fellows swore to 'keep out of disputes and scandals... and not to reveal the secrets of the house' (Kirby, 1888, p. vi). In practice, the election of fellows had become an exercise in nepotism and influence.

The way in which fellowships and other preferments were granted at Winchester (and many other places) at the time is depicted in one of Sarah Williams's letters to her husband, 16 years after he had been elected. The sudden death of the fellow John Lucas, nicknamed 'The Hook' and vicar of Milborne Port, Somerset – a living in the gift of the College – provided a vacancy in the society, she reported, that had been filled scarcely a week after the event (Letter 81):

Huntingford is to succeed the Hook [as fellow], and to remain [as second master] with Dr [Joseph] Warton till Christmas, the living of course goes to your namesake [Daniel Williams], and is to be disposed of the 30th of this month, Dr W has been manoevring for his son Tom [to die tragically; Letter 118] for the next vacancy, and I believe he has met with a repulse; if any man was prepared to leave the world at such short notice it was the Hook, there is some provision for his mother and sister; but his Eleve [obscure] ,is the most pitiable object; I own this event has a little shocked me, as, to our short-sighted judgements there was little prospect of a vacancy in your society for some years, and when I consider that you are almost the senior, I feel with redoubled weight the misery of our present separation.

Philip Williams's election was different in detail, but similar in style. A missive of 11 August 1768 to him by from Lovelace Bigg-Wither (Letter 7) reveals the jockeying for position that went on prior to an election, which on this occasion had been caused by the death in July of Richard Harris, who had been a fellow for 20 years. He was the rector of Widley, which formed part of what is now Cosham, Hampshire, a living that went with the vicarage of the nearby village of Wymering. It was the most lucrative of the college livings, valued at £260 a year (WCA/C8/1/f.1). The appointment required 'the Warden and scholars and clerks of Winchester College' to nominate 'the names of four fellows ...according to the meaning of a decree formerly made in the Exchequer Chamber' (CCED, Vacancy Evidence Record: ID:257065). Harris was an uncle by marriage of Lovelace Bigg-Wither and is buried at Wymering, where he owned the manor (Bigg-Wither, 1907).

In the letter Bigg-Wither considers the possibilities for the vacancy, naming no less than 10 young men, all former scholars of Winchester. The oldest of them was John Geree, aged 28 and supported by John Awbery, a fellow since 1762. He was not successful on this occasion, but was admitted a fellow in 1772. Next in seniority came Edward Loggin, who within a few years was dead, but a much stronger candidate seems to have been John Ballard, a contemporary of Philip Williams, but in the event he was not admitted until 1774. Gossiping in the background were Robert Pope Blachford who, like Bigg-Wither, succeeded to a fortune, and Harry Peckham, the lawyer, who was about to undertake a tour of Europe. He published an account of his travels in 1772, which ran to five editions, yet only in the last one, of 1788, was his name revealed (Brayne, 2008).

A year senior to Philip Williams was Henry Rowland Berkeley a scholar in 1754 by virtue of being founder's kin (his brother, plain Rowland Berkeley, was a scholar two years later), supported by 'Leigh' (perhaps the Winchester warden Harry Lee). Another candidate was the contemporary Robert Taunton, with 'a connection with [William] Bowles', who had been a fellow since 1725. There were two men junior to him, namely Daniel Williams, supported by 'Uncle Price' (probably the fellow Rice Price), and Henry Oglander (brother of John, warden of New College), who had to wait until 1782 to be admitted. The most precocious was Thomas Bedford, aged about 23, for whom the favour of 'Mrs Blackstone' was, however, insufficient.

In the event, Berkeley was elected, presumably favoured by being founder's kin. He spent his days until his death in 1832 as rector of Onibury, Herefordshire, and Shelsey Beauchamp, Worcestershire. It seems that Philip Williams was second in the running, and had only to wait for a few months for his chance. His opportunity came with the resignation in 1769 of William Langbaine, who had been admitted in 1724. In his early life he held parishes in Sussex, and then in 1739 became vicar of Portsmouth, resigning six years later. Finally, in 1760 he followed Lovelace Bigg-Wither's grandfather as rector of Ash, in Surrey. The suspicion is that he was in some way persuaded to give up the Winchester fellowship for Philip Williams, who must have regarded his election in his late 20s as an advance on his fellowship at New College, which he resigned.

The main task of Philip Williams as a fellow over the years was to look after the finances of the school. He was one of the two annual bursars for 18 of the 40 years in the period 1771-1810 (Himsworth, vol I, 1976, pp. l-li). For seven of them he served with a Charles Blackstone: this could be one of two men, either Charles Blackstone senior, who held a bachelor of law degree and the livings of Widley with Wymering and the hamlet of Wyke (now named Weeke and within the limits of the city of Winchester) or his namesake son. In 1783 he resigned his fellowship to make way for his son (as Philip Williams was to do for his son, Charles, in 1819), who had just been ordained priest, but was readmitted five years later (his son keeping his fellowship!), after which co-bursarship with Philip Williams was again in evidence. The reason for Blackstone senior's second term seems to have been to consolidate family interests: his son had obtained the lucrative living of Andover, following the unexpected, early death of the incumbent, his brother-in-law Daniel Williams. Other co-bursars with whom Philip Williams served were Rice Price (another lawyer and in his late years), John Ballard (an exact contemporary), the aforesaid Daniel Williams (a younger man, founder's kin), Samuel Gauntlett (to be warden of New College,1794-1822), Harry Lee (namesake of the warden of Winchester, 1763-1789), Henry Sissmore (lawyer) and Gilbert Heathcote (from a distinguished family at Hursley, near Winchester, later archdeacon of Winchester).

Being a bursar had it advantages, including a modest stipend, together with the insight that comes from knowing the income and expenditure of any institution. Philip Williams seems to have discharged his duties satisfactorily, though was not above seeking to maximise his stipend, as shown by his reaction to a legacy of John Taylor. This good man died in

1777 after 27 years as a fellow of Winchester, during which time he 'enlarged [the] Sickhouse and augmented Scholars' Commons' at the school (Kirby, 1888, p. 15). In 1753 he (or possibly his father) founded a school at Petworth by making a bequest of £2400, the interest of which was to be applied by the incumbents of three named local parishes for the education of ten boys and ten girls (Arnold, 1864, p. 85). He also left £500 to Winchester College, half the interest from which was to go to 'two poor tradesmen' of Petworth and the other half to 'the widows of poor clergymen'. Rather than welcoming such an act of charity, Philip Williams seems to have been rather annoyed; in December 1781, in the only entry in the Minute Book of the Warden and Fellows in his hand, he wrote (WCA/23216):

> It was resolved at the annual meeting that in consequence of the additional trouble occasion'd by Mr Taylor's legacy to Petworth School, ten pounds should be added to the stipend of the bursars.

No applause for philanthropy, but, looking beyond the dateline of this volume, slightly better heart is in evidence over a controversy that surfaced when he sought a co-bursarship in 1809/10, the last year in which he served. John Penrose Cumming, who had himself been a co-bursar four times since 1800, objected to Philip Williams's election, ostensibly on grounds of non-residence, but perhaps for personal reasons as well. He was a man in his 50's, founder's kin, admitted a fellow in 1800, and in possession of two benefices in the gift of Winchester, both in Dorset, namely, Sydling, from 1801 until his death, and Bradford Peverell in his final year. The 'disagreeable business', as Philip Williams then aged 67 termed it, is outlined in a letter of his of 20 June 1809 to Gilbert Heathcote, who was to be the other bursar: Cummings, it seems, without any prior warning, objected at a meeting of the governing body of the school to the election of Philip Williams , who wrote (WCA/22702n):

> It was to be lamented that he did not communicate with me in private, as then his objections would have been brought to an issue one way or other, in a manner less public and offensive to all parties. You may conceive how unpleasant it must have been to a man at my time of life, and so old a member of the society to be abruptly told that he was ineligible, after having been elected twice before [1804/5, 1805/6] to the same office, exactly under the same identical circumstances; and it may have induced me to write to him in a sharper tone, than I might otherwise have done; but I entirely acquit him of selfish and sinister motives of action.

Who could object to such a reasonable and generous letter? Yet it was a requirement of the school that at any one time at least one of the two elected officers had to be resident: how else could the institution function? In December 1800, the Warden and Fellows' Minute Book defined what this means (WCA 23216):

> It is understood by the Society that Bursars may accommodate their Residences to the convenience of each other for the first 3 Quarters of their office, but that they shall be both considered as bound to reside during the last Quarter from Michs.

The requirement is perfectly understandable: the finances of the school could generally be run by one bursar, but when the audit was being carried out in the autumn, both bursars needed to agree the accounts. Heathcote made extensive notes on the business, entitled 'PW – Bursarship Question 1809' (WCA/22702b). In these he argued that Philip Williams was, in effect, 'resident', as he lived only two miles away at Compton, from where he could be quickly summoned, and for 90 days, including the whole of October, was obliged as a canon to reside in the cathedral close. The other question was one of security of 'the books': he had previously conducted his business at 'a room at Mr Washington's - & a Lodging in College Street [Winchester] at which he very frequently sleeps'. To solve this issue, Heathcote suggested that he have a room in the school or if that were not possible he would 'be happy to accommodate [him] during [my] occasional absence, with a bursarial office in my own house' (WCA/22702m). It was storm in a teacup: the two men were elected for the year 1809/10 and as for Cummings, he was dead by the time Philip Williams made his last audit. Perhaps his 'unpleasant' behaviour had been a symptom of illness. Whatever the reason, the rector of Compton had displayed considerable interpersonal skills.

As later chapters demonstrate, throughout his life Philip Williams spun a web of acquaintances and affiliations that must have been the envy of many – what could be better than being established Winchester, with its school and cathedral, and having contacts galore in London and elsewhere, together with family and friends in many parts of the country? Marriage would be his soon, together with a presence at Westminster and a living at Compton, but even after he had resigned his fellowship at New College he continued to go back and use it as a base for studies – and much else.

***

TWO YEARS after he had been elected fellow of Winchester, in the summer of 1771, Philip Williams undertook a grand tour of what in 1707 had become the 'United Kingdom of Great Britain' or the Union. He travelled up to Derbyshire, toured the Lake District and the lowlands and highlands of Scotland as far as Fort William, crossed to Inverness and returned via Aberdeen, Edinburgh and Berwick-on-Tweed. The details are given in a letter from Philip Williams to Lovelace Bigg-Wither written from Fort William and Inverness and contained in the Heathcote papers in the Hampshire Record Office (HRO/63M84/274/1). Carried out two years before Dr Johnson was to set out with James Boswell on his tour of Scotland as far as the Western Isles (Johnson, 1775; Boswell, 1785), it was, by any yardstick, an ambitious trip: it was undertaken on horseback, with the attendant risks of robbery and mishap; it was only 25 years after the English had massacred the Jacobites at Culloden. He was accompanied by two younger men from New College, namely, Samuel Isted and Sir Charles Watson. A letter to the delegates of the Oxford Press at written by him (Letter 16) indicates that he became tutor to Isted at about the same time as he was asked to prepare his edition of Polybius (*see* Chapter 4), which can in turn be dated to some date before December 1768. Perhaps at the age of 29 he took the tour in his stride, but even today on, say, a motorbike, it would be quite an adventure.

It was clearly a mind-expanding tour (though less so than the Grand Tour) with Philip Williams as 'bear leader', a tongue-in-cheek term for a scholarly guide (OED), meaning an amalgam of tutor, chaperone, guardian and guide. It was usual for gentlemen to employ some 'worthy and well-educated but poor man' on such tours (Doody, 2004, p. 454). Samuel Isted, son of Ambrose, who had an estate at Ecton, Northamptonshire, was definitely a pupil of his at New College, Oxford, from about 1769 (*see* Letter 13) and so too may have been Sir Charles. He was the son of the late Admiral Charles Watson, who had been a colonial governor of Newfoundland and a very distinguished naval officer, particularly in the East Indies. He died at Calcutta in 1757 and in recognition of his services a monument was erected in Westminster Abbey and his son was created a baronet in 1760 at the tender age of 9 (Ingamells, 1997, p.982).

There were obviously close links between the Williams and Isted families. In June 1785 Charlotte Isted (presumably on holiday) came up from Bevois Mount, near Southampton, to Winchester to visit Sarah Williams (Letter 97). Also, Philip Williams's stepfather Dr John Gordon seems to have been an acquaintance of Ambrose Isted, a barrister of the Middle

Temple, and may have been the link that brought the two families together. As already mentioned, towards the end of 1768, he advised Philip Williams how to proceed with Samuel as a pupil at New College (Letter 10), with whom he was to form 'a three year connection' as a private tutor. Philip Williams was also 'much honord by having Mr [Ambrose] Isted for a Colleague' as a sponsor at the baptism of his namesake eldest son in 1780 (Letter 28). Much later, in a letter of August 1804 from Philip Williams to his daughters, who were staying at Bath, he writes cryptically: 'I am glad that you like my old flirt H. Isted'. And in March 1805, he notes that his son Philip, then up at Oxford, had a friend G. Isted, with whom he (Philip Williams) was 'to eat oiled butter' in London later in the month (W118, 119).

By the late eighteenth century there had, of course, been a long history of the Grand Tour, when young aristocrats crossed the Channel and set out for Paris, Venice, Rome and all places in between, in a 'rite of passage' to complete their education as gentlemen. They generally travelled by coach, with their own coachman and a bevy of other attendants, including valets, a cook, and a 'bear-leader'. Their aim, as set out in Richard Lassells's *Voyage or a Complete Journey through Italy*, published posthumously in 1670, was to use travel to improve their understanding in various ways – intellectual, social, ethical and political. By the time Philip Williams set out on his more modest tour, the Grand Tour as such had lost much of its appeal and become the province of the macaroni – a fop or dandy who 'affected continental tastes and fashions' (OED). This was not the style of a Wykehamist from the Fens, but he was for some reason attracted to an arduous trek closer to home.

The trip was therefore sandwiched between the apogee of the Grand Tour and stirrings of another style of travel, namely, in pursuit of the picturesque, that movement in the near future that was to blend into the Romantic, championed by the Revd William Gilpin, in his *Observations on the River Wye [etc]*, published in 1782. He had been headmaster of Cheam School for Boys, a small school in Surrey, but in 1777 came to Hampshire as vicar of Boldre, a village near Lymington with a living worth £600 a year. The patron was William Mitford, who was to publish a *History of Greece* (1784-1818) in five volumes. There is no evidence that Philip Williams knew either Gilpin or Mitford at the time, though much later, in 1804, he happened to meet the latter in Winchester, as he told his daughters (W106):

I was fortunately situated yesterday by the historian Mitford, and spent an hour very agreeably under-ground with him in the ruins of Pompeii and Herculaneum.

At the time the trio undertook their tour, planning a visit to the old enemy Scotland must have been tinged with very real impressions of a bloody recent past, not only from taught history but from personal associations. Anglo-Scottish politics were embedded in the personality of Winchester College, and its sister New College. Both institutions had often been suspected of being too Jacobite for their good and at one time the school had even been impugned by a secretary of state. Under Dr John Burton, head master between 1724 and 1766 – and thus during Philip Williams's time at the school – there were often Scottish aristocrats in residence as commoners, such as Lord Elcho, the son of the earl of Wemyss.

In fact, from about 1750, relations between the two parts of the Union had improved as a 'swelling tide of English students attended Edinburgh University… [and] many leading Scots, like Hume, Smith and Smollett, passed a part of their careers in England' (Porter, 2000, pp. 243-4). Hence, when Boswell – a Scotsman, of course – finally persuaded Samuel Johnson in May 1773 to undertake a visit to his native country after 'he had talked [of it] for many years' (Womersley, 2008, p. 401), the tour went surprisingly well. Johnson, who was deeply prejudiced about Scotland and Scotsmen, reached Edinburgh on 18 August via Newcastle-upon-Tyne and Berwick-upon-Tweed, and spent a total of 94 days in the country. He followed a circular route, proceeding via St Andrew's, Aberdeen, Inverness and Fort Augustus to the Hebrides and returning via the Western Isles, through Argyllshire via Inverary, then to Loch Lomond, Dunbarton, Glasgow, then to Auchinleck, where Boswell's family were seated, and finally back to Edinburgh via Hamilton. Two books resulted from the trip, Johnson's *Journey to the Western Isles* and Boswell's *Journal of a Tour to the Hebrides*. For his part, Johnson seemed to be bowled over by what he found and the changes that had taken place (Johnson, 2 ed., October 1785, p. 128):

We came thither too late to see what we expected, a people of peculiar appearance, and a system of antiquated life. The clans retain little now of their original character, their ferocity of temper is softened, their military ardour is extinguished, their dignity of independence is depressed, their contempt of government subdued, and the reverence for their chiefs abated. Of what they had before the late conquest of their country, there remain only their language and their poverty.

For those who might otherwise tour the Continent, or had already done so, visiting Scotland, and especially the Highlands, grew in popularity in the 1760s. Writing in 1759, John Campbell, 3rd earl of Breadalbane, noted that it had 'been the fashion this year to travel to the Highlands' and by 1773 he is complaining that he had had so many visitors that there were 'sixteen often at table for several days' (Levi, 1984, p. 12). The poet Thomas Gray visited the country in 1765 and gained an enthusiasm for tourism that led to his *Journal in the Lakes*, published in 1769, which Philip Williams may well have read.

The tour was carried out entirely out on horseback. A surviving letter to Bigg-Wither (HRO/63M84/274/1) was written on a day of rest at Fort William after spending thirteen hours in the saddle the previous day, riding through mountainous country and arriving late at night, only half an hour before midnight. The sole stop en route had been for an hour and half to 'give our cattle some oats and ourselves some hard eggs'. He had come up from Glasgow, where he had penned a missive to his step-father (Letter 15), on the military road that led north from Milngavie via the Devil's Staircase or Devil's Turnpike, a rocky ridge north of Glen Coe, between Kingshouse and Kinlochleven. As he wrote the letter, he and his companions were 'hovering over a peat fire within 60 miles of Inverness'. The trip had not been without mishap, including the loss at Matlock, Derbyshire, of a 'sumpter horse', or pack-horse:

> …whose withers were so wrung … that we were obliged to send him back, and ship off in consequence our superfluous baggage, so that we have barely a change of linen, and indeed it is the only way of getting thro' so long a journey without the conveniency of a carriage; which along the Devil's turnpike or staircase must I think be crush'd, tho' the Duke of Argyll's equipage comes over it when he reviews the garrisons.

An 'absence of change of raiment' was one of the reasons they had to decline an invitation to dine with the duke of Argyll in his castle at Hamilton later in the tour, though they also held back because he was 'very much throng'd with company'.

It seems that Bigg-Wither, who doubted whether his friend would ever start out (like Boswell thought of Johnson), had kept a 'journal' of some adventure of his own, though Philip Williams confesses: '[I am] too lazy to make my own, as there are but few places we have seen hitherto, out of your rout[e]'. But he does give a few details of some places that his friend presumably did not visit: Windermere and Derwent Water in the Lake District, Corby Castle near Carlisle, where the owner's wife 'has been so generous as to oblige him to live in France to make up for her extravagances in gaming'.

There are many hints that he appreciated natural beauty: Loch Lomond 'has charms'; Corby Castle stands 'on a steep rock cover'd with fine woods and a beautiful river of the name of Eden which give occasion to many apt quotations from Milton' – presumably from *Paradise Lost*; and 'the beautiful river of the Nith [is] crown'd with [a] variety of trees on its banks'. Castles and other grand buildings also came in for some comment: 'Drumlanrig is a desolated old place, the furniture worse than that of Chatsworth, the terraces and waterworks entirely after the manner of the antients…[with] a long gallery of the very worst painted ancestors I ever saw, excepting a good portrait of E. Traquair'; Douglas Castle, 'which like the other Scotch mansions I have seen, is imperfect, and never to be completed [but] what is finished of it, is infinitely superiour to any thing of the Castle kind I have yet seen.' And Inverary Castle, which prompted an extended commentary:

> [It is] a very noble place indeed, but so far from being completed… I suspect it never will in this Duke [of Argyll]'s time, tho' he is very assiduous, as exclusive of the house, at present unfurnish'd, there is a small village up to his gates, which he has begun transplanting, and then I think it will be one of the finest and most singular places in England, and what is very extraordinary in the Highlands, has a considerable platform about it, and such a mountain cover'd with firs and beach…the environs are much superior to the house'…

As might be expected, he visited the site of past battles between English and Scots, which reminded him of the heathland he knew so well from his rides between Winchester and London, and he encountered some gruesome relics:

> I am just return'd from surveying Culloden Moor, which is like Bagshot Heath, except where the dead men were inserted, and those places are mark'd out by a very beautiful verdure. We found a scull [skull] there, and the cottagers are very assiduous in

pressing bullets and other military reliques upon you, which as I did not find [them] myself, I doubt the authenticity of, and wav'd accepting of.

Today, Culloden is a massive tourist destination, run by the National Trust for Scotland, boasting a new visitor centre built in 2008.

In general, the conditions of life in Scotland received no accolades from Philip Williams, though 'some gentlemen came in from shooting, who sent us a tarmegan (a kind of black game) to look at, and then insisted upon our taking a couple with us to our hovel in the evening.' They are 'always sure of good port and clean sheets; but … The latter however are soon frequented by bugs and fleas. We have not yet got the itch, and I hope shall not, tho' we have not done yet with Scotland by a great deal.'

And the accommodation at Fort William invited no praise:

> This is a wretched place; the kitchen up 2 pair of stairs, and our room [up] 3 [pair] - We cast lots every night for beds; I lay over the kitchen, and am amus'd by a stinking ram goat who patrolls all night in the kitchen, I suppose with a view of extinguishing other smells, or at least serving as a scape goat to take of other's blame and filth.

They 'lay [in] a room about 6 foot square, and just by [one of his companion's] bed was plac'd a large gomer to recieve the drippings from the cieling which we supposed to be rainwater, but were soon convinc'd by our noses… was dew of another sort…'.

The food was terrible:

> Last night we had carrots hash'd up with stinking potted butter and sugar. … The land where it is cultivated stinks so sour and acid with the linseed, that the very savour has given me the gripes and forc'd me to pay to pay two shillings for one shillingworth of tincture of rhubarb.

Samuel Johnson gave better reports of his experiences, probably because James Boswell ensured that he was treated to the best. Interestingly, he had 'a box containing a number of curious things he had picked up in Scotland, particularly some horn spoons' sent down to London

(Womersley, 2008, p. 404). These were obviously prized objects, which Philip Williams also noted at Inverness, when he wrote:

> There is a great fair here, and the highlanders come near 100 mile to exchange a little goat cheese for an horn spoon or some such useful houshold furniture.

The tour shows that, although Philip Williams had cast the die in favour of Winchester College, his links with New College were not broken; indeed, like all alumni, he remained a member of his alma mater and no doubt went back from time to time to work on his edition of Polybius.

At the end of December 1771, following the Scottish tour, John Gordon wrote to Philip Williams from Cambridge, relating him the tortured tale of his own failure to get the chair of divinity (Letter 15), commenting: 'A journey upon the Devil's Turnpike is nothing to a Canvass for a University Office.' He had just met one of his stepson's travelling companions, Sir Charles Watson, in Cambridge and writes in the same letter: 'I am exceedingly obliged to you for, and highly pleased with your anecdotes of North Britain, which I had the pleasure of running over again with Sir C[harles] Watson last night, when he did us the favor to spend the evening with us.' Also, within a few years Sir Charles had experienced the Grand Tour proper, at least in Italy: in 1993 Sotheby's of London sold a splendid portrait of him that had until then stayed in the family, painted in 1775 in Rome by Batoni (listed by Adam Williams Fine Art Ltd, New York).

Much later, in July 1784, Philip Williams met Sir Charles in a London coffee-house (Letter 67) and in the same year Sarah Williams almost met him for dinner. She writes (Letter 70):

> We dined yesterday as usual at Compton, and were to have met Sir C Watson in addition to the party, but his servant arrived at the time we did with an excuse that I was sorry for; his being obliged to set out immediately to Weymouth for his health, by the advice of Dr Heberden. Mr Talbot went this morning to meet him there.

The physician in question was probably Dr William Heberden (1710-1801) – known to all doctors from 'Heberden's nodes', bony enlargements of the terminal joints of the fingers in arthritis – whose patients included Samuel Johnson and George III. He studied medicine at St John's College,

Cambridge, where he might have known PW(II). A year later Philip Williams had better luck than his wife, when he managed to dine with Sir Charles in London (Letter 110).

Although the tour of North Britain undertaken by Philip Williams at age 29 was much less grand than that of Samuel Johnson at age 63, it was typical of the many similar adventures he was to undertake in future years, visiting friends and relatives in the Fens and the north of England. Although, embedded in the conservatism of Winchester and the church, he never needed much encouragement to set out for new horizons.

***

THE LETTERS of Philip Williams show that for much of his life he kept in touch with men he first met as a boy at Winchester College, especially those elected to a scholarship at the school in 1755, the same year as himself. This is hardly surprising: they moved in the same small world – Oxford University, the West End of London, Westminster, fashionable salons and assemblies, and the aisles and chancels of cathedrals and other grand churches. There was one individual, however, to whom he was very close, especially in the years up to the death of Sarah, his first wife, in 1787, and more spasmodically thereafter. This was Lovelace Bigg, named here Bigg-Wither, the surname he had to carry from 1789 (despite the comical connotations) as a condition of succeeding to Manydown Park, in the parish of Wootton St Lawrence in north Hampshire and the other parts of the estates of William Wither, the descendant of a family of farmers turned country squires. In all but name the manor and its lands had belonged to the family for centuries. Thus in 1649 it had been purchased by an earlier William Wither from the dean and chapter of Winchester (Kitchin, 1895. p. 176), only to revert at the Restoration and be held on lease it was finally purchased, by the Revd Lovelace Bigg-Wither, in 1863. A major source for this chapter is *Materials for a History of the Wither Family*, by the Revd Reginald Fitzhugh Bigg-Wither (b.1842), rector of Wonston and great-grandson of Philip Williams's friend (Bigg-Wither, 1907).

In some ways, Bigg-Wither was to Williams as Boswell was to Dr Johnson, albeit on a minor scale. The two boys, then men, were probably attracted because they represented near-opposites, but opposites that were, nonetheless, fused together at many points. Johnsonian and Boswellian may not be adjectives that fit exactly the present circumstances, but they help to draw a rough sketch. The few letters that survive show that Bigg-Wither probably regarded himself as the energetic man about town, who had escaped the soft option of the church, for the opportunities of the city. Whilst studying for the Bar in London, he enjoyed the London stage and watched parliamentary debates. A letter of November 1763 to his friend, then staying with his family in Cambridge, teases him not to 'indulge your usual laziness' and mocks him with undergraduate babble (Letter 3):

> You last facetious epistle doth not much convince me of your sobriety, though perhaps you were less affected than the time before. At least you were now too disordered with what I call in the Irish stile dry drunkeness; which may be defined [as] an irresistible impulse to talk or write nonsense.

But he then reports at considerable length on plays he has seen, impressively flexing his muscles as a critic (*see* Appendix V for details). On the actors Charles Holland and William Powell, playing in either Shakespeare's *A Midsummer Night's Dream*, or George Colman's *The Fairy Tale*, which was derived from it, he writes:

> Ah, poor Holland! shall all his industry to please, all his real merit in the lofty parts of Tragedy, be not only abused by [Charles] Churchill, but ridiculed by buffoonery, and eclipsed at once by Powell? ... Holland and Powell may shine on the same stage long with equal lustres; at present the older actor has perhaps the preference. The new one has indeed the advantage of a fine person, a sweet clear and strong voice of great compass, but not yet under proper management.

Then, on *The Deuce is in Him*, by George Colman, a farce then newly performed at the Theatre Royal in Drury Lane:

> ...the apparent distress of Col. Tamper when surveyed by Emily and Capt Johnson, and compared with his pictures, the cool contempt with which his threats and repeated challenges are received, affords a scene equal, I almost think, to any in our best comedies. Miss Pym has her share of merit on this occasion; she is handsome but will hardly make a capital actress.

In the same letter he reports on parliament, including a prophetic observation on a speech by Sir John Glynn:

...after talking of the prolixity of the late debates, he proposed seriously to the house that the two parties should occupy different sides of the room, and the members should try the force of their eloquence by this method. ...Pitt [the Elder] has been so oratorical with his crutches and flannels, that people hardly know which side he is of.

Two years later, still in London, and setting himself a deadline of exactly one hour to write the letter – 'It wants four minutes of two – I write 'till three...' – he again comments on the stage (Letter 4):

We men of business seldom find time enough to see a play; you will therefore the less wonder that I give you no account of the Maid of the Mill from my own knowledge. What I hear from others is, that bad English words are set to good Italian tunes, that it is inferior to Love in a Village, and owes great part of its success to what some may call the absurdities of [Edward 'Ned'] Shuter.

At this time, Philip Williams had just been ordained and was a curate at Adderbury, near Oxford, which invited the jibe:

In Adderbury I suppose you are all minority-men [supporters of Pitt the Elder]; it would be cruel therefore to insult you on the very faint efforts of the Coterie during the present Session. ... Will the clock never strike – Can you get anybody to play at cards or at backgammon with you. How do? How doth sermon-making go on, Kernels are excellent for Lent, Has John Cox read Tristram Shandy? Now it is Three.

Later, as already mentioned, Bigg-Wither married, only to lose his young wife in childbed (Letter 5). A year after her death he married again; his bride Margaret Blachford came with a dowry of £3000 and he settled on her £300 a year from 'estates in Wiltshire' and 'from house property in Pangbourne (Berkshire), inherited from his uncle [and godfather] Thomas Bigg' (Bigg-Wither, 1907, p. 49). When his father died in 1772 Bigg-Wither became a wealthy young man. Aged only 31, he inherited £20,100 of invested capital, and properties in Hampshire – in Sherfield, Andwell, Kingsclere and Wymering (from his mother) – as well as Chilton House and an estate at Woolston, Berkshire. He took up residence at Chilton and did what landowners of the time were expected to do – he became chairman of the county Quarter Sessions. Apparently, between 1784 and 1788 his 'addresses to the grand juries at Marlborough and Devizes... on

Prison Administration, the Poor and Game Laws, and Lunacy Acts …show remarkable ability, clearness of view, eloquence, and common sense' (Bigg-Wither, 1907, p. 51). Subsequently, he also chaired the Hampshire Quarter Sessions and at various times was a deputy-lieutenant of three different counties – surely a record! – namely, Wiltshire (1770), Berkshire (1785) and Hampshire (1793).

Bigg-Wither had been brought up in a well-established family in Worting, near Basingstoke, Hampshire. It seems to have been a relaxed, bucolic sort of place. When in 1734 his father, Walter Bigg, who was the rector, married Jane, the daughter of Dr John Harris, the parish clerk wrote an epithalamium that opened with the lines:

> I rejoice, my good Master, that now you are wedded,
> And the beauteous Miss Jenny have happily bedded…

The saga of the Bigg and Wither clans is of people woven together by marriage, sustained by close links with Winchester College and rents from small estates, church patronage and preferment. It was the world that the novelist Jane Austen observed, lived in, and almost married into, but was sufficiently self-possessed to leave in the pages of her novels. Whilst maintaining the social fabric that supported them, the Withers and their relatives rarely feature in the national record; the exceptions are the jurist Sir William Blackstone, whose *Commentaries* are still in print, and more distantly, the republican poet, George Wither (1588-1667), whose pastorals are found in some modern anthologies.

Bigg-Wither's inheritance was a haphazard sort of business. Since the reign of Edward III, the Wither family had been in Hampshire in the countryside around Basingstoke. In a letter to Philip Williams he tells the story (Letter 133):

> …the Withers … a Lancashire Knight of that name fled the Kingdom (about Edward the Second's time) for killing Sir John Holland; & his Grandson was finally drove out of the North for a similar exploit on a Sir Robert Worsley. The Monks of St Swithin [of Winchester Cathedral] took compassion on their Penitent, & fixed him at Manydown; originally, I take it, as their Steward. Gradually the family secured a firmer possession. In the Civil War they from Tenants became Lords of ye Soil. This unrighteous purchase was however given up at the Restoration. Yet still I owe some obligation to the sagacity if not to the integrity of my old Ancestor Vellum knocking out the brains of the Head of the

Worsleys & cheating the Church, may be even now thought rather venial offences.

The full story, already outlined at the opening of this chapter, is told in the first volume of the *VCH History of the County of Hampshire*, which was also the first volume to appear in this huge undertaking (Page, W., ed., 1911, vol. III, pp. 239-242). In short, Manydown was held by the Withers on a 21-year recurring lease from the dean and chapter of Winchester until it was purchased in 1863 by Bigg-Wither's namesake grandson. The Biggs themselves had a foothold in north Hampshire from 1724, when Henry Bigg warden of New College was presented with the rectorship of Worting, near Basingstoke, in the gift of William Wither (HRO/21M65/E2/1021). When he resigned the living in 1730 to take the wardenship of Winchester College, his brother Walter, Bigg-Wither's father, was instituted in his place. William Wither had hoped to leave his estates to his namesake cousin, who was living at Andwell, an extra-parochial estate of Up-Nately and the property of Winchester College. Failing that, the estates were to go to the male descendants of his aunt Dorothy Bigg (née Wither; 1661-1717), who was the first wife of Lovelace Bigg, seated at Chilton House, Chilton Foliat, Wiltshire, and the grandmother of Philip Williams's friend. As the males of the family did, in fact, not live up to expectations, in 1789, the estates passed to Lovelace Bigg-Wither, following the death of William Wither, who had been a 'bachelor tenant for fifty-six years'.

Bigg-Wither was obviously keen to show his new acquisition to his friend, but had no allusions of grandeur. Three months after he became the owner of Manydown he wrote (Letter 133):

> If you will follow my advice, you shall defer your visit to Manydown till the Summer. Neither the place, as it is now at this season; nor its present inhabitants will contribute much to your amusement. Some months hence, to talk over future arrangements for the spot where my ancestors have vegetated at least four hundred years, where I expect (no small compliments to my Ecclesiastical Landlords) to sleep out the remainder of my days in an independant situation, will be a pleasure to me…

In 1761 Bigg-Wither's father, Walter Bigg, had inherited the Chilton House Estate – often referred to by the name of the village, Chilton Foliat, or plain Chilton – from his brother Thomas, who had in turn inherited it in 1740 from his brother, Henry, warden of Winchester. He,

Thomas, at first occupied the ancient manor house on the site, but after about 1755 built the grand mansion that Philip Williams knew. It was a 'large three-storeyed red-brick building ...[with] service wings... [and] a large farm courtyard' (Crowley et al., 1999, vol 16, 88-109). Demolished in 1965, it was once part of an estate of about 300 acres that had been purchased in 1689 by Bigg-Wither's grandfather, from whom he gained the name Lovelace. His aunt, Elizabeth Bigg, may have occupied the house between 1761 and her death in 1768, when he and his second wife were living at Boswell Court, Middlesex – in what is now Westminster (Bigg-Wither, 1907, pp. 47, 50). Thereafter, the couple lived mainly at Chilton, but also in London (in 1784, for example, in Norfolk Street; Letter 49). They had nine children, the last of whom was born and died in 1783. At the very start of his chaplaincy at Westminster, Philip Williams visited his old friend, telling Sarah (Letter 48):

> I called upon Bigg, whose boy is recovering, but it was so long a doubtful case, that it has laid up Mrs. Bigg with a violent nervous fever.

By the end of the year Mrs Bigg was dead, probably exhausted by child-bearing. He lived on at Chilton until 1789, when he inherited Manydown Park, where he lived for the rest of his life. Three years later the Chilton House Estate was sold, to the Revd John Craven (notable for links with Jane Austen and her family and for being fined £3000 for adultery, termed crim. con., or criminal conversation; Le Faye, 1995, p. 513). The Biggs had held the estate for exactly 100 years, but the only tangible trace of their time was a bequest of the interest from £100 left by Bigg-Wither's father for a school for the poor (Crowley et al., 1999, vol 16, 88-109).

Chilton was the place to which Philip Williams frequently travelled to see his friend, often en route to or from Oxford. In 1771 Bigg-Wither was living there with his 'old parent' when Philip Williams was touring Scotland (HRO/63M84/234/1). Two years later, when he wrote to the delegates of the Oxford press about his progress (or lack of) with his edition of Polybius he was staying at Chilton and in the next year a missive from his stepfather was forwarded to his friend's address (Letter 17). Even after his marriage, in 1779 to Sarah Collins, he was a frequent visitor to Chilton, staying on one occasion for at least a week, which invited her cryptic comment (Letter 25):

> ... pray make our best compliments at Chilton, not forgetting the young ladies; and the knight, whom by your manner of expressing

yourself I for some reason concieved to be Sir W[illiam] Jones, but for what reason he was to be received into the arms of the church I could not so easily discover...

Other visits were shorter, as in August 1783, when he 'launched into the press' his edition of Polybius (Chapter 4), reckoning that 'ten days will carry me through the experiment' and planning to 'give Bigg only one day in my way homewards' (Letter 42). Again in December of that year, Sarah, supporting her sister Charlotte, in childbirth at Moor Crichel, in Dorset, asked rather sharply (Letter 44):

> Let me know whether you go to Mr. Bigg's, how long you stay, whether I am to write to you there, and how I am to direct.

Two years later, he remarked, equally sharply (Letter 98):

> I have just recieved your's and am very much hurt about your Midhurst journey's coming to nothing, and as to the Chilton one, I say nothing about it, till I see you.

Only a month after the death of Bigg-Wither's second wife in December 1784 he visited Sarah in Winchester (Letter 71):

> Mr Bigg was kind enough to sit half an hour with me on Monday, he seemed tolerably well, in spirits, and health, in spite of the black dye, which he had smeared about his hands and face, in such a manner that I could hardly tell how he looked...

Two months later he was 'much better than he has been for some time, not at all black or stuffy' (Letter 84) and again the following May, en route to his in-laws on the Isle of Wight (Letter 96):

> Mr Bigg called here in his way to the Island with his eldest daughter, who is a very elegant figure and bating her mouth has a charming countenance, and seems to have a very pleasing manners... he was kind enough to bring me some pidgeons...

Two years later he made a 'very friendly proposal' for Philip and Sarah to stay with him in London, in a house 'he was expecting to take'. She had often yearned for such a thing, but found reasons to hesitate, saying (Letter 122):

I am not fit company for any one and am afraid least my complaints should increase upon me when I am from home...

Later in the year Philip suggested that they both get away together to his friend's, though plans for her father to join the party – he had just retired from being second master at Winchester College to live in his native Midhurst – were not working out. He wrote (Letter 103):

> If we [Parliament] should break up earlier, perhaps you will go to Chilton; I shan't go without you, and I hate and fly from an election week [at Winchester College].

The attraction of staying with a friend in a substantial mansion on a large estate in the country, in the sure knowledge that he would inherit a fortune is obvious. Besides, it is clear from the letters that Bigg-Wither wrote that the two men enjoyed each other's company (Letters 3-5). Of the two, Philip Williams, who was a year younger, was probably the more exam-clever, whilst his friend was wittier and more worldly. Bigg-Wither entered Winchester as a commoner in 1753/4 (as noted by H[erbert] C[hitty] in the copy of Kirby's *Scholars* in the Fellows' Library of Winchester College) but, as was often the case, progressed to a scholarship in 1755. Similarly, he was not at first successful in his bid to get on the *ad Oxon* roll to New College, but matriculated at Queen's in 1758 and migrated as a probationary fellow to Winchester's sister college a year later, the same year in which his mother died. 'His father's letters to him while at Oxford are full of earnest good advice, and show that Lovelace worked at French and Italian, as well as the usual Oxford studies' (Bigg-Wither, 1907, p. 47).

In 1789 or shortly thereafter, when he moved to Manydown Park, he went as a second-time widower, with six daughters (another had died a year before her mother) and two sons, one of whom died whilst a scholar at Winchester, leaving Harris Bigg-Wither as his heir. He was named after his grandmother Jane Harris, from a family seated at Silkstead, a manor in the parish of Compton, which – like the Biggs – had prospered from judicious marriages and connections with Winchester College. From an early age Harris had health problems, including a speech defect. He was 'tall clumsy and awkward, [and] he would shamble through the house, or lounge on a sofa, adding little to the general conversation' (Nokes, 1997, p. 251). Bigg-Wither realised that his heir would not survive the rigors of a public school and arranged that he receive private tuition. He went up to Worcester College, Oxford, but never graduated. Subsequently, he married a lady from the Isle of Wight, Anne Howe Frith, and the couple lived at Wymering, near Portsmouth, until the death of his father in 1813, when they took over Manydown. Harris might have married the novelist Jane Austen: she accepted his proposal in December 1802, but changed her mind overnight. It was a triumph of honesty over opportunity: she believed in marrying for love, did not love him and therefore eschewed being the mistress of a large estate. Had the proposal been from the Irishman Tom Lefroy, with whom she dallied with in 1796 in nearby Ashe, the story might have been different (Lefroy & Turner, 2007, p.13).

The monument to Harris Bigg-Wither erected in the church at Wootton St Lawrence by 'his widow and their ten children' may tell what Jane Austen might have enjoyed – or not. It seems to have been carefully composed and describes him as:

A man whose heart was full of kind and tender feeling, whose words were few and faithful, and who, with a most sparing display of profession endeavoured by God's grace to prove his faith sincerely and unostentatiously by his works, visiting the fatherless and widows in their affliction and keeping himself unspotted from the world.

It suggests a nice, honest chap ('unspotted' means 'not morally stained', OED), but one who would not have achieved anything out of the ordinary and who really would not have pleased, or been pleased by a sparky young writer-to-be.

Jane Austen was brought up at the rectory Steventon, only a few miles from Manydown, and had got to know the Bigg-Wither family as a girl. When Harris proposed she was therefore paying a visit to a place she knew extremely well and where she had often stayed. She was particularly close to Catherine and Alethea Bigg (they were not obliged to add Wither to their name) and was very friendly with Elizabeth Bigg, who in 1798 had married the Revd William Heathcote, rector of Worting. The sisters may have given their brother courage to propose, since that would have ensured that Jane was kept in the family, and there was great rejoicing when she at first accepted. Although she was at this time completely unknown as a writer, her overnight refusal was a sign that this particular young lady, aged 21, was different from so many female members of the families of Bigg, Wither, Harris, Blackstone – and many others – who had so often accepted a good offer. Her mind must have been in complete turmoil when she and her sister Cassandra, accompanied by Alethea and

Catherine, rattled off in the Bigg-Wither carriage after breaking the bad news to Harris. But the upset did not break her links with Manydown, which endured the awkward moment. One of spectators of the debacle was Mrs Elizabeth Heathcote, whose husband had died at the young age of 30. Thereafter she lived at Manydown until the death of her father in 1813, when Philip Williams arranged for her to live in Winchester in his prebendal house in the close.

A miniature of Lovelace Bigg-Wither aged 23 (*see* List of Illustrations), presumably painted for his first wife, shows a slightly nervous fashionable young man with a powdered wig and lacework cravat. Another painted in the year he died at age 71 (or posthumously) shows a rustic individual, with a ruddy face, heavy jowls and a rather amused, quizzical look. It is difficult to know if he met the life-plan that his clergyman father 'chalked out' for him, to be 'a man of knowledge and a man of business, one who will know how to employ his time and fortune ...[to] be of service to his country, either in public or private life...' His privilege and sheer good luck were enormous. But even so, when, already a very wealthy man aged 48, he wrote to Philip Williams to tell of his good fortune in inheriting Manydown, only four days after the death of William Wither, the messages he gave were mixed (Letter 132):

> You will ... be glad to hear that Mr Wither has left me [£]1500 richer than he needed to have done.

> Presuming you may hear my acquisition much magnified, assert confidently, and from the best authority, that I have not got a year more clear spending money than I had before. The estate is however certainly improvable, though to what extent I cant say.

Jane Austen as a young woman offered a view of Bigg-Wither in a letter written in January 1799, where she related that he had been unable to attend a country ball due to 'a return of his former alarming complaint' at Winchester (heart attack? gallstones? piles?) and commented (Le Faye, 1995, pp. 37-8):

> Poor man! – I mean Mr Wither – his life so useful, his character so respectable and worthy, that I really believe there was a good deal of sincerity in the general concern expressed on his account.

Much later a tribute came from his grandson, Sir William Heathcote (1801-1881), who described him as 'the kindest of parents and most venerable of men'.

In the parish church of Wootton St Lawrence, Hampshire, there is a handsome memorial to him that describes him as:

> ....universally respected, beloved and lamented, as a magistrate he was eminent, active, learned, and judicious, as a private gentleman, he was not less distinguished by those social and relative virtues which adorn the friend, the parent, and the Christian.

Although in the end Bigg-Wither was much, much wealthier than his Wiccamical friend, at the beginning, when the two boys first met at school, they had a similar background. They were both sons of country clergymen, from families with strong links with the universities, and both with estates of some kind. During a period when the value of land increased substantially, particularly in the Home Counties such as Hampshire, Bigg-Wither's fortune became much larger than Philip Williams's, not only because of his good fortune but probably because he was smarter and more businesslike – his Bar studies may have helped – and also because his family network was more established. Philip Williams started from a lower base, with a smaller network, and was always at the disadvantage that the estates he had were small and a long way away, in North Wales and the Fens. Besides, in the rather pushy screeds that his stepfather wrote (such as Letter 10) there is always the implication that his stepson had no instinct for being a landowner. He was scarcely much better himself: referring to land at Tottenhill, near King's Lynn, he wrote (Letter 22):

> The Devil is in all the Law, Lawyers etc., what a plaguy deal of trouble is there even to get rid of an Estate by their means!

Bigg-Wither and Philip Williams were different examples of how wealth creation at the time did not have to come from grand ideas or great industry, but might equally depend on nudges of good luck, shrewd judgment and an ability to prevent human emotions from getting in the way of advancement. Very Jane Austen!

Lovelace Bigg (later Bigg-Wither) writing on 23 February 1765 from London, where he was ostensibly studying law, to his friend, Philip Williams, newly ordained deacon and acting as curate of Adderbury, Oxfordshire (Letter 4).

4. *Tussles with the Classics*

TO UNDERSTAND the life of people like Philip Williams, and especially his work on the Greek historian Polybius, it must be appreciated that in the eighteenth century and beyond the Classics occupied a central position in the life of any educated man and were essential for anyone taking holy orders (Sykes, 1934, pp. 106-7). Philip Williams was steeped in the Classics at school and university and engaged in classical scholarship in a way that could have advanced his standing considerably. He may have learnt some Latin as a young boy in Cambridge, but it would have been nothing to the exposure he was to get at Winchester. Here he would have spent long hours learning Greek and Latin grammar, carrying out translations and compositions in School, the single large classroom in the style (and perhaps the design) of Wren that still stands. Although Latin and Greek were for 300 years the sine qua non of an educated gentleman, the most casual survey of memorial inscriptions in English churches shows that as the nineteenth century progressed many educated and socially advantaged men (and perhaps women) accepted English as an appropriate language for the most solemn of pronouncements. Even so, until 1968, the professor of poetry at Oxford had to deliver an oration in Latin.

The genteel battle that went on between traditionalists and modernists is well illustrated in Boswell's *Life of Johnson*, in which the great man was led to call Joseph Warton, the head master of Winchester College, a 'fool'! It happened in 1776, two years after the death of Oliver Goldsmith, when Johnson had just composed a Latin epitaph for the dramatist's memorial in Westminster Abbey (Womersley, 2008, p. 563-4). The members of his celebrated Literary Club thought it should be in English, but no-one dare tell him, so they – with only one exception – signed an elegantly produced round-robin with the message (Halliday, p. 93):

> ... if we might venture to express our wishes, they would lead us to request that he would write the Epitaph in English, rather than in Latin.

He 'received it with much good humour ... but [said] he would never consent to disgrace the walls of Westminster Abbey with an English inscription. [Boswell's italics]' Also, on seeing the name of Warton as one of the signatories, he commented:

> I wonder that Joe Warton, a scholar by profession, should be such a fool!

Such a statement about the head master of Winchester College is ironic, since it was a school in which the Classics were passionately revered. Some of the early holders of the Regius Professorship of Greek at Oxford, founded by Henry VIII, had been scholars at school, including John Harmar (ca.1555-1613), who was also a prebendary of Winchester Cathedral and rector of Compton, the living that Philip Williams was to enjoy. A similar path was followed by John Harris, who held the chair from 1619 to 1622 and then in 1630 was elected warden of the college. His family became rooted near Winchester, at Silkstead Priors. John Harmar's namesake nephew held the Oxford chair from 1650 to 1660, succeeding yet another Winchester scholar, Henry Stringer. However, as teaching at the university was college-based, professorships had always been little more than a sinecure. That certainly was the case with John Randolph (1749-1813), who was professor of Greek in 1782-3, together with the chairs of moral philosophy and poetry, adding divinity to his portfolio in 1783. At Cambridge, by the late eighteenth century Greek had sunk in importance: Michael Lort, who held the regius chair from 1759 'enjoyed it virtually as a sinecure for twelve years, and left not even so much as a faded reputation as a classicist' (John D Pickles, ODNB).

Joseph Warton himself was obliged to promote the Classics at Winchester (see, e.g. WCM/23643 et seq, listed in Himsworth, vol I), where on all major occasions Latin declamations were de rigueur, notably at the start of Election Week, when the Warden of New College, Oxford, and two 'posers' or examiners were met at the gates in the *orationes ad portas*. This was a ceremony during which scholars – usually in their final year at school – or founder's kin greeted the university visitors in Latin. There were two other annual declamations, namely, one to the Founder and another to 'Elizabeth and Jacob', meaning Elizabeth I and James I, to be delivered on the anniversary of his accession.

'Medal-Speaking' was also – and still is – an important opportunity for Winchester scholars to show their skill at composing verse and prose in Latin (and English) and was rewarded, as the name suggests, by medals (Chitty, 1905, 1906). The concept, in a much-altered form, is at play at many other English schools on 'speech day'. At Winchester the tradition dates from 1761, when Thomas, 2nd Lord Bruce (sometimes misreported as Lord Bute) of Tottenham (created the Earl of Ailesbury in 1776) offered two medals, later increased to three, one in gold, for Latin verse and a Latin essay on alternate years, and two silver medals given every year for Latin and English speeches. Ailesbury is described by Horace Walpole as 'a formal, dull man, totally ignorant of and unversed in the world, and a Tory; very unexceptionable in character' (GEC, *The Complete Peerage*, 1910-1959, vol I, p.63). Later George Pitt, Lord Rivers of Stratfield Saye, Hampshire, added book prizes to the proceedings. The prizes were generally given in the summer on the last day of the Winchester Races.

Following the well-documented rebellion of Winchester pupils in 1793, which led to the resignation of Joseph Warton, all prizes were withdrawn and for a few years a slimmed-down service had to be provided by the warden George Isaac Huntingford and the head master William Stanley Goddard 'at their own expence'. Then in 1796 the Prince of Wales stepped into the breach and the ceremony resumed the following year. As George IV he continued to give the medals and all succeeding sovereigns to the present day have followed his lead. The event was obviously considered to be of great importance: in the early 1900s, Herbert Chitty, the College archivist for 22 years, discovered an almost complete set of winning compositions in 'an old hair trunk' (Chitty, 1907).

The outcome of medal-speaking was anticipated rather like result of a thrilling sports event, with details reported in the *Gentleman's Magazine* and the local Press. On 12 July 1773, for example, the *Hampshire Chronicle* reported (Chitty, 1906):

> After the public breakfast on Thursday at St John's House, the Gentlemen adjoined to the College, to hear the annual performance of the young gentlemen in the School, where Mr [Thomas] Le Mesurier first spoke his Prose Composition on the following subject: *Aut haec cum illis sunt habenda, aut illa cum his sunt amittenda*, for which he was entitled to the valuable gold medal, the annual donation of Lord Bruce.

As well as declamations and medal-speaking, a regular part of Winchester school work consisted of composing essays and verses in Latin and working on grammatical exercises called 'construes'. The standard 'Easter Task' required of pupils was to compose Latin hexameters. Various prizes were awarded each year for the best achievements in all these various exercises. Many examples of this kind are faithfully preserved for posterity (Himsworth, I, under 'Winchester College, Curriculum').

Several Winchester dons (as teachers in the school are termed) wrote bestselling textbooks on the Classics, including Huntingford's *Short Introduction to the Writing of Greek* (1778), which became the school's 'preferred textbook for sixty years, [although] his compositional style was not highly regarded.' (A Robinson, 'Huntingford, George Isaac'. In: ODNB). Much more successful was the Greek grammar by Charles Wordsworth, a nephew of the poet and second master 1835-46 – the first non-Wykehamist to hold the post – whose *Grammaticae Graecae Rudimenta* was, as its title suggests, written in Latin. First published by John Murray in 1839, four years later he took it (rather ungratefully) to OUP, where its sales, together with those of Liddell and Scott's *Greek-English Lexicon*, 'transformed the business of the Learned Press' (Stray, 2013).

Wordsworth makes clear in his autobiography, *Annals of my Early Life*, that he wanted to create a National Greek Grammar so that a pupil from any school, when he went up to university, would recognise the same system of grammar. Although there were at least a dozen different texts used at the time, the main aim was to replace the widely used 'Eton Grammar', which had many defects. It had actually originated at Westminster School in 1595, written by the antiquary and topographer, William Camden, who was, in succession, the school's second master and head. The importance attached to Wordsworth's task was expressed in an unpublished review (spiked as it might offend Eton!) by his brother, who suggested that 'uniformity in grammar is no inconsiderable step towards uniformity in Religion...' (Wordsworth, 1891, vol. 1, p. 186). The new book was a great success, though it took a long time to convince Eton and not until 1866 was it (together with the celebrated Kennedy's *Latin Primer*) formally accepted by the 'nine schools' recognised by the Public Schools Commission. Eventually it was overtaken in 1871 and after a decade went out of print (Stray, 2013):

> Wordsworth was both conservative and stubborn, resisting pressure from the Delegates [of Oxford University Press] to translate his book into English, and only reluctantly agreeing that his nephew could assemble a smaller Greek primer in English on its basis. The new book, published in 1871, soon eroded the sales of its larger sibling ...

It is clear that English classicists were late in making good their stall. They had been overtaken by their German equivalents, who during the eighteenth century had adopted a uniform approach to Greek grammar and its teaching (Wordsworth, 1891, vol. 1, chap. III). The debates of Wordsworth and other Greek scholars were a century too late, though they show that 'that curious alliance between the classical and the Christian' was still very much alive (Stray, 2013). In 1847 Wordsworth left Winchester to head Trinity College (now called Glenalmond College), in Perthshire, and was eventually elected Scottish Episcopal Bishop of St Andrews. Perhaps Philip Williams had hoped that his work on Polybius would in due course propel him to similar heights. The cathedral close was once full of men labouring on the Classics, as he did for many years, though in truth Wordsworth was in a much higher league.

***

ALTHOUGH FOR MUCH of his life, Philip Williams was quietly engaged in classical scholarship, he held no senior university post, never seems to have lectured, and there is no evidence that he ever taught the Classics at Winchester. But somewhere, somehow, perhaps in a casual, part-time manner– more like a serious hobby than a profession or vocation – he worked at producing an edition of the Greek historian Polybius. His magnum opus took 37 years and the work went on until he had passed his 60th birthday. The saga started when he was a young man at New College, Oxford, and was well underway when he became a husband, family man and clergyman.

The only known product of his labours is a leather-bound 1008-page, large folio set of printed sheets in the Fellows' Library of Winchester College. Virtually unknown to modern scholarship, the book was commissioned by the Oxford press (a forerunner of Oxford University Press) in 1767. Specimen pages were approved in 1783, a print run of 500 copies was set, and by 1791 printing was in progress. This continued until in April 1804, 'when the Delegates [of the Oxford press, hereafter called OUP] abandoned the project; apparently because they saw no way of incorporating in it the index from the massive recent edition by Schweighaeuser' (Stray, 2013). All the sheets were burnt, with the exception of a set (probably second proofs) kept by Philip Williams and later bound by his namesake son. The scholarly effort is apparent from the pages, each in two columns, with a Latin translation alongside the original Greek, and many footnotes in English and other European languages.

Philip Williams's edition of Polybius might easily have been overlooked, as probably the only published reference to it until the 1960s was in *A Country Gentleman of the Nineteenth Century* by F. Awdry, published in 1906 (p. 10):

> In 1814 Mrs [Elizabeth] Heathcote [née Bigg, widow of Revd William Heathcote (1772-1802)] in order to be near her son [later Sir William, the 5th baronet] who was a Commoner at the College, rented one of the Canon's houses in the Close. This house belonged to Dr Williams - often called 'Polyby Williams' because he had published a learned edition of Polybius...

In fact, this statement is wrong in two respects, first, Philip Williams did not have a doctorate, and secondly he never actually published the 'learned edition'. The true story is told in a note pasted on the front endpaper of the volume in the Fellows' Library. Written by eldest son, it reads:

> This is the whole of the proposed Edition of Polybius, as it stood on the abandonment of the agreement between the Delegates of the press, and my father; and on his death in 1831 I had them bound in their present shape – all the impression was burnt by consent of ye delegates, & my father, he having returned the Money which had been advanced by them during ye progress of the Work. P.W. 1832

Although Philip Williams had many things with which to occupy himself – his family, his ministry, Winchester College, friends galore, and much else – the abandonment of such a large endeavour is likely to have marked his life. But what exactly happened and why?

By the time Philip Williams matriculated at New College, Oxford, in 1760, classical scholars had for three centuries been producing editions of Greek and Roman authors, both in their original languages and in translations, Greek to Latin and both into modern languages. But the output was gentle: over the years 1759-79, OUP, for example, published an average of only one title a year. Stray describes the process (2013):

> Once the need for an edition of a particular author was identified, or brought to their attention, the Delegates sought a member of the University who would assemble it. He was usually asked to choose an older edition on which to base his work, to collate any

manuscripts which had not been used by previous editors, and in particular to make use of manuscript material held in the Bodleian Library. The men who carried out these tasks, which involved a considerable amount of drudgery, were usually young college fellows who needed the work to keep them alive or at least supplement their incomes. They were paid fixed sums to prepare the editions, and then by the page to see them through the press and correct proofs, Greek being allowed a higher rate than Latin.

In the 1760s, the delegates of OUP identified several authors for whom they judged a new edition to be required, including the Greek historian Polybius (c.203-120 BC). He had written a great work on the rise of the Roman Empire and, amongst other things, was the first to define the attributes that a historian should have, such as attention to sources, impartiality, and awareness of such physical factors as topography and geography. Only part of his work (the first five books) survives in its entirety, but it is enough to show that the one aspect of 'good history' that Polybius did not embrace was the ability to write something that is enjoyable to read. Hence, those who have produced editions of his work have been faced by a huge task and one that is less than joyful.

Between 1756 and 1761 the clergyman John Hampton, baptised in Bishop's Waltham, Hampshire, and educated at Winchester College, published an English translation of Polybius, which eventually ran to at least seven editions. It is inconceivable that Philip Williams did not know of it. The second edition of 1772 was dedicated to Robert Henley, 1st earl of Northington, who took his title from the family estate in Hampshire, now the site of the grand classical mansion, The Grange, which dates from 1804-9. Hampton's reward in 1762 was the rectorship of Moor Monkton, Yorkshire. In the preface of his edition he extols the virtues of classical authors over 'the moderns', but admits that Polybius was an exception:

> Instead of charms that might allure, an energy that might command, or flowing softness that might carry with it the attention of the reader, we meet at every step some deformity which excites disgust, some coldness which offends, some obstacles which expose our patience to the severest proof. ... It cannot therefore be greatly wondered at, that many, even among warm admirers of antiquity, should have been discouraged from perusing writings, which are void of all the charms of nature and of art; which display neither elegance nor strength; neither ease

nor dignity; simplicity nor majesty; but are in every part disfigured, either by tasteless and ill-sorted ornaments, or a negligence that is wholly destitute of grace.

This disarmingly frank assessment, enough to send shivers down the spine of the hardiest publisher, reads like a suicide note, but such was the rarity of the material presented by Polybius that many were prepared to endure his stylistic barbarisms. The Huguenot scholar Isaac Casaubon (1559-1614), who settled in London, produced an edition (unfinished at his death), with the original Greek text and a Latin translation. This was used by the German theologian and philologist Johann August Ernesti (1701-1781) for his 3-volume edition of 1763-4. Then between 1789 and 1795, Johann Schweighaeuser from Strasbourg produced a 9-volume edition, including an index, with commentary that was apparently not superseded until Frank Walbank's *Historical Commentary on Polybius*, published in three volumes between 1957 and 1979 by the Clarendon Press, Oxford.

In this context, it is difficult to discern what the OUP delegates had in mind when they decided in May 1767 to commission their own edition of Polybius. They would not have been concerned about Hampton's English translation since they probably viewed it as 'popular'. And perhaps they did not initially know about Ernesti's. Schweighaeuser was in the future, though he did pay a visit to England in 1770. But OUP had been under a pressure to publish more since the publication in 1756 of *Some Thoughts on the Oxford Press* written by a delegate (member of the board), namely, the jurist Williams Blackstone – a cousin of Lovelace Bigg-Wither. His report was damning, and threatened further action if it was ignored. In was in the backwash of these reforms that Philip Williams took on the ill-fated edition of Polybius.

There was also royal input. In a famous meeting in February 1767 between Samuel Johnson and George III in the royal library at 'the Queen's house' (now called Buckingham Palace), the king had asked the great man of letters about Oxford. In his Life Boswell recorded the meeting in great detail, having 'been at great pains to collect [the particulars] with the utmost authenticity from Dr Johnson's own detail...'. He reported (Womersley, 2008, pp.282-3):

> The King ... asked him what they were doing in Oxford. Johnson answered, he could not much commend their diligence, but that in some respects they were mended, for they had put their press under better regulations, and were at that time printing Polybius.

After the interview, Johnson's literary friends gathered at the home of Sir Joshua Reynolds and pestered him for details; they included Joseph Warton, who had the previous year been promoted to head Winchester College and 'in his frank and lively manner, was very active in pressing him to mention the particulars' (Womersley, 2008, pp.284). Such casually arranged interviews with a monarch were, of course, virtually unknown, and it is inconceivable that news of the event did not soon reach Oxford. As regards the press, Boswell's report cannot be taken as literally true, since the delegates had not yet commissioned their edition of Polybius, and it is even possible that Johnson's inaccurate assertion actually impelled them to do so.

The Orders of the Delegates of the Press show the sequence of events (much of the following is based on the research of Dr C.A. Stray). They met in the Clarendon Building, Broad Street, and included the vice chancellor and both proctors, as well as senior members of the university – professors and heads of college. On 15 May 1767, within a few days of a proposal from William Stafford Done of Christ Church College, the board resolved (Orders, i, f.61):

> That Mr Done be allowed £300 for publishing an Edition of Polybius, provided he shall compleat his Collations and Materials, correct the Press, and publish the Edition entirely. If he should compleat his Collations and Materials, but not print off the Whole Work, the said sum of £300 shall be nevertheless allowed him, provided he or his Representatives shall provide a proper person to be approved by the Vice Chancellor and this Board to correct the Press, and print off the remaining part of the Work.

Done had suggested basing the new work on Casaubon's edition. It was resolved to print 500 copies of the book, the Greek text to be followed by a Latin translation and notes printed separately at the end. The Orders in October report that, on the recommendation of the archbishop of Canterbury (Thomas Secker), Jonathan Toup, a celebrated classical scholar rooted in Cornwall, had agreed to help. However, in November, Done resigned the project, as he was now a country clergyman (though where is not clear) without access to libraries, and the board agreed to offer the commission instead to Philip Williams.

Although the motions of the board seem to have been rather random, any publisher will recognise the process: the press wanted an edition of Polybius and were seeking a young graduate who could be persuaded to undertake the donkey work, with Toup in the background to ensure quality. In fact, the Polybius commission was hardly a gift: only part of the original Greek work had survived, he was a difficult author, the text was long, the financial reward was relatively small, and the scholarly kudos was limited. Only someone with the utmost drive and determination was likely to carry it off. A sign of the low regard in which editorial labour of this kind was held comes from an entry of 14 April 1783 in the order book of John Oglander, warden of New College, Oxford):

> At a meeting of the Warden and Officers Mr [William Henry] Reynell was called before them for having been found by the Proctor drunk in the Street, for having insulted the said Proctor in a most indecent Manner, & having been brought by the Proctor to the Warden, who ordered him to stay within the College that Night. It was unanimously agreed that he should be … admonished to behave with more Reverence to his superiors …confined within College for three weeks … and translate into English Sallusts Cataline War, in such daily Portions that the whole may be finished within the three weeks aforesaid which daily Portion is to be brought to the Sub-Warden or the Senior Officer in College every morning.

Reynell, who had been a classmate at Winchester with Philip Williams, had obviously overstayed his welcome at New College, but it would be another four years before he resigned his fellowship to take a country living.

It seems that at first Philip Williams was not inclined to accept the delegates' offer and wrote for advice to his stepfather, Dr John Gordon, who replied in November (Letter 6):

> Yes I think many things may be urged both pro and con about this same Editorship, which you have [had] offerd you – at all rates it does you great credit, and you are much obliged to the Warden [of New College] …. Somethings I guess you state too high; others too low. Amongst the first may be reckond, I apprehend, the several sacrifices you must make to <u>fame</u> in this instance. Surely there is no occasion so absolutely to part with all your old friends on this account. I have known many a voluminous Editor appear with a sleek skin and a round belly, that implied he had not totally bid adieu to good eating and drinking, when they fell in his way.

He continues with a reference to the Oxford biblical scholar Benjamin Kennicott (1718-1783), still commemorated in the Kennicott Hebrew Scholarship, whose labours were probably well known to Philip Williams:

> What think [you] now of the great Dr Kennicot? And yet what comparison between Polybius and the Bible in 30 or 40 folio volumes! And why not now and then temper severer studies with a poule at Quadrille [a card game] by way of relaxation. I dare say, if the Warden had thought it woud have precluded you from all parties of this kind, he woud not have proposed the thing to you. Your Pupils too – they undoubtedly demand a due share of your care and attendance. But one may reckon I suppose full half the year as vacation in respect to any intercourse with them – and then the Work may be carried on here [in Cambridge] as well as at Oxford, so that I think you will not be so strictly tied down to it, as you imagine – though undoubtedly such a business cannot be undertaken without the resolution of submitting to a good deal of laborious employment.

Then he turns his attention to the likely benefits (in a manner that today sounds like a careers master talking to a teenager):

> And perhaps to balance this the reward proposed may be thought too small – yet it is not an unhandsome one, or what shoud be lightly rejected. But then to eke out this, you may consider many other advantages. It will be giving you early a turn for business. You will gain more knowledge by having your pursuits destind to one particular point of view, than ever can be acquired by the rambling method of going from one subject to another without any other guide than fancy, or some prospect of amusement, as is commonly done when a man's studies are bent to no particular destination. The consultation of other Authors, which you justly deem necessary, will give you an enlarged view of ancient learning, of Authors, Dates &c &c. which you woud otherwise never be tempted to look after.

And he suggests that the production of such a work is likely to launch Philip Williams's career as a scholar:

> As to the Reputation to be got by this, I think, you state it too low. Scholars are still the distributors of fame, and they take care to give it in general only to one another. If you have it in

contemplation to travel nothing will make you more respectable or gain you an easier introduction to Men of Letters, than being known for the Author of a new Edition of a Greek Classic. The course of inquiries too that you will be thrown into by such an undertaking will suggest a number of circumstances to you, that will make travelling more engaging and more usefull. You seem to have no other particular object of pursuit. Philosophic studies, I fancy, you rather decline – and as to Divinity and Compositions for the Pulpit, I suppose you have not formd any strong attachments to, but that a little leisure might occasionally be sufficient to satisfy your inclination that way – and I think it is of vast consequence to have a young man set about something or other in earnest.

It is perhaps a typical letter from a father to a 25-year-old son, who appears rather lukewarm, and overall he is encouraging him to take on the challenge. There is apparently no deadline, nor obligation to complete and he rather regrets that such an opportunity had not been his:

I am sure I heartily wish such an offer had ever been thrown in my way. You never will be able better to undergo fatigue, or sit so disengaged probably to other avocations. Besides as you will not be under articles either to finish it within a certain time, or even to finish it at all – but will be in the hands of liberal men, who will be disposed, I dare say, to treat you handsomely, I think at least you might venture upon a trial of skill with it safely; and determine to go on with it or relinquish if after wards, as it may appear to you on a nearer view. But probably you are one of those, who in the Tatler's phrase (I think) "are ripe for advice". That is I conclude from your PS that you have already come to a determination not to engage in it; and I am only spending my time in giving my sentiments on the occasion to no purpose.

In fact, his guess was wrong and the advice he gave may have swayed Philip Williams towards accepting the offer. Even so, the reluctance remained, as shown by a letter written to the Oxford delegates six years later, on 7 February 1773, from the home of his friend Lovelace Bigg-Wither. He admits he has done little work on the new edition and gives a candid admission of his less-than-enthusiastic attitude to the task (Letter 16):

I entered upon the work at first, rather to oblige the late Dr [Thomas] Hayward [warden of New College], than as a task agreeable to myself, and a three years connection I soon after ~~entered into~~ formed with a young gentleman [Samuel Isted] placed under my tuition, prevented my attention being directed towards the edition so much as it otherwise would have been.

I mean not however by any means to decline the undertaking, unless the Board are willing to put it into hands abler and more inclined to execute a publication of this nature.

As some gentleman may possibly have offered himself for this purpose, I shall very readily communicate what few observations I may have made worthy [of] his acceptance. Otherwise, I shall consider myself bound by the regard I have for the memory of Dr Hayward, and the good opinion the board have entertained of me by intrusting me with this edition of Polybius, to finish it as soon as possible, and I trust in such a manner as may not prove me altogether unworthy of the late Warden's recommendation or the Board's acceptance.

The death of Thomas Hayward so soon after Philip Williams had accepted the commission was unfortunate. Only four years into post of warden of New College, he had started to impose a certain discipline within its walls and might have been able to keep the young man on track. But in the event, only a year after being commissioned to produce Polybius, Philip Williams resigned his New College fellowship in favour of one at Winchester. It was not the act of a young man bent on academic achievement (a rare breed in Oxford at the time) but of one who was in search of preferment. The same letter includes a masterpiece of vagueness, worthy of any author in trouble with his publisher:

> ...the edition of Polybius is in a progressive state and will I hope in the course of the year be in some degree of forwardness, though when it may be ready for the press, I cannot by any means ascertain.

Another four years pass and the delegates give him another prompt, which elicits the response from Winchester on 25 November 1777 (Letter 21):

> I received the favour of your Letter, and can only give a general answer to your Question, that if I am not interrupted by any

unforeseen avocation I hope in the course of the following year to compleat what little matter I may have to offer in a future Edition of Polybius.

He also raises certain editorial issues, suggesting that if the Casaubon edition is to be used as it stands 'there seems no reason why that part of the Book may not be printed off when the Press is ready to receive it', but if footnotes are to be added then obviously the printing must await them. He continues: 'In this case however the Latin Translation may be committed to the Press previous to the rest of the work. As regards Toup's 'remarks and amendations' he has apparently been in touch with the great scholar, who suggests that they are added as an appendix. He also discusses how to handle 'parallel passages' from other 'voluminous Historians' – presumably to compare, for example, Polybius's commentary with those of others – and suggests the use of 'occasional references' rather than extensive quotations. In a disarmingly casual postcript he comments: 'I forgot to ask, if the Book is to be printed with or without [Greek] accents.'

The letter was 'registered' in the Orders without any comment by the delegates; but like any experienced publisher, they did not embark on expensive typesetting before the job was done. The fact that so many basic issues had not yet been settled suggests that Philip Williams has scarcely started the task. Although it is unfair to compare the situation with modern publishing practice, it is incredible that an editor would do any significant work on a complex project without having settled so many basic questions.

During the first few years of Philip Williams's marriage the Polybius project started to take shape. Writing in 1780, his stepfather commented: 'I rejoice ... that Poly (notwithstanding your connections with another Fair) is still in memory' (Letter 27). And by May 1783 the delegates had considered, and accepted, detailed proposals from him, and all seemed to be ready to go to press. The Orders book shows a plan similar to that considered before, but with some very significant differences. The new edition was to be set from Ernesti's edition of 1763-4, rather than Casaubon's, since although the former was regarded as a mere transcript of Casaubon, it did not include so many abbreviations and had been divided into chapters. At the same time the delegates decided upon a folio format with the 'text and translation in parallel columns ... the various readings to be placed immediately under them, and the explanatory Notes at the bottom.' The bound sheets now in Winchester College library show that these decisions were followed through in the typesetting that was soon to start. A letter written by his stepfather at this time is full of chatty advice and enthusiasm (Letter 39):

> I am glad to my heart that the Polybius is going to be launchd. I wish it happily off the stocks, and that it may make in these peacefull times a prosperous cruise. Dr W[illiam]s Commander I think will add to the eclats, and I hope secure a good birth as the Seamen phrase it. I am sorry it is likely to be deprived of the benefit of the Toupian Carronades [by Jonathan Toup]. It's a pity, you had not made a provisional treaty upon that head – to change the metaphor, I conceive no difficulty or even delay need arise about the correcting of the press by your living at a distance. Where there is a sufficient stock of types (as is, I dare say, the case, at the University Press) they can easily be going on with another sheet whilst the first is transmitted to you, and so on. It will be easy for any Corrector at Oxford both to make that fit for your last inspection and also to see that your corrections are properly attended to.

By July 1783 the delegates had approved specimen pages and decided to print 450 copies on small paper and 50 on large paper (for presentation), later increased to 75 copies. It was a busy time for Philip Williams and at the crucial moment he lost someone who had, it seems, been a key supporter and was perhaps even to be a proof reader, namely, Dr Benjamin Wheeler, a delegate of the press and regius professor of divinity, who died a fortnight after the Polybius specimens had been approved and only eleven days after being given a prebend of St Paul's cathedral. The loss did not, however, prevent Philip Williams from pressing ahead and on 13 August he wrote to his wife from Oxford (Letter 42):

> This very day I have launched into the press, and as soon as that business is got into the right channel, I shall set my face southwards, and probably pluck a grape before the old Lady [unidentified].

He was also beginning to get on the preferment gravy train: in November 1783, no doubt due to his stepfather's influence, was given the prebend of Stow St Mary at Lincoln – curiously, due to the death of William Stafford Done, the man who had first been commissioned to prepare a new edition of Polybius, and had only just been promoted to the archdeaconry of Bedford. His wife Sarah, writing in July, who had perhaps spurred him on to 'launch Polybius', did not, however, hold back on her views on his new appointment (Letter 41):

> I have but one objection to your accepting the Bishop's favour [at Lincoln], which is the journey you will be obliged to take, and consequently the long abscence I must endure. ... I am afraid you will feel the loss of poor Dr. Wheeler very materially in your publication ... .I don't know whether you are provided with a corrector and you will perhaps be surprised at my venturing to mention the name of one; but young [Charles] Ballard of Christchurch [Christ Church, Oxford] told Papa that there was a Mr. Robinson of his College, who besides being very equal to the business, was extremely attentive and diligent in whatever he undertook. I hope if you have not seen him, that you have by this time made that matter perfectly comfortable.

The years that followed the start of typesetting of Polybius were full of personal incident for Philip Williams. Most significantly, in 1787 his wife died in childbed, and he was left with four young children. Her death occurred towards the end a period of five years when he had served as chaplain to the Speaker of the House of Commons, Charles Wolfran Cornwall, (D. Gray, 1991, pp. 68). The job itself was pretty minimal. Away from home, living in the Speaker's house in the Privy Garden, Whitehall, he must have had long hours to pore over Polybius. He never mentions the fact, but writing to his wife in May 1784 he asks her to send her bills and his folio edition of Casaubon (Letter 48) which he had forgotten to take up to London. She did so, but in the process discovered that his studies were not high on his list of priorities (Letter 51):

> You have not looked at your Causabon (which I sent last Tuesday) as you would have found the bills pinned on to the first leaf.

In April the next year he is still considering his 'materials' and writes (Letter 88):

> '[Thomas] Burgess of Corpus [Christi College] called on me in the course of the week with some papers of Lord Monboddo's relative to Polybius, not worth a great deal.

James Burnett, Lord Monboddo was a philosopher whose work was ridiculed in Britain at the time but is now better appreciated. Amongst other things, he was one of the first to recognise the links between Greek and Sanskrit. A few days later Toup's papers are forwarded to Philip Williams by the delegates: Toup had died the previous January and had left his papers to the Clarendon Press.

It is entirely understandable that the death of Philip Williams's wife Sarah in 1787 was a major blow for the father of four young children, though within a year the delegates are enquiring over progress. Then in 1789 a new threat started to appear in the form of a continental edition of Polybius, complete with a new translation, notes and a lexicon, edited by the Strasbourg scholar Johann Schweighaeuser. A daily record of activities maintained by the university printer shows the press printing the edition from at least 1791 until April 1804 (Blakiston, 1962, p.34). In November 1798, Philip Williams wrote to 'My Lord', an unidentified delegate, possibly John Randolph, soon to be bishop of Oxford, saying that (Vice Chancellor's Letter Book, 1772-1804, OUP Archives, Shelf OS/E2/1/4):

> the last sheet is now printing off, which will compleat what has come down to us of the original history of Polybius, and will with the addition of Toup's notes, the insertion of Casaubon's preface, and perhaps some others, make about 700 pages folio.

In fact, in the bound-up sheets the pages run to 1008. He wanted to publish what he had prepared thus far as a volume on its own, but obviously the delegates did not see it that way, even though he offered pay for the cost of reprinting some of the sheets. He was candid about the reasons for these revisions, but sounds like an author who knows he has been less than diligent and reminds his publishers that he had warned them. He wrote:

> ...though I might allege many unforeseen incidents in addition to the loss I sustained by Dr Wheeler's death (after which period I made repeated offers to resign what few compilations I had got together to a more experienced and vacant person) as an extenuation of the errors which are to be found in the former part of the edition [,] yet I cannot but consider myself as solely responsible, and therefore disclaim the most remote wish of trespassing upon the forbearance or liberality of the University, which I have already had sufficient experience of, not to require any further proofs.

The master's daughter, Sarah Williams, in Winchester, writing to her husband in early March 1781, addressed to the Somerset Coffee House in the Strand (Letter 35).

He also had another reason for reviewing progress with Polybius, namely, that in March 1797 he had exchanged his stall at Canterbury (where he had met his second wife, Helen Ward Fagg, whom he had married in 1793) for one at Winchester, together with the episcopal living of Houghton, Hampshire, to add to that of Compton. He wrote confidently that:

> ...in consequence of having gone through my offices at Canterbury, and from a change which will take place soon in my own family, to the pleasing prospect of spending the remainder of my days in peace and privacy at Compton, where I presume upon having more leisure than I have ever yet been possessed of, to finish the first volume forthwith, if that should be deemed adviseable, or to advert to the remaining part of the work with as much attention as my other relative duties may admit of.

The Delegates Orders in the opening years of the nineteenth century show fees being paid to individuals for various editorial tasks: making what was presumably the general index, the index of Greek words, and 'preparing Toup's notes on Polybius'. Despite all this, and the printing of a preface (which does not apparently survive), on 20 February 1804 the delegates admitted that it was impossible to add Schweighaeuser's Lexicon Polybianum to the edition and on Monday 2 April 1804 made a final decision:

> Upon consideration of all the circumstances respecting the proposed edition of Polybius - Resolved that it is not adviseable to proceed further in it.

A dozen letters from Philip Williams are known from the period between his second marriage and the fatal decision of the delegates (W94-106), all addressed to his daughters, and although they tell of much 'peace and privacy at Compton' there is not a whisper of the disastrous sequel to all his years of toil. Did he feel himself somehow culpable and had there perhaps been some bitter exchanges before the final decision? Was he therefore too embarrassed to mention it? Or did he, like many a parent, never discuss business in the family? Whatever the reasons for the press abandoning Polybius at the last hurdle (the most plausible being that they had been gloriously outflanked by Schweighaeuser), the accounts for 1803/4 show a total income of £3512.18s.0d, including receipts from the sale of books and bibles and £200 from 'the Revd Mr Williams'. So, after 37 years he had been obliged to repay his advance.

In 1823, seven years before Philip Williams died, the firm of W. Baxter did finally publish an edition of Polybius in Oxford, but it was that of Schweighaeuser, and made from bought-in sheets. At a time when Oxford was narrowly based on the needs of clergymen, and its teaching was poor, it was clear that Continental scholars were winning. The views of the erstwhile editor on the outcome are not recorded. Only two of letters of his after 1823 survive, written to his daughters (W177-8), but neither mentions Polybius.

It must be asked what propelled the shockingly lengthy, and ultimately fruitless efforts of Philip Williams, for whom the project eventually held no promise of income or 'fame'. It certainly shows a dogged stubbornness, but it is sad to think of a man in his late 50's carrying out the sort of editorial drudgery usually undertaken by much younger men. Was he keeping up appearances with others who were completing significant scholarly works, such as the orientalist Sir William Jones, with whom he rubbed shoulders at Twyford? Was he 'showing an example' to his children, especially his sons Philip and Charles, who were going through Winchester College and had scarcely reached adulthood when the project faltered? Or was he even still responding to the distant echos of the encouragement that Thomas Hayward, his warden at New College, might have given to 'a promising young fellow'? Probably none of these had much effect: more likely is that he viewed Polybius as a prelude to preferment, and he persevered with it in the hope of bettering his chances of being made a dean, an archdeacon, or even a bishop. It is evident that his wife Sally took a strong interest in what he was doing, and when she died he lost his prop and his whip. Settled in Compton with his second wife, he allowed the project to lapse and ultimately fail.

It is interesting to contrast the pace of Philip Williams's work with that of Samuel Musgrave (1732-1780), a physician and classical scholar settled in Exeter, unsuccessful as a doctor but now recognised as 'an early proponent of psychosomatic medicine' (A. Cameron, 'Samuel Musgrave', ODNB). Always in financial difficulties, he exercised his skill as a classicist to earn money and sold his notes and materials to the Oxford press for an edition of Euripedes for £250. After publication of the work in 1778, in four volumes, he asked for another £200 from the publishers, but was refused (Stray, 2013). At least the whole business for him was over in a few years, rather than thirty-seven.

5. *Philip Meets Sarah*

DURING THE 1770s Philip Williams lived the life of a bachelor-fellow at Winchester College, where the second master he knew as a pupil, Joseph Warton, had now become head master. His name surfaces most obviously as one of the two annual bursars of the school But more than anything else – his educational attainments, or his family background – the event at this time that most shaped his life, and the Letters, was meeting Sarah, a daughter of the second master of Winchester College, Thomas Collins.

Philip Williams and Joseph Warton would have been well acquainted, in the way that masters and boys are: they had joined the school in the same year, 1755, and Warton's main task as second master was to teach the scholars 'on the foundation'. As a fellow and bursar, Philip Williams must also have got to know Thomas Collins, who in 1766 took over from Warton as second master. Philip evidently impressed this sensitive man and so it was that he fell in love with his eldest daughter, whom he always called 'Sally', though it took him some while to persuade her to marry him. Eventually she succumbed, and on 10 March 1779, a day after signing a marriage settlement, the deed was done and for eight years they were man and wife (W223, 300). They had four children before her untimely death 'in childbed' in September 1787. When they married he had held two church appointments, and when she died he had four, including a prebend. More importantly, between 1784 and 1789 he was chaplain to the Speaker of the House of Commons and spent long periods in London. It was this absence from home that created the letters between him and his wife that are the heart of the Williams Papers (W5-93).

Sarah was the eldest of the three daughters of Thomas Collins and passed much of her young life in his lodgings at Winchester College. Nothing is known of his wife, who may have died young, and during vacations he and the girls probably returned to his home town of Midhurst to stay with his sister. Even if his wife had been alive when he took the job in 1766 she would have lived in school premises, as the warden Huntingford and his sister-in-law and seven children were to do when he was elected in 1789. They probably occupied the 'old chambers of the Masters', where Collins's predecessor, Joseph Warton, had lived before being promoted to head master (Leach, 1899, p. 409). Elsewhere, on the site stood 'Old Commoners', formerly the Sistern Chapel, which Thomas Collins leased from the dean and chapter school (*see*, for example: HRO/11M59/E2/59278). Wherever they lived, and with or without her mother, Sarah must often have seen Philip Williams as the young fellow and bursar going about his business.

Like any father with three daughters, Collins was no doubt keen to see them married. In the stridently chauvinistic atmosphere of Winchester College it must have been very difficult for any contacts between the opposite sexes to be forged. But somehow, the school master, who in many ways seems to have been rather ineffective, was in this regard highly successful (though storing up later troubles; *see* Chapter 15): after Sarah married in 1779, her sisters, Elizabeth and Charlotte, followed in 1781 and 1783, respectively. It seems, in fact, that Philip Williams had asked for her hand 'many years' before they wed, as she admits five years after walking up the aisle (Letter 68):

> I met with a circumstance the other day that has given me a little uneasiness, in rummaging out Papa's papers, I saw a letter in your hand writing, which a little of my mother Eve, tempted me to look at; I found it to be that you wrote to Papa a great many years ago, and which I never saw before, wherein you gave up all thoughts of being connected with me; but there was so much tenderness expressed for me in it, that I cannot now forgive myself for being so foolishly shy, as to be afraid of saying that I liked you; the idea of what you then endured affects me at this moment, and I have done nothing but think of it ever since; but I thank heaven that my folly did not go any farther, and that I am now happy, in one of the best husbands that ever woman was blessed with.

It was the custom for many cleric-academics to wed soon after resigning their university post, but his decision to take a fellowship at Winchester in preference to New College, Oxford, was clearly motivated by other factors. It seems that at his first approach she was too young to contemplate marriage, but he must have persisted. It seems that they were together in parties that went on trips to Kew, and to East Lavington, Sussex, where at some time after their marriage in 1778 the banker-politician John Sargent and his wife Charlotte (née Bettesworth) were seated. Thomas Collins's mother was also a Bettesworth (albeit without the second 'e') and he had in 1764 been presented to the living of nearby

Graffham by Charlotte Bettesworth in her minority. The gift led to litigation, as an ancestor of hers had sold the advowson in about 1750; quite a story, but it seems that Thomas Collins may have held the living illegally (WSRO, I/3/7/p.131; Lavington Estate Archives, MSS9).

The evidence for one of Philip and Sarah's excursions is a poem hastily pencilled on the endpapers of a copy of *The Student's Pocket Dictionary*, published in London in 1777, signed 'Ph. Williams'and still in the Fellows' Library of Winchester College. With the exception of a few words, the pencil has been inked over – perhaps by one of their children. Private love poems rarely survive public exposure, but a few of the lines demonstrate how they got to know each other:

If unaccompany'ed by you,
The classic scenes of Thames or Kew
No longer can my muse inspire,
Or wake to bagatelle the lyre.
Else should the nine [muses] with decent pride
Recount the arteries up-tied,
The silken ladder nicely stopp'd,
With care restor'd the stitches dropp'd,
The tippet lost in storm of wind,
With graver stories of that kind....

No longer can Apollo boast
Of turkey boil'd, of turkey roast,
The pride of Lavington farm-yard,
The joy of ev'ry kingly bard.
All these must pass unheed'd by,
For want of your society...

Again in Winchester we meet,
The lowest end of Kingsgate Street...

Soon the couple were married, she at the age of 22 and he in his late 30's. By comparison with her father at a similar age, Philip showed considerable promise. As well being a fellow of Winchester, he held *in absentia* the living of Bradford Peverell, Dorset, which was in the gift of the College, was editing an edition of a classical author for the Oxford press, and was, or had recently been, chaplain to the politician the Rt Hon. Charles Jenkinson (Chapter 9).

After Sarah and Philip Williams were married they lived in their own house in Kingsgate Street, embedded in a community which they both knew intimately. It is clear, however, that he was less than content with a life in Winchester – its city, cathedral and college – and like most other fellows of the school saw a future elsewhere, whilst she was insecure on her own, even in a setting that she had known since the age of 9. Both of her sisters had married within four years of her own wedding, one to a lacklustre son of a distinguished clerk to the House of Commons and the other to a wilful son of a dissolute aristocrat from a distinguished family.

The early letters show that Sarah was at first rather in awe of her older husband. The manner in which she addressed him, 'My dear Sir', is not particularly austere for the period, but writing to him at Oxford, where he is (ostensibly at least) working on his edition of Polybius, less than eighteen months after the wedding and already with their first child, she uses some phrases that might be interpreted as supplication (Letter 23):

> I hope you will not be displeased at my disobedience…

> I have punctually observed your orders…

> I believe I shall not trouble you again in the epistolary way 'till Sunday…

However, it is a chatty letter, with accounts of visits to the theatre, and the warm tone of a woman who thinks she has made a good choice. She signs off:

> I eat, drink, and sleep as well as usual but I can never be so happy without you as with you; so the sooner you return, the more agreeable it will be to your ever affectionate SW.

***

APART FROM her female charms, there were good reasons why Philip Williams wanted to marry Sarah Collins. The Letters make plain that, although she was not formally educated – few women at the time were – she was familiar with a wide range of subjects. Importantly, she could hold her own with her husband in many matters and was never patronised by him. This is not surprising, as she had spent her childhood in an around Winchester College, where her father was second master. Also, she mixed with a coterie of people from the upper middle classes, including cathedral canons and their wives, and members of prominent families such as the Mildmays, the Ricketts, the Newbolts, the Shipleys and the Heathcotes, all situated to the south of the city, in Twyford, Shawford and Hursley.

One of her attributes was a knowledge of Italian: she may have acquired this from her father, whose linguistic skills were noted when he travelled late in life in Italy in support of his daughter, Charlotte Viscountess Bolingbroke, who was seeking relief from her disastrous marriage (Ingamells, 1997, pp. 102-3). Also, the Winchester head master Joseph Warton was obviously interested in Italian literature and ordered 'a collection of blank verses in Italian by Algarotti', the philosopher and art critic, from a man who was well known to Philip Williams, namely, Paul Maty (Letter 76). He was an assistant librarian at the British Museum and became a controversial foreign secretary of the Royal Society (he might have been a clergyman, but could not accept the Thirty-Nine Articles; T. Seccombe, rev. R. Mills, 'Maty, Paul Henry', ODNB). Shortly after Philip took off for London in May 1784 Sarah went back to her studies (Letter 50):

> I have got some Italian books from [the rectory at] Compton, by the help of which I hope to recover what I have lost these last five years [since her marriage], in hopes that in future I may be of some service to my dear little ones.

She was also had a good knowledge of English literature, especially plays, by Shakespeare, Philip Massinger, and Ben Jonson. On Massinger, for example, she recommends that Philip look at *The Fatal Dowry*, which she says is 'far superior' to a later version, *The Fair Penitent* (reworked in 1702 by Nicholas Rowe). When Philip wrote to her at length about a stage play based on Don Quixote that he had just seen on the London stage, he made a note to read the book, commenting 'you know it by heart already' (Letter 90), to which she replied (Letter 91):

> I am rejoiced that you intend to read the first book of its kind, and hope to have the pleasure of convincing you that you have lost a great many pleasant ideas from having so long delayed it.

However, as G. H. Blore suggested in an unpublished essay, the learning she had was probably not systematic (WCA/E10/14):

> We know from a dozen sources how eagerly the young ladies at Bath snatched up the new and sentimental romances, how many

of them wept over the sorrows of Clarissa Harlowe [in Richardson's novel *Clarissa*]: but it was not the custom for young women (or men) to go back to Elizabethan drama. Perhaps she was only groping at random with such of Philip's books as were within reach and did not carry her studies far.

But her interest was well-founded: on one occasion she showed her appreciation of learning and the company of well-read friends with the comment '… I think it as good as a graduate's books to know where people dined and who they had with them' (Letter 52). Today, undergraduate reading lists of the period, such as the Christ Church 'collections books' are of great interest to historians (Sutherland and Mitchell, 1986, pp. 493-512). Her reading seemed to have included *The Life and Opinions of Tristram Shandy* by Laurence Sterne, published in nine volumes from 1759, though at the time it was not generally highly regarded (Letter 93). And when in 1785 the poet laureateship was vacant, she commented (Letter 92): 'Sir Cecil Wray's probationary ode is a good one and is to be followed by several others.' In fact, the successful candidate was not Wray, an MP who had lost to Fox in the notorious fight for the seat of Westminster in the previous year, but Thomas Warton, the brother of the head master of Winchester College, who had been championed by Joshua Reynolds. Pitt's choice, William Mason, the 'gardener poet', is said to have refused the appointment, though this is not mentioned in his entry in the ODNB. Warton had held the chair of poetry at Oxford and was an intimate of Dr Johnson, whom he helped to gain an MA. In many other ways he was a lion in the Georgian literary world: as an undergraduate, Philip Williams had contributed to a volume of verses edited by him, mourning the death of George II (*see* p. 27)

Sarah and her husband clearly had a shared interest in literature. In 1785, Joseph Warton lent her a copy of a long poem, *The Mine*, by John Sargent, a friend of the family from East Lavington, near Midhurst, which she had obviously seen in preparation (Letter 81):

> … I do not like [it] better in print than I did in manuscript; Dr W says he likes it (which I don't believe) and that it is equal to Comus [by Milton]; [but] the sentiments of the Heroine of the tale are so exactly my own that I could not help being a little affected with it.

In his reply Philip, perhaps feeling upstaged, took the opportunity to take a swipe at a newly published edition of Milton's shorter poems by Warton (though it was elsewhere greeted with great critical acclaim), as well as punning Sargent's work (Letter 83):

> Tom Warton's publication of Milton is, I think, errant trumpery, and the Lavington mine I should be sorry to call mine.

Although Sarah could clearly hold her own on literature, she was no great antiquarian, but on one occasion two years before she died spent enjoyable times rummaging around Winchester College with Joan Smith, a friend of hers who shared her interests and paid her visits (Letter 100):

> ...after church we went to poke out the pictures of Wardens [of Winchester College] that she had heard of in the Warden's gallery, she loves digging into antiquity as well as myself, and you would adore her for stopping to read the names of all the Benefactors; she is kind enough to call upon me often and she is the only consolation I have, she has an extraordinary good understanding, improved by good substantial kind of reading which I love, and the most chearful temper that it is possible for any one to be possessed of – she is going away very soon, for which I am heartily sorry.

Many of the pictures which the two women 'poked out' still hold pride of place in the Warden's Lodgings and College Hall.

Philip Williams was fortunate in having a wife who was intelligent, capable, knew her way round Winchester College and was not afraid to confront problems. Her status in 'Wykeham's world' was sufficiently high for a warden of New College, Oxford, John Oglander, to call on her when he was in Winchester. He had been ill, and looking 'like an old wash leather glove', a verdict she delivered with obvious affection (Letter 66):

> He sat half an hour with me, the children shewed him their doll's things, and I thought he looked upon them with a wishful eye; he was very kind in his enquiries after you.

Whilst serving as the Speaker's chaplain in London, Philip was able to rely on her to keep him informed and do what was necessary to keep him out of trouble. In particular, she oversaw the church at Compton and made sure that he exercised his role as a fellow and co-bursar at Winchester College. In today's terms, she acted as a part-time secretary and personal assistant. She was also not shy at offering the sort of advice that was perhaps not customary from a younger wife, as on one occasion concerning the midsummer meeting of warden and fellows (Letter 102):

> ...of all things be civil to [the warden, Harry Lee] in your correspondence upon the subject, you know that you are more than his match and therefore however smart you may be to him it can be no triumph to you; every trifle is canvassed in such a place as this, which makes me hope you will excuse this hint.

She also relayed to him all manner of news about the school, such as the fact that in June 1785 William Sturges had won the earl of Ailesbury's gold medal for a Latin, writing 'his task (which is a very good one) in a great hurry and without any assistance of any one' (Letter 104). Entitled *Difficilia quae pulchra* (fine things are difficult) copies still reside in the College archives (WCA/23789a, b). She surmised that he 'will probably be as learned as his father [the Winchester prebendary John Sturges jr' (1736/7-1807)], but hoped that 'he may be as good and more agreeable.' In fact, as William Sturges-Bourne (he double-barrelled his surname to comply with the terms of an inheritance) he pursued a successful career as a politician. A close friend of George Canning, who himself was educated at Hyde Abbey School in Winchester, he is remembered for the Sturges-Bourne Acts that reformed the poor law. In 1827, with huge reluctance, he served for two months as Home Secretary, but resisted all attempts to foist on him the office of Chancellor of the Exchequer. The Hampshire Record Office holds the Sturges-Bourne Dyson Correspondence (HRO/9M55), a large collection of letters between Sturges-Bourne's daughter, Anne, and Marianne Dyson, a daughter by his second wife of Sarah's brother-in-law, Jeremiah Dyson jr.

Like many women of her day, Sarah Williams must have been acutely aware of the scholastic gulf between herself and the men she mixed with. And no doubt she looked with some envy at the lives of the blue, or near-blue stockings of mid-Hampshire, such as Georgiana Hare-Naylor (née Shipley), Melesina Trench and Jane Warton, to name but a few.

***

NOT SURPRISINGLY, Sarah Williams's father, Thomas Collins, and his friends and relatives from his native county of Sussex are frequently mentioned in the Letters. He was second master of Winchester College, around which turned the lives of Philip Williams and his wife, and it is therefore important to understand this man and his career.

He was the eldest son of Christopher, an apothecary from Midhurst, West Sussex, and his wife Margaret, née Bettsworth [sic], probably from Wellington, Somerset, where they were married. He and his siblings were widely spread in age: there were at least four sons and two daughters; Thomas was about 17 years older than his younger brother, Charles (an earlier namesake brother had died young), and nearly 20 years older than his younger sister Charlotte. Midhurst was – and still is – a small town best known for the Cowdrey Park Estate. As well as being an apothecary, Christopher Collins appears in the record with an interest in the advowson of the parish of Treyford (united with Didling), two miles southwest of Midhurst (WSRO/QDD/W1(9)R(10)).

It is likely that Thomas Collins received his early education at the grammar school in the town; he undoubtedly won a scholarship to Winchester College (to which his brother Charles followed him in due course), went up to Queen's College, Oxford, four years later and subsequently migrated to New College, which most Wykehamists strove to reach. In 1752, he graduated BA and was ordained deacon at Chichester, and priest at Oxford. In the following year he was presented to the rectory of Coombes, two miles north of Shoreham; it is not clear what link he had with the patron, Sir John Shelley, 5th bt, seated at Michelgrove (now ruined), Patching, Sussex, but he was 'a good deal harassed by [his] affairs' after his death in 1783 (Letter 52). He probably married two years later, in 1755, when he resigned his fellowship of New College *uxore ducta resignans* (NCA, Sewell's Register, ff. 250-51). Nothing is known of his wife – she is never mentioned in the Letters – but they had three daughters, Sarah in about 1759, Charlotte two years later and Elizabeth in about 1764.

Thomas Collins acquired another living in 1764, when he was instituted to Graffham by the offices of Richard Bettesworth (probably a relative of his mother), who was the father of the patron of the living, Charlotte Bettesworth, then a minor (a situation which subsequently led to litigation), who had inherited the advowson from her mother née Orme. Much information about the life and career of Thomas Collins at this period can be found in a run of documents in the Lavington Manuscripts in the West Sussex Record Office (pieces 84-94 passim), which are thought to have originated from the politician John Sargent junior (1750-1831), who married Charlotte Bettesworth in 1778. The couple were seated at Woolavington, near Graffham, and nearly a decade later Sargent exercised his patronage as lord of the manor of Woolavington to give

Thomas Collins the rectorship of Graffham (boundary changes make it difficult to untangle the extents of the parishes in the area.)

Charlotte and John Sargent and others in West Sussex were part of the coterie of friends and relatives of Philip and Sarah Williams. On a visit to Midhurst in July 1783, for example, Sarah wrote (Letter 41):

> Mrs. Sargent has spent two days here, and looks quite well, though she is drinking porter by way of avoiding a consumption, which she is in hourly dread of.

Much else happened for Thomas Collins in 1764: as well as the birth of his third and last daughter, he went back to New College as a chaplain, graduated MA, and BD (12 years after graduating BA) and was appointed head master of the choristers' school (which became defunct within a few years; Edmunds, 1996, Ch. 4). Two years later he was elected second master of Winchester under Joseph Warton as head. How this came about is not entirely clear, though by December 1766 he was writing letters to parents about the minutiae of their sons' education, albeit from Midhurst in the holidays, and was therefore apparently well established (HRO/62M73/F7).

The whirl of events that engaged Thomas Collins in 1764 may indicate that it was in that year that his wife died, possibly at the birth of the youngest daughter, Elizabeth, though this is not proven. After his election as second master, he presumably came to live in the school with his three daughters, aged about 2, 5 and 7 years. It was not uncommon for families to do so: Warton and his much-loved wife Mary had six children. And Collins was not the only man to live in the college with a bevy of females. Huntingford, when his brother died young took his sister-in-law and her children under his care, and moved them into the college when he became the warden. There are similarities, in that both men had 'the problem of marrying off' several young ladies. Huntingford's strategy was to give preferment to the prospective husbands, but Collins did not have that luxury, as will be seen.

When Thomas Collins came to Winchester College as second master, or usher, to Joseph Warton in May 1766, he walked straight into a pay dispute (HRO/21M65/B9/6/1-19,WCA/23216/pp.3-6; WCA/605, 619, 23358). Although the affair scarcely deserves a footnote in labour history, it does reveal the lowly status given to teachers at the time and illustrates the setting in which Philip Williams was to spend much of his life. Just before Collins's arrival, acting on instructions of the warden and supervisors (or posers) of New College, Oxford, the warden and fellows of Winchester had passed a resolution that the head master and usher were to be paid £250 and £100, respectively, and that they were to desist from taking gratuities or 'presents' from pupils. The warden of Winchester College, Harry Lee, later pointed out that the 'stipend only' scheme had followed an earlier proposal to pay the masters from the proceeds of two legacies, topped up by gratuities, which had been opposed by Warton's predecessor as head, Dr John Burton. At the time, 'the tipping system was in full vigour' (Leach, 1899, p. 369) and it had been common practice for the parents of scholars on the foundation to hand out gratuities of 10 guineas a year. Not surprisingly, Warton and Collins, who may have been promised such perks 'at the interview', were not pleased with the new measures. Although they were content with fixed stipends, even though the amounts were considerably less than they might have expected from a church living, and were pleased to exclude children 'whose parents are known or confessed to be really and truly necessitous or indigent', they failed to understand why they should not be rewarded by 'parents who are known to be in easy and affluent circumstances...[who] voluntarily without any solicitation or Demand offer...a decent Gratuity...'.

By October the affair had hotted up and the masters decided to put their case to the ultimate arbiter, the bishop of Winchester, Benjamin Hoadly, who was the visitor to both Winchester College and New College. Although a cripple, Hoadly was a worldly man, a whig, a low-church propagandist, one of the most prominent churchmen of his time, who invited much venom in Winchester, where he was rarely to be found. They met him to explain their claims. Also weighing in was former usher Samuel Speed, rector of Martyr Worthy, near Winchester, who had been edged out of the school for his whiggism. In the precise and meticulous manner that was his way, he spoke up for the masters, quoting Wykeham's statutes and seeking to clear his own name by saying: '...with full ease of mind [I] received the voluntary presents of the Rich and able: and cannot yet be prevailed upon to reproach myself for having done it.' In mid-November, Hoadly – who was a colossus of theological debate – and his wife even went out to Martyr Worthy to visit Speed. In a school where the Classics were paramount, it might be supposed that its masters were in a strong position when it came to interpreting the statutes of the College, which were, of course, written in Latin. They based their case on the difference between demanding gratuities, which the statutes forbade, and accepting them (WCA/23358):

...the Founder, as the Masters humbly apprehend, has obviously and fully exprest his Intention, in the Three Words, *exigere* [exact], *petere* [demand], & *vendicare* [claim]. William of Wykeham would not have used only Three Words, yet have meant Four, would not have laid such a snare for his Masters ...To add this Fourth Word, accepere [accept], a word of quite a new Sence and meaning, appears to be, to all Intents and purposes to make a new Statute....

In a letter to the bishop the former head master, John Burton, diplomatically pointed out that 'if the Warden conceives the least glimpse of your L[ordshi]p's inclining to the opinion that the Statutes have left us no power of prohibiting voluntary presents he will rejoice to terminate the Dispute...'. A few days later Warton and Collins got their way, when the warden and fellows passed a resolution to pay them £150 and £100, respectively, with no mention of the question of gratuities. The next day, Harry Lee, in a joyfully worded letter to the bishop, reported the outcome, with the rider that masters 'would be favourable to the poorer sort of Scholar, especially to the sons of Clergymen...'.

The whole affair is redolent of pique and donnish self-interest, and even shades of Reform. But the potentially corrupt situation whereby masters depended for their livelihood on tips from boys and their parents was not settled finally until the death in 1845 of head master William Stanley Goddard – who succeeded Collins and then Warton – under the terms of his will, which 'settled £25,000 stock on the Head and Second M[aster] on condition that they should receive no gratuities from the Scholars' (Kirby, 1892, p. 399 et seq.). Goddard had come to the school as a quirister after the bankruptcy of his father, 'a prosperous merchant... thanks to Thomas Collins... who was the brother of one of his father's City friends' (R.D.H. Custance, 'William Stanley Goddard', ODNB). Ensuring that Winchester acquired an effective head in the form of Goddard is probably the single most significant achievement of Thomas Collins's career.

The Letters illustrate only the end of Thomas Collins's career, and then only from the point of view of Sarah. She does her best to shield him from matters that might agitate him and depicts an anxious man at his wit's end with unrest in the school. Rebellions were, of course, a fact of life in boarding schools, and Winchester had its fair share, notably the ones of 1774 (Kirby, 1892, p. 404) and the wildest of all in 1793, which forced Warton into retirement and led to 35 expulsions. Although not otherwise documented, it is clear from the Letters that Thomas Collins experienced a similar event at the end of his career and only a year after it had been necessary to call on the chairman of the Hampshire Quarter Sessions to quell a 'town and gown' riot (HRO/1M44/44/1). In corroboration, Kirby's *Scholars* (1888) shows that eight boys left the school in 1784, six of them for no stated reason. Such events must always be distressing to schoolmasters, but Thomas Collins, who was prone to anxiety, was excessively affected. Perhaps he had 'come to the end' of teaching, seeing no way in which he would ever get the headship in succession to Joseph Warton, who in the event did not end his term for almost ten years. Like many a person facing retirement, Collins himself did think that he might be asked to stay on for a while, but that was not to be. The flavour of the affair is provided by Sarah Williams, writing in May 1784 (Letter 52):

> Papa is still very unhappy about the shocking business at College, and he will write to you about it in two or three days; there are two [boys] to go away which he and every other reasonable person thinks sufficient, especially as there is more come out, which will justify the saving the others; but he is afraid that what has been done will not satisfy ... the W[arden] of N[ew] Col[lege] ... However, he is determined to do nothing more, let them do as they please. It is a circumstance much in favour of one of the poor boys that are to go, though it makes the matter more burthensome to Papa, that he is affected by it to a degree, which can hardly be conceived.

In the following month she addressed the same theme (Letter 55):

> The idea of Papa's staying is at an end, so you will not mention it, it would interfere so much with Goddard[']s designs that it is not to be thought of, and it would be very unpleasant to Papa you may be certain. He is now ready to be off with his two horses (which turn out beyond expectation) as soon as they will let him resign; as to the other business [the rebellion], he is rather more easy, because something is now to be done, which they hope will finally settle matters, if the Warden of New College [Oxford] does not interfere ... the young couch of roses [surely a nickname] and another boy are to go at the election; they were produced on the scrutiny as most guilty, but not a word of this to any one as it is to be done with the utmost secrecy.

Much later, his successor William Goddard faced similar problems, which were often related to the territorial instincts of scholars, who fiercely guarded rights of entry to the buildings granted for their use, including 'School', the fine building – still extant – in which they were taught by the second master. Thus in February 1787, Sarah reported to her husband (Letter 118):

> ...it has been a very lawless time at College, for Mr Goddard has been very ill indeed, with a fever, which has turned out to be of the intermitting kind, so that all danger is I believe over, and to add to all Newhouse was taken ill too, and the boys were certain that the Warden and Dr [John] Ballard [a fellow] were to go into the school, which people believed.

After retirement, Thomas Collins went to live with his much younger sister Charlotte at or near Midhurst. Three years later he became a trustee of Midhurst Grammar School (which closed in 2008), and it was almost certainly due to him that the Wykehamist John Wooll in 1799 relinquished his New College fellowship to head the school, en route to the headship of Rugby. The history of the school shows that there were many links between it and Thomas Collins's in-laws, the Bettesworth family, which must have favoured him (Row, 1913, pp. 25-64 passim).

Six months after her father had retired, Sarah painted a less than charming picture of his successor and his wife, with an interesting side swipe at her father's teaching methods (Letter 71):

> I have seen Mrs Goddard and she has returned my visit, she is very civil, and well behaved, and tolerably well-looking, though not of the first order of females in any respect, Goddard very fussy, has been down to consult me several times; he last night told me that his wife had a cold, but he hoped it would not last, for of all things he dreaded the idea of a sick wife, L'Ingenu [by Voltaire] exactly. He is the oddest compound I ever saw, to which his education under Papa has not a little contributed.

There were at least two memoirs of Sarah's father, both published in 1806, one a notice in Dodsley's *Annual Register ...for the Year 1804* (vol. 46, p. 489) and another as an extensive footnote in John Wooll's *Biographical Memoirs of ...Warton* (pp. 45-46). Wooll refers to 'a noble spirit, and a mind superior to every selfish consideration', with 'a contempt of money, such as to preclude the meanness of avarice, or the servile blandishments of sycophantic dependence'. He was not 'terrified by the power of the great' and bowed only to 'a superiority of talents and virtue'. Wooll continued:

> As a master, he was sedulously accurate in imparting the first rudiments of classical learning, and in impressing the necessary foundation of grammar, without which, he well knew, no real scholarship could be obtained.

The note in the *Annual Register*, which Sewell transcribed verbatim into his register at New College, refers to his 'literary attainments' (though he seems to have published nothing) and 'his generosity and noble disinterested spirit' and then goes on to extol 'his fortitude and Christian resignation under the severest trials', explaining:

> Within the short space of about 12 months, the venerable old man had lost no less than three of his descendants; his daughter, Charlotte Viscountess Bolingbroke, and two of her children, the hon. George and Mary St John. He had fixed his residence in Bath since the death of his daughter.

Many readers of the *Annual Register* would have heard of the scandalous life of Charlotte's husband (*see* Chapter 15); Wooll goes further, referring to 'many years of accumulated sorrow and anxiety, originating in the guilt of others, and arising from sources to which he naturally looked forward for comfort and felicity'. Sarah would, of course, have known the gentle and the endearing, if somewhat unworldly aspects of her father's character before she died. Although the full extent of the consequences of her brother-in-law's unfaithfulness were in the future, she must have known that the marriage was well on its the way to ruin.

A view of Thomas Collins written in draft by G.H. Blore, who taught history at Winchester College, depicts him as (WCM/E10/14/1/1-2):

> ...a kindly conscientous man, beloved by his daughters, not disposed to push his own interests, but taking it to heart when anything went wrong with his charge. When he retired he might expect to [have] had enough backers to have been elected a Fellow [of Winchester], but he made no effort and was seriously annoyed with those who urged him to apply. He was a sensitive soul, seeking above all peace of mind, and he found it in a rural retreat at Midhurst in Sussex.

In fact, it is unlikely that Thomas Collins would ever have been elected a fellow, though it seems that, much to his distress, Philip Williams had raised the matter (Letter 59):

> You said something to Papa in your letter, which put him out of humour, about his going to the Warden [of Winchester College, Harry Lee] concerning a fellowship; it happened to come very inopportune; as he had just had a recent instance of very uncivil treatment from the Warden, proceeding merely I believe from his having the misfortune of not being a gentleman, I shall tell you more of this matter when I write on Monday; in the mean time let me intreat you never to mention the subject above to him again, from what you have already said, you have been the innocent cause of great uneasiness to me...

Eventually, he comes to terms with the status quo (Letter 82):

> Papa is perfectly easy upon the subject of the fellowship, he does not abound in wealth, but he has enough for his comfort, and he has what is better than twenty fellowships, a consciousness of having done his duty, and injured no man, I wish I may be able to feel the same if I live to be as old as he is.

He had not 'failed': no second master had in fact ever been granted a fellowship – certainly not during the eighteenth century – though some received a prebend, as did Thomas Collins himself in 1775, when he was collated by the bishop of Chichester to the bursal prebend at Chichester, one of four at the cathedral reserved for Wykehamists. It fell open at the death of Samuel Speed, the second master before Warton, who himself, as head master, was rewarded more generously in 1788 by the king with the 10th prebend of Winchester.

6. *'Tear, or lock up my letters'*

THE UPS AND DOWNS of all three of the families of Thomas Collins's daughters form the subject matter of much of the Letters. There are also many insights into the life lived in London by Philip Williams, serving as chaplain to the Speaker of the House of Commons, and his behaviour as absentee rector of Compton, near Winchester. For her part, Sally forebore his frequent absences with unconcealed distress: her letters tell the tale of a woman – albeit one supported by servants and a diaspora of friends and relatives – morphing from a bright young thing into a rather embittered, but loyal and faithful wife. She struggled with something close to manic depression, whilst he sought preferment in the manner of the times – which meant near-continuous socialising with the great and good.

All the while, they had to keep up their end in the polite society of Georgian Winchester, which centred round the cathedral close and the assemblies and race meetings patronised by a wide range of people. These included a huge number of churchmen of all kinds and their families – high-flyers such as Jonathan Shipley, William Buller and Beilby Porteous; academics and polemicists such as Thomas Balguy and Robert Lowth; and those tarnished by Edmund Pyle's 'dawdling' epithet (*see* p. 189), such as Matthew Woodford and Thomas Rennell senior. Philip and Sally knew them all, as well as a cast of the local well-to-do and aristocrats (pretended, descended and real) that they often mention.

There are 89 letters written between Philip and Sarah, 24 from him and 65 from her (*see* Concordance, Appendix I). His letters mainly cover the first two sessions of parliament he served, namely, 1784 (6 letters) and 1785 (17 letters), with only a single letter from the 1787 session (Appendix III). Ten of her letters cover the period from their first year of marriage to the commencement in May 1785 of his appointment as chaplain to the Speaker, all but one written from Winchester (the exception being from Midhurst) to him at various addresses – at New College, Chilton Foliat, Lincoln, Ely and the Somerset Coffee House in the Strand (W29-39). It is clear from these that even before he was able to justify his absence from home on the grounds that parliament was in session, he took every opportunity to travel. Two letters were written in 1783 by her from Moor

Crichel, Dorset, where she was supporting her sister Charlotte in childbirth, whilst he and servants held the fort at Winchester (Letters 44 and 46). The letters she wrote whilst he was at Westminster cover all three of the sessions, with 18, 26 and 9 letters, respectively. There are none from either party for the session of 1786, during which evidence from elsewhere suggests that he was prevented from serving by illness. There are also a few other letters, including one written in 1783 from him at New College to her staying with relatives at East Lavington, near Midhurst (Letter 42).

Since the routine when he was away from home was for them to write each other one letter a week, many of his must have been destroyed or lost. Indeed, he expressly instructed her to keep their contents private, writing in a postscript (Letter 103):

> I hope you either tear, or lock up my letters.

It was the practice for him to send a letter on a Saturday, with the contents laid out day by day, as he had probably been schooled to do at Winchester. Her reply, which was much freer, was usually written on a Sunday and posted the next day, arriving on the Tuesday. When in London, he benefited from the privilege of free postage granted to all parliamentarians, including his employer, the Speaker. Similarly, during the brief period 1782-84, when their brother-in-law, the Hon. G. R. St John, was a member of parliament, she also benefited from free postage when he was in Winchester. Thus, she wrote (Letter 46):

> Mr. St. John being from home and of course no frank to be had, I did not think it worth while to write without one, especially as there was a letter of mine upon the road when I received yours.

Therefore, the availability of franks, to some extent, regulated their correspondence, as she acknowledged (Letter 29):

> I forbear all reproaches and hope you will not omit writing to me continually even without franks should they not hold out.

The same point is illustrated in the two following examples:

> I wish you would buy Mrs Smith's verses for me, they cost only two shillings, and are published with her name to them, and you may send them down in one or two franks (Letter 51; *see* p. 184).

I should be glad to have the enclosed carried to Sage, and let William [his servant] wait for what I have sent, and you will put it into the next frank (Letter 97).

Another beneficiary of free postage was Philip's father-in-law, Dr John Gordon, who on one occasion, obviously wanting to limit costs of postage by not using too much paper wrote (Letter 15):

[I] forgot to get a frank of the B[isho]p [and] therefor obliged to croud these things in.

In July 1784 Sarah worried that new franking regulations (*House of Commons Journal, General Index XXXV-LV (1774-1800)*, p. 772, resolution no. 2559) would cost them dear for packets received from Oxford (Letter 66), but he assured her otherwise (Letter 67):

The franking being withdrawn will not affect me, as I shall have my Oxford packet sent under cover to Mr [Charles Wolfran] C[ornwall].

First introduced in 1652, free franks for parliamentarians lasted until the reform of postal services by Rowland Hill in 1840 (Robinson, H, 1948; Bottomley, 1988). The cover of the letter was generally stamped FREE and, in principle, had to be signed by the nominal beneficiary. A few of the letters from John Gordon to Philip Williams, which variously were sent from Cambridge, Lincoln, London, and even Saffron Walden, show some of these features, such as FREE and LINCOLN stamps (Letters 19 and 370), the endorsements 'Free John Lincoln' and 'By favor' (Letters 19, 129) and the bold flourish of an unidentified signatory on four letters from Cambridge (Letters 11, 13, 15 and 17), possibly that of John Green, bishop of Lincoln at the time, though the mail probably often went via his official London residence.

On another occasion, sending a letter from Cambridge to Oxford, John Gordon hoped to reduce costs by having his daughter post the letter from London, as he explained (Letter 11):

...Fanny sets off for Town on Tuesday and I intended by way of œconomy, as I forgot to get a Frank for you, that she shoud convey this so far to save postage...

***

THE CORRESPONDENCE between Philip and Sarah Williams that forms the basis of this volume was a happy accident of separation. Unlike many other letters, they were not written to arrange business or send orders (except incidentally), but rather to nourish the bond between two married people. They were the equivalent of the conversation that couples have when the children have gone to bed and the day is nearly over. They were a means of conveying news, discussing problems, airing issues, scoring points, even having rows. And, of course, they were private, intended for no other eyes.

It so happens that at the time these letters were written the public postal system in Britain was undergoing a revolution. Whereas at its inception in 1635, post-boys took letters on horseback from 'post to post', in 1784, John Palmer, an enterprising theatre owner from Bath, demonstrated that a system using mail coaches was much faster. The first experiment, between Bristol and London, was carried out at an average speed of about 8 miles an hour, reducing the time taken from 36 to 16 hours. Within a year similar services from London were running to Portsmouth and Southampton, starting in May and August, respectively (Binnion, 1976, p.39). In the year before the advent of mail coaches, post from London via Hartford Bridge and Alton arrived in Winchester at about 6 pm on Sundays, Wednesdays and Fridays and via Petersfield at 7 pm on Tuesdays, Thursdays and Saturdays (Sadler's *Hampshire Directory*, 1784). The city also had a relatively fast passenger coach from the capital: Collier's service, for example, left London at 4 am and reached the White Hart Inn, Winchester, at about 2.30 pm.

The task of the local 'postmaster' was to collect letters for his district and hand in letters for onward delivery. Postage was paid on delivery, at a rate per sheet, unless a frank was provided by the sender. Free delivery was accorded to members of parliament and others. Philip Williams often made use of the privilege of his patron, the Speaker, Charles Wolfran Cornwall. For most of their time apart, Sarah and Philip abided by a strict arrangement, whereby he posted his letter in London on a Saturday, to arrive in Winchester on Sunday, and she replied with a letter posted on Monday to arrive on Tuesday. His letters seemed to have been written in instalments during the week: hence he wrote in one, 'I had written thus far, when I recieved your's…' (Letter 123). She was keen to receive his letters, writing on one occasion (Letter 52) '…you are very good to charge your memory with so many trifles for my entertainment', but More often it was he who expressed his satisfaction, as in the following examples:

Upon my return from the house received your last letter, which gave me great pleasure, and made me think more of you than I wished to do ... (Letter 73). I hurried from home to read your letter which, without any nonsense, is a period I look forward to with impatience, as soon as one Tuesday is over; it is a thanksgiving day to me, and the five minutes I am reading it give me much more real comfort than I shall experience on Thursday with the immaculate [the archbishop of Canterbury]...his chaplain etc, etc, who are to dine here (Letter 67).

She took pains to reply immediately, but could not always do so:

I am got up rather earlier than common that I may not disappoint you, being prevented from beginning my letter as usual upon Sunday night (Letter 55) ...We came home rather late from Compton, last night, so I could not begin your letter till this morning [Monday] (Letter 69).

However, when he did not adhere to his side of the bargain, she complained vigorously:

You will not surely be a worse correspondent to me than Rachel [Landy; a friend], who has written every Sunday and Wednesday since I came here. If you are going out, or have not time, I beg you will direct some [postage paid] covers here for her and she will fill them up on the days above mentioned (Letter 44)...Remember to write next Saturday if you do go out, because I shall otherwise have no letter 'till Tuesday which would half kill me (Letter 51).

And failure to reply to questions brought prompt reminders (Letter 99):

... you say nothing of Mrs Elyott's business, indeed you do not say a great deal of any sort, it is very hard to deprive me of the least part of the very little comfort I have, write more next time...

Failure to receive word from him at all was extremely upsetting (Letter 74): 'I have been in the utmost anxiety for these last two hours expecting your dear letter ...as it brings me the only pleasant moments I spend in the week.' His replies were often so terse that you can almost hear his crossness – or was it his form of raillery, a much prized conversational style of the time? (Doody, 1994, Note 59, p. 458; Letter 42):

Why do I answer your letters so soon; but that I love you, and you know it, and why don't I mention the children, but that I love them and they don't know it? Depend upon it that yourself and them possess my mind more than ever will appear, 'till you can dissect it, and so much for that business'

His sister Anne also admonished him, addressing him as 'Phee' and writing from Eastbourne in 1784: 'I know you are not very fond of using the Pen, when it is not absolutely necessary' (W194). And his excuses could be rather lame (Letter 88): ' I wrote you a shorter letter than I wished, least I should not come back in time, and so it proved, for I was pinned down to a card-table till near eleven.' There were also variations to the routine, as Sarah suggested on one occasion (Letter 50):

In future I shall write to you on a Tuesday, because Monday is [a] 12 o'clock day [for the post], and if I am interrupted you will be disappointed; and if I answer your letter Sunday evening, my spirits will be too much affected by the receipt of yours to wri{te} any {thin}g but nonsense, which can {only} make {you} uneasy.'

And sometimes it was her turn to experience problems:

Should the like happen again, you may be very certain that there is no cause for it, but some neglect in the post-office, you and my children have my whole and sole attention in this life, and wherever you are concerned I am scrupulously punctual, my letter is always ready by half after ten... (Letter 79)...Contrary to custom I have not been able to begin this letter till this morning [Monday]...(Letter 111).

When Sarah had moved out of the city to live in the rectory at Compton, she had the added trouble of collecting mail from Winchester, delivered by the new mail coach service between London and Southampton (though there were also active posts at Compton and Shawford; *see* Letter 118). This sometimes led to problems, not least when the postmaster or his staff had difficulty in reading addresses (Letter 119):

Owing to your letter's being carried on to Southampton on Saturday I have but just got it; Martin has played me the same trick before with a letter of my father's, for which reason I have always sent by some of the people for your letter on Saturday; it seems Martin can't read and if Todd is not in the way to look at the letters, the maid does it, who I believe is almost as illeterate [sic] as Martin, they assured me that they had looked at all the letters and there was none for me; it had poured with rain and no body had gone from Compton, so I dispatched Prince to Mrs Green, who said that Martin certainly had a letter for me; this comforted me, because I knew there was nothing wrong about you, so I waited, I won't say with much patience his return to day.

Sarah's letters to Philip were more often than not laced with problems, frequently expressed in distressing language, and it must have been with extreme trepidation that he opened them, though he generally put on a brave face. On one occasion he wrote (Letter 83):

Tuesday brought me your letter which always brings me some uneasiness, when you speak of yourself, and the more so, as it is not in my power to remedy it, or your own either, and yet as it proceeds only from your affection for me, I cannot but love you the better for it.

In the last of his letters to survive, he tries to express the fact that, because he and Sarah are making plans for her to move up to live with him in London (one of several such attempts), they will no longer need to communicate by letter. But what he wrote probably came closer to the truth than he wished (Letter 108): 'I hope in my next I shall desire to be troubled with no more of your letters.'

It is interesting to speculate on the moment the letter was opened. Was it opened there and then at the post, and read walking in the road, or was it guarded and cherished for reading at home? Read with joy, with trepidation, even fear? However it was read, the sheer range of purposes served by the letter was immense. Between spouses it was a means of 'keeping the romance alive' of nourishing the marital bond, even a billet doux to be ripped open and replied to immediately, or torn to pieces! It was for arranging rendezvous, discussing issues (family, political, gossipy, personal), solving problems, 'letting off steam', thinking things out, remembering loved ones, ordering the events of the past days and weeks, apologising, negotiating, impressing, correcting, disabusing, even misleading. It was for effecting commissions, assuaging mental stress (especially for Sarah), reminding the children of their father, local news (keeping Philip Williams in the know about Winchester College), running the parish (Compton), sending bankers' drafts, family business, giving orders, chastising, advising, directing, seeking views and approval, moulding moral and social norms, asserting authority, amusing, reporting on well-being or not – and much else!

**

ONE OF THE GREAT ASSETS of any collection of letters is that they act like a record of a counsellor and his client. Bit by bit the corners are lifted on the mask, so that the writer is revealed. Thus, Philip Williams, as a newly married man and young father, is disinterested in his parish at Compton, hopelessly out of his depth buying presents for the children, less than understanding of the challenges faced by a young woman with several children, fond of the good life in London, prone to go off to stay with old school chums, and unhelpful in running errands (in London) for his wife and friends. Also, in the eyes of his wife, he is not doing well in the greasy task of seeking preferment, and she is losing patience with his failure to bring home the clerical bacon. And yet, she says, he is 'my greatest blessing in this life' (Letter 104) – or did she feel she had gone too far in her lament and feared repercussions?

When Philip Williams wed Sarah Collins he was aged 37 and she was 22. Their substantial age difference is perhaps apparent in the earlier letters, where she invariable addresses him as 'My dear Sir'. The terminations in her early correspondence (Letters 23-70), which ended simply 'S.W.', are also relatively restrained, centring on assurances of fidelity, with phrases such as 'Adieu, yours entirely', 'Your ever affectionate', 'Adieu my dearest and believe me eternally yours', and 'I am ever yours most entirely'. Sometimes she puts on the pressure for a reply: 'Write to me as soon as you have this and don't think me, who loves [you] so well as I do, unreasonable' (Letter 35). Occasionally she mentions the children, as in 'God bless you and my dear children is the eternal wish of yours S.W.'. For his part, in the few letters from 1783 and 1784 (42, 48-9, 60, 63, 65 and 67) he addresses her as 'My dearest woman' and 'My best' and terminates with '...believe me more than ever if possible, Your's Ph. Williams', or 'your's most dearly and affectionately' and 'Adieu my dearest and take care of yourself'.

Notwithstanding the formality of opening and closing letters, the variability of their terminations speaks of genuine warmth and affection, which is even more apparent in the later letters. Invariably, from 1785 onwards they mutually address each other with 'My dearest love' and the terminations are warmer and more insistent. In February he ends with 'Once more adieu, I long to see you – which will be on good Friday', and

CAPITUM ROBUR TRIUM

Philip Williams.

(*Left*)[1] a coat-of-arms claimed by the Williams family on a bookplate (W414) and (*above*)[2] that of Owen Tudor.

(*Below*)[3] St Mackraeth's church, Llanfachraeth, on the west coast of Anglesey, in an earlier form of which Rice Williams was rector, in succession to his father-in-law.

Two faces of Phillip Williams: (*above*)[4] aged 81, the 'contented elderly rector', painted in 1823 by George Sharples, and (*left*) [5] aged 67, the 'earnest senior fellow', by George Hayter (later knighted) in 1809. (© *Winchester College*).

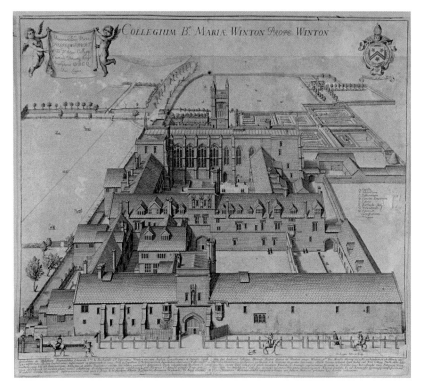

(*Above*) [6] Winchester College from College Street, an engraving by David Loggan, originally made in about 1675 and much as Philip Williams would have known it, except for 'School' (*below*)[7], completed in 1687, possibly by Sir Christopher Wren.

Winchester College: (*opposite*)[8] from the east in 1777 (© *Hampshire Record Office*), (*above*)[9] a chamber, where scholars slept, and (*below*)[10] dons and scholars mark the fifth centenary of the school in 1893.

(*Above*) miniatures of Lovelace Bigg (later Bigg-Wither) as a young man, aged 23 [11], and later in life [12]. (*Below*)[13] Chilton House, Chilton Foliat, near Newbury, where he lived in his early years, often visited by Philip Williams, depicted on a map of Wiltshire by Andrews and Dury,1773.

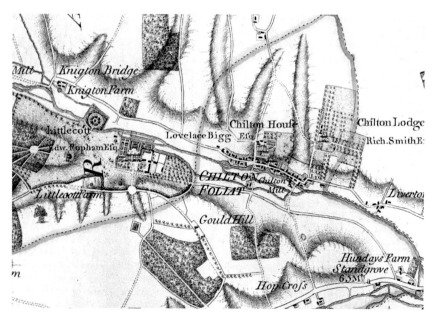

(*Above*)[14] Manydown House,
Wootton St Lawrence, near
Basingstoke, inherited
by Lovelace Bigg-Wither in
1779, now demolished, and
(*right*)[15] a statue of his
cousin, the celebrated jurist Sir
William Blackstone (1723-
1780), which stands in the
Codrington Library, All Souls
College, Oxford.

(*Next page*) [16] Winchester
College from the Warden's
Garden, 1827, by George
Shepherd (© *Winchester College*).

later letters end with 'Ever your's till death' and 'Ever my dearest dear's, not forgetting the blessed children'. More curtly, 'Ever your's' is frequently used by him, but other terminations speak of his affection, such as 'God bless my ever best and dearest' and 'Adieu, God preserve you and the fœtids', the last using their rather unattractive code word for 'the kids'.

In these later letters, when the stress of bringing up a family alone in Winchester is apparent, she often writes extensive endearments, almost always starting with the mildly pious 'God bless..', as in 'God bless you my best and dearest life and I am ever yours', 'God bless you and them, my dearest, dearest love as ever yours', and, in her last letter, 'God bless you my dearest and send you safe to your affectionate S.W.'.

Personal letters, of course, enable relationships between couples to be more fully explored than any other type of source. In the case of Philip and Sarah this is particularly fruitful, as she was very uninhibited in expressing her feelings; in fact, as will be seen, she was undoubtedly on occasion clinically depressed and in the present age would probably have sought the support of a psychotherapist or more. Philip did his best to reassure her (Letter 48):

> I am returned home on purpose to write to you, and tell you once for all that you and my children are scarcely ever out of my thoughts, and that it will ever be the case 'till we meet again, and so much for sentiment, or what is a better thing, real affection and friendship.

Simple human virtues were also highly valued by Sarah (Letter 47), who would rather have Philip 'a country curate... with some feeling and humanity, than [a man] at the top of his profession .... if it is to be purchased by the sacrifice of every amiable virtue and sentiment.'

Sorting out her father's papers in the summer of 1784 when he retired as second master of Winchester College, she came across a letter of Philip's written 'a great many years ago' at a time when he had given up hopes of 'being connected' with her and realised how close she had come to not marrying him (Letter 68). Nothing is known of their courtship, but she was clearly familiar with London, had friends and acquaintances there (especially the ubiquitous and 'agreable and good-humoured....Miss Pyke'; Letter 111) and in one letter there are hints from him of earlier years spent in and around the capital (Letter 103): 'He [George Gordon] and I are going a scheme to morrow to spend the day at the awning place. I shall avoid going through the foul clothes room again…'.

She often wrote to him to express dissatisfaction with her lot, as a mother of small children with an absent father. He occasionally showed extreme tolerance, which she acknowledged (Letter 87): 'I have this moment your dear letter which though short is sweet, as it assures me that you do not love me the less for the extreme uneasiness I gave you whilst you was at home.' On another occasion she expressed her love and her desire to be in bed with him (Letter 102): 'The abundance of affection I have for you, never suffers me to be at rest, I don't think you are absent from my thoughts ten minutes in the day, and too often you are present at night.' Receiving news about him from the many people fresh from London who dropped in to see her was a trial (Letter 102): 'Mr Jenkinson gave me a good account of you, but I thought I should have burst out a crying, whilst he was in the room, and I did before he got down the stairs, all this, because he came to tell me that he had seen you.'

A month later she returns to the same theme, a sort of 'row in writing', but seems to draw back from pushing home the point (Letter 107):

> … I am hurt at the idea of having given you any uneasiness, but when you consider my unhappy situation, you must forget the petulancies that in spight of myself will escape me; when I married you I thought myself th one of the happiest of the human kind, and at present circumstances being so much the reverse, I cannot bear up with that composure of mind I ought to do, and to say the truth I'm afraid my temper is not quite so good as heretofore, but enough of this heart-breaking business.

Eighteen months later, and having moved out to the rectory at Compton, she looked back at their eight years of marriage in a letter concerning a parental bar on the marriage of Philip's stepbrother, George Gordon, at the age of 22 (he married five years later). After deprecating 'long engagements', and querying the concern of George's father about a 'settlement before marriage', she gives a disarmingly frank view of her own experience that must have left Philip wondering (Letter 115). Three years earlier she had made a sharper and probably truer comment on her lot as a married woman (Letter 58):

> I wish I could forget the happy hours I have spent with you, a sad contrast to those I now drag on.

Fortunately, he had probably learned to tone down her diatribes and was perhaps heartened by Sarah's assessment in the same letter of the forthcoming marriage of his sister, Anne (Nanny) to the Revd Theodore Gould: 'Your sister has I doubt not fixed her affections upon a worthy object and will meet with the reward she so justly deserves.' Two months later he reported that he was to officiate at their wedding (Letter 123). But her reply was, again, terrible to contemplate (Letter 118):

> ...my scheme of happiness has been cruelly destroyed and I have no resource from which I can expect relief; my every wish, every thought and affection is fixed on you and those dear children that belong to you, and whilst I am deprived of you I lose all comfort of my life; my mind is quite distracted and I have not the power of turning my thoughts to those things that might afford me ease; all I can expect is to get on, and I thank God that as yet my health is good.

There are several references in the Letters to an intimation of hers that death was impending – a fate not uncommon in otherwise healthy young women of her age. In a letter written five months before she did die, she even expressed a view about his remarriage, in the setting of a similar situation faced by their physician Dr John Littlehales, whose first wife Maria Anne Parry had died 18 days after the death of a son (there is a memorial inscription in Winchester Cathedral, alongside that of the Jane Austen). She wrote (Letter 124):

> ...people are outraged at our friend Dr L's behaviour, which I am afraid is not quite what it should be; that he and Miss Lea [Lee] are engaged I believe there is no doubt, and why should they not? It is what most of their friends approve, and wish; but they should be a little more decent and circumspect as to externals; I own it would hurt me, if I thought you would be ready to enter into new engagements after so short a separation.

For his part, Philip Williams could pen the sort of missive that must have outraged his wife, like one written with obvious boredom (a fragment only, Letter 101), without consulting her earlier letters about an errand (dunning Mrs Elyott's debtor) or his son's wish to have a 'knife with a silver blade to eat his dinner with' (Letter 99). In fact, he seems to have liked annoying her and loved 'to be scolded and lectured' (Letter 103). Yet again, he could be very loving (Letter 106):

If I have any dignity it is derived from you, and if I have any pride, it is in exhibiting you to my acquaintance, and you know as well as I do, that I look forward with the utmost impatience to the time when my whole life and existence will be devoted to you and my family, and our domesticity be separated only by the sisters three.

Although most of his letters give the impression of him having a fine time in London, the stress of being apart for such long periods does occasionally surface, as at the end of July 1785, only a week before the parliamentary recess. His words may not have made every heart sing, but the message is clear (Letter 110; *see also* p. 251)):

> Never was a being more tired, and almost wearied of existence, thank God for it; it is in consequence of having so good and so dear a woman, that ~~he has~~ I have been so long separated from, otherwise every possible attention and kindness have been shewn me, and which in a state of celibacy would have rendered my present situation not only palatable, but agreeable.

Like many wives, Sarah Williams had to share her husband with his friends. One of those was Lovelace Bigg-Wither (*see* Chapter 3), who had been a party to their marriage settlement (W223). Four years later, returning from New College, Oxford, Philip wrote (Letter 42): 'I shall set my face southwards … I mean to pay no visits northward, and give Bigg only one day in my way homewards.' Bigg-Wither was often in London and tried to encourage Sarah to go up and enjoy some of the capital's benefits, though she was loathe to spend the money (Letter 97):

> If Mr Bigg is in town at the musick [at Westminster Abbey], say what you please about yourself, but do not promise for me; the pleasure I shall receive from such an excursion will not answer the expence of it, and I will not deprive myself of every comfort, and live in the wretched manner I do, to whirl my money away in chaise hire.

In the very year she died he had offered to accommodate her and Philip at a house he was to rent in London, though it is not clear if this did in fact transpire, and in any case her response was ambivalent (Letter 118):

> …with regard to my coming to London, I shall not do it before Easter, afterwards I must try it, because my situation of body will by that time be full enough for me, though from the experience I had last year [perhaps a miscarriage], I don't promise myself much, except spending my money… .

7. *'Dear little creatures'*

THE LETTERS SHOW that Sarah Williams was not best suited to bearing children – as she put it 'the truth is I breed very ill' (Letter 124) – though she did give birth to four, all of whom survived into adulthood and long after. Eighteen months after the birth of their third child, Charlotte, whilst supporting her namesake sister Charlotte in childbed at Moor Crichel in Dorset, she wrote (Letter 46):

> I have news now that will perhaps surprize you, but I hope it will not alarm you, as I am very well, though you have lost another something, whether boy or girl I can't tell. This adventure happened to me yesterday afternoon, not owing to any fright or over exercise, for I have not been out of the house above four times since I came, and that but short walks. I am afraid it might be the hurry of Charlotte's accouchement, and sitting in a crump by her the whole time; be it what it will, I am not otherwise hurt by it, than that there is a propensity in my constitution to these affairs, which is not pleasant to me. It was at so early a period that at present I do not think it will make any difference as to my plan of returning [to Winchester], at least if I'm pretty well.

Eight months later she is pregnant again, and parliament obliged by taking its recess at a time that allowed Philip to be at home, and not to sit again until two months after she is delivered of their fourth child, Charles, on 29 November 1784. A few months before the event she wrote (Letter 68):

> I am ... glad that it is, as it is, for I could not at all bear the idea of your being from home, at the time of my lying in; I don't think I should have had strength or spirits, to have gone through the fatigue of it, with nurse Spencer alone just dropping into her gro[o]ve; if you do know by the next time you write next the day, you are likely to be at home, do set my tortured heart at rest, and if you are to stay two or three months longer, let me know the worst; for my patience is quite exhausted.

After the birth she obviously had gynaecological problems, that only Philip and nurse Spencer were privy to, which took her to the Winchester surgeon Charles Lyford (father of Giles, who attended Jane Austen in her last days). She wrote (Letter 87):

> I have at last plucked up spirits enough to consult Mr Lyford about what I told you, and have great reason to rejoice that I have had resolution enough to do it, for he tells me that had it been neglected much longer it might have been of bad consequence, and now he can put me in a method to prevent farther mischief; he says the sole cause of it is the having had children who were larger than my frame would admit of; I thank God that it is no worse; my mind has been cruelly wounded altogether of late, but I have never lost my rest, which supports me through all, I have managed this last business in such a manner that no one but nurse Spencer knows any thing of the matter.

Later, she takes a great interest in the arrangements for the impending lying-in at Shawford House, near Winchester, of Lady St John (née Jane Mildmay), a daughter of her close friend Mrs Carew Mildmay (née Jane Pescod; Letter 117):

> ... she is in a great fuss ... has put up a bed in the drawing room for her, because it is more airy, I think she will worry herself to death with anxiety, she has been to Lyford, to know inhow many minutes he can get to Shawford, and feels much comfort from his assuring her that he can be there in eleven minutes.

The surgeon may well have been sugaring the pill, as Shawford is more than three miles from St Peter Street, Winchester, where Charles Lyford lived.

Sarah Williams also took a great interest in, and perhaps envied, the experience of Mrs Freston from Farley, probably Farley Chamberlayne (rather than Farleigh Wallop), near Compton, about six miles from Winchester (Letter 118):

> ...she (Mrs F) the most vulgar, little good-natured trundle that can be, is just recovered from her lying in of a fourth child, which she suckles when convenient to herself, and she told us that she never knew when her children came into the world, so little trouble did it cost her, and all this in consequence of her taking for three

months before, every night before going to bed a lent-fig chop soaked in oil and drinking some oil after it, and she is persuaded that if every body would adopt the same method, the system would be entirely changed. One lives to learn, but the remedy is as bad as the disease.

***

NOT UNEXPECTEDLY, children feature large in the letters of Sarah Williams, and occasionally in those of her husband. His comments, when they came, were – even allowing for some tongue in cheek – short and rather brutal (or was it raillery?), such as 'whip Phil and Bess once a week for my sake, if not for your own' (Letter 48) and 'take care not to instill too much learning into the foetid [an unattractive nickname for their first-born, Elizabeth]' (Letter 63), though the latter brought a swift riposte from her (Letter 64):

You need not be afraid that poor Bess will be over-learned; I hope to make her in the first place a good Christian and that foundation no learning or folly will I trust undermine. It is my opinion that neither men or women can know too much. I lament that I haved not otherwise employed many idle years, which have been given up to vanity, I should then have been more better qualifyed to instruct my dear children, however if they are not very dull, what I know, they shall know.

Bringing home gifts after his absences was, of course, required, though he seemed to have had no idea what to buy. She was frequently offering him ideas: 'bring Phill any trifle that is cheap, and a shilling business for the little one' (Letter 58); 'Phill says he will have a fiddle when you come down, and he deserves it' (Letter 56); 'don't bring them play-things, suppose a knife and fork each to eat their dinner with, Phill has 6s. that you are to spend for him and he wants a knife with a silver blade' (Letter 94). As 'Phill' grew older, he had his own strategy to encourage his father (Letter 69):

… I enclose a letter to you from Phill which I believe conveys his wishes to you. I desired him to indite and little Molly [Strong; a servant] to be his {secre}tary so whether you will be able to understand it is doubtful I think.

Later on, displaying a familiarity with Ben Jonson's *The Silent Woman*, Sarah tells Philip that his namesake son talked 'of nothing but his cow and his horse which he says you are to bring him, he is so fond of animals that he will be qualified for nothing but to act Captain Otter', a bear keeper in the play (Letter 102). When Philip Williams did deliver, Sarah made sure that he was aware of the outcome (Letter 55):

> The children are delighted with your box, and as proof of it, they are not yet tired of it. Little Charlotte has no share in it, and Phill seems inclined to withdraw his pretensions, by which means I hope what is left may be preserved, Phill having already disposed of handles and spouts; he depends upon your bringing him a fiddle which I think is not a good thing; but whenever you do come I must have a large naked jointed doll for Betsy, that I may make cloaths for it for her to take on and off...(Letter 56) The doll is expected with more impatience by Bess, than myself, for I shall be put upon immediate duty to clothe her...

As it happens, it was her sister Charlotte who made at least one doll, perhaps a later one, 'as fine as a queen' (Letter 102).

***

HEALTH was a frequent matter of concern, whether it was fears of Charlotte getting whooping cough; or Bess with shortness of breath and looking 'very clouded about the eyes', perhaps a cold, or the measles (Letter 115); or Phil eating 'too much gooseberry fool' from which he rapidly recovered to be 'quite stout again, little brisket as strong as a house' (Letter 57). Charlotte had 'a course of Physick for a breaking out on her bottom... least it might be some remains of the small pox...' (Letter 69).

Smallpox was, of course, a constant fear until modern times (the last case in the world was diagnosed in 1977). Recent research has revealed the extent of the disease and the measures adopted to contain it in Winchester, Southampton and Salisbury (South, 2013). There were virulent strains of the virus, with about a mortality of one-third, and mild forms that only killed about one in a hundred. Those who survived the disease were naturally immunised against further attacks. Others could be protected from infection by inoculation with the mild strain of virus – a small part of a smallpox scab was inserted in a cut in the skin – though there were risks. There are two major incidents recorded in the Letters, one in March 1781, and another three years later, when Sarah wrote (Letter 62): 'The small pox is very bad still in our street. I bless God a hundred times that my little dears have had it.' People were extremely chary about going out, and those with the disease were often taken to the relatively remote location of St Giles's Hill, at the east end of Winchester, where 'the inoculating doctor' Dr John Smith, practised. Sarah reported (Letter 64):

> I should tell you that our friend Mrs Pryce ventured to the flower de luce [a pub, now called the Wykeham Arms] through all the terrors of the small pox, though there was an old woman died of it, but a little before, just by, and our neighbour Schmit's maid was carried to Gile's hill with it full out upon her but the day before...

By this time Sarah was a mother with experience, but at the time of the first outbreak in 1781 she was wife of two years with two very young children. The panic she exhibited is understandable (Letter 34):

> I have all the horrors of the small pox before my eyes. Master Jenkinson and his maid are to be inoculated at home tomorrow. I have heard besides that the small pox is in other places in the town. Whilst people desisted from inoculating in their houses at this end of the town [The Jenkinsons lived in St Thomas' Street, then called Calpe Street] I think we have so little communication with the Soke and High Street that there would have been no danger of infection, but now it is once begun here it is most likely that other people will avail themselves of such an example as Mr. Jenkinson and that it will become general in the street. I must observe to you that the practice of beginning to inoculate at home unless the disorder was to become universal is an action neither neighbourly, or commendable in any light, at least that I can view it. Mr. Barker [a surgeon] called upon me this morning very kindly to inform me of what was going forward (otherwise I had no account of it but from our own servants) and to advise me to speak to [John] Smith the Inoculating Doctor to know whether he thought my children might be safely inoculated; now I cannot think that either of them is of a proper age, the girl [Elizabeth, 14 months old] being about her teeth which she does not cut remarkably well, and the boy is so very young [Philip, three months old] that I should be afraid, though many people think the time of sucking the best.

Although inoculation with the mild form of smallpox had long been practised in the East, the first published account in England was in 1703, in the *Philosophical Transactions*, written by Lady Mary Montagu, who had observed the procedure in Istanbul (then Constantinople). The 1770s and 1780s seem to have been bad years for smallpox in Hampshire and yet the Winchester corporation advised against inoculation (Lefroy and Turner, 2007, p. 9; HRO/W/B6/28/5-8), which carried about a 1 in 50 chance of death. One victim was a 10-year-old daughter of the Winchester College head master Joseph Warton. Winchester prebendary John Mulso, in a letter of November 1773 to Gilbert White, reported plans for the inoculation of his family:

> ...Mrs Mulso is gone to settle with Dr Smith (an inoculating Dr) about taking Charge of my 4 Children and 5 Serv[an]ts for this critical Event. They will all be together in my House: Jack [presumably his younger son, John, aged 14] is not now apprized of it, but as soon as Dr Smith has judged for him, he shall have his choice.

The Dr John Smith mentioned in this letter was celebrated for his inoculations, with premises on St Giles's Hill, Winchester. In 1771 he was practising in 'a very convenient house by Weyhill', near Andover, where he inoculated 'servants at two guineas; coffee, tea and sugar excepted.' (Carpenter Turner, 1986, pp. 50, 167). It was not until the early 1770s that Benjamin Jesty, a farmer from Yetminster, Dorset, discovered that vaccination with cowpox protected against smallpox, though he was vilified locally at the time for using animal material (Pead, 2009). The credit is usually given to Edward Jenner, who independently made the discovery in 1796, and introduced vaccination (*vacca*, Latin, cow) into medical practice, though Jesty was recognised towards the end of his life. A pioneer of the technique and a friend of Jenner was John Ring (c. 1752-1821), who was a pupil at Winchester College for two years before going up to London to train as a surgeon. His major medical work, in two volumes, *A Treatise on the Cow-Pox* (1801-3), has been reprinted in recent years. In an age when the Two Cultures were one, he also wrote Latin verse and published a celebrated translation of Virgil.

Sarah, a young woman in her twenties, was understandably nervous about making a crucial decision to inoculate her children or not and urgently sought advice (Letter 34):

I shall consult my father about it and in the mean time I wish you would let me know as soon as possible whether, if it should be thought expedient that the dear foetids undergo the operation, you have any objection; you may be assured that my fears shall not betray me in to doing any thing rashly or contrary to the advice of my best and ablest friends and I will make myself quite easy, as I am certain that I have but one object, which is the good of my children and of those who belong to them. Mrs. Watkins has inoculated her boys, but she takes them to [St] Giles's hill as soon as they sicken, for which I am extremely obliged to her, as she does it merely because she would not be un-neighbourly.

In Philip's reply, which does not survive, he apparently suggested that he come down to Winchester, and passed on an offer from the Speaker and his wife – perhaps to take the children up to Westminster – which Sarah declined (Letter 35):

...with proper care our dear children will be in no danger of infection. If it should spread I think it would be most advisable to have them inoculated or to remove them; it has been in two or three houses in the town I find, but I don't hear that it is about at present. I keep the children entirely out of the town, and as soon as I hear that Master Jenkinson has sickened I shall not suffer them to go into the street, but send them the back way through the college for their walks. ... I should not perhaps have been so much terrifyed when I wrote to you last, if Mr. [Joseph] Barker when he called upon me, had not desired me to send for Smith the inoculating doctor, and advise with him about the propriety of inoculating the foetids. Now I think with all his caution he would not have said so much without reason; however let this rest, for the present I flatter myself we are safe enough. I shall take all possible care, and if it is the will of providence that we do not escape, I shall be contented with having done my duty.

Much later her sister, Elizabeth (Betsy), Mrs Jeremiah Dyson, had her children inoculated by Dr Smith, but he declined to visit them when they went through the fever and frettings that the process involves, which upset her greatly, particularly as 'she has done great things in complying with Smith's wishes' (Letter 91). Sarah approved (Letter 92): '... the children have had the small pox in the most favourable way that can be, though I believe Betsy thinks Jerry [their eldest son, Jeremiah Dyson] has been in great danger...'.

THE CHILDHOOD ILLNESSES that are a frequent item in Sarah's domestic litany and are generally treated without seeking medical advice: Bess's stomach ache is treated with 'a course of Liquorice tea'; Phil catches the same infection and receives 'Rhubarb'; her sister's child, Mary St John, is treated for a fever with 'magnesia', which seems to be effective (Letter 116). For herself, fearing a fever, Sarah takes 'balm and barley water' and feels much better for it; for 'harvest bugs which I have scratched and my gown has fretted in such a manner upon my elbow' she used 'Turner's white' (Letters 70 and 107). None of these treatments would, of course, stand up to medical scrutiny today, and even at the time there is an element of disbelief. Philip Williams in London reported that he 'had a cold and pain in my teeth, which induced me to buy a quack medicine, which smelt so formidably of pitch that I was afraid to use it ...' (Letter 108) – even so, he told his wife that he would bring it down with him when he came home!

As Sarah was frequently pregnant, she often complained of morning sickness – but more than that she often had more worrying symptoms, including 'numbness in my fingers, pain in my head and stupor' and 'nervous tremblings' (Letters 55 and 115). She considered being 'bled in a great hurry', a frequent treatment at the time, but shied away from what she obviously regarded as a practice likely to lead to 'lowering' and heightened nervousness. In the last year of her life, pregnant and pinned indoors by bad weather for ten days at the rectory at Compton, she is near breakdown (Letter 116):

> ...I have so little exertion about me, that I can hardly prevail upon myself to crawl out even when it is fine; my whole employment is teaching my children all that is in my power, and thinking of you and incessantly lamenting my own miserable condition which is almost insupportable; my bodily inconveniences become more numerous as I advance, my sickness is at times very bad, but I know that I am as well as most people are in my situation, and you never heard me complain when I had the happiness of living with you as your wife...

Opening letters like these was obviously a trial for her husband, who on several occasions encouraged her to consult a doctor. Good health, he insisted, 'is of too great importance to me as well as yourself, not to be purchased if money can procure it, or any other method that you may be able to suggest...' (Letter 65). On another occasion he wrote: 'I beg you will have recourse to Dr Littlehales without any scruple...', though he rather spoilt the effect by adding: 'As you are getting so ill-tempered, I beg you will vent a certain portion of it upon Phil; to prepare him for a change of manners against my arrival' (Letter 108). In Sarah's final year of life he seemed uncertain as to whether her problems were physical or psychiatric, though he recognised the value of medical help on both counts (Letter 123):

> Surely my dear you should have recourse to the medical people if you have those disagreeable feelings which you express; and if they arise merely from a depression of spirits, still I would have you represent your real state to [Dr John] Littlehales, as it will admit of some palliation.

Sarah recited her own views on healthy living in the context of their friend John Monk Newbolt, nicknamed The Blade, who led a rather debauched sort of life with 'lazy mornings, and convivial evenings' whom she thought should 'stick to tea and cards only, for the remainder of the winter [and] follow old Parr's maxims'. She was probably referring to some advice she had read in an almanac, probably by the physician and medical author Bartholomew Parr (1750-1810). She went on (Letter 84):

> ... I am sure I am the better for following them in a degree, I don't eat above a third part of what I used to do, and I seldom walk less than two hours every day, and I was never better in my life, I take my three dear children upon the St Cross road [Winchester] every day without fear of being molested ...

Even though the 'dear little creatures' were her 'only comfort' they gave her 'a great deal of trouble'. Before he had reached the age of four, Phil was proving difficult, though the threat of going to Winchester College tamed him, as well as his siblings (Letters 54-5):

> [He] grows very bold and of course is hardly to be managed by such a feeble creature as myself, and they all know that I am afraid to touch them, but they have {great} dread of being sent to College. ...Phill almost Master; he has found out that I am afraid to touch him for fear of hurting myself; I have been obliged to part with my bedfellows, though they were very quiet, but I was afraid they might kick me whilst I was asleep.

Later she and Bess slept in 'the great bed', with 'Poney and Chatty' [a maid and daughter Charlotte, respectively] in 'the little bed', so that, as she told her husband, she 'slept what you call a round robbin, which is more than I did any one night, when you were last absent' (Letter 71).

A major event, almost a rite of passage, was when their elder son got his first set of trousers at the age of 4 years 4 months, which Sarah announced proudly and he quickly put to the test:

> This day has been productive of a very great event in our quiet family, that of Phill's first step towards manhood, and it is the opinion of every body that he looks better en cavalier than he did in his Ankees's as he calls them, little Molly took him out to shew him, and he came home with eight pence which had been given him by different people, 6d he is to spend upon what he chooses to morrow, and the rest he gave away to a black sailor to day, he is a generous boy and I am proud of his disposition ... (Letter 91). Phill does indeed look better in Articles, he exhibited a piddling before the Miss Tripps this morning, do what I could to prevent him, to shew them how cleverly he could manage matters...(Letter 92)

His delight at reaching this stage of life is expressed in a letter, written on St Valentine's Day 1785, and probably dictated to nursemaid Molly Strong (W195). He explained that there is a fair in Winchester that Philip and his two sisters are going to, but not Charles who is 'to Littel'. He continued:

> I Shall have some briches a ganst Easter and be a man very Soon now you and William [his father's manservant] wont No me when you comes home....the Dormiel [dormouse, a nickname] Chattey [Charlotte] Wants to no when Dear papa come home and Willey fawks [forget?] for I wants to see poor papa and never to go a gain...'

Much though the children impacted on her life, she was at first determined not to disrupt normal living (Letter 50):

> I have made a resolution never to give up any-thing to them, and what is more I have kept it; they dine with me, little one and all, every day.

But gradually, she was worn down by the daily routine (Letter 82):

...I ...am glad when the time comes to go to bed, and am sorry when I am to get up in the morning, the children read, and we then walk out for about two hours, the rest of the day, that is not employed in eating, I work very hard for the children, and I think of you twenty times in the day till my heart achs, I look forwards, and I look backwards without seeing any thing but wretchedness for me.

On one occasion she wrote (Letter 105): 'I am so tired that I can hardly hold my pen...'. Her lot was scarcely improved in her final year of life when her sister, Charlotte, was obliged to go to Paris to assist her husband's lover, Mary Beauclerk, in delivery of an illegitimate child (*see* Chapter 15). Sarah was literally left holding Charlotte's legitimate babies, and supervising their care – as well as managing the drunkenness of their charges. It got a lot better in March 1787, when she wrote (Letter 124):

A great load of my cares departed yesterday with my sister's nurses, and the children are at last settled with Mrs G Cole much to my satisfaction and at about half the expence.

Of her own four children, the last, Charles, was the most difficult to rear, not least because he would not breast-feed and Sarah was therefore obliged to wean him when he was only three months old. She makes sure that Philip has all the details:

I work very hard for little Charles, and Phill's shirts are begun...(Letter 71)... Charles continues as he is at this time, for one of his compl{aints} (and the most tiresome to me), has been such a whimsical way of sucking, that he never came to me without putting himself in a tantrum and it was just the same if he was offered Pap...(Letter 74)...I tell you that I have experienced a most vexatious, and cruel disappointment, in being obliged to wean my dear little boy [in another hand: 'Charles, my father, born 1784'], the history of which is this, for these last five weeks he has thrown himself into terrible passions at particular times when he has been brought to suck, at others sucking perfectly well, but latterly it has got quite intolerable, and he would seldom suck without Molly and myself patting, and jogging him the whole time, and that after crying till he had frightened me out of my senses. By this whimsical mode of going on, and a great failure of appetite for my dinner on my side, my milk has decreased continually which has made me a little doubtful for some time past that I should be under the necessity of parting with the child; last Wednesday he was brought to me early in the morning, and with some difficulty he sucked. After breakfast I went to him again, he was in such a tantorum that he turned as white as a sheet, and terrified me in such a manner that when he attempted to suck, I found the milk was gone, it returned again after a little time, but I was not long in resolving upon what it was right for me to do, I therefore immediately gave it up and he has not sucked since; I have the comfort of seeing him look, (so far from worse) better than he did before; upon the whole I believe it is best as it is, and I feel myself more at ease in my mind since I have taken this step than before, for I had the constant dread upon me of injuring the child, every time I thought of you (which I could never do without great agitation) and how often that has happened I need not tell you...(Letter 77).

Her fear of failure to breast-feed, and therefore having to rear by 'dry-nursing', were expressed several years later, when she wrote: 'Mrs Hare's last child is dead in a fit, for the credit of dry-nursing, it was one of the finest children I ever saw, and is one of the thousand that are annually destroyed by this pernicious mode of nursing' (Letter 119). One rationale of the benefit of breast-feeding is that young babies are thereby protected from infectious diseases by their mother's antibodies, a fact which in essence was known to Sarah, who wrote that 'many people think the time of sucking is best' for inoculation against smallpox (Letter 34). Attitudes to breast-feeding in the eighteenth century were not uniform – *plus ça change!* – though between 1760 and 1850 there seems to have been an upward national trend in breast-feeding in Britain, with the duchess of Devonshire promoting the cause, though there were considerable local variations (Vickery, 1998, p. 107).

Philip Williams's only contribution to the subject, made several months after Sarah's trauma, was the curt observation that 'it is not fashionable to suckle your own children' (Letter 106). Commenting on the period, Vickery writes:

What a national increase in breast-feeding says about the complexities of maternal emotion for individuals ...remains obscure. In fact, when eighteenth-century ideologues urged the 'natural duty' of breast-feeding, their principal lure was that the practice was beneficial to the mother's health.

31)   Sat. 23rd July 1785

My dearest Love,

            We went on Sunday to Twickenham, of drive to which
through Richmond Park, & down Richmond hill, I had never been before,
& indeed it beggars all description, as does Mr Ellis's villa, & of
ground behind it, which is so well contrasted to ye Thames & ye
ground before it. What was Pope's habitation serves as merely
rooms of passage to ye two wings which have been added, & ye field
which is likewise added to ye pleasure-ground is one third more
than ye original, & is sweetly retired & planted with great variety
of shrubs — Mr Ellis is a great florist, & has a great collection of
exotics — A carnation tree with more than 50 upon it in full bloom
struck me more than any thing. Mr C. & myself wished you to have
been of ye party, & who knows but another year may accomplish it —
our party was very small & comfortable, only Mr & Mrs Hatsel, &

The Speaker's chaplain, Philip Williams, writing on 23 July 1785 to his wife, Sarah, in Kingsgate Street, Winchester (Letter 110).

In fact, Charles continued to give Sarah troubles, flying into tantrums, expressing great 'crossness' and on one occasion 'crying ready to kill himself for nothing that I can find out' (Letter 100). On a happier note, she seems to have enjoyed teaching the basics to the children, telling her husband that 'Bess reads as well as you can' (Letter 81)… 'I am happy to tell you that I think [Phil] will soon be as good a scholar as his sister. I have by dint of perseverance got him to attend and he comes on very well' (Letter 56) 'Charlotte was yesterday three years old, to-morrow she begins learning her letters, which is an increase of employment for me' (Letter 93). Sarah gives more detail on progress in the 'schoolroom' in the summer of 1785, when Bess is five and half, and reading *The Adventures of Gil Blas of Santillane*, a picaresque novel by Le Sage, originally published in 1715-35 in French, and subsequently in a variety of English translations. Phil is four and a half, but struggling against his older sister and even 'sensible' Charlotte, who is only three years old (Letter 94):

> I have begun with Chatty[Charlotte], who is a sensible little hussy and knows above half her letters already; Bess is reading Job and by way of recreation a 1s. Gil blas that I have bought; Phil does as well as his idle disposition will permit him, and I don't find but that he is full as capable of learning as the girls, the little darling is got wonderfully quiet and for his months uncommonly forward; we have given Bess the new name of Crabb, which angers her much…

Once Sarah and her children had moved to Compton, to live in the rectory, they were sent to a preparatory school run in the village by a member of a long-established farming family, Richard Goldfinch. In 1772 he had announced that he was giving up teaching, but subsequently took it up again (Drew, 1939, p. 122). In February 1787, when Bess was seven, Phil six and Charlotte four and half years of age, she reported that 'Betsy is to begin learning French tomorrow if she is well enough, and Phil had prepared paper etc to write to you, but he has such an everlasting clack that he must let it out to old Goldfinch, who made me a formal speech to day desiring it might be put off till Easter' (Letter 115). Later in the same month 'Mr Goldfinche's boys said their catechism to day in the church with Betsy at their head; she is a queer thing, for I had been trying to persuade her and had given the matter up, but when the boys were called out she marched with them'…(Letter 118). The curious decision to give their eldest daughter the name 'Crabb' (see above) and calling her a 'queer thing' echoed later events: she suffered all her life from a psychiatric illness of some kind, as harrowingly portrayed in Philip Williams's later letters to his daughters (W94-177).

Growing children, especially perhaps boys, often bring worries, and anticipating the day that Philip and Charles were older, Sarah saw with horror what was happening with the connivance one of their friends and bon viveur, the Revd John Monk Newbolt, rector of Winchester St Lawrence, Faringdon (Berkshire) and Chilcomb, Hampshire (Letter 97):

> ...there is a sad bill against that said Blade, but as it was mentioned to me by way of a secret don't say any thing about it; he has had the weakness to leave the key of his cellar with the boys and given them leave to invite their friends if they would run the risque of being found and you may be sure they availed themselves of this permission and to the full extent of it, there must be some explanation with him upon the subject when he comes down, Dr [Joseph] Warton knows nothing of it, but the boys were in a shocking condition. Oh! the times when boys are brought so forward.

Death and disease were a constant feature of life: Philip Williams reported that 'the old lady is at last going at the top of the street [in Westminster], all putrefaction and ulcers' (Letter 108), whilst in three successive sentences in one letter, Sarah passed on grim news from Compton (Letter 118):

> Mrs Wareham is dead, which I am not sorry for, as I believe she is released from a load of misery; they are in a very bad plight indeed, he spends all the money he can get at the alehouse and will soon destroy himself, and Symonds the [Winchester] College brewer who is her brother, will do something for the children. ...Old Murden is going at last very fast, a mortification has begun, and very luckily for his wife, who would not otherwise have had sixpence, there is just now a vacancy in the Widows' College [College for the Widows of Clergymen, Winchester], which is I believe secured for her. ...Mrs Wool has had a third paralitic seizure and lies in a senseless state.

In the same letter Sarah wrote of a shocking event at Winchester College, where the head master had gone to see his son, a young man in holy orders who lived in the school, and found him dead in a chair. Philip

Williams had no doubt heard of the tragedy, but Sarah filled in the details for him (Letter 118):

> Dr Warton is I hear much shocked at the mode of his son's death, as he was the person who found him first, he could hardly persuade himself that he was dead; he [the son] had desired the servant to bring him some Jelly into the parlour, which not being enough the man carried him in some more and set it down upon the table, he observed that he leaned back in his chair, but not apprehending anything, he left him and the Dr went in just after to wish him a good night, and finding that he did not speak supposed that he was fainted away and immediately seized his hand, which when the house was alarmed he could hardly be prevailed upon to quit. I sent to know how they did and had but an indifferent account; he [the son] had done his duty but the Sunday before. I understand Dr Littlehales has pronounced it to be a lost case for some time…

In his biography of Joseph Warton, John Wooll described his son as 'a man of high talents and superior information, but who had long laboured under a lingering and obstinate disease…'(Wooll, 1806, pp. 74-5).

8. *'Pray, let Molly be restored to you'*

SARAH'S LIFE would have been much more irksome without the help
of servants. One in particular served her and the family for at least three
years, and probably much longer. This was Molly, variously also called the
Poney and the Veteran (the Williamses were not very adept at choosing
nicknames), who nannied the children and generally helped in the home.
Her maiden name does not surface in the Letters, but she later married
William Strong, a man with a wooden leg, who ran an alehouse in
Compton (W197), possibly the Bridge Inn at Shawford, the only such
establishment in the parish listed in 1859 (White, 1859, p. 127). She may
have been the woman depicted in February 1781 by Sarah in a
masquerade in the city (Letter 31):

> I set it down in my own mind who would be the best character in
> the room and so it proved. You will not be at a loss to guess that I
> mean the Veteran who made the tightest little Irish sailor you ever
> saw, and looked as if she had just been blown from the mast of
> one of the ships at Spithead. I am told by every creature that was
> there, that she was by far the most entertaining mask in the whole
> assembly, by means of large trousers and a short sailor's petticoat
> she was so much disguised that you would never have found her
> out to be a Hannah Snell [the woman who famously disguised
> herself as a man and served in the Army and Royal Marines].

Sarah came to depend heavily on Molly, who became a companion and
almost one of the family. Sixteen years after she had left, and now a
married woman, she wrote to Elizabeth and Charlotte, both spinsters
(W197). The letter is in a good hand, but with spelling that is almost
entirely phonetic, though with a great improvement on that of an earlier
missive (W195). The letter is reproduced on p. 145 and the transcription
of a section below follows in all but minor detail that published in *The
Wykehamist*, (11 February 1970), which was probably made by Virginia
Clanchy:

131

My dear young Ladys: I hopes you will pardun my persumtion in sending these fue lines to inkwire after your health for sence Master & Mrs [Philip Williams and his second wife, Helen née Fagg] have gon gurnying, we hear no title [tattle] of you, and the Village is so mopish & mollonkolly, & our William himself methinks is some how infected by it for he be not hafe so nimbul as useall, but that mought be hoing to his nue Legg not being so lite as the ould one, which snapt in two like tuch wood, & down he comed souce into the hog truf.

Her husband attributed the rot in his old leg to a dog repeatedly relieving itself on it, to which Molly retorted in the letter: 'An sure enmuf says I, we shall all decay, whether p---d upon or not.' The same tale, with the same word, rendered in Philip Williams's hand as 'p-s-d', is included in a long, waspish, comic poem, perhaps by him (W249). Obviously not intended for public consumption, this curious and vindictive verse is in the voice of Molly Strong and is directed against the Winchester physician, Dr John Littlehales, whom, she says, she will eschew in favour of the vet: 'Dr Cumley shall manage my business as he does our Alderney cow'. And she complains:

An't you ashamed, Mr Littlehales, to sham such a letter to dear Miss Bettsy…

The village had obviously taken it out on a man otherwise regarded as a model doctor, who, according to Molly, 'knows nothing of the rheumatiz, or what ails my precious bowels' and is advised 'to stick to your hospital business'. He had, she relates, also committed other acts, including stealing Philip Williams's cherries and spreading rumours that Molly 'was infected by a dram' and that Charlotte Williams wore a 'garland and a bridle'. Such parish-pump incidents are perhaps of little importance on their own, but illustrate how Molly, long after she had left the service of the family, kept in close touch with Philip Williams and his daughters, of whom, she said (W249):

Poor little dears I have loved them ever since their dormouse slipt its tail

And they cried and I told them not to mind it, and to be brisk as bottled ale.

It seems that she was equally loved by Philip Williams's eldest son, who in a letter written in 1793, when he was a 13-year-old scholar at Winchester College, asked his father to: 'Give my best love to my [step]mother, as also to Dear Molly…' (W178).

The weekly wash was one of Molly's tasks, though Sarah was fearful of her tendency to perform everything with excessive vigour (Letter 56):

> I am going to dine [at Compton] to day, and I take the children and Molly with me, being afraid to leave them at home, as we have a great wash in hand, which is an attraction Molly is not able to resist and the children would be burnt or scalded, if I was to leave them without any body to superintend.

In July 1784, shortly after her sister Elizabeth Dyson had given birth to a son, and two maids had suddenly left her, Sarah sent Molly to Compton to help. Philip was worried that his wife would suffer as a consequence, but she countered (Letter 66) that '[Elizabeth] would have been left without a creature if I had not spared Molly to her, which I could very well do not having a young child myself at present.' At a time when she was expecting a visit from his two sisters, he persisted, showing husbandly concern (Letter 67):

> I know what you are at, making yourself a maid to accommodate other people – beware of overfatiguing yourself. … pray, let Molly be restored to you before that time, and do not think of going out upon their account; they [his sisters] beg and intreat that you will not, as they come to visit you merely and the children.

But she was not to be shaken (Letters 68-9):

> … you are mistaken about Molly, I can manage very tolerably without her, and the child at Compton might be lost, if I was to have her home; in about ten days they will be able to spare her. …Molly horse is to be returned forthwith, for the ease of your mind, more than of mine as we have gone on very well without her.

Six months later, shortly after he had returned to Westminster, she was again without Molly, who had gone to Midhurst to help Sarah's father in retirement, living with his sister, who was planning to come to Winchester, though the scheme had its problems (Letter 71):

I had a very kind letter from Papa the day after you went, in which he said that my aunt was ready to come whenever I liked, but that their household was in such disorder in consequence of Molly's frailty, that he wished her to stay a little to arange matters, ... I have lived one week by myself, and I trust, I may pass twenty in the same manner, I don't know that I should be [better] if I had a companion, I rather think I might be worse, therefore I have written to Papa to desire that the Veteran may remain where I am sure she is more wanted... I am on the whole much better than when you left me...

Sarah's last child to survive, Charles, had only been born two months earlier, and it seems as if her aunt was planning to help her, though surely Molly would have been a better bet. Two months further on, though, she is very grateful for the return of her nursemaid (Letter 84):

... I take my three dear children upon the St Cross road [Winchester] every day without fear of being molested, which gives the Poney time to do a little needle work, a thing that is at present much wanted with us; Charles is become very good to the comfort of poor Molly Horse, who has been worn to death with him.

In fact, Sarah was soon to lose 'the Poney' – a name once given also to Molly, but now it seems applied to another maid. She first considers a friend of Molly's to take her place; she would engage her were she older than her twenty years, but instead she passes her on to a friend, wife of a canon, and hires another for herself, aged 'upwards of thirty' (Letter 85). Within a few months the deed is done: the Poney has gone to work with a namesake of Sarah (probably the wife of Dr Daniel Williams, a fellow of Winchester College) and is to be 'succeeded by a St Cross nymph a daughter of Mrs Cornwall's wash{er woma}n' (Letters 94 & 107):

Mrs Williams has produced a little girl, after being about six months mistaken, and Mr Williams took the Poney off in a whisky on Friday last, which had I been somewhat more wealthy I would never have consented to, as I do not expect to meet with her like again, I have got a girl, who is much recommended to me, who seems good natured and in time will do very well, but for obvious reasons can never be a Poney as you will see when you come home.

Why Sarah changed her maid is not entirely clear, but the reasons do not seem to have been financial. At the time a new tax on maidservants was being considered in Westminster and formed part of Pitt's second budget, presented to parliament on 7 May 1785 (Hague, 2004, p.194). It involved 'sliding scales of payment and a bewildering range of exemptions'. However, it would not have impacted on Sarah, as mothers living with 'two or more' children were exempt. As might be expected, the tax was extremely unpopular and was repealed within seven years, although an analogous tax on manservants that had been introduced eight years earlier lasted until 1937 (Steedman, 2007, p.16). Sarah took the opportunity to air her views on this and other matters with her husband, who of course served the House in which the bill had been passed. Her interest was perhaps quickened by the fact that she had probably met Fox, the Whig politician (*see* Letters 55 & 52). She was certainly not adverse to wading into the debate and using it to further her own domestic agenda (Letter 95):

> The tax on maid servants is as little relished here as with you, it will fall, except in some degree qualified, particularly hard upon us little people with large families, but I am sick of taxes, debates and every thing thereunto belonging, when they bring in a bill to oblige husbands and wives to live together, they shall have my hearty concurrence, these last three days we might have spent together, without an act of parliament, but I dared not to think of it.

Rarely did Philip mention such political issues, but early in his chaplaincy he asked for Sarah's views on other domestic matters (Letter 60):

> How do you like these new taxes? Ribbons, gauzes and callicoes for the ladies, and horses for the men; it is supposed the window tax will be modified in some shape or other – I sincerely wish it.

Later in the same year she gave a reply which displayed a sound understanding of the issues raised in Pitt's first budget presented to parliament on 30 June 1784 (Hague, 2004, pp. 180-81; Letter 62):

> I have {n}o objection to the new taxes, as taxes we must have, [though] the coals seems the hardest of digestion as it affects the manufactures, [but] candles is such a very trifle that it does not much signify.

Nearly three years later, in February 1787, Sarah and Philip were considering a plan, long in the making, for her eventually to move up to London whilst he served the Speaker, living in a house to be rented by his friend Lovelace Bigg-Wither. For some reason Philip's manservant William wanted to move on, and Sarah is given the task of hiring another, presumably acceptable to them both. There were plenty of reasons for her not taking a maid up to the capital, as depicted graphically in the novels of the day, such as Richardson's *Clarissa* with its notorious rapist Lovelace. So, she finds a 'creditable looking' man who has been working for Mr Poole Bathurst, seated in Gloucestershire, a brother of Wykehamist Henry Bathurst, who rose to be bishop of Norwich. Their father had 18 children (including Poole) with his first wife and 13 (including Henry) with his second wife. The manservant is leaving because he cannot dress Bathurst's hair, though 'he says he can dress a wig very well': this was important, as Philip wore a wig, and did so until his dying days, though natural hair was by this time gaining favour (Doody, 1994, Note 134, p. 505). She wrote to him at length (Letters 117 & 118):

> ...I sent to Mrs Bathurst about him and she speaks very highly of him, and the Warden's servants give him an excellent character for good-temper, he would wait till Easter for our place, and I should prefer taking a servant from a distant county to one of the Winchester breed; if therefore you would like him I will talk more to him, I know it is William's wish to settle, as he calls it, by Easter … .I should tell you that this man has been used to London…

> Our new man has been over to day and I told him of everything that he was to do, and he objected to nothing; he has lived one year with Mr Bathurst, and before that he lived eight years with a Mr Willis an attorney at Dorchester of which place he is a native; he said that he never dressed Mr B's hair above six times, that it was the same with all his men servants, he said they hurt him because he chose that her maid should dress his hair. You know they are strange people, but Rachel Corfe the Warden's housekeeper gave so good an account of him that I was tempted to engage him and he is to come in a month, which will be about ten days before you come home…

Eventually, perhaps after working for six or more years with the family, Molly had plans to leave – probably to marry – but not until after the planned stay in London. The impending loss weighed heavily on Sarah at a time when she was expecting another child. She exhorted Molly 'to postpone matters till after the next child is weaned, but without effect', which made her wish she had not agreed to 'Mr Bigg's very friendly proposal' (Letter 122). Philip, too, was concerned but optimistic (Letter 123):

> I am very sorry about old Molly, but your own character is so established that I am sure you will have offers enough, and now she has got this crotchet in her head, she will never descend from her third heaven.

He also asked what the new man's name was and suggested that 'his cloaths' be made before they go up to London. In her last surviving letter (Letter 125) Sarah reported that the servant had arrived, was called William and that there was 'nothing to find fault with as yet, he is a great man for church musick and will assist the Compton choir...'. Also, that the 'suit of cloaths that Craddock has of ours will fit him'. She was probably referring to Robert Craddock, a tailor, who lived in the parish of St Swithun, Winchester (HRO/1790A/13).

***

MONEY was rarely far from the minds of Sarah and Philip Williams (*see* Appendix VI for money values in the late eighteenth century). He received small rents from estates in the Fens, plus emoluments and shares of the profits from his clerical appointments and his fellowship of Winchester College. His major commitment for the last three years of their marriage, as chaplain to the Speaker, brought no income at all beyond bed and board and was designed rather to bring preferment, which in the event was long in coming. Like the bursar that he was, he seems to have held the purse strings of their domestic expenditure, and provided funds for Sarah only as required. After four years of marriage she commented rather tartly (Letter 51):

> I am much obliged to you for your budget which was better worth examining than I fear the m{onies}s will be...

The Letters often mention the fortunes of others. Thus, Charles Blackstone, who often served with Philip Williams as a bursar of Winchester College, was set to marry, but 'the young lady must be married, before she is 25, or forfeits great part of her fortune (which is about £5000) by her father's will' (Letter 103). As it happens, Blackstone did not take a wife until seven years later, when he married Margaret Bigg, a daughter of Lovelace Bigg-Wither (Bigg-Wither, 1907, Pedigree VI).

In another case, it was the lady who was the fortune seeker and 'could she have staid to have fanned the flame a little, by what I hear she would most likely have completed her conquest, which would be worth pursuing, as his mother has a large fortune at her disposal and at present allows him [£]600 per annum...' But there was a snag, which Sarah spotted (Letter 116):

> ....if I was a man and she was as handsome as Helen, with all the virtues of Penelope into the bargain, unless she could get rid of that un-harmonious nasality she might remain a spinster all the days of her life...

A nephew of Harry Lee, the warden of Winchester College, 'contrived to make a Shropshire heiress a Miss Hodges fall in love with him', which amazed Sarah (Letter 96), but as the Lee family had been seated since the 1300s in Bridgenorth in the county its offspring might have been a suitable match for an heiress. Members of the Lee family had also emigrated to the US in the 1600s and prospered there, two descendants signing the Declaration of Independence.

Lower down the scale, a former servant 'has made a conquest of a fortune who is going to set him up in an alehouse, [but] she has no prize...' (Letter 119). And at the very top, Philip spread a little Westminster gossip about Richard Atkinson (1738-1785), a merchant and director of the East India Company (Letter 98):

> The talk at present is about Mr Atkinson the contractor's will, who has died worth £25,000 and left his friend Mr Robinson £700 annuity for his life, and remitted him a debt of [£]12,000. ...
> All these riches were acquired by impositions upon Lord North, or at least the greatest part of them.

None of these fortunes was ever going to come to Philip and Sarah, whilst closer to hand they watched with incredulity as their brother-in-law Jeremiah Dyson, son of a self-made parliamentarian who had left him well provided for, spent money like water. Philip Williams visited Dyson's uncle and trustee, and shared the horrors with his wife (Letter 72):

Would you believe it, that since August [17]82, they have spent £3,700, and run in debt £800. How they are to raise a sum to discharge the creditors is more than I can devise at present, and I have only time to desire you not to be vexed about it. Their prospect is a good one, and their present hardship will be, to live upon £600 a year – great difficulty doubtless.

Giving her views on the matter, Sarah cites the sums of money she regards as required for their way of life (Letter 75):

...they may live better at Compton upon 600£ (getting rid of all incumbrances), than we can at Winchester upon 500£ surely,... he has no room for useless men, horses, and dogs,... to think that they should have frittered away such a sum of money, without any pursuit to justify it in the least...

One of the 'incumbrances' was a carriage, which the Dysons could ill afford, though Philip opines that the 'possibility of their remaining at Compton [two to three miles from the city] without a carriage will never do' (Letter 76) – though Sarah herself had to cope when it was her turn to live there! Although Jeremiah Dyson had not spent quite as much as they feared, he eventually had to take a 'place' at Westminster with a salary, albeit of only 300 guineas a year, as detailed elsewhere (see Chapter 15). People without a family could, of course, get by on much less, especially if they lived in less expensive surroundings than Winchester (Letter 96):

Mrs Harris has left Miss Freeman for her life every thing she could dispose of, which is about 30£ per annum and her furniture live stock etc, which with what she has already will make her an income of about a hundred a year, and enable her to be at the top of things at Fareham [Hampshire], where she means to fix her abode.

Failure to make ends meet eventually, of course, could have dire consequences. Sarah told her husband the sad tale of 'the poor woman Mrs Ashby alias Dutton of suspicious character', obviously well known to them (Letter 92):

She and her daughter and a maid have contrived to run in debt near three hundred pounds, great part for eating and drinking, and after watching for her for some time one of her creditors has at last got at her and carried her to prison where it seems she is quite penny-less…

She reported that the prebendary William Lowth jr had been to see the unfortunate woman in prison and the most likely outcome was 'a subscription' to pay off her debts. After the death of their friend and neighbour, Scottish physician Dr John Makkitrick, Sarah herself expressed considerable irritation that his brother, also a physician but with the surname Adair (W.P. Courteney, rev. M Beavan, 'Adair, James Makittrick [sic]', ODNB), refused to settle the expense of a daily newspaper they shared and 'was shabby enough to go off without taking any notice of [the] debt…' (Letter 69).

Those unable to live on their income could, in theory at least, move to a more remote location than Winchester. The Dysons toyed with the idea of moving to Wales (where Philip Williams had his roots – *see* Chapter 1), and the same strategy was planned, and perhaps undertaken, by Mrs [Lucy] Elyott, though Sarah was obviously not impressed by the scheme. Probably a relative of Philip Williams, the lady in question had six years earlier lost her husband, the Revd Edmund Elyott (Letter 125):

> I went to Mrs Elyott's, and found them rather out of spirits, determined as I think upon a very rash scheme from which I endeavoured to persuade them; they are immediately going to quit their house, and to go and live in Wales, either at Abergavenny or Monmouth, where they certainly may live cheaper and the house-rent will be trifling; they say it is a case of absolute necessity …I wanted her to hire a couple of rooms and then if she would part with one maid and be contented to dine upon one thing she might live just as comfortably in my opinion as she did before and amongst her friends; but she would sooner banish herself to the mountains than give up things which are really mere luxuries, she has spent some idle money since poor Mr E's death that would now be of service to her; I wish anything could be done for her relief, but what, and where it is to come from I know not.

The upshot of this tale is not known. Mrs Lucy Elyott was a close friend of Sarah Williams and lived in Winchester with her two daughters, Lucy and Sophie, and her son George. She was present in June 1782 at the baptism of Charlotte Williams, as a representative of her sponsors (W418). Her husband 'Ed Elyott A.M.' deputised as a sponsor at the baptism of Elizabeth Williams two years earlier, and was almost certainly the rector of

Litchfield alias Ludshelfe, Hampshire, and died in or before March 1781. Sarah chaperoned Lucy at balls held in the city. As detailed elsewhere (*see* p. 185), Mrs Elyott owned a house at Newmarket, and there is much in the Letters about Philip Williams's tardy behaviour in seeking to find out why she was not being paid rent. The Elyott family and Sarah were all friends of the Bower and Bisset families. The Bowers were long seated at Iwerne Minster, Dorset. Anna Catherina Napier married Thomas Bowyer Bower in 1767 and their second son, Henry, entered Winchester as a scholar in 1784.

There are also several mentions of the Elyott family by Philip Williams's stepfather Dr John Gordon and it seems that Mrs Elyott was related to Philip Williams's mother; a mention of 'Aunt Elyott' (Letter 20) suggests that one of her sisters – perhaps Mrs Elyott herself - married an Elyott, though one would have thought that, when writing to Philip, Sarah would have called her 'your Aunt'. The same source mentions 'Lady St John, Hollis Street', probably Holles Street, in Mayfair, and a 'Lady St John' was party to a covenant involving Philip Williams's maternal grandparents (W217-218). The Elyott link goes back to Philip Williams's childhood in Barrow; the family bible shows that 'Mrs Barbara Elyott' was a sponsor at the baptism of his sister Anne in 1747 (W418). Also a series of letters from L'Abbé T Elyott, living at Massa di Carrara, Tuscany, and elsewhere in Italy, to Philip Williams's sister Anne, refer to her as 'a cousin' (W180-193).

It is clear that Sarah was schooled not to spend a penny more than necessary. Hence, as Winchester race week loomed, she wrote (Letter 104):

> … I have been very busy, not making, but new trimming, my finery for the races, which will cost me nothing but for hair-dressing, a circumstance that makes the hurry a little more supportable to me; I shall be able to rub on perhaps another fortnight without any remittance and then you need not trouble yourself as I know where to get a supply and without having recourse to illicit practices.

She was also self-effacing in the extreme with regard to her husband's expenditure, writing 'I should like of all things to go to the Messiah in the Abby', but urging him instead to go, as it would 'give me as much pleasure as going myself' (Letter 93). On another occasion she wrote (Letter 51):

> I am glad you are going to Westminster Abbey; I would sooner go
> without a new gown than you should be deprived of such hearing
> and seeing; and if you think it extravagant put it down to Sally.

And when he was in funds, probably after disposing on one of the small
fen estates inherited from his mother, she accepted that she would have
no share of the proceeds, but not without some bitterness (Letter 91): 'so
you have sold the estate without my consent, and will spend the money
too, I suppose'.

It is hardly surprising that she found herself short of funds on many
occasions, as, in addition to paying for all domestic expenses, she also had
to settle various taxes, such as those due on servants and horses (Letter
107). Her strategies for coping were varied: 'I have borrowed ten pounds
of Papa, which will last me I hope 'till you come home...' (Letter 64); '...I
am sorry to tell you that I am a Bankrupt, not being possessed at present
of a farthing; I did not like to borrow more of Papa; if you can spare it, a
small recruit by Mr Dyson will be very acceptable' (Letter 68); '...I shall
be a Bankrupt I'm afraid before you come home, what with taxes,
insurances, hospital etc. money has flown at a strong rate lately, I never
spend upon myself you may be certain' (Letter 97). Her most extreme
action was to raid money intended for the poor: staying with her sister in
Dorset, she announced (Letter 109):

> I have taken ten pounds of the Charity Money, which will I trust
> carry me on till you come and that is as much as it will do.

On top of all this, the practice of making money by clipping tiny amounts
of metal off coins meant that she was from time to time 'plagued with
light gold, ...[with] a great number of guineas that are deficient in weight'
(Letter 125).

***

ALTHOUGH THE COUPLE lived for much of their time at 'the lowest
end of Kingsgate Street' (*see* p. 89) – probably meaning at the southern
end – which is an urban or suburban area of Winchester, they had a
garden and a greenhouse, both for pleasure and produce, and exchanged
vegetables and the like with neighbours. Also, there were occasional gifts
of game for Sarah from her sister Charlotte and her hunting-mad husband
in Dorset (Letter 84):

I had a letter from Mrs St John the other day, and a present of woodcocks and a snipe, which would not keep, or I should have sent them to you, one of the birds I gave to Miss Jenkinson for her mother, two of them I had last night for supper for Mrs Blackstone and Mrs Smith [perhaps her friend Joan], whom I persuaded to take their bread and cheese with me, and I had the mortification of being obliged to eat the snipe myself…

Sarah is at her most poetic when writing about the garden, which she looks after with her 'poney', an unattractive name for a maid (Letters 53 & 62):

Our garden is in high beauty, the poney and myself gardeners in chief, you may smell the honeysuckle into the street; the fraxinella is as tall as Bess, and the great orange-tree in full bloom; but I would rather live close to a pig stye with you. … I have been in the green-house but once since you went, but I believe everything is in a bad state there, the myrtles on the outside of the house are dead, this affects not me, I have too many cares of another sort.

As the year gets under way her spirits rose, quickened by some funds she is expecting from the sale of a small fenland estate he inherited (Letter 92):

I have had a thorough rummage in the greenhouse, and find that I am not worth a single geranium, the myrtles and oranges are in tolerable condition, except Mrs Balgrey's (as Steevens the gardener called her [possibly Dr Thomas Balguy's cousin and housekeeper, Sarah Drake]) tree, which like it's mistress is withering; the myrtles before the house are coming forth at the root, my beautiful cypress (which perhaps you might call Cyprus vid. cypress vine in a former letter of yours) quite dead, at least down to the root, I have planted a Virginia cedar to succeed it, but I hope we shall be in possession of the 550£ before it reaches half way.

And when they moved out to Compton, which was definitely in the country, she takes even more interest and writes to her husband with the sort of enthusiasm you might look for in, say, a Gilbert White. Even in a letter written as early as February, she finds much to write about, including sea cale (*Crambe maritima*), described in *The Times* as a 'new Culinary Vegetable' (30 April 1795; Letter 116):

… our garden flourishes, we have brocoli, with largish heads, and our cucumber bed is made and the seeds put in, under my own auspices, and I think we shall succeed; we are going to have a bed of sea cale, which is something of the nature of asparagus and comes in earlier; I have got seeds, but I hope to get plants.

By the third week of March of the same year, there is much more to report (Letter 122):

The spring is very forward here – our trees are all out in bloom, and the kitchen garden things are all running to seed. There is a great plenty of hop-tops for you, and I have had a present of a hare this morning which I should be glad to keep for you, if it was possible; our asparagus beds are made, and we have a sea kale bed, which is I think a better thing; we do not shine in cucumber beds, owing to a scarcity of materials, my carnation trees are in the finest bloom and the admiration of the whole world…

She obviously loved the garden and in an undated fragment of a letter Philip warns her not to overdo it (Letter 112):

I have only time to add how much I build upon seeing you this day 3 weeks at the farthest. Adieu, my dearest love – don't stay out too long in the garden this tempting weather.

But her enjoyment was tempered by crippling worries about her health as she goes through what was probably her seventh pregnancy (of which two ended in miscarriages), six months before she was to die (Letter 122):

I fear I shall not see any of {these} things brought to perfection, I really and truly {do not} think altogether well of myself, I have {no ve}ry alarming complaints; but I have some internal feelings that tell me I have not strength enough to encounter alone the situations into which I am thrown; it is astonishing how the least trifle overcomes me; I think I could endure any thing, if I was not separated from you; but it is tedious to dwell always upon this ever-[en]during subject, would to God that I had other feelings or a different constitution.

***

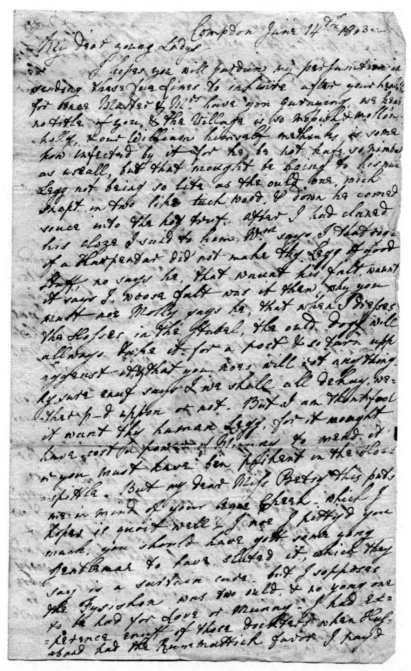

Mrs Molly Strong, a much-loved maid, writing in June 1803 to Philip and Sarah Williams's daughters, Charlotte and Elizabeth (W197; see also p. 131).

THE GEORGIAN HOUSEHOLD was often threatened by crime, with residents scuttling home before curfew and locking up their valuables (Vickery, 2009). Although Sarah suffered many troubles, crime was not one of them, though she was kept in the picture by a friend who presided at the Winchester Assizes, Sir Henry Paulet St John Mildmay, Sheriff of Hampshire and later a local MP. Together with Canning, he was one of the 'Winchester faction' loyal to Pitt the Younger. He had married into the Mildmay family seated at Shawford House, Twyford, and told Sarah about a case involving a brother of Earl Fitzwilliam and a Mr Dickinson from the Isle of Wight. It was a tangled tale yet the villain was clearly Fitzwilliam. Sarah regaled her husband with the details (Letter 120):

> Sir Henry returned in the evening from his attendance on the judges, full of F's trial … there was a great deal of family history came out, amongst the rest that he used to sleep out when the family were in London for five or six nights together, which Mr Jekyl [counsel for Fitzwilliam] attributed to his aversion to that greatest of all curses a wife, and he added that he understood Mr F had the misfortune of being united to a lump of deformity both of body and mind; by the account I hear from all parties of her temper, it is so extremely bad, that if he had no other crimes one could half excuse him for leaving her …

There was, however, one incident in which crime got close to hand, after Sarah had gone to live at the parsonage house in Compton. It took place in nearby Twyford, where 'Mrs Vane' lived (probably the widow of Godfrey Woodward Vane, who had died two years before; HRO/15M51/1/4; HRO/1M44/75/20). She reported (Letter 117):

> …we are under great alarm in this neighbourhood from Mrs Vane's house having been attempted the night before last; it happened very fortunate for her that the family were up remarkably late that night, and her coachman was scarcely got to sleep before he was awaked by an uncommon noise of the dogs, which continuing a great while, he went down stairs and found there was somebody trying to get the door open which they had split entirely down, and upon seeing that the family were alarmed there was a whistle heard, and they were off; I am not terrified by this, but it makes us more vigilant...

A fortnight later and the matter is still hot news in the village (Letter 119):

Mrs Vane's alarms continue, her house was really once attacked, and the servants are persuaded that it is attacked every night. She has removed her plate, and valuables to Winchester which will probably allay the Phantoms. Mr Travis says his house has been attacked but upon being cross questioned, the only proof he could [give] of it was that the dogs in the inside as well as the outside of his house barked violently and the whole family got up without being able to discover any traces of a two-legged creature's having [been] near the place.

It seems that Sarah Williams thought Robert Travis a romancer. This disparaging view of him might have been a sideswipe at his views on social reform. Amongst other things, he set up a local cottage industry in Compton, with the women 'carding and spinning yarn and knitting stockings' and 'a system of industry for employing the infant poor …from four years old… spinning flax', which is woven into 'linen and woolseys' for the use of the parish (*Hampshire Chronicle*, 18 July 1788). He was 'a young man of Winchester society, who lived [at Silkstead Priors, Compton, Hampshire] with his wife for 20 years' (Drew, 1939, p. 124).

Sarah and Philip also shared news about a burglary that had taken place at the Speaker's house in Westminster, which was covered in plodding detail (*Hampshire Chronicle*, 7 February 1785):

Friday se'nnight [28 Jan], or very early on the Saturday morning, the house of Woolfran [sic] Cornwall, Esq, Speaker of the House of Commons, in Privy Garden, was broken into at the back part, next the Thames. They cut a hole in the window-shutter of the dining parlour, and having entered the house, took from thence the Speaker's rich gold gown, or robe of state, several suits of clothes, silk breeches, a number of silk stockings, about two dozen silk handkerchiefs, two gold snuff-boxes, one of which had been made a present to the Speaker by Mr [Henry] Flood [Winchester's MP for the year 1783], and was remarkably elegant: They took likewise a small sum of money in a purse, which, we have been informed, was rather under seven pounds: They afterwards had the audacity to break open the next house, but being disturbed, made a hasty retreat to their boat, and got clear off. It is said they were seen to come from Lambeth, and were eight in number.

Philip did not, however, seem too concerned about the event (Letter 73):

We have and are to have a watch, who is constantly to sit up all night in the lower part of the house; but the misfortune is, that the steed is stolen. However it makes us not apprehensive of a second visit. Some of the S[peaker's] wearing apparel has been discovered in an empty house at Lambeth, and one man taken up whose boot corresponded exactly with the print of his foot in the garden, but that is not sufficient evidence to try him upon – no tidings of my hat.

Amongst other things, it is an interesting example of the degree of justice that might be at hand: *The Times* later (26 February) reported that a William Sharp suspected of the crime had been acquitted after a trial at the Old Bailey, even though boots matching impressions in the Speaker's garden had matched those found in his house. The incident encouraged Sarah to take precautions in Kingsgate Street, Winchester, though she obviously felt immune from the attention of criminals (Letter 71):

I condole with you upon your losses, and to qualify yours as much as I can, I have taken care of the beavers that hung up in the passage, they have been {w}ell brushed, and deposited in a place of security, as well as our more valua{ble} furniture, but I think no one will attack such a poor creature as myself, with four helpless children.

She worried, however, that Philip might be attacked, perhaps by a highwayman, when he rode down from London on horseback and urged him to take a carriage (Letter 70):

I wish that you may come down with Mr Jenkinson [either Philip's patron Charles, or his brother John], rather than ride over the Arabian sands of Hounslow and Bagshot.

There was, however, another reason for him to come down in a coach, such as a Diligence (Letter 81):

...you will I suppose come home in the Dilly; for if you come on horseback it will be two days lost to me...

9. *Williams at Westminster*

ALTHOUGH PHILIP WILLIAMS never seems to have taken part in practical politics, either in Winchester or nationally, nor was there any trace of it in his family, he was clearly attracted to the seat of power. Even before he had graduated at Oxford his taste for Westminster might have been heightened by a typically long letter from his friend Lovelace Bigg-Wither, who had been granted a seat in the debating chamber of the Commons by the jurist William Blackstone, member of parliament and brother-in-law-to-be (both married a Clitherow). Active in the tory cause at Oxford for many years, Blackstone had been handed a seat for Hindon, Wiltshire, to which he was elected unopposed in March 1761. In November 1763 Bigg-Wither described the visit to his friend (Letter 3):

> On the grand day of privilege Blackstone seated me in the gallery, some altercations passed between Beckford and Rigby, and the house was growing warm, when a wretch of an Irish Lord, Lord Digby, moved to turn all strangers out, the house did not approve of it at first, but another fellow, a friend of Hunt's, Lord Carysfort, seconded the motion and out we went[.]

The gallery in question had been necessary to accommodate the MPs brought to Westminster by the Act of Union with Scotland in 1707. The participants named in Bigg-Wither's letter can all be found in Namier's *History of Parliament*. William Beckford was the son of a sugar planter from Jamaica, and a member for the City of London. Richard Rigby was the member for Tavistock and 'man of business of the Bedfords in the House of Commons'. He seems to have misidentified 'Lord Digby', since an Irish peer of that named had been a member, but died in 1757. The speaker in question was probably his brother, Henry Digby, who hung on the coat-tails of his uncle, the leading politician Henry Fox. Lord Carysfort was a mediocre politician who within a few years was obliged to sell the furniture at his country seat, Elton Hall, near Peterborough. The bluestocking Elizabeth Montagu explained why in a letter to her husband (Blunt, 1923, I, 159):

All this has been brought upon him by an enormous expense in kept women. He used to have one always within a few miles of his country house.

At the time, parliamentary debates were held in St Stephen's chapel, which was destroyed by fire in 1834. It was a rather makeshift affair: the Speaker's chair was placed on the altar steps and voting took place by the 'ayes' and the 'noes' passing though the right-hand or left-hand doors of the choir screen. MPs in the chamber sat in the former choir stalls facing one another, but there was no formal arrangement in terms of political parties, which scarcely existed at the time. As already mentioned (Chapter 3), Philip Williams's friend Bigg-Wither, not knowing that he was peering into the future, noted a proposal from Sir John Glynn 'that the two parties should occupy different sides of the room'. Glynn (or Glynne) sat for the Flint Boroughs, Flintshire, and, as commentators wrote, 'gets up and jokes', but is 'little better than a chattering caff [probably 'cafard', a hypocrite]'. Nonetheless, the idea he proposed, treated with such contempt by Bigg-Wither, has, of course, come to pass.

Blackstone was Vinerian professor of English Law at the University of Oxford, with chambers in the Middle Temple. His lectures, which morphed into his *Commentaries on the Laws of England*, codified the status quo and yet conversely stirred the heart of social reformers such as Jeremy Bentham, who made a rare return to Oxford to hear them: his view of England was that it was 'cold, selfish, priest-ridden, lawyer-ridden, lord-ridden, squire-ridden [and] soldier-ridden' (Porter, 2000, pp. 416, 419). Both Philip Williams and Lovelace Bigg-Wither had, and continued to have, close connections with the Blackstone family, the former via Winchester College, several of whose fellows were of the family, and the latter by means of multiple family links. For example, the Revd Henry Blackstone (1722-1776), fellow of Winchester College, and vicar of Adderbury, Oxfordshire, where Philip Williams served as curate to qualify for ordination as priest, was the son of Charles Blackstone and his wife, Mary, a daughter of Lovelace Bigg of Chilton Foliat, Wiltshire, and Dorothy Wither.

Philip Williams was to gain his own personal experience of Westminster as a chaplain, first to Charles Jenkinson (1729-1808), later the lst earl of Liverpool, and then to the earl's brother-in-law and cousin, Charles Wolfran Cornwall, Speaker of the House of Commons, both of whom had links with Winchester. As G.H. Blore elegantly put it (WCA/E10/14/1/1-2): 'His lucky star rose in Winchester and continued to shine in London.' Jenkinson was born in Winchester, the eldest son of Colonel Charles Jenkinson and his wife Amarantha Cornwall. They lived on the east side of Calpe Street, now renamed St Thomas' Street, in house later numbered No. 9, south of Minster Street and virtually opposite the parish church that gave the street its name, now demolished (HRO/113M96/W/1, HRO/COPY/487). It was replaced by a new church, now redundant, on Southgate Street. Although Jenkinson's father had been educated at Winchester College, as founder's kin, he for some reason was sent to Charterhouse. Cornwall too was a Winchester native, as well as a Wykehamist, and had various freehold and leasehold estates in the city at Priors Barton and on Tegdown (HRO/13M85W/169). A large melodramatic memorial to him can still be seen on the south wall of the nave of the church of St Cross Hospital, Winchester.

Amongst other things, the role of the chaplain was a means for churchmen to evade the limits on plurality and to do so without any need to engage in the 'cure of souls'. There were no limits to the number of royal chaplains, and there were extended limits for 'the several degrees of nobility, temporal and spiritual: thus archbishops and dukes might have six [chaplains]... viscounts and bishops four...' (Sykes, 1934, p. 147). It has to be said that many people had a poor view of chaplains in general, as expressed by the character Lady Delacour in Maria Edgeworth's *Belinda*, published in 1801 (p.317), who describes the breed as:

> The meanest sycophant...fawning to my lord the bishop, insolent
> to the poor curate...greedy for preferment...

Such sentiments would of course have made uncomfortable reading for Philip Williams, though it unlikely that he spent much time delving into novels, which were largely regarded as trivial compositions intended for ladies to pass the time. And he might have been heartened when Lady Delacour moderated her views and is made to say:

> I am not so *illiberal* as to condemn all chaplains for one, odious as
> he was.

There is some uncertainty about the exact timing of Philip Williams's appointment by Jenkinson, though it was probably at some time after his election to a fellowship of Winchester in 1769. The introduction to a typescript transcription of some of the Williams Letters, made anonymously in about 1935, but ascribable to J.S. Drew (Winchester Cathedral Library, W10/7), refers to his appointment as 'Chaplain to

Charles, [1st] Earl of Liverpool', giving as a source the 'Andrews MSS, Lambeth Palace Library'. This source cannot now be recognised (pers. comm., R. Cosgrave, 2012) and it should also be noted that, at the likely date of William's appointment, Jenkinson would not have qualified for an entry in the Register of Noblemen's Chaplains, still accessible in Lambeth Palace Library (F5/1/13-14), as he was not enobled until 1786, when he became 1st Baron Hawkesbury (named after one of his estates); it was only in 1796 that he was raised to an earldom. There seems little doubt, however, that Williams's appointment as his chaplain took place. There are, for example, several references to 'His Honour Jenkinson', including one in the first surviving missive from Philip to Sarah, written from New College in August 1783 (Letter 42):

> His honour Jenkinson, Lady Cope [Jenkinson's second wife] and company are to arrive this day at Sir Banks's, where they are to remain sometime, and then to separate for their respective schemes into Huntingdon and Hampshire.

Sir Banks Jenkinson, seated at Headington, Oxford, was the 6th baronet of Walcot and Hawkesbury, and died without issue in 1789, when the title descended to Charles Jenkinson. Again, a year later, when Philip Williams had started his term as chaplain to the Speaker in London, he was obviously still close to Jenkinson (Letter 63):

> I read prayers, and after breakfast his honour carried me a very fine ride over a very fine country, and was very communicative and very entertaining.

Also, he and Speaker Cornwall seemed to have had open access to the politician's country home at Addiscombe, near Croydon. He must have felt close to the reins of power at this place, conveniently situated close to Croydon Palace, long a retreat of the archbishops of Canterbury; he called the head of the Church of England of the day, John Moore, 'the immaculate' (Letter 67) and brushed shoulders him with from time to time at parliamentary dinners. He also got to know a chaplain of his, Dr Thomas Drake, 'a very good sort of man, and as we are both much restricted in our time, and take our airings pretty regularly, we have made an agreement to accompany each other, as often as we can make it convenient' (Letter 67). In May 1784 he wrote to Sarah (Letter 49):

> The family went down to Adscombe this evening. I was much sollicited to be of the party, but have cut it under the promise of going down the next time.

The duties of the Speaker's chaplain were light but varied: as well as opening parliament every day with a prayer, he acted as a spiritual companion to his patron, a sort of 'divine personal assistant'. Many young clerics sought a position as a chaplain to a patron, in the hope of greater things. Royal chaplains were particularly well placed for preferment, but others could expect advancement, especially if the patron himself went up in the world (Sykes, 1934, p. 151 et seq.). Unfortunately for Philip Williams, Jenkinson's career hit a bad patch in early 1770s, and Cornwall was a relatively elderly man who was never going to gain higher office.

Like Blackstone for the tories, Jenkinson for the whigs had been extremely active in Oxford politics and when in 1768 he stood for the University of Oxford as the 'government candidate' he was defeated, largely because the dons cherished their independence. The full story is complex, but essentially he was caught in a whirlpool of change at the university, which was emerging from a long period when its tory-cum-jacobite sentiments set it against whig administrations and entering a phase of better relations with the new monarch, George III, and his ministers (Sutherland, In: Sutherland and Mitchell, 1986, pp. 137, 141, 152-71 passim). In 1769 Jenkinson married Amelia Watts, who died the following year giving birth to Robert Banks Jenkinson, a future prime minister. The motherless young boy often 'spent Christmas and part of the summer' in Winchester with his paternal grandmother, and in the company of his sister Elizabeth and her husband Charles Wolfran Cornwall (Gash, 1984, p. 11). Thus it was that in some way an ambitious politician operating in Oxford and London, with family links to Winchester, came into contact with a young man with a fellowship at Winchester, following one at Oxford, and made him his chaplain. Jenkinson, who had to work hard to make way in the world, may well have been attracted by Philip Williams's relatively modest background. For all his achievements, this son of an undistinguished Oxfordshire family is now regarded as 'a bureaucrat rather than a politician' and even, in the words of the painter Nathaniel Dance, 'a common kind of man whom luck and perseverance have made' (Gash, 1984, pp.8-9). In that pioneering satire *The Rolliad*, written anonymously, he is 'skilled in courtly lore' and a favourite of George III:

Jenky, pursue Ambition's task,
The King will give you whate'er you ask

The historian Norman Gash paints picture of him as a sort of 'Mr Malaprop':

> The pompous formal manner he affected in society created amusement in the royal family, despite their appreciation of his loyalty and usefulness. His attempt to assume the air of a man of fashion, his mispronunciation of the occasional French phrase...brought him ridicule in smart London circles. Yet with much of the pedant about him, he had some of the pedantic virtues: industriousness, an appetite for knowledge and a zest for writing.

After a period of considerable success under Bute (whose sons had been at Winchester College in the 1760s), Jenkinson 'looked as if he had settled for comfortable obscurity', but in December 1778, midway through the American conflict, he was appointed secretary of war under North (Cannon, J. 'Charles Jenkinson', ODNB). It seems likely that Philip Williams was his chaplain at this stage or earlier. Certainly, he seems to have taken a deep personal interest in the minister's brief, as suggested by a copy of the second edition of 1775 of the *Speech of Edmund Burke, Esq. on American Taxation, April 19, 1774*, now lodged in the Fellows' Library at Winchester College. In his unmistakeable hand there are detailed comments spread over 16 pages offering a minute critique of the text, from the viewpoint of someone who opposed Burke. There is no doubt that this would have been Jenkinson's stance: in a letter of 1775 Burke complained to Rockingham that 'Jenkinson governs every thing' (John Cannon, 'Charles Jenkinson', ODNB).

The background to Burke's speeches is well known: in the wake of the Tea Act being given royal assent in May 1773 and the Boston Tea Party of the following December, the great orator, a Protestant Dubliner, argued that the benefits of co-operation between Britain and the American colonies were far greater than any advantages to be gained from insisting on the right to exact taxes. His beautifully crafted speeches set a new standard of political debate and influenced minds far beyond the House of Commons. Philip Williams's notes are written in a small neat hand in the margins and outer spaces of the text. Although it is difficult to prove, they seem to have been made when the events were fresh to mind. In his mid-30s, and exposed for the first time to the hub of power, the chaplain was therefore probably preparing himself for casual discussions with Jenkinson and the other parliamentarians he dined with, to ensure that he could keep his end up. Or perhaps he was merely filling in the time that spread before him in London.

Whatever his intention, it is evident that he had combed through the *Journals of the House of Commons* and made a careful textual analysis of Burke's words in the context of past parliamentary debates. His remarks are therefore more those of a lawyer than an orator, more inclined to polish a contract than sway an audience, and some – especially the early ones – are pedantic in the extreme. In this regard he was not unlike his master, of whom it has been written that 'no ray of wit, humour or levity pervaded his speeches' (Wheatley, 1884, cited by Cannon, 'Charles Jenkinson', ODNB). For example, in response to Burke's sneer about 'the public promise of a Peer' (Burke, p. 26) Philip Williams wrote (with idiosyncratic spelling):

> It is unfair to call it so. The letter was written officially; by a secretary who indeed happened to be a pear. But whose was the promise? The promise not of the pear but the secretary. Nor is it a promise to repeal a tax; but a promise only that the repeal shall be proposed to the house.

And, on the Stamp Act, he commented that 'many have thought ... that the timid repeal of that act did cause all the disturbances that have succeeded [it]'. There is much else (*see* Appendix IV) showing how Phillip Williams – and, perhaps the ministry of George III – thought at the time. In retrospect, the Taxation of the Colonies Act 1778, which repealed the Tea Act, was too late to stop the American War of Independence (1775-1783) and its sequelae.

Whenever it was that Philip Williams served Jenkinson, the appointment may have ended by the time of his marriage to Sarah Collins. However, Jenkinson's brother-in-law, Charles Wolfran Cornwall, then sought to draw him back to Westminster. After he had been elected Speaker of the House of Commons on 1 November 1780, he asked Williams to be his chaplain (Letter 26), but he declined, presumably as he wanted to stay with his bride of 11 months – or at least she wanted him to do so. Instead the post went to a second cousin of Cornwall, namely, Folliot Herbert Walker Cornwall [sic], who was only 26 years of age. Four years later, Philip Williams was offered the post again and this time he accepted. He served for nearly five years, but the Letters only cover 1784/5 and 1787, because of an illness that seems to have kept him at home for the whole of 1786 – certainly there are no letters at all from that year.

The period after 1784 was an exciting time to be at Westminster: Pitt the Younger had just become prime minister at the tender age of 24 and was radically to reform the public finances, and much else. Cornwall was not perhaps the ideal man to rise to the occasion and endure long debates, as Philip Williams noted (Letter 67):

> The day proved so wet in the afternoon that I could not stir out, even to the house which sat late, and the Sp[eaker] eat nothing but a slight breakfast till 1 o'clock on Tuesday morning, which made him very unwell.

The authors, of *The Rolliad*, whoever they were, noticed more his need of constant refreshment (22 ed., London 1812, p.67):

> There CORNEWALL sits, and, O unhappy fate!
> Must sit for ever through the long debate;
> Save when by Nature's sovereign will,
> Sometime to empty, sometimes to fill…

and:

> Like sad PROMETHEUS fasten'd to his rock,
> In vain he looks for pity to the clock;
> In vain th' effects of strength'ning porter tries
> And nods to BELLAMY for fresh supplies…

John Bellamy was the deputy housekeeper who first set up catering facilities at the Houses of Parliament in 1773 and is today remembered by an eponymous bar in the House of Commons. His pork pies (or was it veal pies?) were, according to an apocryphal story started by Disraeli, the subject of the dying words of Pitt the Younger.

Philip Williams was the 39th chaplain to serve the Speaker since the Restoration, and the 28th since 1700: inspecting the list of holders of the post shows that he was fairly typical (Gray, 1991, pp. 57-80). They were drawn almost equally from men educated at Oxford and Cambridge, most with an MA degree (a virtually automatic award for graduates). At 42 years of age he was in line with most, though it happens that the two men who served before and after him were both aged only 26. Most, but not all chaplains held only a parish living before appointment, so Philip Williams, who already held a prebend at Lincoln had a headstart. However, divinity was not his major subject at Oxford and it is noticeable that many other chaplains acquired bachelor degrees and doctorates in divinity (some awarded by Lambeth), generally after they had finished at the House of Commons.

Interestingly, according to a resolution of the House made in 1700 (Gray, 1991, p.15) either a doctorate in divinity or at least the 'dignity of a Dean of the Church' was required by anyone who presented state sermons on three key dates, namely, 30 January to mark the 'martyrdom of Charles I', 29 May for the Restoration of Charles II and 5 November for the Gunpowder Plot. A comment by Sarah Williams in a letter to Philip written in August 1784, a few months after he had started at Westminster, confirms that, although he lacked the basic requirements, he did address the House on occasions. Referring to Pitt the Younger's tutor and secretary, George Pretyman (1750-1827), who had delivered the sermon to mark the Restoration of Charles II (Letter 67), she wrote (M/PW/56):

> I see there are some sarcasms upon Dr Prettyman's sermon in the newspaper; beware of the martyrdom of poor King Charles; get your sermon ready that you may submit it to the inspection of the wise ones...

He, too, was critical of the sermon: after he had gone 'in the lumbring state coach to hear Dr Prettyman at St Margaret's, [he] was not much pleased either with the matter or manner' (Letter 67). When he did preach, he seemed to take it in his stride, though he was not always impressed by the congregation (Letter 73):

> I performed at the abbey, as the Morning Chronicle told you, to a set of lazars, people without noses, and the dregs of hospitals; afterwards paid Davison's bill in the city; settled some matters with the [Winchester] College banker, and the patent stove man, and returned home and was quietly inhumed for the remainder of the day.

He friends in Winchester no doubt noticed what appeared to be his rising fortunes. A report in the *Hampshire Chronicle* (7 February) noted: '[It was] ordered that the thanks of this House be given to their Chaplain, for his sermon preached before them on Monday [31 Jan], and the same to be printed.'

The 11th prebend of Canterbury presented by the king to Philip Williams on 4 May 1789, a few months after the death of Speaker Cornwall, was a typical reward: throughout the eighteenth century all Speaker's chaplains (with the exception of one who died in post) received a similar dignity after completing their stint in the chamber. Most became canons of Westminster or Windsor, several received preferment at Christ Church, Oxford, or Canterbury, and a few elsewhere. It is clear from Philip Williams's correspondence that he hoped in the long term to gain even more, but the chances of this were slim. Sarah expressed her own ambitions for him, at the same time teasing him about his neglect of his parish at Compton, where a friend had deputised for him (Letter 68):

> When I (that is when you are) am Bishop of Winton I shall remember him [Thomas Heathcote]; there were prayers only at Compton at the thanks giving, and a very good congregation, which I am glad of, as it is a proof that they deserve to be attended to...

After receiving their stall, very few Speaker's chaplains in the eighteenth century advanced any further, although Philip Williams's predecessor, Dr Folliot Herbert Cornewall (1754-1831), did gain the minor bishopric of Bristol after 17 years (and thereafter Hereford and Worcester). Other exceptions were the few who became deans, and three others who gained bishoprics, namely, Dr Francis Gastrell (1662-1725), who became bishop of Chester ten years after completing his chaplainship, Dr Richard Terrick (ca.1710-1777), who gained London after 22 years, and his successor Dr Charles Moss (1763-1811), who gained Oxford after 16 years. In short, the chaplainship of the House of Commons was a certain path to a stall, but only rarely did it lead to further advancement.

For her part, Sarah, only a year after he had taken up his post, and pregnant, was expecting more from his time in London than actually seemed likely (Letter 85):

> I felt disappointed at your letter, I did not expect that you would get anything in the present scramble, but I had pleased myself with the hopes that it might lead to a certain promise at the next thing that falls; for till that is the case I do not look upon your advancement as at all forwarded by any vacancy that may happen; for if the whole bench of Bishops were to go off, competitors would start up like Hydra's heads; you see what my poor head is roaming upon, and I have an additional reason to wish to be with

you, in my present situation, which becomes very oppressive to me, from unusual sickness and countless inconveniences.

The routine of the Speaker's Chaplain has changed very little since the Restoration, according to Dr Donald Gray, who has himself held the post (Gray, 1991). They have a 'uniform' which has not changed since Philip Williams's day. They dress in a room set aside for the purpose, part of the Speaker's house, 'to which there is an entrance in the Lower Library Corridor'. They don a black silk priest's gown, over a black silk cassock, with black silk stockings, court shoes with silver buckles, and white linen 'preaching' bands at the neck. They wear white gloves, a long scarf (or tippet) with the royal arms embroidered at its extremities, and carry a black three-cornered chapeau and a white handkerchief. In one respect, however, there has been a great change, reflecting different views within the Church of England on the ordination of women. In 2010 the 79th Speaker's chaplain, Mrs Rose Hudson-Wilkin, already a royal chaplain, became the first woman (and the first black person) to be appointed to the post. The break with tradition was made by the Rt Hon John Bercow and led the dean of Westminster to break with tradition in another way, by appointing a separate chaplain for the Abbey.

On a typical day, at the opening of proceedings in the House of Commons the chaplain enters the chamber in company with the Speaker, the Sergeant-at-Arms, and the Speaker's Secretary. They bow to the chair, advance seven paces, bow again, and then the chaplain starts prayers (the secretary meanwhile having left the chamber), by reciting Psalm 67. The chaplain then greets members with 'The Lord be with you', to which they reply 'And with thy spirit', which invokes the words 'Let us pray'. At this point the members turn to face their benches and, in an age when they would have worn swords, would probably have knelt on the seats. Then follows the three-fold Kyrie ('Lord, have mercy upon us ...') and the Lord's Prayer, succeeded by prayers in turn for the sovereign, the Royal Family and parliament itself. The service ends with the prayer 'Prevent us, O Lord...' and the Grace.

Although generally referred to as the Speaker's Chaplain, as they are appointed by the Speaker (and cannot appear in the House in his absence), they are in fact chaplain to the House of Commons and in modern times have a pastoral role that reflects this. The norms of the job were revealed in 1833 when the Select Committee on the Establishment of the House cross-examined John Rickman, the Speaker's Secretary (and coincidentally the son of the rector of Compton, Hampshire, who *The* preceded Philip Williams in the living). He explained that each chaplain was expected to serve for three years (hence there were generally two chaplains per parliament), though he had 'known one serve five, and another four years': in fact, the record suggests that the four and a half years that Philip Williams served was not unusual. Although terminated by the death of Cornwall in Privy Garden, Whitehall, in January 1789, a new appointment would in any event have soon been required. To guard against the possibility of parliament being dissolved during the recess, an address was presented to the House at the end of each session 'to confer some dignity in the Church on the Chaplain'. Rickman told the committee that 'the usual consequence of the address is a Stall at Westminster, at Canterbury, at Windsor, or at Christ Church, Oxford', and a departing chaplain was put on the list until there was a vacancy. No salary was attached to the post but 'eight guineas a year are given as an allowance in lieu of stationery ... out of the Speaker's allowance.' Hence, although Philip Williams would ultimately gain from his time at Westminster, he had first to finance his entire time in London, which must have placed a severe burden on the budget of the Williams household in Winchester.

As Reform crept through the corridors of Westminster, the eagle eye of change alighted on the automatic appointment of the Speaker's chaplain to a senior post in the Church, merely for three years of saying prayers at the opening of parliament. Armed with the evidence of John Rickman quoted above, and much else, the Select Committee decided to abolish the automatic appointment of chaplains to 'some dignity in the Church' and replaced it with a salary of £200 per annum. Philip Williams did not live to see the changes, and most of his generation escaped the new order. But one who did not was his brother-in-law, Jeremiah Dyson, who had some very difficult questions to answer about the role of the Deputy Clerk to the House of Commons (*see* Chapter 15).

Of course, those with an eye to preferment made it their business to watch the obituary columns of the national newspapers and other important sources of information, such as the *Gentlemen's Magazine*. The Letters are peppered with observations on who had died where and what had happened as a result. Hence, in March 1787, referring to very recent events, Philip Williams wrote (Letter 123):

> A stall has been vacant last week at Gloucester in the Chancellor's gift, and disposed of immediately to Dr [Samuel] Horsley, so that poor Warton has no chance I fear of any thing through Lord Weymouth.

Horsley went on to be successively bishop of St David's, Rochester and St Asaph's. He had played an influential role as one of the secretaries of the Royal Society, of which he was a fellow, but it ended acrimoniously. The reference to 'poor Warton', probably meant Joseph, head master of Winchester College, though it could equally well have been his brother, Thomas, who in 1785 had been appointed Poet Laureate. Joseph had obtained a prebend of St Paul's in 1782 and the year after this letter was written was given a prebendal stall at Winchester by prime minster Pitt. Thomas Thynne, 3rd viscount Weymouth, regarded as an ineffective and corrupt politician, was seated at Longleat House, near Warminster, Wiltshire.

At the level of the parish priest, Philip Williams's attitude to 'doing the duty' was made crystal clear in a letter to Sarah (Letter 123):

> I met our old friend Dr Hodson yesterday in the park; I understand though not from himself, that he is going into orders; a very wise resolution, and which will at least put £40 a year into his pocket.

Typical of the many exchanges between the couple is Sarah's interest in the parish of Crawley, near Winchester (Letter 92):

> Old [Henry] Taylor of Crawley is dead, which is lucky enough for your namesake, as he will now be able to fix himself for life, Brush I understand has given up all thoughts of Milbourn Port, the business will now of course be settled at the midsummer meeting; Mr [Edmund] Poulter has his reasons to be pleased, as I hear that Crawley is worth 500£ which is no bad beginning.

This paragraph concerns the 'musical chairs' of clerical appointments in the gift of the bishop of Winchester and Winchester College. Thus, when Henry Taylor died his living went to Edmund Poulter, whilst that at Portsmouth went to Henry Oglander, and Daniel Williams obtained Milborne Port, Somerset, following the death of John Lucas. All but Taylor and Poulter were Winchester fellows and Portsmouth and Milborne Port, Somerset, were College livings. Thus it sounds as if Oglander was in line for Milborne Port, but after the death of Taylor he took Portsmouth, leaving Daniel Williams free to take his place. Poulter later became a cathedral prebendary. The list of livings held at one time or another by Poulter and Taylor is a clear demonstration of the almost industrial approach of greedy clerics of the period. 'Brush' is perhaps a

The Lincoln canon, Dr John Gordon, writing on 31 December 1780 to his stepson, Philip Williams, at Winchester, congratulating him on the birth of his namesake son (Letter 28).

nickname: the Church of England Clergy Database contains no-one of that name at anything like a reasonable date.

The Canterbury stall gained by Philip Williams for his time at Westminster was quite a prize, to be added to his other preferments, although some observers were extremely scathing of the metropolitan see, particularly after Reform became respectable. For example, Sir Egerton Brydges (1762-1837) in his autobiography, published in 1834, remarks that Canterbury was 'richer in inanimate than in animate attractions' and calls it 'the feasting and sleeping spot of Speaker's Chaplains and powerful noblemen's tutors' (vol I, pp. 39-40, quoted by Gray, 1991).

Many of the chaplains appointed were related to the Speaker, albeit distantly, and the cosy relationship between the two is revealed in a letter written in January 1792 by William Wyndham Grenville, the stopgap Speaker who had taken the chair for six months after Cornwall died in office (and later served briefly, and reluctantly as prime minister). Thus, Charles Moss, his chaplain in 1789, who served the next Speaker until 1791, was Philip Williams's immediate successor (and, even more than he, a beneficiary of preferment, starting with a sub-deanship from his father at the age of 11!). Moss had, apparently, made an excuse to write to his former patron in order to make him aware that he was keen to obtain the bishopric of Norwich, the incumbent nearing the end of his life. Grenville explains that William Pitt the prime minister is 'so hampered with engagements' that he is unlikely to be able to make the appointment for some while, but the former Speaker confirms that he is ready to be 'of use in promoting whatever arrangement might be more convenient' (Letter dated 26 January, 1792, Charles Moss Papers, Duke University Library, Durham, North Carolina, USA, reproduced by Gray, 1991). In fact, Moss was rewarded with a stall at Westminster and had to wait until 1807 for his bishopric, when he gained Oxford.

As a footnote to Philip Williams's time at Westminster, as mentioned above, there are no letters to Sarah from London in 1786. This was due to illness, as shown from the fact that, although he delivered an address to the Commons, as was customary for the chaplain, in August 1784 and July 1785, he was unable to do so in 1786, when it was given by the Rev Thomas Heathcote, 'who ...officiated during the illness of Mr Williams' (*Journal of the House of Commons*, vol. XLI, p. 155). Thomas Heathcote was a Wykehamist and close friend of Philip Williams, who spent much time in London and at the time was rector of Stone, Kent. He was a son of Sir Thomas Heathcote of Hursley Park, which lies south of Winchester, close to the village of Compton where Philip Williams was rector – and where Thomas Heathcote occasionally deputised for his friend.

Philip Williams's illness and his recovery are set out in a very preachy missive of April 1786 from John Gordon (Letter 113). He writes about a 'late alarming malady' that 'Mrs Williams undoubtedly at first managed to underwrite ... so much, as to keep down our solicitude' and 'God be thankd for his mercy in giving so favorable an issue to so threatening an appearance'. He went on to describe an illness of his own:

> It appeard aukward and unlucky to be detain in the country just at that critical point of time; but the attack appeard neither dangerous, nor likely to last long. ... Perhaps you may be disposed to think meanly of such a disorder as St Anthony's fire; as I myself once did. But I have learnt better; and I woud rather wish you to take my word, than put it upon your own experience. How it got the name of saint I know not, but surely not from it's nature, which believe me, has nothing saintlike in it.

St Anthony's fire is today interpreted to be either ergotism, erysipelas or herpes zoster (shingles). In the case of John Gordon it seems most likely to have been erysipelas, which resolves in weeks, though can be fatal (Queen Anne died from it) or herpes, as ergotism is a long-term illness associated with exposure to milling products and is a more severe disease, with convulsions and gangrenous complications.

Gordon's son George had also been unwell, though not with tuberculosis as feared. And the letter shows that, whatever Philip Williams's problem, Rachel [Landy] a servant much-loved by Sarah, had been a 'faithful Nurse' and a Winchester physician (who was to become locally well known) had been giving advice to both of the sick:

> He and I are much obliged to your friend Dr [John] Littlehales for his advice, as well as you are for his effectual care and attention, and successfull assistance: for which he cannot easily be paid too much, though your generosity seems to bid fair to try the experiment.

10. *Fancy Free in London*

ALTHOUGH LONDON in the late eighteenth century was not remote for the people of Winchester, travelling up on horseback could take the best part of two days. In the spring of 1785 Philip Williams assured Sarah of his safety midway on the journey to his lodgings in the house of the Speaker, alongside the Privy Garden of the Palace of Whitehall (Letter 86):

> I got here (the red Lion at Bagshot) about ½ past four, having had one of the finest spring days I ever felt, eat a broiled fowl, and slumbered over newspapers and Carver's travels through America [*Travels Through America in the Years 1766, 1767, and 1768*, London , 1778, by Jonathan Carver] till near 10 o'clock. I breakfasted at Popham Lane [at the Wheatsheaf Inn], where there was no fresh butter, and the substitute, some bad currant jelly, gave me the gripes. I fell in there with Dehany who came to inquire about the hunter's dinner, and wanted me to go home with him. I met old Keates in one of the Exeter Dillys; his son meant to go from Portsmouth to Midhurst next Tuesday. I shall finish when I get to Privy Garden, and I hope with a better pen.

The journey itself started him on the explosion of social activity that marked his time in London: the people he met en route were probably Philip Dehany from Farleigh Wallop and the Revd Richard Keats, vicar of Sparsholt, who went on to be a chaplain to the duke of Clarence and William IV, travelling up from Exeter in the Diligence coach.

At the start of his appointment as chaplain to the Speaker, acquiring the right dress was, of course, a high priority (Letter 48):

> Yesterday I sallied forth to Mr. Stone's who is to furnish me with a gown and cassock, and as good luck would have it he supplied my predecessor and the Speaker, and therefore knew the trim of it, and insists upon my having weepers, as he says it is not like going to dine with a bishop, for you will dine, Sir, with the greatest men of the kingdom.

Then a week later he reported on his first day in the job and innocently lays out his less-than-arduous routine (Letter 49):

> I took possession of my office, rode down [by coach] with my colleague Mr Man, backwards, and read prayers to about five people; was in a funk from the novelty of the scene, and hearing my own voice in the h[ouse] of commons. My master had been in the same apprehensions the day before in the H[ouse] of Lords where the heat and crowd was so great, that he and the chancellor bawled at one another without being able to exchange a look. It is very convenient going with the Speaker to the House, as his carriage waits 'till I have done, and then brings me home without any trouble, when I lay aside my robes, and am a free agent for the remainder of the day.

During the five years Philip Williams served as the Speaker's chaplain in London, a post without any income, he must have had many hours of spare time. Almost all of the letters he subsequently wrote to his wife reveal the trouble-free existence he enjoyed. Not for him closeting himself in the library to work on his edition of Polybius. Nor to work on the College accounts, which were in certain years his responsibility as one of the bursars. Nor, as far as the evidence of the Letters goes, to perform any sort of pastoral role at Westminster. Instead, he engaged in a round of visits to friends and acquaintances, visited the theatre or the circus, dined regally with a wide range of parliamentarians, some of them household names, and carried out the odd errand for Sarah and others. She continuously regretted his absence and displayed a degree of cynicism about the business of parliament:

> (Letter 96): ... I begin to think that we shall never meet again, if the remainder of the Irish Propositions are each to produce a debate of the same length as the last, when are we to expect an end...not in the next month I fear...

> (Letter 51): What is said about the length of the sitting of Parliament? Is there any chance of your being down before August?7 But what is this all to me, you will only be down for a short time to go away again for a very long one, for I clearly anticipate what is to be my fate from your total silence upon a certain subject, I believe I dwelt too much upon in my last.

(Letter 54): {Notwith}standing what you say, these late nights {through to} mornings must retard the breaking up of Parliament, because they are not able to raise a house again the same day; I do not see any symptom of a wish in the leaders to part, and this cool weather, which is so seasonable for them, will make them feel less the necessity of doing it.

Whilst in London, Philip Williams enjoyed a wide range of diversions and entertainments (Porter, 1994; White, 2012). One of the more intellectual kind was offered by the French reader and exhibitionist, Le Texier, although in the event the man himself did not perform. Philip Williams was brutally honest about the event (Letter 80):

Not understanding the French I was very near asleep and should have been quite so if it had not been for the conversation of Mr and Mrs [Nathaniel] Dance [of Cranbury Park, Hursley, near Winchester] whom I sat next to. And yet there were 60 people at ½ a guinea an head. One half hour was consumed in handing about tea and lemonade.

He had been given a ticket by 'Bob Jenkinson', who may have been his patron's son, Robert Banks Jenkinson, a future prime minister, and at this stage an earnest teenager, who later was to spend several months in Paris perfecting his French (Norman Gash, 'Robert Banks Jenkinson', ODNB). Le Texier gave French readings at his house in Lisle Street, off Leicester Square, in the manner of an actor, assuming the countenance of each character and even in Paris (but not in London) changing costume. He performed to a 'fashionable circle' according to one contemporary account, which continued (Boaden, 1825, p. 414):

The whole wore the appearance of an amusement in a private house. On ascending the great staircase, you were received in M. le Texier's library and from that instant you seemed to be incontestibly in France... . You then passed into the reading room, and met a dressed and refined party, who treated him as their host invariably. His servants brought you tea and coffee, in the interval between the readings, silently and respectfully. Le Texier, too, himself, came into the library, at such pauses, and saluted his more immediate acquaintance. A small bell announced that the readings were about to commence.

Every week in London was different for Philip Williams and none is wholly representative. A flavour of his life at the beginning of his office is perhaps given by a letter he wrote to his wife in July 1784 (Letter 63). On the Saturday he rode down to Addiscombe House, near Croydon, the country house of his patron Charles Jenkinson. He drank tea with 'Lady Harry Beauclerk ... and her daughter the maid of honour (a virgin of 50)' and then 'sauntered in the gardens 'till supper time'. He might have learnt something of the ways of the capital from Lady Beauclerk, a courtier and hanger-on who constantly sought patronage for herself and her children. He rubbed shoulders with his patron's second wife, Lady Cope, and their daughter Catherine, who was 'getting very fat and coarse'. On Sunday it was down to business: 'I read prayers, and after breakfast his honour [Jenkinson] carried me a very fine ride over a very fine country, and was very communicative and very entertaining. Poynte Ricketts and his wife... dined there ... she is a very good-natured woman, and seemed happy to see a Winchester inhabitant.'

On Monday he rode up to London before breakfast, then called on a family friend, Miss Elizabeth Pyke, and caught up with gossip that a modern tabloid might have headlined 'Brewer's wife runs off with Italian toy boy', though he wrote: 'People talk about nothing but this worsted stocking Mrs Thrale's marriage with Piozzi the singer, and leaving her children (3 or 4 daughters) to take care of themselves.' He perused the newspapers and was 'sorry... though not surprized' to see the name of an acquaintance of theirs in the list of bankrupts. On Tuesday he dined with Jenkinson at Speaker Cornwall's house and then walked in the park alone, as Mrs Cornwall was tired. The highlight of the day was 'dear Sal's letter, though it contained much that needed a response'. He was lucky, he thought, to miss his brother-in-law's uncle and trustee, Samuel Dyson; before returning the visit he decided to await the arrival of the man's 'shatter-brained nephew'. A week later, he 'paddled into the city, and called upon' him (Letter 65).

Wednesday brought a letter from his sisters, safely housed in Eastbourne, and a visit from the Dean of Hereford, Nathan Wetherell, who wanted to send another of his sons to Winchester College. They 'took an airing to Dulwich ... and walked about a college founded by one Allen [Edward Alleyn] a player'. On Thursday he accompanied the Speaker's wife to see *The Death of Major Pierson*, an epic picture by the American painter John Singleton Copley of an incident in the Battle of Jersey, 1781, when the French, acting as an American ally, tried to seize the island. He deemed it to have 'very great merit'. In the evening he passed the time visiting

'Kensington Gardens, which were very refreshing, and not over-crowded'. Here he picked up the fact that the playwright 'Sheridan has a considerable hand in the Morning Herald'. On Friday he spent a long day, 'that is from four 'till one', in the house of commons, after which he paid some visits and played 'at chess with the automaton, who beat me after a struggle of near an hour by my mistaking an Hungarian knight for a bishop.' The Mechanical Turk or Automatic Chess Player was an ingenious, but fake mechanism based on magnets, first exhibited in 1770.

Whilst in London, Philip Williams's life was split between Westminster, socialising with the great and good, and friends from Winchester and elsewhere, going to the theatre and incidentally engaging in much that the capital had to offer. It cannot be said that he exhibited a serious involvement with affairs of state in his letters to Sarah, but there are pithy asides showing that he was very conscious of being close to the seat of power. On one occasion he enthusiastically reported a near-miss diplomatic gaff (Letter 63):

> The Speaker was very near taken in to meet the French Ambassador who dines and sleeps at Addescombe [the home of Charles Jenkinson] to night, but the cat was let out of the bag …which I am sorry for as it is a disappointment to Mrs C[ornwall] who was to have been of the party, and begged me to say nothing of the matter.

He enjoyed many parliamentary dinners, often with ministers on one day and the opposition the next. Shortly after assuming his office he wrote to Sarah with the details (Letter 67):

> We had a superb entertainment; soups, removed by fish, removed by venison and veal, two courses of 18 dishes each and a desert. We sat down to table just before six, and rose from it about nine.

As usual, he gave her the names of the company, many of whom were leading figures of the day: 'Rose expressed himself very highly obliged to your father, and perfectly satisfied with what had been done' (his son, George Henry, who was to become a government minister himself, had been admitted as a scholar to Winchester College in 1781, though the ODNB says he was 'educated at Geneva') … 'Banks but a poor soul'… 'Wilberforce very pleasant and the life of the company' (Letter 73). On one occasion the diners included a future prime minister, Henry

Addington, a Wykehamist, of whom he wrote, prophetically: '[he] is a very promising young man, and asked after you' (Letter 78).

One of the great tours de force of Pitt's new government was the disputed election in May 1784 of a member to represent the City of Westminster. The whig leader Charles Fox, who had assured himself a seat in parliament for the rotten borough of Orkney by buying off its twelve voters, also contested Westminster, with the support of the Prince of Wales and Georgiana, duchess of Devonshire. He hoped to win one of the two seats by beating Sir Cecil Wray. The initial result seemed to confirm it (6,234 versus 5,998), but there was much talk of electoral irregularity and the High Bailiff therefore allowed a scrutiny of every vote cast. In the event, fraud on both sides was found, though the result was confirmed in Fox's favour, but not until the following March, when Pitt suffered his first defeat in the house (Hague, 2004, pp.173-4, 190). Philip Williams was obviously as fed up as everyone else with the business, which did not show Pitt at his best (Letter 78):

> In the evening I attended the debate about the old bore, the Westminster Election, where if they dont put an end to it some how or other, the ministry will be foiled, and so they ought to be.

Two days after its resolution, with a members' vote of 162 to 124 in favour of Fox, Philip Williams and his patron were much relieved, though he assured his long-suffering wife that the affair would not by itself lengthen the sitting (Letter 80):

> The Speaker came home at seven o'clock this morning; thank God, the business of the Westminster election is at last over; but you may be satisfied that these late nights by no means retard the ordinary business, as that comes on previous to the debate.

One of Pitt's great ideas was to reform parliament. It sparked fear in the strongest of heads imbued with Old Corruption. Philip Williams's stepfather, Dr John Gordon, revealed his hand in a letter written in June 1782, replete with the business of farming rents (Letter 38):

> I am afraid these confounded Reformers will dissolve the Parliament if not the Government. Only they are a most dangerous race – they know nothing but the art of cajoling the dupes the People. A contemptible system!

He would have had little in common with the Revd Christopher Wyvill (1738-1822), founder of the Yorkshire Association, which was set up to foster modest reforms, such as removal of some of the most outrageous rotten boroughs and extension of the vote to copyholders and others. A packed house attended the debate, but the vote on 19 April 1785, 248 to 174, was a resounding defeat for Pitt's government. Philip Williams's comments a few days after the event say much for his politics (Letter 90):

> Monday brought on the great and long expected debate of reform, and the house was filled so early that I suppose I had an audience of 200 members. I sat there near 10 hours, and I desired John to wake me when the house broke up with an account of the division, which he did at 20 minutes past four on Tuesday morning, with, 'Sir, Mr Pitt has lost it by 74.' I thanked God for it, and slept very heartily after the news, and trust that this cursed spirit of reform is laid during my time at least. I never saw the Speaker [Charles Wolfran Cornwall] so interested about any political measure, or so exhilarated by the event, and I trust my old Lady though no great politician, will join the majority with a satisfied countenance.

He and Sarah obviously were of the same mind (Letter 91):

> I am heartily pleased with the denouement of the reform business, which has ended as I guessed it would, for it could never be expected that those gentlemen, of respectable names, would vote themselves out of the house; let them act up to the spirit of the present constitution and they will find it needs no amendment, strict honesty of principle, and constant attention to the good of the publick, will alone be sufficient to correct every abuse and place things upon a firm footing, but (without reflecting upon the present times), such a reform is not to be expected in any times, when we consider the frailty of human nature.

Extreme radicals such as Thomas Paine, whose *Rights of Man* was first published in 1791, must have hardened the opposition of people like Philip Williams and it was not until the end of Wyvill's life that 'the moderate reform movement he had always advocated' began to take shape (H.T. Dickinson, 'Christopher Wyvill', ODNB).

Another of Pitt's great causes was reform of Irish-English trade, to relieve the poverty suffered by the largely Catholic population of Ireland, governed by its own parliament in Dublin. A raft of restrictive regulations and customs duties obliged Ireland to trade in ways that favoured England and choked off its own ability to develop its own economy (Hague, 2004, pp. 185-91, 195-6). Adam Smith's *The Wealth of Nations*, published in 1776, had put trade on the agenda of all enlightened politicians. It was a huge challenge for Pitt, as he not only had to persuade Westminster of his propositions, but also to ensure that they were passed by Dublin. Ultimately, the ambition was too great and had to be abandoned. In March 1785 (Letter 83) Philip Williams called it 'this abominable Irish business' and was concerned that it might 'abridge our Easter Recess', and three months later it was still affecting his domestic plans (Letter 98):

> Monday closed the scene of these Irish propositions, or rather Tuesday morning 5 o'clock, at which time the Speaker returned home. If Mr Pitt chuses to have them pass into a bill this sessions, it will take up probably 5 weeks longer before they can pass the Irish house and be returned back again; and in that case it is supposed when the other remaining business is got through, that our parliament will be adjourned for 9 or 10 days, and meet again for that single purpose. If so, I shall come down to Winchester, and return for that day – but nothing at present is known for certain.

Sarah, who supported Fox, called Pitt 'our sapient Premier' and commented that 'at best he is a very corked business, and he must take care, or he may find himself stuck in the Irish mire after all' (Letter 99). Domestically, her main concern was to know when her husband might come down for the summer, but – as so often was the case – writing in late June and early July he was unable to give a definite answer:

> ...it seems now to be the opinion that parliament will rise about the [Winchester College] election week, and I trust it will be prorogued, instead of being adjourned. However, nobody can answer for Wil: Wilful and I believe he has got into an Irish bog, and is not at present determined how to extricate himself ...(Letter 103).

The Lords have come in for a little dose of Irish politics; they rose at four this morning, with a majority for government of 58 to 27. They resume the debate next week, and then return the proposition to the commons, which if altered, may occasion another bustle of a day with us. The talk is of parliament's rising the latter end of the week after this; I hope in my next to speak positively about it, for though I feel enough anxiety on my own account, believe me that I feel doubly on your's (Letter 106).

In fact, this session of parliament ended on 2 August 1785 (Namier and Brooke, I, 1754-1790, 536). Although adoption by the House of Lords of the resolutions on Ireland of the administration of Pitt was regarded as a triumph, a vote on 13 August in Dublin dashed hopes that they would succeed (Hague, 2004, p. 196).

Philip Williams could hardly have been closer to events as they unfolded. In mid-July 1785 on a Saturday he rode down to Addiscombe with his patron Charles Jenkinson, who was dragged away the next day to a cabinet meeting called unexpectedly by Pitt. When he returned, he brought with him the lord chancellor Edward Thurlow, whose company Philip seems to have enjoyed (Letter 108):

> After church I took my ride, and Mr J brought back the Chancellour with him, who with Mr and Mrs C[ornwall] made our party. I enjoyed old swashbuckler amazingly, whom I had long wanted to see. The goosberries were damned musty, he preferred beef to mutton which was not good at this time of the year, and after the women were gone, he talked of blowing somebody to hell.

The experience was perhaps typical of Thurlow. Then a man in his 50s, he was a lawyer of relatively humble birth, who was serving as lord chancellor for the second time in his career, and had gained a reputation for a formidable appearance, crushing retorts and insolence. He was also a clergyman and held several livings. Commenting on the propositions to reform Irish-English trade, Charles Jenkinson wrote: 'In carrying the business through the House of Lords, the chancellor is the most firm and able person that government has... .' (Buckingham MSS, 187, quoted by GM Ditchfield, 'Edward Thurlow', ODNB.)

Another of the events that Philip Williams witnessed at close hand during his term as the Speaker's chaplain was the trial by parliament of Warren Hastings, formerly governor-general of Bengal. In one of the greatest speeches ever made at Westminster, on 8 February 1787, the playright and politician Richard Brinsley Sheridan spoke for five and a half hours, accusing Hastings of a range of misdemeanours carried out by him and the East India Company. The level of interest in the affair throughout the country can be judged by the fact that the *Hampshire Chronicle* of 26 February devoted almost an entire page to it. Sheridan was acting with Burke and Fox in a business that occupied 148 days of parliamentary time and ended with Hastings's acquittal. History has tended to view him as a something of a scapegoat for a rotten system, but one whose highhandedness brought him ruination. Commenting on the affair, Sarah exhibited her knowledge of Roman history, by comparing Hastings to Marcus Licinius Crassus (ca 115BC-53BC), the famous general who amassed huge wealth in expanding Rome's influence. He was ultimately defeated in Syria by the Parthians, who according to legend killed him in the symbolic way she describes (Letter 116):

> I was much pleased with the newspaper account of Mr Sheridan's speech, which carried conviction with it even to his oponents, but why? (for I am no politician) if they acknowledge the guilt of the man, do they at the same time declare against his impeachment; of what use is it to convict an offender of his importance, of the most flagrant acts of cruelty, rapine and oppression, before an Assembly of the whole nation, if he is to escape unpunished; you remember the miserable end of Crassus amongst the Parthians, who for his thirst of riches, had melted gold poured down his throat; a dose of the same sort administered by the Begums [high-ranking Hindustani women], would hardly be more than he deserves; it will be a disgrace to the nation if some notice is not taken of such enormities, and an encouragement to future Governors to behave in the same way.

Sarah's involvement in the affairs of the day conflict with the views of Winchester history don, G.H. Blore, who in an unpublished essay written before feminism had got into its stride, suggested that (WCA/E10/14):

> [although Philip Williams] met the great men of the day... he is too discreet to tell her much of interest, and perhaps he guessed that to enlarge on them might only irritate Sarah, who was often weighed down by domestic cares.

It must not be imagined that Philip Williams routinely spent long periods in the chamber listening to debates. More often than not for much of the day he was socialising in some way, either meeting fellow Wykehamists, or occupants of the cathedral close, who often spent time in the capital, attending parliamentary receptions and dinners. He and Sarah also had a few longterm acquaintances who lived in and around London. One of these was Miss Elizabeth Pyke, whose exact relationship to the couple is unknown, though she appears in 1780 in a record of the baptism of Elizabeth Williams as a sponsor 'of Bennet Street St James['s] London' (W418). Clearly, living in central London was a challenge for her (Letter 76):

> ...at the ancient music... [she] was frightened to death almost at the croud and bustle in getting away, added to the pickpockets and rogues who tore the diamonds from several ladies heads whilst getting into their carriage. She very quietly pulled out a few pins she had and put them into her muff.

By this time she had either moved permanently out of the centre of the city, or had a second house elsewhere. On one occasion he rode 23 miles to see her, but she had left that morning to go to Oxford for the races. She tried to warn him of her plans by letter, but he and the missive crossed en route. He wrote (Letter 67): '[I] dined at Egham very sulkyly by myself, and returned home in the evening after a fruitless bump of 45 miles at least.'

Amongst those of his Winchester acquaintances he met frequently were Beilby Porteus, bishop of Chester, and Jonathan Shipley, bishop of Asaph, with whom he was comfortable to invite himself to dine (Letter 80). On one occasion Porteus and Shipley were fitted in around a bevy of other people he met, including the physician William Heberden and the Welsh antiquary and academic Michael Lort (whose mother was the daughter of Edward Jenkins, a vicar of Fareham; Letter 78):

> On Tuesday I called on the Bishop of St Asaph, who looked sadly and mentioned Elizabeth [a daughter] as getting worse and worse. I called likewise on Mrs Stinton, (of whom I got intelligence by Mr Graves) who has lodgings in Sackville Street; she is still in mourning, but grown as fat as a pig – a Lady Jane Lyon, sister of the late Lord Strathmore, lives with her. In the evening I went to the Bishop of Chester, who sees company (as it is called) that night, and met Dr Heberden and Lort; sat about ½ an hour, and a flight of Cantabs being announced, I fled the Pit.

At other times he dined with a clique of people who lived near Winchester, including Thomas Heathcote, son of Sir Thomas, from Hursley Park, Mrs Ricketts and children from Twyford House, the 'little Newbolt' and the Blade (John Monk Newbolt), rector of the Winchester parishes of St Maurice's, St Mary Calendre and Chilcomb, who seems not to have been able to tolerate the London smogs (Letter 83):

> The Blade's bellows were so oppressed, that he was obliged to leave town on Thursday afternoon at two o'clock, and I never saw any thing of him.

Such socialising was essential but was often a bore, as he found in February 1785 (Letter 76):

> I waited for your letter till I almost lost my dinner and read it in my way to the Chaplain's table, where I dined with [John] Sturges [a Winchester prebendary, 1736/7-1807], and spent a very dull afternoon; our company was his brother Majendie, (a Cambridge prig) an officer in the guards, and a son of J. Buller's, a captain in the navy, and a solemn little ugly coxcomb. We broke up before six, a time when in London you can call no where, which drove me to the play, where I saw the new actor Holman perform Hamlet for his benefit, and really very tolerably.

The actor he saw was Joseph George Holman (1764-1817), who had first appeared on the London stage at the Theatre Royal, Covent Garden, in the previous October. *Hamlet* with him in the title role was advertised in *The Times* to be played for his benefit on Tuesday 15 February 1785. There was soon more entertainment to hand when his close friend Lovelace Bigg-Wither was in town (Letter 78):

> ...he tempted me to mob it into the pit, to see Mrs [Sarah] Siddons in Zara [in Congreve's *The Mourning Bride*], which character she sustained in a very great stile, and was recieved with the applause she deserved.

Later in the year it was *Peeping Tom of Coventry*, a comic opera by John O'Keefe (1747-1833) taken from the story of Lady Godiva. It had first been performed, 'By COMMAND of their MAJESTIES', as an afterpiece, at the Theatre Royal, Haymarket, in 1784 and continued to be staged for two generations. The tone of the piece can be gauged from a verse in a song that appears near the end (Donoghue, 2003, p. 98):

> When I was a yonker and liv'd with my dad
> The neighbours all thought me a smart little lad
> My Mammy she call'd me a white-headed boy
> Because with girls I lik'd to toy.

Opportunities for regular entertainment in London had been transformed in the late 1770s by George Colman the Elder (ca. 1732-1794), a celebrated playwright and theatre manager, who took on the Theatre Royal Haymarket in 1776. Philip Williams sent a colourful account of an evening there to his wife (Letter 103):

> I went to Coleman's on Tuesday to see ... peeping Tom – wonderful good acting – the farce has not much to boast of and yet I defy any crab (love to the fœtid [their daughter, Elizabeth]) to keep his countenance when Edwyn who acts the taylor is first acquainted with Godiva's intended expedition through the streets. A little nephew of Wenman's whom he brought there, would I thought have at least and I dare say did bep— himself with laughter.

Attending public performances often not only involved drama on the stage, but also in the surroundings. Riots, booing and other forms of disorder were not infrequent and the process of arriving at and leaving the playhouse or concert venue was also itself often a challenge. Philip Williams experienced at least two episodes of this sort. On one occasion, after dining with his cousin, Charles Nalson Cole, he looked into the Little Theatre in the Haymarket (also known as the Theatre Royal) where he witnessed a rare – perhaps unique – event (Letter 80):

> Whilst Wilson was singing one of the airs in Gretna green, a man leaped over the stage box, went and seized him in the king's name, and forced him off the stage. This you may suppose occasioned a great tumult, and Wilson was called for by the audience to give an account of the proceeding; who said this bailiff had arrested him for a debt he was not conscious of; that his affairs about four months ago were very derangé, when the manager of Covent Garden had advanced him a sum of money, which he had deposited in the hands of an attorney by name Turner No. 7 Spring Gardens, who had appropriated it to his own use, and had now seized his person under the pretence of his having fled from bail. The bailiff however had the prudence to make a precipitate retreat, otherwise he would have been torn to pieces, and Wilson resumed his part as quietly as if nothing unusual had happened.

Gretna Green was a musical farce, performed as an afterpiece, written by Charles Stuart and John O'Keeffe, with a score by Samuel Arnold, which had opened two years earlier. It involved a parson, Rory, played by

Richard Wilson (1744-1796), an actor born in Durham who had a colorful life. He had at least five 'wives', was frequently in debt and died in the king's bench prison (Geraldine Cousin, 'Sarah Maria Wilson', ODNB).

Even the more sedate setting of a performance of classical music might give something to talk about, as Philip Williams noted in March 1787, when he witnessed the rough side of the Prince of Wales, then a young man in his mid-twenties (Letter 123):

> Miss [Gertrude] Mahon was seized with an hysteric fit at the antient music the other night, and attended by Dr Halifax to her carriage; when he returned the P of Wales brutally enough came up to him, and said, Doctor we say here she is with child, and his blackguard uncle made a coarser reflection.

There were at least four brothers of George III's wife, Queen Charlotte, who might have been the 'blackguard uncle', including her favourite, Charles, who in 1794 succeeded to the German duchy of Mecklenburg-Strelitz.

Classical music performed by professional musicians was in short supply outside the capital and Philip Williams, encouraged by his wife, took advantage of his time at Westminster. A setpiece of the year was 'The music', by which was meant the annual performance in Westminster Abbey by the Royal Society of Musicians of sacred works by Handel, who had been commemorated on the 25th anniversary of his death in 1784. All profits went to charity, namely, the 'Decayed Musicians, Westminster Hospital and St George's Hospital'. In 1785, Philip gave Sarah an account of the events, which were held on the 2, 6 and 8 June (Letter 98):

> Wednesday [1 June], Folliot Cornwall [his predecessor as Speaker's chaplain] came up from Windsor to us for two days, for the sake of the music, which Sir Banks [Jenkinson], who arrived here for that purpose, gives up at last, having catched cold at the rehearsal on Monday. Folliot and Mrs C[ornwall] went to the abby on Thursday [2 June], which was crowded, and from some mismanagement more tickets were sold than could be admitted, which occasioned some confusion. I met H[enry] Oglander [a fellow of Winchester College] returning from thence sine watch. They talk of an additional day, very much to the disquiet of Silence, who goes to see and hear peeping Tom at the Haymarket one night, and the Messiah in the abby the next morning [8 June].

Tickets cost one guinea and despite measures to the best efforts of the organisers it seems that there was considerable chaos, with pickpockets taking advantage of the situation. The problem of hundreds of fashionable people descending on the abbey in carriages at the same time had been envisaged by the organisers, who gave strict instructions about which doors were to be used by which ticket-holders and announced that 'it is intended to stop Delivery of Tickets, when a sufficient Number has been disposed of to fill the Places allotted for the Company' (*The Times*, 1 June 1785).

Philip Williams spent many an evening playing cards, including 'commerce', a game, in which exchange or barter is the chief feature, as in March 1785 when he visited an unidentified friend who was obviously known to both him and his wife (Letter 83):

> I went in the evening to old Flabby's, where were four whist tables, and a commerce one. I met with the Miss Manners there…
> I played at crown whist with a conceited little puss, who seemed to have nothing good about her but her diamonds, Sir Matthew [White] Ridley's wife.

The 'conceited little puss' is described elsewhere as 'not the Pink of gentility, but very good humoured' (J.M. Ellis, 'Sir Matthew White Ridley', ODNB). On another occasion he escaped before the party got too wild. Having 'heard the Stuarts called over the coals by a pragmatical preacher at Whitehall' – by which he meant the sermon was preached during a state service held on 29 May to commemorate the Restoration of Charles II – he went off to dine, probably at the house of Winchester friend George William Ricketts. The company included 'The Blade', John Monk Newbolt, and a bunch of other chums. He primly told his wife (Letter 98):

> We did not dine till six, and I left them at nine, when I dare say they had recourse to the four kings, as they were very stupid, and had drank wine enough.

His social life, however, was not all cards and coffee, and he occasionally was called upon to preach, as at St Mary's chapel, Park Street, in the heart of Mayfair (Letter 83):

> I forgot to tell you I preached for Mrs Forrester on Sunday, who has an interest as I supposed in Park-Street chapel, her husband having built it. I sat in the same pew with Dean Coote and his

wife – the latter paid me high compliments upon my sermon, which I believe was a better [one] than the Dean could have put together.

The chapel, now demolished, was at the southeast corner of Park Street and Green Street, and is described as a 'modest Georgian preaching box' (Sheppard, 1980, pp. 252-56). It was built in 1762-3, half the cost being borne by the Revd Pulter Forester of Cosgrove, Northamptonshire, and half by the builders. Rarely without some link to many of the people he met, Philip Williams was no doubt aware that Dr Charles Coote's daughter Grace had in 1780 married a fellow Wykehamist, Henry Bathurst, who went on to become bishop of Norwich.

London, as ever, was a city in which anything might happen. Philip Williams regaled Sarah with some of the sights, and incidently gave his view of the annual meeting of Wykehamists that took place in London each year (Letter 88):

> … I had two escapes this morning, one of very narrowly missing the sight of an execution of nine men at Kennington as I returned from my ride, through the turnpike, ignorant of what was going forward; the crowd of spectators was inconcievable, and had I been a quarter of an hour later I had plumped into the midst of it … My other escape was from hurting myself by a fall down stairs, my heels flying up, which very slightly sprained my wrist, and bruised my hip, but not enough to prevent my going with T[homas] Heathcote in his carriage who was waiting at the door for me, to the Wykehamist's meeting, which was of all stupid assemblies by far the stupidest, and very thin, the numbers not exceeding 73 – and by the old Wykehamical notions not keeping pace with the rest of the world, dinner was on the table precisely at four, the consequence of which was that one third of the company came too late, and Tommy and myself were distanced.

On another occasion, he and his horse got tangled up with a contingent of guards on the north side of Hyde Park, presumably returning from a review at or in the vicinity of Buckingham Palace (Letter 108):

> As I was going through St George's fields on Saturday I met the guards returning from the review, and I could not get my mare by, upon which I was afraid I should have been obliged to have returned to town with them, and the men observed the chaplain

[change of ink] was come just in time to march before them into London. A second attempt however proved more successful, and I left a charming corps of officers at the next turning.

Gentle folk had to be careful when treading the pavements in London, with pickpockets and snatch thieves galore. Also 'mobs' of disadvantaged men might roam the streets is search of objects of detestation: denied the vote, how else could they express their distress? Clergymen, in particular, it seems, could be in danger, as Philip Williams depicted in an incident that involved a friend (unidentified) of his brother-in-law Jeremiah Dyson and George Pretyman (subsequently Sir George Pretyman Tomline) and a mob taking its protest to the House of Commons (Letter 103):

> I forgot to tell you that Dyson's friend, Nicoll, saved Dr Prettyman from the mob last week – he was walking home after his ride, and overtook a great croud following three clergymen, one of whom seemed very much distressed and frightened upon which as Nicoll tells me, he accosted him with saying, I don't like to see any gentleman used ill, and I desire you will take refuge in my house. He with some difficulty got him in, and his maid let down the chain, which prevented the mob forcing the door, and they soon after went to the house of commons. Nicoll made the Dr take a large glass of madeira, which he stood much in need of, his face being whiter than his wig, and conducted him afterwards safe home. He had endeavoured to get into the house through Mrs Bennets chamber, but found the mob in possession of the door-way, who followed him back and prevented his going home into George Street, and hustled him down new palace yard towards the water when his deliverer appeared and saved him probably from much ill usage, if not a ducking. The Dr called the next day upon Nicoll, and was very thankful indeed for his civilities.

Pretyman had been tutor to Pitt at Cambridge and became a close adviser to the prime minister, who had appointed him a canon of Westminster. He seems to have lived in the 'Westminster village' near Philip Williams, perhaps even in the same house in Privy Garden. Later in life he became bishop of Winchester. His encounter with 'the mob' showed the dangers faced by clergymen at large in the capital. Even in the highest circles, churchmen might feel uncomfortable, as the Speaker's wife found at Court (Letter 103):

She took leave at the drawing room yesterday, and was complimented by the princesses upon her nephews preaching so well at Windsor, which the second said was the more welcome as they had but three good ones, though her sister said four, and Mrs C[ornwall] rejoined that she was worse off at Whitehall. So I think the clergy were tolerably slabbed.

('To slab timber' was to take off its bark and throw it aside as useless, though the OED only records the earliest usage in the USA in 1835.) He also reported:

Mrs Adams and her daughter (the American ambassador's wife) were the chief objects of notice, and had a fashionable appearance, owing to his having succeeded Silas Dean at Paris.

John Adams (1735-1826), one of the Founding Fathers of the United States and its 2nd President, replaced Silas Deane, who suffered from allegations of financial irregularities, in Paris in 1771 and in 1785 became the first US Minister to the Court of St James's (ambassador to Great Britain). Adams and his wife Abigail were greeted at Court with some hostility. Philip Williams took a great interest in the American question, as evidenced by the existence in the Fellows' Library at Winchester College of a heavily annotated copy of the 2nd edition of Edmund Burke's Parliamentary Speech on American Taxation, delivered on 19 April 1774 (*see* Appendix IV).

From time to time Philip Williams used his time in London to see the sights. Excursions of this kind were early forms of tourism, which it is claimed 'was born in the seventeenth century, and Englishmen were the first to practice it', though the word – often used pejoratively – did not come into print until 1811 (OED). Fashionable folk from London were, in particular, amongst the earliest tourists. On one occasion he went in a party to view the former house of the poet Alexander Pope. He was accompanied by the Speaker's wife, Mrs Cornwall, John Hatsell, a formidable clerk to the House of Commons, and his wife, and a sister of Charles Agar, archbishop of Cashel, County Tipperary, Ireland, who belonged to the family of the earls of Normanton, seated at Somerley, Harbridge, Hampshire (HRO/21M57/C3-C20; Letter 110):

We went on Sunday to Twickenham, the drive to which through Richmond Park, and down Richmond hill, I had never been before, and indeed it beggars all description, as does Mr [Welbore]

Ellis's villa, and the ground behind it, which is so well contrasted to the Thames and the ground before it. What was Pope's habitation serves as merely rooms of passage to the two wings which have been added, and the field which is likewise added to the pleasure ground is one third more than the original, and is sweetly retired and planted with great variety of shrubs. ... I forgot to mention Pope's grotto, which goes under the turnpike road and admits you to the shrubbery, at your return from which you are struck with the Thames which catches the eye at the end of this souterrain cavern, and is at once unexpected and noble – it is a most enchanting place.

The poet's house at Cross Deep, Twickenham, had been purchased after his death and extended by Sir William Stanhope, brother of the earl of Chesterfield, whose daughter Elizabeth married the politician Rt Hon Welbore Ellis (later 1st baron Mendip). The house was demolished in 1808, but the grotto survives beneath buildings of Radnor House School.

During the time that Philip Williams spent in London in the years 1783-87 the weekly letters he received from his wife might have made him aware of her lot in Winchester. Faced by all the problems of a mother of four children, she had to endure the details of his jolly life in a city that was daily enjoying the fruits of the Enlightenment and Britain's growing power in an expanding world. The generally light-hearted accounts of his daily affairs and his enjoyment of a continual round of parliament, parties and plays must have been hard for her to bear. Marital politics determined that he had to go away, had to live the London life, had to mix with the great and the good, in order to secure the preferment he needed to support her and the family. It was a theme, however, that wore thin with time and she was not sufficiently naïve ever to swallow the line wholeheartedy. The Letters show that she was not in a strong enough position to call him back to Winchester, though ironically it was there that the seat of his security lay.

***

PHILIP Williams's long absences in London had one advantage: he was, in principle, available for the many errands that Sarah asked of him. The reality was slightly different, but places like Winchester had a constant traffic of people visiting the capital and therefore an in-built courier service. Thus she asked (Letter 115):

If you hear of any body that is coming to Winchester soon I wish you would let me know, for I want a few trifles from Sage's which it is not worth while to pay carriage for; you was to ask Mrs Cornwall about another sort of lamp for me, and let me know what is the price of it.

And in June 1784 she asked him (Letter 53) to 'buy Mrs Smith's verses…they cost only two shillings, and are published with her name to them, and you may send them down in one or two franks.' These were *Elegiac Sonnets, and other Essays*, which had just published, by Charlotte Smith of Bignor Park, Sussex, who was propelled into authorship by her husband's debts. Sarah might have been especially interested in the book, as the author knew, and mlater came to live at Woolbeding House, near Midhurst, the seat of Sir Charles Mill, who was well known to her father. On another occasion she spelled out her needs in detail (Letter 64):

You are very good to remember a word I drop'd about a silver teapot, which I assure [you] I do not want, for I am past the age of ostentation and vanity, but if you intend to have one, as a useful piece of furniture, let it be as plain as possible, and large enough to make tea for us, when we are in a domestick way, we will say for our two sisters you and myself and one more, which is as many as our private parties generally consist of. I daresay that what would suit Mrs Cornwall [the Speaker's wife] would do for us, because their family parties are not large.

Her requests were manifold: sometimes it was green tea, or Souchong tea 'from Davison's' (Letter 70); a 'moderate sized chest of oranges' for her father's successer as second master, William Goddard (though they arrived 'so very bad, as to be scarcely eatable'; Letter 84); or 'two yards of callico, like the enclosed patt{ern} from Gatty & Gildort's in New Bond Street' for her sister Elizabeth (Letter 84). She also asked him to buy some tea-spoons and sort out a bill at the same store, as she had no money (Letter 111):

… I have not had a penny for above this week past, I am now wholly upon tick; there are some table cloths, two at 14s.-6[d] each and three napkins but what they were I never heard, owing for at Gatty's and a yard of linen at 5s.

Sometimes he was given the chance to beat impending changes to tax law, as well as be generous (Letter 69):

I have sent for some second mourning things to Sage's before the new tax takes place, which come to about two guineas; if you can pay it I will send the bill in my next, and if you have about thirty shillings more to spare {I} will have a new gown for the winter like {one} your sister has which I will send a pattern of in my next, with directions where to get it; but if you cannot afford it I shall very readily go without it.

One of Sarah's requests reveals the importance of a kind of publication that might not be thought a priority for educated people (Letter 116):

The things that I thought I wanted from Sage I can do without and I am in no hurry for the lamp, but the Almanack I should be glad to have.

Almanacs of various kinds have been published virtually since the invention of printing. In the eighteenth century, as well including the usual pocketbook items of astrology and predictions of the future, they provided snippets of information on a huge range of subjects, including astronomy, politics, history, the Classics and religion (Capp, 1979). The Letters contain several other equally enthusiastic mentions of an almanac (77, 84-5, 115 & 117).

Couriers were sometimes of great dignity, such as Dr William Buller, dean of Exeter, who was in London 'for a week or more', prompting Sarah to tell her husband that he had offered to 'bring down your shirts that want repairing, if William [Philip's manservant] will pack them up in a small compass' (Letter 87). Like many men he prized a neat clean shirt (Vickery, 2009), but his reply obviated the divine from acting as a postman (Letter 90): 'You will rejoice to hear that William was mistaken about the chapter of shirts, and that upon another review, they all appear perfectly sound.' Whether he was lax about worn collars and cuffs, or could not be bothered will never be known. He was, however, not above demanding Sarah to retrieve a handkerchief he had lent his brother-in-law, Jeremiah Dyson, which she did (Letters 98-9).

The Letters tell the long tale of a debt relating to one or more houses at Newmarket, Suffolk, belonging to a 'fussy person', Mrs Lucy Elyott, who was a relative of Philip Williams of some kind (Letters 93, 101-103 and 107-109). 'Mr Weatherby (the racing callender man)' had let them for her and the tenant owed her money, but would not reply to letters. (British horseracing still depends for its central administration and registration of

Dr John Gordon, writing from Lincoln on 22 September 1787 to his stepson, Phillip Williams, sending his condolences on the death in childbed of his wife Sarah three days earlier (Letter 128).

thoroughbreds on the enterprise founded by James Weatherby.) Sarah asked her husband to call at an address in St James's in the heart of the West End, where she believed he lived. Understandably he was not keen to act as a debt collector – besides, Jeremiah Dyson apparently owed Mr Weatherby money, 'and when he pays him, it would be a very good opportunity to talk to him' (Letter 90). Sarah was indignant and had visions of the business going sour, as had apparently happened with the small estates they owned in Cambridgeshire (Letter 102):

> Was I in London myself, I should fly to do it; consider her helpless situation, and do stir your stumps in her cause and endeavour to get some intelligence for her, that it may not turn out a fen estate business, if you will not, say so at once.

Eventually, after a muddle about the correct address for Weatherby, he did call, but only to find a son at home, and subsequently had to sort out the affair with him by letter, 'as he is only visible early in the morning'. The story demonstrates how difficult it was to pursue debts, but equally how useful it was to have a London agent.

Whilst Philip was away, Sarah had to look after the house, and on one occasion turned her attention to its decor (Letter 87):

> I have done more than you could expect, Pewsey [a workman?] has not only been spoken to, but the room is painted and looks very neat, the cracks are hardly to be seen, and there is some of the paint reserved, in case any of the pannels should crack again, which the wise ones do not think will be the case, as they are well filled with putty, and painted over before the room was done, the outside of the house too is to be painted tomorrow which is absolutely necessary and ought to have been done two years before, the expence will be very trifling.

She is well pleased with the parlour, which 'looks very smart the cracks...quite hid' (Letter 91), though she baulks at the task of putting back a portrait (now probably lost) of his father, PW(II), preferring to lock it up in his study – or was this an excuse to get rid of an irksome object? When all was done she dined in the room with the children and 'a good, and pleasant boy' that she is looking after and lights a fire to 'help to get rid of the smell'.

For much of the time she is conscious that her father is acutely aware of her predicament; and he is by nature a worrier. Living in retirement in Midhurst, he writes to her in a way she cannot ignore (Letter 116):

> Although I have had another letter from Papa about the Almanack, he wishes to have it sent to me … and he can tell somebody to call for it; he is likewise very impatient for us to have an Iron Oven, and thinks that Mr Dyson stated the matter to us in such a way as to make it appear perfectly ridiculous, when he is so much in earnest, that he wishes to have the ordering of one forthwith from the same person that made his.

By instinct Sarah was extremely thrifty and if she had a free hand it is unlikely that she ever acquired an 'Iron Oven'. Such things dated from about 1730, on the Continent, where cast-iron ovens and stoves were made, with progressive improvement of designs as the century wore on.

Another of Sarah's tasks whilst they lived in Winchester was to keep an eye on her husband's horse, which was grazed in College Meadow – one of the perks of being a fellow – where, she reports, 'there is for his comfort more grass than in other places' (Letter 95). On other occasions she tells him (Letters 53 and 97):

> Your horse has had his blister and it has taken effect beyond what they expected, and they think he is in a very fine way. …James Wells desires me to say that your old horse has been a little indisposed with the fret, and it has been thought expedient to bleed him which has done him good, he grows very fat and has the whole range of the meadow.

Blistering horses with an irritant such as cedar oil is still done to treat lameness in horses. This would have been well known to James Wells, the Winchester College ostler, on whom Sarah called for all matters equine, including paying the tax on horses, though he became less available as time went on (Letter 118):

> I cannot summon James Wells as I used to do when I lived at Winchester, besides he is much less discerning in these matters than he used to be, before he entered so deeply in the oat-trade.

11. *'Filled with inhabitants of opulence and gentility'*

ALTHOUGH SARAH WILLIAMS had much to contend with bringing up a family, especially when her husband was away in London, she was well established in Winchester society. It was a city with a population of 3,500-4,000, set to rise to more than 6,000 by the first census of 1801, with a vigour than came from its position as the county town and administrative centre of Hampshire (Cooper, 1999; James 1988). Moreover, it was the heart of a huge diocese that still reached to the banks of the Thames at Southwark, included Surrey, the Isle of Wight, the Channel Islands and much else. Even though the bishop of Winchester was as likely to be at his official residence in Chelsea, or at Farnham Castle, as in his palace in Winchester, the cathedral close was still occupied (in theory, at least) by a dean and twelve canons and was still the *raison d'être* of the city. In the way that words can wound, it has ever been dealt a blow by the words of Dr Edmund Pyle, a Winchester canon from 1756 until to his death twenty years later, who, in a letter to his Cambridge tutor, Dr Samuel Kerrich, wrote (Hartshorne, 1905, p. 266):

> The life of a prebendary is a pretty easy way of dawdling away one's time; praying, walking, visiting; - & as little study as your heart would wish.

Fortunately for divines, the world in general did not read these words until his letters were published in 1905. He had much else to say about life in the close, including an assessment of the health of his patron, Hoadly, and the canons, who in 1753 were 'blocking' his advancement:

> The number of prebendaries, viz, twelve, three of 'em above 70 years of age, and a fourth who has been fistulous for some years, cut, over & over, in vain, & twice at death's door by the great discharge from the wounds that are open still, together with the Bishop's extraordinary good health, are the circumstances which are thought to make my chance for success herein a good one.

Notwithstanding the requirement for 'strict residence', when canons were obliged to live in their prebendal house in the close, many of them spent most of their time elsewhere. Though absentees were often to be found in London, Newton Ogle, the dean during most of Philip Williams's time at Winchester, was seated in Northumberland. In one of her letters, written in early summer 1785, Sarah Williams commented (Letter 97):

> ...this last week has allmost emptied the close, the Bullers and Sturges's gone, the Mulsos upon the eve of going...

Even today the Winchester cathedral close and the area around Winchester College still have a feeling of not being public spaces. In modern parlance they are a campus, and 200 years ago they were even more separate from other parts of the city. The cathedral and college were then part of the same continuum of middle-class culture that spoke to God and learning, wisdom and prudence, and sound finance, and respected royalty and rank when it suited. With this set of values went all the ills, to modern eyes, of privilege, snobbery (social and intellectual) and chauvinism. Also, as laid down in Wykeham's statutes, the bishop of the day was the visitor to Winchester College and, when disputes arose, he was the ultimate arbiter, as in the case of the warden John Nicholas, when Trelawney was the bishop. A letter of his written in 1711 to the Oxford physician Dr John Radcliffe was included in an anthology of published quotes on Winchester (incidentally edited by a daughter of a porter of Winchester College; Dawson, 2014), in which the prelate complained (Locke, 1912, pp. 157-8):

> I have been now neare four years, and made three journies [from Farnham?] on purpose, persuading the Warden and Fellows of Winchester College to make up theyr differences among themselves, and if that could not be done to take in the assistance of the Dean and Prebendaries of Winchester, telling them they did not know what mischief they might do themselves by forcing me on a Visitation.

Similarly, in 1757, when John Purnell, warden of New College, reached for the more lucrative post of warden of Winchester College, bishop Hoadly overruled him. Instead, he appointed Christopher Golding, who, in the words of Dr Edmund Pyle, 'no more dreamt of this advancement, then he did of being Pope; [and] was very nearly frightened out of his wits' (Hartshorne, 1905, p.301).

Within the minds of those whose lives slipped easily between close and college (and occasionally strayed into the city) was a huge range of opinion. There was the distinguished divine Dr Thomas Balguy (1716-1795), who bridged the gap between university and cathedral. He had spent nearly 20 years at St John's College, Cambridge, where he gave lectures on moral philosophy. He was also deputy to the university's public orator James Tunstall, a successor to Philip Williams's namesake father, and he may have been the link that brought him – the young son of the former orator's widow – to Winchester College, for which Hoadly as bishop was the visitor.

Pyle was obviously very pleased that Balguy had come to Winchester (Hartshorne, 1905, p.309):

> I have had amends made me by very good company in the close, especially Dr Balguy's our new prebendary, who is a special clever man...

The poet Thomas Gray visited him in the close and referred to him in a doggerel poem as 'Balguy with a Bishop in his belly', but when in 1781 he was offered the bishopric of Gloucester, he declined on grounds of poor eyesight (Nichols, 1812, p. 220). Balguy knew Philip Williams and his stepfather Dr John Gordon, a fellow native of County Durham, who wrote from Lincoln in 1775 (Letter 19): 'Dr Balguy calld this morning and spoke kindly of you'. Ten years later, Philip called upon him in London (Letter 73) and it clear that Sarah also knew him and his cousin, Sarah Drake, who kept house for him (Letter 92).

Equally heavyweight in the close were three generation of Sturges, grandfather, son and especially grandson. Their track is similar to that of the Philip Williams: it started in East Anglia, moved to Winchester and then took root in London. Grandfather John and his brothers Charles and Thomas lived in the 'greater Cambridge' area – which included the diocese of Ely, and more loosely, Lincoln and Norwich, of whom it was said (Nichols and Bentley, 1815):

> The Patron and relative of these three worthy and learned brothers has been Bp. Trimnell of Lincoln and Winton.

Actually Charles Trimnell was bishop of *Norwich*, elected in 1708 and translated to Winchester in 1721 – but the element of patronage is clear: John Sturges senior (d 1740), became a prebendary of Winchester shortly after Trimnell's translation. His mother, Mary, was a sister of Trimnell;

and his wife, Margaret née Lowth (sister of Robert), was no stranger to the close: her father had been a Winchester prebendary and her brother, Robert, became bishop of London (Blore, 1944). In demonstration of the interlinked world in which these clerics lived, Charles Sturges, a brother of John Sturges senior's namesake father, married a sister of Ambrose Isted of Ecton, Northamptonshire, whose son Samuel was later tutored at Oxford by Philip Williams and went on a Scottish tour with him (*see* Chapter 3). John Sturges's namesake son also held a prebend at Winchester (as well as Chichester), between 1759 and his death, in 1807 at Alverstoke, Hampshire, where he was rector. He was a doctor of civil law, became chancellor of Winchester and served as a chaplain ordinary to the king. Speaker Charles Wolfran Cornwall appointed him as one of his executors (WCA/29910). He married first Judith Bourne, and then a sister of William Buller, briefly bishop of Exeter. By all accounts, Sturges junior (1736/7-1807) was not great company (*see* p. 176). A breakfast in London with him and a jobbing curate from Winchester did little to stsrt the day well for Philip Williams (Letter 78):

> On Monday Sturges and [Bradnam] Tawney breakfasted here, but like two affirmatives they produced a negative ... In the evening I attended the debate about the old bore, the Westminster Election, where if they don't put an end to it some how or other the ministry will be foiled, and so they ought to be.

He is playing with logic here, around the fact that 'two negatives make an affirmative'. Meanwhile, in Winchester, Sarah was required to cope with Mrs Sturges junior and other canons' wives. She writes (Letter 77):

> I have had many invitations, and amongst the rest one from Mrs [Robert] Hare to sup, which I refused supposing it might be a convivial affair, but I had a still greater escape, for I have since found out that it is to be a solemn for Mrs [William] Buller and Mrs [John] Sturges; I am determined not to leave my own fire-side...

The grandson William Sturges (1769-1845) was a scholar at Winchester College, from where Sarah Williams told her husband of his success in 'medal speaking' (Letter 104). He is remembered for the Sturges-Bourne Acts concerned with reforming the poor law.

Another prebendary, but of a different kind, was Dr William Buller (1735-1796), who with his wife socialised with Philip and Sarah, especially the men in London and the ladies in Winchester. In Nigel Aston's ODNB article he is described as 'a dutiful, orthodox cleric whose family associations and connections held the key to his advancement'. The crucial link was his marriage in 1762 to Anne, daughter of John Thomas, bishop of Winchester. He was elected dean of Exeter in 1784, and at the end of his life gained the Devon bishopric. The advancement clearly caused him to shed commitments in Winchester, where he failed to administer the will of local physician, and neighbour of the Williamses, Dr John Makittrick. Sarah commented, somewhat acidly (Letter 64):

> You must let me know what the newspaper account comes to, as there is an advertisement in the paper desiring every body to make their demands, and Dr Buller (for Dean I never can call him) has resigned the management of the whole to Dr Adair [brother of the deceased], who seems to be ready for a straight waistcoat …

William Buller was regarded as being rather lightweight. Thus, Philip wrote from London (Letter 76): '…[he] has been here cackling, and boasts of having intimidated the Warden [of Winchester College] from appealing to the commissioners of the windows upon the grounds I left with him…' And Sarah shared the jibe (Letter 92):

> Monday Bess and myself paid a visit at St Cross, the Bishop [of Chester] and Mrs P[orteus] we found well, and very civil and pleasant, their tone rather altered, upon the subject of a certain Dignitary of whom they were very fond when they were last here, wondered how it was possible that he could so ill understand the window tax act, we see what trifles turn the scale.

Elsewhere (Letter 91) she calls him 'a chatter-box to say the best of him', adding 'the Dean will not be much flattered to hear upon his arrival on Wednesday, that they have smuggled a dinner at the Sun on the Monday before to get rid of him…'

There was an army of other prebendaries who in one way or another impinged on the lives of Sarah and Philip Williams, including the Hebraist and English grammarian Robert Lowth, the socialite Sir Peter Rivers Gay, Thomas Rennell jr, 'Demosthenes of the pulpit' as Pitt called him, the letter-writer John Mulso and others. The fellows of Winchester College were not in general appointed to prebends, though the patronage of the bishop occasionally extended to them, as in the case of Philip Williams and the rectorship of Compton. Closer links between cathedral and college were literally wrought when John Nicholas, the warden of the latter from 1679, and a canon from 1684, gained permission from the dean and chapter of the former agree to a gate being made in the close wall. However, during the later period covered by these letters, Philip Williams was virtually unique in straddling the two camps, with a fellowship of the college (from 1769) and a prebend of the cathedral (from 1797) – he was also a prebendary of Lincoln. Although his roles were relatively humble – he was one of the bursars of the college and treasurer of the cathedral – his duopoly at Winchester at the time was only equalled by head master Joseph Warton, who in 1788 was given a stall at the request of Pitt.

Although the cathedral close and college were major elements of the social context in which Sarah lived, there were plenty of other opportunities to socialise, especially in Compton, where her husband was rector, and the adjacent villages of Shawford and Twyford. There was the inevitable, ongoing round of visits to maintain contact with the people she knew and to meet newcomers. There was a constant flow of visitors to the city, which since the 1760s had been served by seven turnpikes. A contemporary view of the place surfaced at Westminster during an incident involving Francis Seymour-Conway (1718-1794), viscount Beauchamp, seated at Ragley Hall, Warwickshire, as Philip Williams reported (Letter 88):

> Lord Beauchamp brought the Speaker upon his back the other day by proposing that instead of transporting the felons to Africa, the king's palace at Winchester should be converted into a place of confinement for them; he bullyragged him very handsomely, and said he might with as much propriety desire the convicts might have a castle built for them in Ragley Park, as in a city, the residence of a bishop, the seat of a great public school, with a church and college in it, and filled with inhabitants of opulence and gentility. In short he made him look very silly, and ashamed of the absurdity of his proposition.

The old palace had been commissioned in 1682 by Charles II, who chose Wren as his architect, but died before its completion. When Lord Beauchamp rose to his feet it had in fact already long been used to house prisoners from the various wars of the eighteenth century, and was later to house refugee clergy from the French Revolution, but clearly it was felt by local residents not to be suitable for 'mere felons'. In 1796 the War Office took over the buildings, which were destroyed in 1894 in a catastrophic fire. A military complex called Peninsular Barracks was then built on the site, which in recent times has been developed into private residential accommodation.

Opportunities to mix and mingle for people like Sarah, albeit with appropriate chaperoning, were provided by the fixed events that animated the city every year, including the Assizes and the Quarter Sessions, the meeting of the Hampshire Fox Hunt Society in April, and in July, election week at Winchester College and horse racing on Worthy Down (Shurlock, 2012). At other times, there were the occasional balls and assemblies that brought together people from a wide area in north Hampshire.

During late June and early July Sarah could expect to have to accommodate her sister, Charlotte, brother-in-law the Hon George Richard St John, and family. Her husband, however, took a rather dim view of it (Letter 106):

> The fatigue of people in your house during such public times is too great for our premises or establishment, and I shall vote them lodgings another year close by, so as to make the victualling with us not inconvenient, and the same at the music meeting, for the being all squeezed together like brenbutter destroys all the pleasure, if there is any, of such festivities.

Even so, in 1785 they all came, together with St John's half-sister 'Miss Beauclerk'. Sarah reported (Letter 104):

> I found the St John baggage when we came home and they are to be here tomorrow and to begin the week with the play, whether I shall go myself depends upon how I am tomorrow…

She had earlier complained (Letter 102) of being 'dragged to the Maid of the Oaks', which she described as 'a wretched choice', which is rather strange as John Burgoyne's play is known as a 'cheerful comedy of country life'. It was based on a real-life fête champêtre held at his home 'The Oaks', near Epsom, that later gave its name to the famous horse race (Thomson, 2006, p. 120). To mark the start of race week in 1785, Monday 27 June, the Winchester theatre programme included two popular comedies, namely, *The Provoked Husband* by Sir John Vanbrugh and *High Life Below Stairs* by clergyman James Townley.

In the event, Sarah did not go, but shared in much else during the week, giving her husband a very full and gossipy account (Letter 105):

Our Races have been very full; the balls crowded, and particularly the last, with good company; the brides were two of the Clanrikarde [Clanricarde] family and a Mrs Osborn (Miss Adeane) of some place near Romsey who is married to a Major Osborn who got a good deal of money the last war, I believe in the East, who is nothing very famous, got extremely in liquor and is to be Steward the next year; Lady C[lanricarde] is I dare say a good kind of woman but very plain and awkward, ditto Mrs Osborn; the St Johns came to me on Monday and went to the play, but I stayed at home; Tuesday and we all went to the Ball. Mr St John danced with Miss Mildmay, Mr Dyson with Miss Beauclerck and Charlotte with Mr Streatfield and of course Mrs Dyson and myself joined Mrs Mildmay in the window.

Wednesday we went to the Race and did nothing more. Thursday to the Ball again; which if I was not the flattest of human beings I should call a very pleasant one indeed. ... Mr St John danced with Letitia Mildmay, Charlotte with Mr Pitt and Miss B[eauclerck] with Mr Parry. Mr Dyson retired to a whist party and was seen no more till four o'clock; there were a number of pretty women, but Mrs Fitzroy (Miss Keppel), Arabella Ogle, and Miss Beauclerck were the reigning favorites; Friday we were persuaded to meet the Shawford party at the Blade's [John Monk Newbolt] and go to the play which compleatly did me up, and yesterday the St Johns left me, in order to prepare for a Fete at Lord Radnor's on Thursday...

This passage reveals the custom of the day at formal balls, whereby ladies who were much beyond the age of 25 were not expected to be invited to dance, but joined groups of 'elderly' women, to converse and play cards. Whether on such occasions in a small city like Winchester the gentlemen called the next day to enquire after the young ladies with whom they had danced is not clear (Doody, 1994, Notes 54,65, pp. 457-8).

It was a busy time for anyone with an interest in the turf, with major meetings at Basingstoke, Stockbridge, Salisbury and elsewhere. Events were originally scheduled at Winchester for the week commencing Monday 20 June, but only two weeks before the meeting it was decided to put them back for a week to avoid a clash with the meeting at Stockbridge (*Hampshire Chronicle*, 6 June 1785). No doubt to puff the event, the local press reported on 20 June:

(His Royal Highness the Prince of Wales, it is said, intends paying us a visit…whence he is expected to go through Southampton, on a visit to the Earl of Radnor at Radnor Castle, in Wiltshire, where he will remain until the Salisbury Races commence.

In fact he did not come to Winchester, though, as this letter relates, he did stay at Longford Castle, which is still the seat of the earls of Radnor (Old and New Radnor Castles once stood in mid-Wales). Sarah caught up on the news of Lord Radnor's ball when she dined with the Mildmays at Shawford. Also in the party were her sisters Charlotte and Elizabeth, the latter's husband, Jeremiah Dyson, plus Miss Beauclerk, George William Ricketts and John Monk Newbolt, who, perhaps taking note of her earlier advice (Letter 84), 'drank tea'. Then they all went off to the theatre in Winchester (Letter 109):

> … we all went to see Rule a wife and have a Wife most wretchedly performed, as I have formerly seen Garrick and Mrs [Frances 'Fanny'] Abington in the same play, which is rather a favorite of mine.

The only relatives Sarah had in the neighbourhood, other than her sisters, were the Revd Edmund Elyott (ca 1725-1781), rector of Litchfield, Hampshire, and his family: 'Mrs [Lucy] Elyott' especially is mentioned many times in the Letters (*see* p. 140). In 1784 Sarah chaperoned Mrs Elyott's namesake daughter Lucy Elyott during race week. She knew she would be tired but confided with Philip (Letter 61) that 'those who will not go a little out of their way to serve their friends do not deserve any; amongst my faults I do not reckon selfishness.' She later gave him a full account (Letter 58):

> …Charlotte and myself, chaperoned Lucy Elyott, and a friend of her's from Fareham, [Hampshire] who though a very good natured girl, was no addition to our party; the races upon the whole were rather thin, and the appearance of gentlemen of the county at the member's ball remarkably so, a proof I fear of the decline of Charles's interest in these parts; Lord Northington and Sir W[illoughby] Aston, Captain Luttrel[l], Colonel Sheriff and a few more stragling people were all that I recollect of any note, except Sir W Gardener and his Bacchanals, though there was a tolerable appearance of West-Indians and promiscuous people from Southampton; the member's supper was very elegant indeed, the ornamental part extremely admired by those who understand such matters; for me, I was so hungry that I was glad to attack the

more substantial part, and both Charlotte and myself thought ourselves much obliged to Mrs Littlehales [wife of Dr John Littlehales], who did for us what we should never have done for ourselves, [namely], seated us in two very good places, and provided us with every thing in the eatable and drinkable way we could want.

There was obviously a need to fight for a place at such events:

At the steward's ball we were still more fortunate, by means of our good friend fatty Leeke we got seated at supper before the doors were opened; there was a great deal of wine, whether good or bad I cannot tell, but the gentlemen seemed so well pleased with it, that there was hardly a man who could stand in the room by two o'clock. I wish these orgies could be put an end to, but where there are wine and men, the effect will I fear be always the same; there was an Assembly on the Wednesday, which we had nothing to do with; we went that day to the course, and saw a horse beaten that Sir H Featherstone had given six hundred guineas for not long before…

Equally demanding at the end of the summer term was election week at Winchester College, during which incoming scholars were elected to the school and leavers to New College, Oxford. It is clear that neither Sarah nor Philip relished the prospect of this set piece, which had (and still has) a succession of standard events interwoven with the business of the week (though elections to New College are no longer part of it; Letter 109):

Tomorrow begins the election week, which you are so fortunate as to miss; the Bowers are at Mrs [Lucy] Elyott's, and the Binghams are to be here and to dine one day with me; Charlotte and Miss B[eauclerk] are to dine with me on Friday for the Domum [the end of year celebrations] and I suppose we shall go to the play as the Superannuates [pupils obliged to leave] bespeak it; to morrow, (being afraid to say no) I have engaged to go to Miss Woodford's play [possibly a home theatrical; see Letters 122 and 124]; so that I shall not want {em}ployment this week.

Amongst her acquaintances was a Mrs Spooner (Letter 56), who 'dresses a turtle herself … which it seems she is very famous for, and does not chuse that her servants should have anything to do with it; it will be a great day for her, as she bespeaks a play in the evening, which I have happily got myself excused from attending, by not seeing her when I paid my visit.'

Another acquaintance was a Mrs Pitt (not known to be related to the prime minister), who prompted Sarah to give her views on taxation and politics (Letter 56):

..[she] seems to feel the increase of taxes already, for she has got rid of all superfluous garments, being I believe, except for some very light drapery, perfectly in fresco; I did not tell her, that I did not approve of the new tax; it is not that I have an objection to taxes; you know it is my maxim to pay them without grudging, but I think this comes so home to people in a middling station; and is so advantageous to the great that I cannot like it, and I could give you my reasons for it, if you were here and I could tell you why I do not like W[illiam] P[itt] too, but this I leave for future discussions at breakfast.

New taxes introduced by Pitt were listed in detail by the *Hampshire Chronicle* (12 July1784) and included: 1/2d per lb tallow candles; 3s.per chaldron of coals, or 2s. per ton; 1/6d. per yard, printed silks and linen, stained [dyed] in GB; 4d. per yd, square silk handkerchiefs; 3d. per yd, cotton stuffs.

Many of her friends and acquaintances were, understandingly, from the cathedral close and she also seems to have made occasional visits to Twyford to the highly intellectual household of Jonathan Shipley, who was also on Philip Williams's calling list in London (Letters 80, 90 & 100). He was bishop of St Asaph, but rarely or never visited his remote Welsh diocese, which was the custom of virtually all the diocesans of such small sees (Sykes, 1934, p.356-65). Her circle also included Beilby Porteus and his wife; in 1773 he had been appointed to the sinecure of the mastership of St Cross Hospital, later adding to it the bishopric of Chester, and in 1789 being translated to the see of London. Nonetheless, Sarah reckoned it 'better sport' to dine with the ladies of the close, though thought it proper 'to make an attempt to tea there [chez Porteus] before they go [up to London]' (Letter 95). The bishop was renowned for his sermons (Letter 91) and the performance of younger clergymen were judged by his standards; at St Michael's church, which Sarah sometimes attended, a Mr Rawlins 'gave … a sermon that had it come from the Bishop of Chester would have been talked of for this next month' (Letter 100). Apparently Porteus also had a gargantuan appetite, as she noted (Letter 115):

I dined at the Bishop's on Tuesday … I was very near sick with looking at a Hog's harslet that the Bishop eat of with gout; there were only ourselves and I was beat half a dozen rubbers at Cribbage I believe, for we played a great many and I lost them all.

Philip Williams also often saw the bishop and his wife in London and delivered a typically terse verdict: 'I like them very well, notwithstanding they are shabby in some respects' (Letter 88).

He rarely if ever comments on matters ecclesiastical, but with regard to sermons in one letter he revealed his dislike of Methodism and 'enthusiasm' in general and delivered a damning report of a son of William Cook, dean of Ely (Letter 78):

> ...[he] preached an hour, and poured forth a rhapsody of methodistical nonsense, and had the appearance both of an enthusiast and madman. He ought to be silenced and punished into the bargain if there was a possibility of it, as I am told that in the afternoon, when he has little or no audience, he preaches and is as passive as other men.

Another of Sarah's frequent acquaintances was Sir Peter Rivers Gay and his wife; a flavour of their times together is conveyed in a missive probably written in August 1784 (Letter 66):

> I dined at Sir P Rivers's on Thursday, with Mrs Lee [unidentified, but possibly related to Harry Lee, warden of Winchester College, though not his wife] and Mrs Spooner etc their two spouses were both ill at home, so that our party run short, but we had no cards, which pleased me, as I should have lost my money, and it was a wet day, which had obliged me to be extravagant enough to have a [sedan] chair...

Her state of mind did not, however, always match such events (Letter 74):

> I have had numberless invitations to cards; which of course I have refused, and shall continue to do so, not meaning to drink tea out of my own house, except once with Mrs Goddard [wife of the second master of Winchester College], and at Mrs [Lucy] Elyott's, I sit a compleat Grooby, hard at work [sewing?] with my nose into the fire all the day, that I am not eating, or suckling, or walking, the latter I have not omitted to do one day, not withstanding the very unfavourable weather, I am very sensible of the good effects of constant exercise, for I was never better, in spite of the

wretched state of my mind, than which nothing can be more unpleasant.

She clearly does not get on with Goddard and his wife, who have recently wed, and in telling her husband about them reveals her views on acceptable social behaviour and the protocols of visiting (Letter 74):

> I had company yesterday to dine: Mr and Mrs Goddard, Miss and Mrs Dyson, and Mr [Thomas] Bargus [a curate], to say the truth I do not think the Bride improves much upon acquaintance, new married people never know how to behave; they are too apt to think and talk only of, and to each other, and he is so queer an animal that it is a difficult task for her to manage him, she is too much at home for me, though she is not forward, but there is no embarassment in her behaviour which one would rather expect at first amongst strangers, she is to receive her company this week, and I believe I have spoiled a great deal of sport for their guests; for it seems he intended not only to have sat tup [sic] with her, (as the phrase is) but to have returned his visits at the same time that she did hers, full dressed, which was so ridiculous that I could not help telling them I thought so.

Her views were perhaps tinged by the fact that Goddard had been a protégé of her father and had succeeded him as second master, and she may even had a soft spot for him, having once admitted to 'a sentimental walk home' after dining at Compton (Letter 50).

Mrs Robert Hare was another 'cathedral wife' often mentioned by Sarah. She comes across as very convivial, if not rather pushy, and fond of parties and spending time in London. On one occasion Sarah reported (Letter 118) that 'Mrs Hare's tongue was upon full stretch all day' and on another that she is waking up the world at the approach of spring (Letter 75):

> We are turning Lent into the carnival here, nothing but balls and concerts, to morrow there is one at the George under the auspices of Mrs Hare, who has pressed a number of gentlemen into her service and obliged them to subscribe a guinea each...

At such events – which were 'subscription balls' as opposed to private balls – a guinea might give each subscriber three tickets, one for themselves and two others for ladies of their choice. In February 1787 the Revd John Monk Newbolt asked Sarah to a 'numerous and pleasant ball at the George', where she would have had the company of her friend Jane, Mrs Carew Mildmay from Shawford. But she declined the offer, explaining her reasons to her husband (Letter 117):

> … my heart goes not that way and another thing I should have felt the force of if I had been disposed to go, and my pride would have kept me at home; if you had been here I am certain that you would not have subscribed and therefore I should have felt that I was an intruder.

Also, she was not altogether comfortable with Newbolt, who was nicknamed 'the Blade', a word used in the eighteenth century for 'a gallant, a free-and-easy fellow ... generally familiarly laudatory, sometimes good-naturedly contemptuous' (OED). He was the son of an apothecary, held two livings in Winchester, and deputised for Philip Williams at Compton from time to time (*see*, for example, Letter 64). Sarah was very concerning about the effect of his lifestyle on his health and advised him 'to stick to tea and cards for the remainder of the winter' (Letter 84). He was probably close to the disgraced MP for Winchester, Henry Penton, who 'left his ice house for Mr Newbolt' when he ran off with his wife's maid in July 1785 (Letter 60).

On another occasion Sarah sought to decline an invitation of his to dine with him and others, and then proceed to an assembly at St John's House, Winchester, but he skilfully deflected her (Letter 124):

> Mr Newbolt was here the other day to give me a good account of you, and to begin the campaign by an invitation to dine with him on Thursday to meet the Shawford people and which is the worst part of the story to go afterwards to the Assembly; I pleaded an engagement with Lear [a fellow of Winchester College] who is to come to Compton after the College meeting, but the Blade with his usual good humour smoothed that business in an instant by saying he would send to Mr Lear to come to his house; so that if the girls go, I cannot be out of the scrape…

In February 1785, the spirits of 'the sisterhood' – the word used by Sarah for the cathedral set of ladies (Letter 95) – were quickened by the sight of the prebendary Thomas Rennell (later to be dean) courting Sarah Blackstone, eldest daughter of the jurist Sir William Blackstone (Letter 75):

> …wonders will never cease! for on Tuesday Mr Rennel gives a ball in honour of Miss Blackstone, he has had a room new painted

upon the occasion, it is to be a very famous affair and happy are the people who are so lucky as to be in the number of his favorites, he is in a fair way to wipe off the rust of his black letter binding, I am told that he puts on a clean shirt every day.

Three months later and the gossips are hard at work (Letter 82):

Mr Rennel[l] goes on at a great rate in the road to matrimony; he has made his offer, and has been accepted, the old man (a bad appendage for the Lady) is so charmed with the idea, that he has sent him word, he will give him 600£ per annum at present, and leave him 20 000£ at his death. My authority for all this is Mrs Price through the medium of the Tripps, the offer was first made to your ex socius [ex fellow of Winchester College], before any thing of the kind was even hinted to the Lady, which may be the more classical way of making love, but it is certainly not the most gallant; the scandalous chronicle says he has used Miss Brereton ill, which I rather doubt, as he seems to have an excellent heart. ...The Rennels don't seem to be in a hurry, the Chariot is building, the wedding trappings prepared, and what they wait for I suppose they know, but we who are most desirous of knowing, cannot find out.

The dowry had probably been negotiated by a brother of the late Sir William Blackstone, namely, Charles Blackstone (1720-ca 1804), who in 1783 had resigned his Winchester College fellowship in favour of his namesake son (and was readmitted in 1788). In July 1785 the anticipated event finally took place, as Sarah reported to her husband (Letter 111):

So your friend Rennell is married at last, they are gone to his father's near Stamford for six months ... it is said that by the time the chaise got to the Flower de Luce [a pub, now called The Wykeham Arms] he kissed her at such a rate as to be heard by the people in the street, I think in such a case myself, I should have stopped the chaise and left him to himself, like a pig as he deserved.

Amongst others to whom Sarah paid frequent visits were Lady Anne Chernocke, widow of Sir Villiers Chernocke and a source of 'so much news and scandal' (Letter 79), and members of the Jenkinson and Cornwall families, notably 'the old lady' Mrs Amarantha Cornwall, the widow of Col. Charles Jenkinson, whose will, proved in August 1785, includes generous legacies (Cecil and Reade, 1908). These families were related more than once by marriage and had come to Winchester from Oxfordshire. They included three children of Col. Jenkinson and his wife, namely, Elizabeth (wife of Speaker Charles Wolfran Cornwall), Charles, a distinguished politician later 1st earl of Liverpool, and John Jenkinson, who pursued a parliamentary career as MP for the rotten borough of Corfe Castle on the back of his brother. They all lived in Calpe Street (now St Thomas's Street) near the parish church, which was replaced by the church, now redundant, which stands in Southgate Street. Sarah seemed to enjoy visits to their households, which she in any event was virtually obliged to maintain, as Philip Williams was – in his early years at least – a private chaplain to Charles Jenkinson and chaplain to Speaker Cornwall and the House of Commons (*see* Chapter 9). Amongst the friendly gestures that Sarah made to the Jenkinsons was the gift of a woodcock 'which would not keep' (Letter 84).

One letter written in April 1785, and unusually for Sarah was set out day by day (as Philip always structured his missives), gives a week's-eye-view of her life. Her sister Charlotte was in London, showing her face to the St John relatives at Marlborough House and elsewhere. Her husband, the Hon. George Richard St John, was well out of the way, staying with the Dysons at Compton rectory. For Sarah it had been a busy week dominated by a meeting of the Hampshire Fox Hunt Society (Letter 89):

> Tuesday I went to a route at Mrs Blackstone's my neighbour, both their rooms as full as they could hold and as hot as ovens, I played two rubbers at whist and lost my money... Wednesday Mr and Mrs Dyson dined with me, and Mr [George Williams] Ricketts, who was very nervous with the idea of his exhibition [a horse race] the next day, we dined in the drawing room and found it most comfortable this hot weather; Thursday the day of Mr Hayne's ball and the race, Mrs Dyson being employed in hair-dressing, the chaise carried Sophy Elyott, little Bess [her daughter Elizabeth], and myself to the course, where I had the pleasure of seeing Mr Ricketts not victorious, but with his neck safe upon his shoulders, ...[there were] as many carriages as are usually at our races, all the people from the Alresford side of the country were there and formed a considerable party at Mr Haynes ball ... I remained quiet upon the occasion and saved my money, had Mr Ricketts won, he intended to have given a dance and of course I could not have avoided going... the beauty Miss Shakspear [Shakespeare] was at the race and ball, with her brother ...she is very handsome and one of the faces you so often see in [Henry

William] Bunburys drawings. Friday I drank tea at the Tripps with Mrs Price who sets out to-morrow upon her Welch [Welsh] expedition ... we had no cards which I heartily rejoiced in; yesterday I spent at home, and was indifferent all day in consequence of having eat pork two days together [...] by the assistance of Dr Cawte I am pretty well to day and have been at Compton, with my darling children – they are writing you a true history of themselves...

A constant companion of Sarah's was Jane, Mrs Carew Mildmay, seated at Shawford House, Twyford, near Compton. As well as attending social events, Sarah and her sisters were sometimes taken off to cricket matches, including one occasion on which they were bound for the downs above Itchen Stoke, a small village near Alresford, about 6 miles from Winchester. With some relief she wrote (Letter 66):

Monday morn, a dreadful wet day, and of course no cricket, which Charlotte and I are very glad of; it is curious that we were both going to a place we disliked, out of civility to the rest of the party.

In the eighteenth century, cricket was played in a number of locations in the vicinity, including Flower Down, Compton Down, Basley Down, and Peartree Green (Southampton), by village teams from Hursley, Twyford, 'Worthy', Sutton Scotney, East Stratton, 'Micheldever, Weston, West Stratton and Northbrook' (essentially the Bedford estate), as well as urban teams from St Bartholomew Hyde (Winchester) and Southampton (Buckley, 1935).

When Sarah moved out from the house in Kingsgate Street to live at Compton, in the rectory vacated by her sister Elizabeth and brother-in-law Jeremiah Dyson – probably at some time after July 1785 (Letter 105) – it became harder for her to keep in touch with her Winchester friends. During one dire period in early spring she had been incarcerated indoors with a 'terrible cold and cough ... incessant wind and rain' and, with one exception, had not seen 'a human creature' for ten days (Letter 119). At such times she was trapped, as she had no carriage and relied on the generosity of others to get about. On one occasion a family friend, Dr William Buller, came to the rescue (Letter 118):

The Dean of Exeter has before this time told you that the Fœtid [Elizabeth Williams] and myself dined with them on Monday, he and Miss Buller very civilly called to desire that they might send the carriage for me, to a mere family party, which was literally the case, except two officers who added much to the pleasure of the party. I made Prince come to escort me home in the evening, knowing that there are posts in Compton as well as Shawford.

She seems to have been wary of 'posts', where presumably mail was collected and dispatched, and perhaps horses exchanged, and might therefore be frequented by travelling strangers. Later in the same week it was the turn of Mrs Carew Mildmay to give her a ride into Winchester for a reception being given by a prebendal wife, Mrs Robert Hare. Sarah was clearly very apprehensive and expected 'all the horrors of a genuine Winchester party' (Letter 118).

Duty was the main driver that Sarah kept in touch with many of the people she knew and visited repeatedly in Winchester and district. There were relatives, people from Winchester College, friends and acquaintances of her husband (mostly Wykehamists), cathedral canons and other churchmen and their wives, and suchlike. None of them, with the exception of her sisters and Mrs Carew Mildmay, could be called close friends, but there was one person who without doubt was in that category, namely, Joan Smith, often give the courtesy title of 'Mrs' (Letter 79):

> There is a very old friend of mine in this neighbourhood, whom I hope to get to me for a day or two before she leaves it, a Joan Smith who was concubine (as she called herself) to Mr [Nicholas] Preston at Alton Barnes [Wiltshire].

How the two became acquainted is not clear, though Sarah was much the younger (Letter 82):

> Mrs Joan Smith dined with me one day last week and we had great satisfaction in talking over ancient matters; she remembers me when I was a foetid, and is besides a very sensible, pleasant woman, I wanted her to stay some days with me, but that was not in her power.

In June 1785, just before race week, Joan stayed for a few days with Sarah under her 'chearless roof'. As already mentioned, after attending together a service at St Michael's church, only a short walk from the College, they went to 'poke out the pictures of Wardens' (Letter 100). Later in the summer they spent a day together with 'some Wiltshire acquaintance' before Joan moved on (Letter 107):

She goes to Southampton to-morrow to take a fortnights dipping, then into Wiltshire for a few months and then she returns to Lady St John [probably the wife of Sir Henry Paulet St John Mildmay, 1st bt] – to spend the winter.

For his part, most of Philip Williams's firmest friends came first from his family, living in various parts of East Anglia, and then from those he knew as a schoolboy and undergraduate at Winchester and Oxford. Also, he gained a new coterie of friends and acquaintances – many seated in Sussex - from Sarah, through her Midhurst-born father Thomas Collins. Much later in life, after the death of Sarah, his prebend at Canterbury and his second wife Helen (née Fagg) expanded his footprint and introduced him to a large circle of clerics and minor aristocrats in Kent. Like any other Georgian who sought advancement, he was not shy of seeking favours from more elevated people, such as his patrons the Rt Hon. Charles Jenkinson and Speaker Cornwall.

There were also endless opportunities to keep up with his family and friends, through his stepfather, Dr John Gordon, and visits paid to his sister Anne and her husband at Fornham, near Bury St Edmunds, Suffolk, to the mysterious 'Mrs Pyke' and other friends in London, in the cathedral close and college at Winchester, the courts of New College, Oxford, and the dinner tables of Westminster. For reasons that are not hard to imagine, he forged particularly strong relationships with school friends who owned substantial estates, especially Lovelace Bigg-Wither, seated grandly at Chilton Foliat, near Newbury, Berkshire, and then even more grandly at Manydown Park, Wootton St Lawrence, in north Hampshire (*see* Chapter 3; Letters 3-5, 7 & 132-33). His family had long been established in the county and were influential in Winchester College; it was undoubtedly through Lovelace's father that he obtained his fellowship at Winchester. Of a similar ilk was the Derbyshire squire and minor poet Francis Mundy, whom he visited in his 60s at his estate, Markeaton Hall, (W390-395). In addition to these, the Letters make plain that he had many lesser friends of various kinds, old and young, who came into and out of his life, many with links to Winchester and New College, including Harry Peckham, John Ballard, Henry Bathurst, William Buller, Thomas Heathcote, Richard Hollist, Ambrose and Samuel Isted, Sir Charles Watson, John Monk Newbolt, Michael Wodhull, and many others.

***

THE LETTERS include many mentions of plays attended by Philip Williams or his friend Lovelace Bigg-Wither in London (*see* Appendix V) and by Sarah in Winchester. Even though London was of course the hub of drama, Winchester had long had a place of sorts where plays were performed and in 1785 it acquired a custom-built theatre on a site in Jewry Street (then called Gaol Street). No longer standing, the site is now occupied by a modern building appropriately called Sheridan House. The moment that Winchester, in common with other provincial cities, sought to catch up with the London stage is captured by Sarah in the Letters. The material has been studied from the viewpoint of theatre history by Paul Ranger (1976, 1996) and is here only presented as a backdrop to this study. Before the New Theatre opened, productions had been presented in a makeshift venue over the Butchers' Shambles, comically portrayed in Thomas Warton's *Prologue on the Old Winchester Playhouse*. This was written in about 1781 for *The Orphan*, a tragedy by Thomas Otway (a Wykehamist), with lead character Monimia, which had first been produced in London in 1680:

> Whoe'er our stage examines, must excuse
> The wondrous shifts of the dramatic Muse;
> Then kindly listen, while the prologue rambles
> From wit to beef, from Shakespeare to shambles!
> Divided only by one flight of stairs
> The monarch swaggers, and the butcher swears!
> Quick the transition when the curtain drops
> From meek Monimia's moans to mutton chops!

The skit 'lately spoken' appeared in the *Gentleman's Magazine* of November 1781 (vol. 51, pp. 531-2) and was later published in Warton's *Poems on Various Subjects*, published posthumously in London in 1791 (p. 191). It was a case of the city of Winchester being shamed by the home-educated boy from Basingstoke, brother of the head master of Winchester College, introducing the celebrated dramatist and poet Otway, who a century before had spent a year in the school before going on to Oxford. The dire state of theatre in the city, and its tendency in earlier days to 'corrupt' boys from the College, is glimpsed in a municipal order of 6 May 1715, transcribed in 1856 by the town clerk Charles Bailey (HRO/W/B2/6):

> ...whereas complaint has been made of disorders committed by the Players acting Interludes [light acts between plays] within this city, and that it tends to the corruption of Youth, and that some of the young Scholars of the School of the College of St Mary's [Winchester College] have laid out of the College on this occasion...the said Players [be forbidden] to act or play any more

Comedies or Tragedies within this city, and that they…do depart…

Alas, the New Theatre did not live up to expectations for long. It fell into decline in the late 1820s, and in 1861, when it had been renamed the Theatre Royal, it closed (Ranger, 1976). A snapshot of it in 1818 noted that it had 'all the requisite qualifications for a place of public amusement but two, namely, cleanliness and convenience' (Ball, 1818, 'The Fifth Walk').

The list of those who subscribed to a fund to erect the theatre of 1785 (HRA/106A10W) contains mainly the names of local worthies, but was short of those from close and college who would have been known to the Williamses. One who is there is *bon viveur* John Monk Newbolt, 'The Blade'. Sarah told the back-story of his involvement, albeit rather half-heartedly, to her husband (Letter 69):

> I suppose Mr Dyson told you that we were going to have a play house in Winchester; the Blade is so indefatigable in the pursuit, that I believe he will bring it to bear, there are one and twenty subscribers already and there are only four and twenty required; it is not of much consequence to me, if I like any amusement it is a play, but my avaccations [avocations] in a different way are so many that I shall have little leisure or money for any thing of that kind…

Clearly the theatre was desired most by those, like Newbolt, who were frequenters of the London stage and wanted to have something closer to hand. Even Sarah, in her sniffy manner, was willing to sample what was on offer (Letter 97):

> Tomorrow the Winchester Theatre opens, not to a crowded audience I guess, the great Patrons of the stage Mrs Hume and the Blade being absent, some people think it will be damp, others prophesy that it will tumble down, as being built in too slight a manner, and if neither of these dreadful calamities take place, in about a fortnight, by which time people will begin bespeaking, I may venture thither perhaps and try to drive away care…

It had 'commodious dressing rooms' and the same dimensions as a theatre in Southampton run by the prime mover in the project, the enterprising theatre manager Thomas Collins (not Sarah's father). He also ran theatres in Salisbury, Portsmouth and Chichester (Ranger, 1987). Local builders and coal merchants, Messrs William Kernott and John and Thomas Dowling put up the building at a cost of £600 (HRO/106A10W/1; Ranger, 1976). *The Hampshire Chronicle* (6 June 1785) reported: 'Our New Theatre opened on Wednesday evening with the celebrated Comedy of *The Rivals*, which was performed to a brilliant audience with universal applause.' An advertisement in the previous edition of the paper had declared that it would open on the Monday, but in the event a bitter dispute delayed the opening, as detailed by Sarah Williams (Letter 99):

> ...they are determined to worry poor [John] Downes [an attorney] to death; the business as far as I can collect, (after making proper allowance for the thousand lies that are every moment coming forth) is this; when the thing was first proposed last year, it seems that Kernot[t] [the builder] and Mr Downes had a dispute, and which became so violent, that the latter bound himself by an oath to inform against the players if they acted, and his mother and sister were too rigid to suffer him to break it, and the spirits of these good ladies being once raised they have been incessantly goading the poor man, till they have obliged him to take the very injudicious step he has done, to which Silver-tongue [unidentified] has not a little contributed by defying them to put their threats in execution etc. At one o'clock last Monday Mr Downes announced his intention, and a number of people met together at the Theatre in the evening, when it was agreed that there should be no play, and if they had pulled the old Keats house down at the time, she deserved it, but they did not make much riot that night but since I am told they have burnt him in effigy, and they have been all round the town with musick singing the enclosed ballad, which is said to be the joint production of Sir W. Gardner and C. Gauntlett; Kernot[t] was obliged to make some trifling apology, upon which the triple alliance, (for there is it seems an aunt who possesses the family spirit in a high degree,) a bated something of their rigour and the players were permitted to proceed without farther molestation on Wednesday, he has put an advertisement in the Winchester paper that I hope to send you, but they are so much in request that I am afraid it will hardly be in my power to get one, Mrs Courteney I am hurt to say has behaved in a shocking manner, has made use of the most abusive and vulgar language, such as would have been beneath a Bil[l]ingsgate fish woman; for the sake of our poor friend that is gone, I shall continue to visit her, but I suppose no one else will.

The attorney John Downes occupied a house opposite the new theatre: the *Hampshire Chronicle* (6 June 1785) ran an advertorial telling his side of the story:

> Mr DOWNES of this city, having been very unjustly ridiculed and vilified in consequence of some inveterate enemies, he begs leave to solicit the attention of the public to a printed account, intended to be circulated to his vindication, containing the true state of his conduct from the time the New Theatre was first proposed to be built opposite his Dwelling-house, the particulars thereof being too long to be inserted by way of [a] paragraph in a newspaper.

The 'advertisement' that Sarah hoped to send to her husband was therefore probably a printed sheet circulated (for a fee) with the newspaper. The nature of the dispute is not clear, but Downes and 'the triple alliance' may have been objecting to the placing of the theatre opposite their house, at a time when 'planning applications' had not yet been devised. William Kernott, who with others had been commissioned to build the theatre, seems to have persuaded John Downes to back down. Sarah kept Philip in the picture, acknowledging that the new building was, indeed, better than Warton's 'butchers' shambles' (Letters 100 & 104):

> The players are now permitted to go on without molestation, I suppose I shall be obliged to go, when they bespeak and if I can bear any amusement it is a play. ...I went last Wednesday to the play for the first time, the house is very neat, and by far too capacious for the company, but the players appear to a much greater advantage, than in the other wretched hovel...

The theatre came into its own just in time for the 1785 race week in Winchester, when the city thronged with visitors in search of entertainment. The *Hampshire Chronicle* (4 July 1785) reported that the theatre 'was remarkably crouded' and the 'performances gave general satisfaction, and went off with spirit and vivacity.' Mrs Powlett Powlett bespoke *The Provoked Husband*, or A Journey to London, by Vanbrugh, with 'A SONG by Miss Sharrock' at the end of the play. This was followed by a two-act comedy, *High Life Below Stairs*, by playwright clergyman James Townley (1714-1778), which involved 'the standard plot of a master who dons the functional yet humorous disguise of a servant to witness and to assess the behaviour of his employees' (LL. Eckersley, 'Townley, James', ODNB). The play might have raised a frisson of excitement in a city in which one of its members of parliament, Henry Penton, had recently deserted his wife for her lady's maid. This great scandal casts a light on attitudes of the Williamses to sexual impropriety.

In Winchester the Pentons occupied Eastgate House, a mansion at the east end of the Broadway, where on 28 September 1778 George III and Queen Charlotte had spent four and a half hours after travelling from Windsor to Winchester for a royal visit (Kirby, 1892, pp. 412-414). The two parliamentary seats of the city were in the hands of the dukes of Chandos, seated at Avington House in the upper Itchen valley, and it was by their influence that two Henry Pentons, father and son, held one of them between 1749 and 1796 (Carpenter Turner, 1992, p. 127). After being educated at Winchester College and Clare College, Cambridge, the son was returned to Westminster in 1761. He later gave his name to the quarter of Pentonville in the London Borough of Islington, which he developed in the 1770s. The family was obviously known to the Philip and Sarah Williams, who in 1780 wrote (Letter 25):

> The Pentons are coming down and I have paid my compliments and promised as much on your part when you return [from the home of Lovelace Bigg-Wither at Chilton Foliat].

Henry Penton jr's affair with his wife's lady's maid, Miss Catherine Judd, seems to have started in the early 1780s. They had two daughters and were eventually married in January 1812, five days after his wife's death (Thorne, *History of Parliament, 1790-1820*, vol IV, p. 762). A spoof advertisement placed in the *Hampshire Chronicle* after race week, on 28 July 1783, suggests that by that time the scandal was public knowledge:

> FOUND. On the 10th day of June last, in a field near Winhall [meaning 'Winnall', a district of Winchester], belonging to Henry Penton Esq. A Switch-Tail BAY MARE, about 14 hands high, who has been used to both saddle and harness. The owner may have her again, by applying to Benjamin Carter at Winhall, on describing her marks, and paying the expenses.

The affair first surfaces in the Letters in February 1785 and continues to the end, mostly in letters from Philip Williams, who was of course aware of happenings from the gossip machine of Westminster (Letters 72-3, 90 & 106):

> I am afraid that Penton is much playing the fool; he pays visits I hear with her in the carriage; than which nothing can be well more silly –I have since seen them riding together. ...Poor Penton has, I

hear, bedevilled himself – he and his new associate already quarrel like cat and dog; they are at present in lodgings in Kensington, where she has miscarried. He never goes into public, and was shamefully absent from the H of Commons the other night. ...Mrs Penton was at the drawing room on Thursday... Sloan wrote to him desiring him to attend the house on last Monday, but he neither came, [n]or answered his letter. I am sorry for him. ...Pray what is the history of Penton; is he gone abroad or not?

In fact, he had taken his lover, who was 'not seen by ladies', to Italy, where he 'had her taught music and languages' (Thorne, ibid, p. 763). The lot of a woman who breached sexual morality was, indeed, awful at the time: Fanny Burney in her novel *Evelina* recounts how a misbehaving countess at the opera sat for 'the whole night in her box without any woman's speaking or curtsying to her, or taking any more notice of her than you would of a post, or a beggar woman' (Doody, 1994, p. 199). Sarah for her part heaps on the opprobrium, no doubt deeply conscious of the plight of Penton's wife Anne (née Knowler), by whom he had had three sons and a daughter (Letter 107):

Mr Penton goes on in such a way that there is little to be said for him, he is certainly abroad and for some months (he has left his ice house etc. for Mr [John Monk] Newbolt [a clergyman friend])[,] he drove her in the Phaeton down Winchester Street, and whatever she proposes he implicitly complys with, whenever he has friends with him, she never leaves the room for a moment, abuses him in the grossest terms before the servants, and is quite frantick; it is said that she really is disordered in her senses and has attempted to destroy herself but such is his infatuation that he will not part with her; I have heard a story of him which is so shocking that, I cannot repeat it by letter, the very idea of it quite chills my blood, and I shall never see him again without shuddering, I hope it is not true.

Philip, too, was adept at piling on the outrage they both felt, even though it was a time when sexual morality was often very loose, at all levels of society (Letter 123):

Penton is pursuing the high road to destruction; Newbolt could not get access to him, whilst here...[he] is going to buy an house in Piccadilly for which he is to pay £3000, to settle upon Miss Judd. Young Gulstone is returned from abroad, who is his ward, and had declared he will never go into his house again, to be witness of such unmanly treatment, as she was in her tantrums one day when he was there, and spit in her limber-ham's [lackey's] face.

Penton's behaviour made him 'a social pariah' and led to much talk of his resigning his seat (Thorne, ibid, p. 762-3). He sat in opposition to Pitt, though was of uncertain value in the House as 'he could not be relied upon to attend'. However, he hung on until 1796, when he vouched health as his reason for retiring. Before stepping down he 'treated the House to a witty speech against the tax on dogs'. His grand mansion in Winchester, Eastgate House, stood to the east of St John's Hospital and and assembly rooms, on land granted to Winchester College in 1544 after the dissolution. Subsequently, it was sold on lease to Sir Henry Paulet St John Mildmay, the son-in-law of Sarah's great friend, Mrs Carew Mildmay. It was demolished in 1846-7 to make way for new houses. However, the Mildmay name lived on in the name of a pub, the Mildmay Arms (and more recently a veterinary practice, now relocated). The landlord reminded clients of his loans policy by placing a non-functioning clock on the building (no tick!), which is still there.

Watching other people on 'the high road to destruction' who are 'quite frantick' and 'disordered' in their senses was a means by which Philip and Sarah were able to reassure each other that they were not in the least attracted by the behaviour of people like Henry Penton and Catherine Judd. And yet, Sarah, as she spared no opportunity to say, was thoroughly miserable when he was away and might have wondered whether she should have married another – perhaps someone like Mr Thomas Heathcote. But seeking a male friend to provide support, even within a totally platonic relationship, was impossible for someone in her position. She was living in a neighbourhood where she was known to a multitude of willing spies, besides which her religion spoke against anything but obedience to her husband. What she thought cannot be known; but what she did was beyond doubt to be wholly faithful; when she signed off 'yours entirely' she meant it. Philip, too, even if he found celibacy irksome, lived in the house of the Speaker and his wife and was in frequent and constant contact with Winchester folk for whom gossip was food. Though he paid visits to friends and acquaintances throughout London – a city where female companionship was freely available – the likelihood of him being a Boswell or a Pepys is slight.

12. 'Doing the duty' at Compton

FOR FIFTY YEARS Philip Williams was rector of the parish of Compton. It lies about two miles from the centre of Winchester and abuts the former parish of St Faith's Winchester to the north, Otterbourne (with which the Compton benefice is now twinned) to the south, Twyford to the east and Hursley to the west. On foot it can be reached from the cathedral in little more than half an hour. The dean and chapter of Winchester were lords of the manor and leased much of the land to farmers. They also held the advowson of Compton. Earlier rectors included John Harmar, sometime warden of Winchester College (and one of translators of the Authorised Version of the Bible), who was presented to the living in 1595, whilst G.I. Huntingford, another warden, was curate in about 1774-1776 and later chose to be buried in the churchyard.

The parish was studied in great detail by local historian John Summers Drew (Turnbull, 1992), who in 1939 published *Compton, near Winchester: Being an Enquiry into the History of a Hampshire Parish*. Many of his original notes remain and have been used in this section (HRO/116A05). In 1780, only a year after Philip had married Sarah, the bishop of Winchester collated him to the living of Compton in place of Thomas Rickman (rector 1776-1780), who had resigned. The parish was in good shape: Rickman's obvious care in keeping the parish records in a fluent copperplate hand was an asset (HRO/1M76/PR1). Also, his immediate predecessor, Newton Ogle (rector 1775-1776), dean of Winchester, had in 1776 made new arrangements with the tenants to commute the tythes, achieving an increase of a quarter in the income. And his predecessor, Robert Shipman, rector 1765-1775, had spent considerable sums on repairs and improvements to the rectory, which had been built – in 1758, according to White, (1859, p. 126) or ca 1737, according to Drew (1939, p. 140) – during the long incumbency of Charles Scott, rector 1724-1763. Fifty years later, after Philip Williams's death, his successor, John Old Zillwood, formerly chaplain to Winchester gaol and bridewell, rebuilt the rectory (White, 1859, p.126).

Initially, Philip and Sarah chose not to live in Compton, but stayed in their house in 'the lowest end of Kingsgate Street', Winchester, subsequently letting the parsonage house to her sister Elizabeth and husband Jeremiah Dyson. In July 1781, the couple had married at the tiny church of St Swithun's-over-Kingsgate church, Winchester: she was 19 and he 23 (*Alleg. Marr. Lic. Winch. 1689-1837, Harleian Soc*, I, 238). Between 1782 and 1785, they had four of their children baptised at Compton.

Although Philip Williams was collated to Compton in 1780, he was not inducted until the following March; in January 1781 Thomas Rickman was still conducting marriages. On the last two pages of an Incumbent's Notebook of Compton Philip Williams noted (HRO/1M76A/PI1):

> Mr Rickman vacated the living of Compton by Cession February 1 1781 and Mr Williams was instituted into this rectory the same day, and inducted by the Rev Mr Rickman March 18, 1781.

Wheels were turning within wheels. In 1780, Rickman had himself gained the living of Ash, Surrey, which was one of the most valuable livings in the gift of Winchester College and went with a 'good house' (WCM/C8/1/f.1). The vacancy arose from the death of William Langbaine, who had earlier gained the living after the death of Dr John Harris, who was of a family seated at Silkstead Priors, Compton, and a maternal grandfather of Philip Williams's great friend, Lovelace Bigg-Wither.

The Compton parish registers show Philip Williams's hand starting in May 1781, with his first marriage on Christmas Eve 1781, and continuing, almost all in his hand, to 1824, when he was 82 years of age. The only extensive period when he was not able to officiate continuously at Compton was during the five years after May 1784, when he served as chaplain to the House of Commons. He was, however, able to do the duty during vacations. The parish records showed that amongst those who officiated in his absence were John Faithfull, son of an inn-keeper from Overton (once in 1785), Thomas Brereton, son of a local upholder, or upholsterer (once in 1785), J. A. Birch, not traced (several times in 1786), Dr [Daniel] Williams (once in 1788, the year before he died), [Bradnam] Tawney (once 1789) and John Woodburn (once in 1793). The closest he came to having a longterm curate was Edward Smith, who officiated at several marriages between 1789 and 1799. From 1811, his son Charles, who was in his mid-20s, often served as curate. Until 1823-4 he officiated at almost all baptisms and missed only two weddings. The parish clerk, who witnessed nearly all weddings until March 1801, was George Cole, followed by Will Selwood until 1822.

Clearly, a number of different people helped him to 'do the duty', including 'Mr Goddard' (probably the man who was to be the future head master of Winchester), who is mentioned by Sarah as a possible curate (Letter 52). Thomas Heathcote seems also to have 'done the duty' at some time (*see*, for example, Letter 68), though the first trace of a Heathcote in the parish registers is in 1820. It is clear that many of the men who officiated at Compton had links with Winchester College. The 'assistant masters' at Winchester were often called on to help out at Compton, as had the sometime warden of Winchester, G. I. Hungerford, later to be bishop of Gloucester, and also a Robert Stanton Woodham, who took a wedding for Thomas Rickman in June 1780. According to Foster's *Alumni Oxonienses*, he was from Kingston, Jamaica – probably from a planter's family – matriculated at New College at the age of 15 in 1773, proceeded to BA in 1780 and was an assistant master at Winchester, In 1791 he obtained the living of Spanish Town on Jamaica. Many of the others who served at Compton were in some way related to Winchester College, which is hardly surprising: it was a useful reservoir of ministerial deputies. William of Wykeham would have been pleased.

Compton was essentially an agricultural parish. A terrier of 1844 recorded that the parish comprised 2099 acres, of which 1197 were arable, 188 meadow or pasture and 522 downland. Since the reign of Elizabeth I it had been the home of people named Goldfinch, who had progressively farmed more and more land. Drew (1939) comments:

> It is indeed not too much to say that for six generations the Goldfinches of Compton were one of the best-known families for miles around, and that they had come to be regarded as a sort of institution by the whole district.

They were pioneers of farming on a large scale and their house, Compton Manor Farm, and its buildings were constructed and maintained in a grand manner. Responding to a survey of 1805, the Goldfinches were unable to state exactly how much land they farmed; it included more than 1100 acres rented from the dean and chapter of Winchester alone. However, within a few decades it seems that the farming instinct had gone. In 1856 White's *Directory of Hampshire* noted (p. 126):

The latter [Joseph Goldfinch] has lately removed to West Brompton [an area of London now in the Borough of South Kensington and Chelsea].

At his death in Bayswater at the age of 80, the family became 'extinct' (*Hampshire Advertiser*, 2 April 1870). With the end of the Goldfinch era most of the land came to be farmed by the Heathcotes of Hursley and their tenants.

Only one member of the Goldfinch family seems to have ventured outside farming, namely, Richard Goldfinch (1727-1789; one of eight namesakes in a dynasty that ran from the late sixteenth century; Drew, 1939, p. 140), who set up a private school at Compton which he ran until Whitsun 1773, when he handed it over to William Scardefield (or Scarvill). He had been for 'many years Writing Master to the Rev Mr Cotton's [Hyde Abbey] School at Winchester' and intended moving the Compton school the short distance to Twyford (*Hampshire Chronicle*, 30 November 1772; see also HRO/1800AD/60). Richard, described as a 'Gent' at his burial in April 1789, went back to managing his estate, but continued to run a school of some sort on a small scale in the village for the children of the well-to-do. Drew (1939) writes:

> Mr Goldfinch was 60 years old in 1787 and he seems to have had several boy pupils as boarders, while Bess and Philip Williams (aged 7 and 6) [children of Philip and Sarah] attended the school daily. The mention [in the Williams Letters] of little John Jenkinson, whose family were very much of the "quality", shows the social class from which the pupils came.

'Little John Jenkinson' was a namesake of his father, who served as the MP for the rotten borough of Corfe Castle, Dorset, from 1768 to 1780, when he stepped aside in the family interest of Henry Bankes, who had come of age. Jenkinson's great-great-grandmother had been a Bankes and the two families were close. The full name of 'little John' was John Bankes Jenkinson and Richard Goldfinch's school seems to have prepared him well for Charterhouse, then Christ Church College, Oxford, and a career in the Church. He rose to become bishop of St David's. He was a cousin of the prime minister Robert Banks [sic] Jenkinson, 2nd earl of Liverpool.

During the early part of 1787 there are several references in the Letters to Goldfinch's school (*see* 115-6, 118, 120 & 125). In 1750 Richard Goldfinch had married Elizabeth Hockley, who gave him three children before dying in child-bed five years later. In 1757 he married Ruth Blake, a lady about 20 years his senior, who predeceased him in 1784. Sarah reported the event to her husband (Letter 64):

> The old Dowager Goldfinch is dead, and Mr [John Monk] Newbolt was kind enough to bury her yesterday.

The school at Compton did not endure, though a preparatory school of separate foundation at Twyford did, and still thrives.

The changing times that slowly replaced 'old corruption' by reform between the generation of Philip Williams and his namesake lawyer son are reflected in the lives of his predecessor, Thomas Rickman, and his son. An article in the *Compton Parish Magazine* (almost certainly by John Summers Drew) noted that the 'parish books and register in his time are a model of neatness and precision' (W233). It described him as 'very enigmatic', but with modern searching methods it can be shown that prior to coming to Hampshire in 1776 he had been vicar of Newburn, on the outskirts of Newcastle upon Tyne (HRO/21M65/E4/4/83). It is almost certain that here he had the ear of Newton Ogle, who also came from that part of the country: he had been appointed dean of Winchester a few years earlier and, as already mentioned, served as rector of Compton in 1775-1776. The 'neatness and precision' of Thomas Rickman may have influenced his son, John, born at Newburn, who was educated at Guildford Grammar School and Oxford and pursued a career as a Westminster statistician and civil servant. His entry in the 1893 edition of the *Dictionary of National Biography* says that his father 'descended from an old Hampshire family', as supported by the catalogue of the Hampshire Record Office, which has a large number of items from the mid-sixteenth century, relating to yeoman farmers and the like with the name, mainly from the southwest of the county, including Christchurch, where Thomas Rickman spent his last years.

After graduating, John Rickman went to live at Christchurch with his father and spent his time studying political economy, which led him in 1796 to make a proposal for a national census. His idea was given to the local MP, George Rose, by whom it reached Charles Abbot MP (1757-1829, later the 1st Baron Colchester), who was a keen administrative reformer. In 1801 he steered a bill through parliament that led to the first national census. When Abbot was elected Speaker in 1802 Rickman became his secretary and thereafter was responsible for many statistical surveys. In this capacity, in a way that echoes that of Philip William with

Speaker Cornwall, he lived in a house alongside the official quarters of the Speaker. Elected a Fellow of the Royal Society in 1815, he was responsible for all national censuses up to 1831 and was working on the 1841 census when he died.

Philip Williams first went to live at Compton with his wife Sarah in about 1786. It might have been an idyllic experience, but he lost her in child-bed and lived there alone for several years until his second marriage in 1793, to Helen Fagg, who clearly enjoyed the life of a rector's wife. At his death he was followed at Compton by John Old Zillwood, a native of Dorchester, Dorset, who represented a break with tradition: he was neither a Wykehamist, nor a member of New College. He was presented to the living at the relatively advanced age of 46 and stayed until his death in September 1871.

***

THE LETTERS illustrate the key role of the rector's wife in ensuring that the parish was well served. Sarah seems to have gone to church on most Sundays at Compton, though at other times she attended St Michael's, Winchester, in the parish in which she and Philip resided during the early years of their marriage. The key requirement at Compton was to have a 'deputy' to 'do the duty'. There were a number of local clergymen on whom Sarah called. For some time it seems to have been William Goddard (though his name does not appear in the parish registers), but in July 1784 he took over from Sarah's father as second master at Winchester College (later to be its head), and was presumably too occupied to continue. She set about finding a replacement during the ensuing week, which was the occasion of the Winchester races (Letter 62):

> Goddard will be in town in a day or two and I desired him to call upon you – he will be glad to leave the cure of Compton, and I shall speak to Mr Heathcote when I see him at the Balls.

'Mr Heathcote' was probably the Revd Thomas Heathcote, a son of Sir Thomas Heathcote of Hursley Park, near Winchester, who was a Wykehamist and rector of Stone, Kent, between 1772 and his death in 1811. He was often in London in the company of Philip Williams (e.g., 'T Heathcote' in. Letter 49) and Sarah knew the family, as evidenced by the following (Letter 29):

Just as I had finished my broth and was preparing to get into the carriage we were detained by the Hursley Family, who were introduced before I knew any thing of the matter, and having sent their carriage to turn, which I believe went half the way to Southampton, they sat with me for three quarters of an hour

Her approach to Heathcote was obviously successful, as a week later she is suggesting to her husband that there should be a sermon for a thanksgiving day that had been set for 29 July, to mark the ending of hostilities with the United States, France, Spain and Holland. The *Hampshire Chronicle* of 26 July 1784 noted:

Thursday next [29 July] is the day appointed for a General Fast and Thanksgiving, for the conclusion of the late bloody and extended war. The Forms of Prayer appointed to be used on this occasion may be had of the Agents for and Distributors of this paper.

And the following week it reported:

…[the event] was observed in this city with the highest degree of decency and solemnity. The shops were entirely shut up. The Mayor and Corporation went in procession, with their formalities, &c and heard divine service at the Cathedral Church. And to the honour of the inhabitants, the evening was not disgraced by illuminations, fireworks, or any riotous demonstrations of joy, ill befitting, in our opinion, the solemnity of the occasion.

However, Philip did not feel that the village justified such festivities and left Sarah in no doubt of his views (Letter 63):

I shall not wish Heathcote to take any notice of the thanksgiving; in so small a place n'importe, and pray tell him so.

Not calling his friend 'T. Heathcote', as he usually did, introduces some slight doubt of identity, but there seem to be no other candidates. Her response is equally uncompromising (Letter 64):

…I have written to him [Mr Heathcote] about the thanksgiving, and if he cannot do the duty I shall get it done, if I make a sermon myself; as I think the obligation indispensable upon you to take care that there shall be no relaxation in the attendance upon your flock in your absence, and particularly on such a remarkable occasion as this in question it is no excuse to the Comptonites, that you have bought some oxen and must go to prove them; it is very audacious in me to say this, but I trust you will not be angry, and so in spite of you there shall be [a] service on the 29th.

Subsequently, Sarah often refers to 'Mr Heathcote' carrying out duties at Compton, where she and her sisters 'spent a snug day' with him soon after he had taken over. He proved to be 'an excellent gossip' and offered to bury a local man who had died, but 'Mr Westcombe [probably Nicholas Westcombe, who had the misfortune of being murdered in 1813] came in the handsomest manner ... some time ago, and offered to take the charge of any occasional duty that might happen at Compton' (Letter 68). At other times Mr Heathcote was 'full of civility and good humour...', 'smiling and good-humoured as ever...a great favourite' (Letters 69 & 72).

Subsequently, Sarah found it harder to obtain the help of deputies as acceptable as Heathcote and in April 1785 reported (Letter 85):

Taskins performed this morning to about a dozen people besides myself, and I made Old Cole ring the bell earlier this afternoon, that we might dine time enough for him to get to College Chapel; that chatter-box Phil told him he preached in an o{dd way} and frightened me for what he might {say} next, so I sent him away crying the moment Mr [Bradnam] Tawney left us; they all observed to him that his articles and coat were very dirty and shabby (and to be sure they did not smell very strong of the cranberry) which he excused by the badness of the day.

The Compton parish register of banns show two men doing the duty in June 1785, namely, 'Mr [John] Faithful[l]', who is described as a curate and was a son of William of Overton, Hampshire, keeper of the Poyntz Arms, and Thomas Brereton 'Assistant Minister'. who was from a local family; in 1789 he was collated rector of St Michael's church, Winchester. One or other of these men was obviously quite pleased with the set-up, as Sarah advised Philip that 'we dined with your Deputy who is I believe not displeased at your long absence...' (Letter 104).

Bradnam Tawney, mentioned above, appeared frequently in the Letters. A graduate of Magdalen College, Oxford, and ordained priest in 1768, he was one of those many would-be incumbents who never got a living. He was not a Wykehamist, and held the relatively humble position of a chaplain of the College between 1769 and 1799 (Suzanne Foster, pers. comm., WCA/F16/192). He was clearly something of a hanger-on: in February 1785 he breakfasted in London with Philip Williams and the cathedral prebendary John Sturges jr, the two 'not being well paired' (Letter 78); at various times he called on Sarah in Winchester where one day he 'brought …no intelligence of any sort' (Letter 116) and on another gave her the details of a sordid squabble between two men, whom Philip knew in London (Letter 103), resulting in a case for defamation at the Winchester assizes (Letter 119):

> All this will be fine fun for the lawyers but sadly distressing to the young lady [a witness]; this I had from Mr Tawney, who told it to me in as plain terms, as he could have told you, thinking I believe that he was saying what was quite decent and right.

Tawney was obviously a jobbing curate and served both Compton and Twyford, but not with total success. Sarah's report goes some way to explaining why this man was not getting a living (Letters 119 & 120):

> Mr Tawney… is in mauvaise odeur at Shawford [which is within the parish of Twyford] and not without reason, though I believe he meant no ill, but nature did not make him a gentleman…

Although he continued to serve Compton – and on one occasion Philip, with hopes of coming down from London, graciously gave him 'an holiday on Easter Sunday, and probably the Sunday after' (Letter 123) – Sarah was obviously uncomfortable in his presence and did not shrink from providing more evidence for the unfortunate man not being a 'gentleman' (Letters 124-5):

> I am obliged to bolt my dinner whole when Mr Tawney is in course at the College, for before I can help him and the children he has finished, I could excuse his dining with me at all when he has so much duty. …I don't know how to get rid of your Deputy, for he has so little notion of propriety that a hint has no effect upon him, if he shews an inclination to go, I shall not press him; but I am the more civil to him, because he is quite odious to me and one great satisfaction I have, is his not dining with me any more…

Eventually poor Tawney found some favour, as a minor canon of Winchester, with the livings of St Thomas's and St Clement's.

Sarah did much else to satisfy the cure at Compton. Her letters are full of parish news, to keep the rector in the picture – generally of death, disease and similar disasters (e.g. Letter 118) – but on one occasion when he first went up to Westminster, before he had even started work, she asked for his permission to make changes to fabric of the church (Letter 50):

> I am charged with a petition to you from Shawford and Compton to have a casement or two opened in the church, which I think perfectly right and necessary, but I could say nothing 'till I had your orders; you will be so good as to signify your consent in you next letter.

He readily granted permission (there seemed to be no churchwardens) with the sort of order that either reveals him at his worst or exercising raillery (Letter 49):

> You will order the blacksmith at Compton to make two casements in the two chancel windows, and that instantaneously.

She apparently asked their brother-in-law Jeremiah Dyson, who lived in the parsonage house, to arrange it, but two months passed without any progress, inviting the comment: 'Only think of his being too lazy to order the blacksmith to make a casement!' (Letter 63) – to which Dyson might have offered a rich reply!

Much later, towards the end of her short life, Sarah was concerned that Thomas Houghton, who was about to leave his farm at Compton, might 'forget to pay us the remainder'; that she has been told that 'he is a thousand pounds behind hand, with Lady Charnack [Chernocke] and Lady St John', but does not believe it as 'the weird sisters would tear him to pieces skin and all before they would suffer it' (Letter 119). A week later she was much more relaxed about the matter (Letter 120):

> There is no occasion to be under any alarm about Houghton, though he is very much behind hand, I believe he has a good deal of property either [in] his or his wife's [name].

If Sarah had lived a long life she might have retreated from intruding on her husband's affairs, but it seems unlikely. For his part, he seems to have accepted her involvement willingly.

13. *A Fenland Family*

PHILIP WILLIAMS never forgot that his family had found its feet in Cambridge, and it was there and in the surrounding fenlands that he probably felt most comfortable. There were plenty of opportunities for him to keep in touch. His widowed mother married a Cambridge don, his sisters never left the Fens, and there were many other members of the Williams diaspora whom he frequently visited, as if Hampshire could never quite provide the security he needed.

Like Anne Williams's first husband, the man she married in her widowhood, John Gordon, was a 'bright young thing' who never scaled the heights of academia and relied on a materially more rewarding career in the church. He had been brought up in north-east England, a son of John Gordon, of Whitworth, County Durham. He matriculated as a sizar at Peterhouse, Cambridge, in 1745 and two years later migrated to Emmanuel College. He seems to have prospered there, as in 1751 he was elected to the Gillingham Fellowship, founded by a gentleman of that name, with the advantage over other fellowships that the 'possessor has a dividend arising from a particular Estate' (*Cambridge University Calendar*, 1807, p. 241). However, for some reason in 1759, he migrated back to Peterhouse; possibly the move was related to his institution to Henstead, though the living was not apparently in the gift of the college. Although his marriage in 1762 would have required him to resign his fellowship, the couple made their home in Cambridge, at Cotton Hall, which was probably a remnant of the manor house of the Cotton family, locally prominent politicians, that came to be owned by Trinity Hall, and stood opposite Pembroke Hall (Lysons, D and S, *Magna Brittannia*, Vol II, 1810; W. Fenton, pers.comm.).

John Gordon seems to have had a good relationship with Philip Williams, a man of 20 years of age when he first knew him, halfway between fa son and a younger brother. He wrote to him as someone who understood the 'clerical game' and had a similar education, gossiping about church appointments and slipping in Latinisms, as others might arm-wrestle (*see* Letters 15 & 18). But he was not a man to upset: much later, in 1785, referring to his stepbrother, George Gordon, Philip Williams commented:

'...a very fine young man he is; the image of his father, but I trust with a better temper' (Letter 73). One potential minefield they had to tread was the division of the spoils of the estate and lands of Philip's father, part of which he had owned in his own right and the rest in settlement from his father-in-law. John Gordon took an interest in these matters and discovered one great big snag, to which he applied his considerable skill for negotiation and disputation. He found that the marriage settlement between PW(II) and his young bride not only stipulated equal rights of inheritance to all the children but also required him to pay her a lump sum of £1000 – which he had not done. As John Gordon explained, this 'non-performance ...in the Lawyer's phrase infects the whole deed [the settlement] and renders it of no validity' (Letter 10). Hence, he was called on to reach agreements that not only guarded the interests of himself and the two sons that subsequently Anne bore him, but also those of Philip Williams, his two sisters, and his grandfather's sister, Aunt Bell, whose 'fortune' had been determined in chancery. These letters do not reveal the upshot of this delicate process, but, even though Gordon's tone is insistent, there is no evidence that anything other than a decent and reasonable solution was found.

In 1765 John Gordon received his doctorate in divinity and became a chaplain to John Green, the bishop of Lincoln (and successor to PW(II)'s living at Barrow), who had been in post for four years and was a man in his 60s. Like many Cambridge academics turned churchmen, Gordon might have preferred a post at Ely, but, in his early 40s, still retained hopes of higher office in the University. In 1771, after the death of the regius professor of divinity at Cambridge (the more distinguished of two such chairs, the other being the Lady Margaret professorship), he cherished being elected to the position, but was outmanœuvred by Richard Watson (1737-1816), who since 1764 had held the chair of chemistry. The parvenu's ride to London to be dubbed Doctor of Divinity is colourfully described in a letter of John Gordon's (Letter 15). He called 'foul', but Watson had the ear of the chancellor of the university, the duke of Grafton, and was obviously a clever man: in the Mathematical Tripos, taken by all ambitious undergraduates, he graduated 2nd Wrangler in 1759, whilst ten years earlier John Gordon had seemingly been ranked 16 out of 22 Wranglers and Senior Optimes, which were not then listed separately. The approach of Watson to his new chair was simple (quoted by Sykes, 1934, p. 350):

> I reduced the study of divinity into as narrow a compass as I could, for I determined to study nothing but my Bible...

Watson went on to become bishop of Llandaff, which only had the relatively tiny income of £500 per annum and was generally a stepping stone to greater things. The previous nine bishops had, for example, only held the Welsh see for an average of five years – of them, Jonathan Shipley for less than a year! But Watson was obliged to serve for 34 years, though for the last 25 of them he chose to live *in absentia*, on the shores of Lake Windermere. His episcopal stagnation was mainly due to the fact that he spoke his mind and was a reformer of sorts (notably campaigning to equalize the incomes of all bishoprics), though he was vilified for his non-residence by Victorian historians. In the last century he was one of only two eighteenth-century churchmen singled out for a whole chapter in Sykes's landmark study *Church and State in England in the Eighteenth Century*, (Chapter 8; the other was Benjamin Hoadly, bishop of Winchester), which sought to re-examine the period. Whilst he does not totally exonerate Watson from charges of non-residence, he is sympathetic, commenting 'Watson's life refutes at once any whisper of insincerity of speech or innate lethargy of disposition' (Sykes, 1934, p. 371).

At about the time that John Gordon lost to Watson, he preached a sermon which has been seized on by students of the American Revolution. He delivered it in Great St Mary's church, Cambridge, to commemorate the accession of the king, as the Cambridge Calendar required, on the 22nd Sunday after Trinity, which in 1771 was on 25 October. Only a doctor of divinity was qualified to do so, and it was designated a Scarlet Day, i.e. a grand occasion on which all doctors wore full academic dress. The subject he chose was *The causes and consequences of evil speaking against government considered* and the 17-page pamphlet that resulted from it is back in print today. At a time when the Enlightenment philosophy of Locke espoused the idea of 'government with the consent of the governed', Gordon rejected the idea that all men were naturally equal, and ridiculed the fact that groups 'of the lowest artificers have been formed to dispute and decide on the most abstruse questions'. He probably also chose the occasion to score points against his professorial foe, Watson and his type, as Gascoigne noticed (1989, p. 210):

> His sermon probably typified the intellectual confusion of many in Cambridge, who were increasingly concerned at the growing assertiveness of 'the lower orders' and who recoiled from the radical conclusions that self-proclaimed custodians of whiggery like Watson drew from the familiar contractual view of government, and yet were still too influenced by Cambridge's

whig traditions to return to the Filmerite views of government and society.

Sir Robert Filmer was an advocate of patriarchial authority and Gunn (1983, p. 169), writing on eighteenth century political thought, especially in North America, claimed that even more than him 'Gordon attracted [the] accusation of preaching divine right'. He wrote:

> The American troubles brought with them more urgent need for lectures on the merits of obedience and, accompanying the rise of extra-parliamentary activity, a new readiness to challenge any limit of authoritarian language...

Perhaps Gordon discussed these matters with Philip Williams, who also took a great interest in the growing unrest in the American colonies (*see* Appendix IV). His stepfather's conservatism was captured in a biography of the Christian apologist and theological utilitarian William Paley (1743-1805), in which Gordon was described as 'an avowed tory in religion and politics' (Meadley, 1809, pp. 46-7). In his *Principles of Moral and Political Philosophy* (1785) Paley was to make many reformist claims that might have unsettled a man like Gordon, including 'it is a mistake to suppose that the rich man maintains his servants ... the truth is they maintain him' (op. cit., 8 ed., Boston, USA, p. 153). At a meeting of the Hyson Club (founded in 1757, at which Cambridge intellectuals met for tea and conversation; named after hyson tea, or dragon tea, from China), Gordon clashed 'with his usual heat' with Paley and the reformist John Jebb (1736-1786) about church government. When most of the members of the Hyson Club rallied in 1772 at the Feathers Tavern in the Strand to press for abolition of the need for University members to sign up to the 39 Articles, it is unlikely that Gordon's name was on the petition presented to parliament. Mrs Edwyn Jervoise, the Williams family historian, may have been repeating whispers of a man out of step when she noted that Gordon was 'a most nasty man apparently' (W294).

John Gordon spent the rest of his years immersed in the affairs of the huge diocese of Lincoln, where he was a prebendary, archdeacon, and later precentor. No doubt he shared the gossip and the clerical and academic politics of this part of the country with his stepson, Philip Williams: it was, after all, the world known to his father PW(II). He keeps him up to date with the living and the dead (Letter 11):

Death has been very busy both here and at Ely lately. There have died here, whom you know — Poor Mr Bennett, the Bedel; and Mr Cowper and Mrs Barnerdiston, of Bene't College. And at Ely old Mr Cole and Mrs Greene.

Over a period of nearly 30 years he served three different bishops: John Green until his death in April 1779, then Thomas Thurlow until he was translated to Durham in February 1787, and finally, George Pretyman (later Sir George Pretyman Tomline), appointed at the tender age of 36. It was an appointment engineered by Pitt the Younger, whom he had tutored at Pembroke College, Cambridge, and for whom he later acted as a private secretary, much favoured for his mathematical skills. One of his sons, John Pretyman, was to succeed John Gordon as archdeacon of Lincoln and many years later, in 1820, Sir George himself was translated to the bishopric of Winchester.

At Cambridge John Green had already held the regius professorship of divinity, the mastership of Corpus Christi College, and the vice-chancellorship, before being appointed to the see of Lincoln in 1761. He had been domestic chaplain to the duke of Somerset, chancellor of the university, and it was his successor, the duke of Newcastle, who propelled him to high office. He was also close to Philip Yorke, 2nd earl of Hardwicke, who had become the university's high steward in 1764. A strong supporter of whig politics, Green engaged royal disfavour in 1772 by voting for a bill for the relief of protestant dissenters. George III commented that 'Green, Green, he shall never be translated'. (John Gascoigne, 'John Green', ODNB). Green's successor at Lincoln in May 1779, Thomas Thurlow, was an Oxford man, who was 'well-liked' and a 'devoted and affectionate husband' to his wife Anne, daughter of William Bere of Lymington, Hampshire (E.I. Carlyle, M. Johnson, 'Thomas Thurlow', ODNB). During his eight years at Lincoln he was a 'persistent seeker of recipients for benefactions'. In 1780, during the Gordon Riots, he was lucky to escape with his life, dressed as a woman. It was this man who quickly rewarded John Gordon, as he related to his stepson in the form of a play-script (Letter 19):

After Dinner — Tete a Tete [.]

Bishop: 'Pray how long have you your House at Cambridge for?'

Chap[lain]: 'My Lord, I have it only from year to year.'

Bishop: 'So if you had an offer elsewhere, you coud quit it when you pleased.'

Chaplain: 'At ½ a year's notice.'

Bishop: 'Well I suppose if the Precentorship shoud become vacant, you woud have no objection to taking it.'

Chaplain: 'No, my Lord, it woud make me the happiest man living.'

Bishop: 'Well Sir you will easily guess that I have had many applications for it – but I rejected them all – being determind to offer it to you, if ever it became vacant.'

Gordon's letters often tell of the tribulations of his office, including the toil of arranging the visitations of the bishop and accompanying his lordship, who was often seated at the bishop's palace at Buckden, then in Huntingdonshire, now in Cambridgeshire. Sykes describes in huge detail the sheer physical labour of the bishop and his entourage, trailing like a travelling salesman around the diocese to perform the three main episcopal functions of ordination, visitation of the clergy and confirmation (Sykes, 1934, pp. 92-146). It was one of Sykes's main criticisms of Benjamin Hoadly, bishop of Winchester that he was lame, and he should never have been enthroned (though his determination perhaps now looks heroic), since 'a prelate unable to ride on horseback, to ride abroad save in a carriage, and to walk without the aid of a stick was manifestly unfitted for …his office'.

The effort of attending the bishop gave Gordon an excellent excuse for his habitual tardiness in letter-writing, which he ascribed to (Letter 6):

> …a certain indolence and listlessness which my illness left behind it; in the next place for the Bishop [of Lincoln]'s carrying away with him all of a sudden from hence to Buckden, where I had the honor to be pretty closely employd in his Lordship's service for about a fortnight.

In the next year, after a 'comfortless Visitation through Leicester and Lincoln shires', he was met on the road with the terrible news that his wife was ill with smallpox, though it was probably a mild form and she survived the attack (Letter 9). And again, in 1774 he wrote: 'At my return from the North, I was called upon almost immediately to attend the Ordination at Buckden' (Letter 17).

He endeavoured to sweeten the toil of his travels by meeting with his stepson, as in April 1770 (Letter 11):

> It might have been managed, when the Bishop [of Lincoln] comes [on] his Visitation into Buckinghamshire, which he sets out upon about the middle of May, and will be at Stony Stratford Wednesday 16th, Buckingham Thursday 17th, Aylesbury Friday and Saturday 18th and 19th, High Wycomb[e] on Sunday for confirmation etc. At some of which places, I shoud hope it might not be very inconvenient for you to let us have a peep at your old face. I am to procede upon my own Visitation [as archdeacon] sooner; which I propose to begin on the 23 inst. and hope to conclude at Lincoln on the 7th of May.

John Gordon was never chancellor of Lincoln – for much of his time it was Dr George Stinton (some of whose sermons are back in print) – though when the biographer James Boswell unexpectedly spent a day at Lincoln, on 25 May 1778, he wrote to Dr Johnson, telling him that he had encountered 'the Reverend Dr Gordon, the Chancellor [sic]', and recording that he 'received me with great politeness as a stranger, and when I informed him who I was, entertained me at his house with the most flattering attention…'. (Womersley, 2008, p. 717).

Gordon's letters are extremely wordy, display a penchant for disputation and reveal a person well able to take care of himself in the kitchen of church politics. He may also have fancied himself as a player in local politics. Between 1767 and 1789 he corresponded (BM Add MSS 35608-80, 38223-471) with Philip Yorke, 2nd earl of Hardwicke, and Charles Yorke, both powerful men in the University of Cambridge and in East Anglia in general, and to Lord Hawkesbury (later 1st earl of Liverpool), who was the first patron of Philip Williams. Local politics in Cambridge from the late seventeenth century to the end of the eighteenth is complex, but involved a gradual transition from a tory ascendancy that emphasised landed interests towards parliamentary reform Pitt-style, with influence moving from the Cotton 'banner', to an alliance of Hardwicke and Yorke interests and later on to Manners and Mortlock (Roach, 1959, pp.68-76). Dr Gordon is a good example of the cleric who exemplified the fact that church and state were brothers and they both prospered best when a healthy respect was shown for the status quo and the social hierarchy of the land. He and Philip Williams must have shared similar views on many things, but he was the better operator.

***

ONE OF THE JOYS of John Gordon's marriage to Anne Williams must have been the acquisition of two ready-made daughters, Frances ('Fanny') aged 21, and Anne ('Nanny'), aged 15. Although their brother was away at New College, Oxford, they still retained a playful relationship with him , even when they were well into their 20s, as shown in a postscript to one of their stepfather's missives in the hand of one of them (Letter 13):

> The Girls my Dear Phee have nothing particular to add except to repeat their very particular request that Master Phee will at Christmas comply with the Dr's aforementioned desire of making a visit at Finch Place – now don't be an Old Fogram thats a good Boy but come and enliven us with a few of thy Witty Crambos upon the Popes birthday or what else thou pleases – so shall thou be the favorite darling of thy maiden S[is]ters.
>
> F[anny] and N[anny] Williams

The sisters were, however, trusted with going out into the world, as Gordon told Philip Williams in May 1770 (Letter 12): 'I have just heard from Nanny – the Girls are both well, but London I'm afraid will turn their heads.' But four years later they appear to have got into the swim (Letter 18):

> Fanny was probably launched on board the Vengeance yesterday, which is a 74 Gun Ship built by Mr Randall, Mrs Panton's neighbour in Q[ueen] Anne Street and they were all to be present at the ceremony, which I suppose woud not be a dry one. She by accounts is to frisk her tail tomorrow at an Assembly at Shooter's Hill with Do. [the same] party, returns to Town on Tuesday, and proposes to see Camb[ridge] on Thursday.

Elsewhere, in November 1778 (Letter 22), John Gordon talks of 'Fanny's Law' – the meaning now lost – and writes:

> ...[she] has had what she used to call some terrible nips or pinches from the Old Man. The Language and Phrase are entirely her own. The meaning, a violent pain in the head and face,

attended with much swelling (which has at last broke and discharged very much) probably arising from a stump, the remains of a Tooth imperfectly drawn some years ago.

He paints a picture of life in the country around Cambridge in the dark days of January. The details are obscure, but the events involved the 'Dittonians', presumably a family from Fen Ditton, a village near Cambridge (another possibility being Ditton Green, near the Upend estate of his wife), and the local parliamentarian Thomas Bromley (1733-1799). His title, the 2nd Baron Montfort of Horseheath, related to a small village near Haverhill where the family, which had made its fortune in Barbados, had an estate. Gordon wrote (Letter 17):

> The Dittonians all well, and so are all other friends. A Rumpus just taken place with the Allixes – Ball there on the 12th Night. Nanny [Anne Williams] invited. Fanny [Frances Williams] at Newmarket – but though Downey was asked from the same House where she was, no notice taken of her. In the mean time she returns to Camb[ridge] and both the Miss W[illiam]s are invited to a ball at Lord Montfort's on the same day. Fanny thinks of accepting the invitation – but Nanny considers herself as engaged. During this suspence, Mrs A[llix] hearing of Fanny's return home, and fearing it shoud seem, lest she shoud come uninvited as she was, and teach Nanny any bad lessons about her. Dear Charley – sends to say, she is sorry, she cannot receive her – upon which both sisters went to Horseheath and on their return next day were stopt at a little Alehouse by the water for 3 or 4 hours. No explanation yet.

Clearly, Lord Montfort was enjoying an expensive lifestyle and three years after Gordon wrote this letter the estate at Horseheath had to be sold, due to the extravagance of him and his brother Henry. The letter shows that the sisters were close to the Allix family, from Swaffham Prior, near Cambridge. Thus in November 1767 John Gordon reported (Letter 6): 'Nanny left us this morning with her Swaffham parents.' Peter or Pierre Allix (1690-1717) of French extraction was a prominent churchman in his day, followed by his namesake son (1705-1758), who served as a vicar of Swaffham Prior.

Like all fathers, John Gordon was ever watchful of approaching matrimony for his stepdaughters. There is never a mention of such a possibility for Frances, but in 1769 he wrote (Letter 11): 'Aunt Bell ...

announces the arrival of a ring from the faithfull Dean to Nanny, and is pleased to wish it was upon another occasion.' This rather cryptic remark presumably means that Anne Williams, aged 22, had received an engagement ring and was anticipating, as 'another occasion', the wedding. In the event, the romance faltered and much later, in 1789, her stepfather may have revealed the name of the suitor. He rejoiced at the appointment of Richard Beadon (1737-1824) to the bishopric of Gloucester, adding (Letter 131):

> We once liked one another very well. I only thought Nanny shoud have been the Bishopess.

Between 1768 and 1770 Beadon had been junior dean at St John's College, Cambridge, and in 1778 he married Rachel Gooch, daughter of the Ely prebendary Dr John Gooch (Nigel Aston, 'Richard Beadon', ODNB), who was 'an old Oxford acquaintance' of Philip Williams (W137). A few years earlier, in 1774, his 'Aunt Bell' had herself being 'smuggled away' by a 'faithful dean' (Letter 18), though an age difference of 30 years surely points to another man! Beadon's career at Cambridge had many parallels with that of Philip Williams's father. In 1768 he was appointed public orator of the university and in 1775 sought election to the mastership of St John's, but failed, by one vote. Thereafter, he prospered in the church and married, but unlike PW(II) he was successful in gaining appointment as master of Jesus College, Cambridge. He also served for a year as vice chancellor of the university, which Aston attributes to his 'exceptional administrative competence'.

Philip Williams's younger sister did eventually marry, but had to wait until the age of 40 before walking up the aisle with the Revd Theodore Vincent Gould (ca 1735-1815). He was a clergyman in his 50s, who for ten years had had the living of Fornham All Saints with Westley, near Bury St Edmunds, Suffolk, and was to serve the parish for 38 years as its 'belov'd and respected rector' (Anon, 1827, pp.135-6). He had been a fellow and tutor at Clare Hall (refounded in 1856 as Clare College), Cambridge, where he graduated 5th wrangler. He was an acquaintance of the poet Thomas Gray, whose friend Norton Nicholls, at a time when the older man was ill, complained that 'Mr Gould's incessant, impertinent Babble, will not let me sleep quietly, nor Mr. Gray talk...' (Mack, 2000, p. 558). We can only speculate what men like Gould, Gordon and Williams thought of Gray's bitter satire, *The Candidate*, published in the 1770s, which lampooned the earl of Sandwich's attempt to be elected High

Steward of the university and ridiculed his overtures to the faculties of Divinity, Jurisprudence and Medicine (Kaul, 1992, p. 226):

> When sly Jemmy Twitcher had smugged up his face
> With a lick of Court whitewash, and pious grimace,
> A-wooing he went, where three sisters of old
> In harmless society guttle [gorge themselves] and scold.

Mr Gould and his bride were married by her brother Philip, who reported to his wife Sarah (Letter 123):

> I have only time to add that Theodore Vincent Gould has this moment introduced himself to me, and from what little I have seen him, I rather like him. I was shaving and dressing, [and] therefore could not pay much attention to his person. He seems to have lost some of his teeth. Tomorrow we are to go to Doctors Commons for a licence, and on Wednesday I am to make use of it.

The comments of Sarah Williams on the prospects for her stepsister are those of an 'experienced wife', albeit one ten years younger. Possibly recalling the problem her sister Charlotte had in arranging a suitable settlement after marriage, she sounds caution and uses the opportunity to air some harrowing gripes about her own marriage (Letter 115):

> I cannot imagine what can be Mr [John] G[ordon]'s scruple about the settlement before marriage, I daresay your sister can clear up this matter to your satisfaction, but I think there should be as little cause left for uneasiness as possible after marriage; cares and anxieties will obtrude themselves when they are least foreseen and expected; look at ourselves, who set out with every prospect of happiness and for a time were happy as we could wish, but now with an affection that I will venture to say has not decreased, I am a most wretched, unhappy creature, separated from the only person I wish to live with, and only meet him to look forward to a repetition of the same misery; if such then are the fruits of the happiest marriages, ought not every precaution to be taken beforehand, that is in our power? Your sister has I doubt not fixed her affections upon a worthy object and will meet with the reward she so justly deserves.

And on the ceremony itself she is less than generous. She uses a family nickname for her stepsister that is an early form of 'dervish' and may indicate her lively character (Letter 124):

> So the Dervise slides quietly into the matrimonial noose on Wednesday! May she have all the comforts I have experienced in the state, without my wretched appendages; as dear and excellent a husband and if she has children may they be as healthy and promising as mine are and for the rest I hope she will be more fortunate; give my love and best wishes to her and in some months I will write to her, long after the time of congratulations is over, all that I leave for sentimental friends, and appoint you my substitute for the present; you will of course tell me in your next whether they stay in town and all their future motions…

The marriage, between a clergyman in his 50s and a 40-year-old spinster, seems to have been a happy one. In surviving letters between Philip Williams and his daughters, written after the death of their mother, there are many mentions of apparently joyful visits to Fornham, where he sometimes gave the sermon (W99). The couple had one daughter – a risky business for a 40-year-old woman. She was named Anne after her mother and in 1816, the year after the death of her father (for whom a memorial was erected in All Saints church, Fornham; Anon, 1827, pp.135-6), she married his successor to the living, William Webb, the newly appointed master of Clare Hall. Philip Williams, who must have been pleased that a strand of his family had eventually reached the 'top table' at Cambridge, confided the forthcoming event to his daughters (W141):

> …the new rector of her father's living, or rather the new master of Clare hall College is the man, and well qualified in every respect does he appear to me for a connection of this sort, under forty, and in other circumstances, desireable. As it will not take place for some time, it is only mentioned to her relations, and you will keep counsel accordingly.

***

PHILIP WILLIAMS had two stepbrothers, Charles and George Gordon, who lived in and about Lincolnshire. Although 20 years his junior, they are an important part of the fabric of his letters and travels. It is evident that as soon as his widowed mother Anne married the Revd John Gordon, on 7 June 1762, the couple wasted no time in starting a family.

6he two boys were born in the biologically shortest time possible: Charles was a honeymoon baby and George was baptised in Cambridge in December 1763. The only reference to them as children by their father is in 1769, when they were perhaps five and six years old; it contains what is probably a coy reference to the Devil's Arse or the Peak Cavern, a spectacular limestone cave with a narrow entrance at Castelton, Derbyshire (Letter 11):

> The Boys are mightily pleased with the Geographical Pastime, talk with great familiarity of the place where the great Sir Isaac Newton was born,† and of the wonders of the Devil's A- of peak.
>
> †I am out, they tell me, it is the place where he received his Education

Newton was a 'local boy made good', who first attended day schools in the village of Woolsthorpe, Lincolnshire, and then the nearby King Edward VI Grammar School, Grantham. His scientific and mathematical discoveries probably did more to change the direction of the University of Cambridge, and indeed the intellectual and cultural complexion of England, and ultimately Europe, than any other single happening (Gascoigne, 1989, p. 2). In 1792 Dr Gordon's second son, George, became rector of Sedgebrook with East Allington, only a short distance from Woolsthorpe.

As the boys grew up John Gordon toyed with the idea of sending them to Winchester College, but in the end he settled for Rugby School, in the Warwickshire town of that name, about 60 miles west of Cambridge. It was obviously closer to home and he may also have got wind of the fact that the school was in the process of being reformed and given a new head master. This was Thomas James, educated at Eton College and King's College, Cambridge, who was to take the number of pupils at Rugby to a high of 245. Just before his arrival, in 1777, the school had been reformed by an act of parliament that gave assistant masters a salary (long before Winchester College masters; *see* pp. 96-8) and brought in new rules and regulations. James built on this, literally adding new schoolrooms and introducing the methods of discipline and teaching used at Eton, notably a tutorial system, boarding houses and the use of senior pupils or monitors to regulate discipline. He also extended the curriculum and introduced a wide range of extracurricular activities. In short, he made a school that was more modern in outlook than Winchester College. Like many boarding schools of the period, including Winchester, he had to contend with pupil insurrections. In 1777, after he had left, the school was struck by its Great Rebellion, which was only quelled by the local militia. In 1806 the Warwickshire school appointed Wykehamist John Wooll as its headmaster.

Both the Gordon boys left Rugby for Cambridge, but it seems that they were not at first inclined to follow in their father's footsteps. Charles went up first, as a sizar and then scholar, to Pembroke College, at the young age of 15, but did not graduate. Instead he joined the Army with a commission, presumably purchased by his father. After a few years he tired of military life and went back to Cambridge, to Trinity Hall, and graduated in 1788. In the previous year, no doubt with the helping hand of his father, by now precentor of Lincoln, he had been instituted vicar of Wellingore, Lincolnshire, and by the grace of the bishop of York collated to the vicarship of Edwinstowe, Nottinghamshire (where popular belief has it that Robin Hood married Maid Marion). After graduation his Wellingore appointment was regularised by the processes of 'cession' and 'collation' on the same day. The process reeks of the sort of manoeuvres that men like John Gordon revelled in. Perhaps he can be forgiven for helping a son who seems to have lost the plot. But he advanced no further and died at the early age of 39.

George, unlike his older brother, thrived at Cambridge: he went up to St John's College and graduated 14th wrangler. In his final year he was one of two Chancellor's Medallists, chosen for excellence in 'classical learning'. Two years later, in 1786, as a Senior Bachelor, he was one of the two Members' Prizemen, for the 'best Dissertations in Latin Prose' (*The Cambridge University Calendar*, 1807, pp. 63 and 68). He seemed set for the law and when studying in London at Lincoln's Inn he often dined Philip Williams, or joined parties of people from the Fens and elsewhere (Letters 90, 98, 101, 103, 106 and 123). At about this time he seems also to have fallen in love, but was not allowed to marry, as we discover in a letter of Sarah Williams (Letter 115):

> ...your brother George's is a disappointment and of that sort which is apt to make a lasting impression, upon a mind like his, that is a good deal locked up in itself; on the other hand he is too young to marry yet and set down ... and I always deprecate long engagements, and it is to be hoped that at two and twenty he may get over it...

John Gordon was an argumentative man of fixed ideas and it is hardly surprising that this trait got in the way of the desire of his son to marry as

(*Previous page*) [17] On the way to St Cross and Compton, a view of St Michael's church, Winchester, from Culver Close, 1826, by George Shepherd (© *Winchester College*).

(*Above*) [18] Joseph Warton, a headmaster of Winchester College 1766-93, son of the rector of Basingstoke and, (*below*) [19], his immensely philanthropic successor, William Stanley Goddard, a protégé of Sarah Williams's father, Thomas Collins (© *Winchester College*)

(*Above*) [20] a 1008-page set of proofs of the ill-fated edition of the works of Polybius that Philip Williams worked on for 37 years, and (*right*) [21] a long note, revealing the fear that he and many others had of the 'dangerous turbulence of Democracy'.

Two very different caricatures by James Sayers of Charles Wolfran Cornwall, Philip Williams's patron, and Speaker of the House of Commons: (*left*) [22] doing business in the House, and (*below*) [23] 'Gulliver casting a damper upon the royal fireworks at Lilliput'. (© *National Portrait Gallery, London*)

(*Right*) [24] Folliott Herbert Walker Cornewall [sic], second cousin of the Speaker of the House of Commons, Charles Wolfran Cornwall and his chaplain before Philip Williams, a portrait of 1813 by William Owen (© *National Portrait Gallery, London*).

(*Below*) [25] Privy Garden, beside the Palace of Whitehall, where the Speaker's chaplains lodged in his official residence.

Charles Lord Hawkesbury

Drawn from Life by C.Benazech, & Engrav'd by C Warren

Publish'd according to Act of Parliament. Jan.y 7.th 1791.

ADDISCOMBE

(*Above*) [26] the politician Charles Jenkinson, 1st baron Hawkesbury (later the 1st earl of Liverpool), for whom Philip Williams was at one time a private chaplain (an engraving of 1791 by Charles Warren, after Charles Benazech; © *National Portrait Gallery, London*) and (*left*) [27] his country seat, Addiscombe House, Croydon, then in Surrey, a frequent haunt of Philip Williams.

Some of many people Philip Williams knew in London and elsewhere (*clockwise from top left*): [28] Harry Peckham in about 1762, later recorder of Chichester (by Joseph Wright of Derby); [29] Michael Wodhull, minor poet and book collector; [30] Jonathan Shipley, bishop of St Asaph; and [31] Beilby Porteus, bishop of London, and an anti-slaver (mezzotint ca 1800, from portrait by John Hoppner; © *National Portrait Gallery, London*)

WINCHESTER, 1798.

TO BE RUN FOR,

On MONDAY the 17th of September inflant,

THE CITY PLATE,

Confifting of Four large Pieces, of elegant workmanfhip, gilt with gold; the winning Horfe to have the whole. Horfes of all ages are allowed to ftart. Catch weights. Croffing and joftling will be allowed as at former Races.

The following Horfes are now in training:

CRIB-BITER, a horfe that never ftarted for this Plate before, was got by Young Harry, his grandfire Old Sir P——t who won this Plate feveral times.—The odds run in favour of this horfe.

SELL ALL, a noted *Stallion*, got by Old Deceitful: he has won the Plate feveral times, but never deferved it; he always got it by croffing and joftling.

BLUE PIG, alias DICK BACON. This horfe won two Plates when he ran for the late D*** of C*****s, after which he was entered in the name of L**d T****e, but running *booty* no dependance can be placed on him.

DOCTOR, an old horfe and pretty ftaunch; has won this Plate before, but it is thought, as he has been played tricks with lately, he will run on the wrong fide of the poft.

GALLIPOT. This horfe has alfo won feveral Plates, but it is thought he will ftand but little chance, having made the bargain not to take the whip hand.

FEARFULL. This horfe has ftarted before and won, but, being very fhy, it is thought he will ftand no chance.

SKIPPING JACK. This horfe has alfo won two Plates, but being now no better than an *old hunter*, cannot poffibly win.

RUSHLIGHT, who has won a Plate; and it was thought at that time he would make a famous ftaunch horfe and fhew fome blood; but, being turned out in P*****'s lawn, got a kick from fome of the above horfes, fo that it is thought he can never win another.

SHELL-FISH, a dungy horfe that never won nor never will.

DICK DREADNOUGHT. This horfe has ftarted three or four times, always came in fecond, but running FAIR could never gain the Plate, though it is the wifh of the Jockey Club he fhould.

Other Horfes expected to enter at the poft, viz.

SQUIB, alias SAM the YOUNG DEVIL, or STOCKBRIDGE PUNCHINELLO; JEW JACK; BANKER; BUTTERFLY JOHN; TOM POST-MAN; &c. &c. &c. &c. but none of them ftand any chance except Squib, he having been in training fome time and has the art of *turning* quicker than any of the reft, though they are all pretty well verfed in that manœuvre, except Fearfull and Dreadnought.

All Difputes to be decided by the majority of voices, Yes or No.

To ftart from the Town Clock at Eleven in the Forenoon.

Printed by PETER QUIZ, (for the independant Members of the Jockey Club,) at the Sign of the Stallion, near the Devil's Ditch.

(Opposite) [32] The Square, Winchester, 1827, by George Shepherd (© *Winchester College*). (*Above*) [33] a spoof race card, lampooning Winchester worthies including the grandee Sir Henry Paulet St John Milday, Henry Penton MP, surgeon Joseph Barker, one of 'the tribe' of Earles, attorney John Ridding, draper John Silver, grocer and soap-boiler RH Lloyd and upholder John Crabb (©*Hampshire Record Office*).

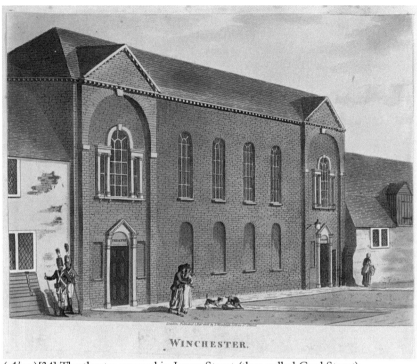

WINCHESTER.

(*Above*)[34] The theatre opened in Jewry Street (then called Gaol Street), Winchester, in 1785, a print of 1803 by T. Woodfall Villers (© *Hampshire Record Office*). (*Below*) [35] No 11, The Close, Winchester, the prebendal residence allocated to Philip Williams in 1797, when he resigned a stall at Canterbury for one closer to home, though he never occupied the house.

(*Above*) [36] the namesake elder son of
Philip Williams and his wife Sarah, who
pursued a successful career as a lawyer
(a sketch by George Woodley) and
(*right*) [37] the stern gaze of his younger
brother, Charles, who pursued a quieter
path as tutor to the Stanhope family
(earls of Chesterfield) and rector of
Gedling, Nottinghamshire. (© *Winchester
College*)

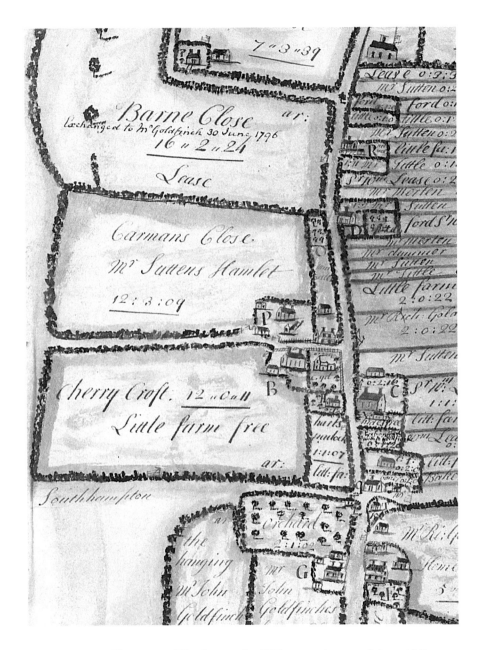

[38] Compton village, near Winchester, in 1735, scarcely out of the middle ages, a detail from a map by William Burgess of Sir William Heathcote's estate, showing the church and rectory, facing each other on opposite sides of Carman's Lane, still so named (© *Hampshire Record Office.*)

(*Above*) [39] the church of All Saints at Compton, the village near Winchester, where Philip Williams was rector for 50 years.

(*Right*) [40] a native of Winchester, George Isaac Huntingford, once a curate at Compton, where he is buried, a warden of Winchester College and successively bishop of Hereford and Gloucester.

(*Opposite*) [41] Lydiard Park, Lydiard Tregoze, Wiltshire, once the seat of the St John family, an engraving of 1808 by F[rederick] Nash. (©*Lydiard House & Park, Swindon*)

Two sisters, two memorials: (*right*) [42] to Sarah Williams, who died in child-bed aged 30, in All Saints church, Compton, near Winchester, and (*below*)[43] in the church of St Mary, Lydiard Tregoze, the hatchment of Charlotte Viscountess Bolingbroke (née Collins), who died aged 44 in 1804, estranged from her husband.

GEORGE RICHARD.
VISCOUNT BOLINGBROKE & ST JOHN.

[44] The 3rd viscount Bolingbroke, George Richard St John, who married Charlotte Collins, sister of Sarah Williams, and gave her a title, but did little to make her happy. A portrait by John Hoppner. (©*Lydiard House & Park, Swindon*)

a young graduate with no profession. In 1791, at the more conventional age of 27, George did get a wife, a 'Miss Tomlinson of Lincoln'. By this time he had given up the law, been ordained deacon and priest in swift succession and been instituted rector of Gumley, near Leicester, by his father's third episcopal patron, the bishop of Lincoln George Pretyman. Thereafter he followed a glittering church career, with many parish and cathedral appointments, including the deanships of Exeter and later Lincoln. In 1819 he might have been bishop of Peterborough, one of the least well endowed sees, but declined the offer.

Thus, although both of John Gordon's sons had started life with the idea of not entering the church, even with a father in a position of influence, neither had found a path sufficiently agreeable or rewarding to compete with a career as a cleric. Charles Gordon may not have had the steadiness and intelligence of his younger brother, nor the temperament to enjoy a military life; but surely George had the necessary qualities to become a lawyer. A late surge of piety may have inclined them to the priesthood, but it was no doubt laced with a large dose of pragmatism. For those who wanted to follow a gentlemanly lifestyle, there were perhaps few better options.

***

A FIXED POINT in the family landscape of Philip Williams in the Fens was a maiden aunt, a sister of his father, generally referred to as Aunt Bell. Her full name was Heleonora (or Helenora) Theabella Williams and she appears in the manuscripts of William Cole (1714-1782), the antiquary and diarist of Bletchley, Buckinghamshire, who wrote (W241): 'I have often dined with her at Mr James Bentham's at Ely, where she and her Sister boarded.' They were in learned, but eccentric company: Bentham was an accomplished cathedral historian, whose *History and Antiquities of the Conventual and Cathedral Church of Ely*, first published in 1771, was very successful in its day and is now regarded as a classic of his kind. Cole was privately amazed that 'so good a book should come from such Idiot appearance', but it does seem to have been Bentham's own work, albeit aided by others. He also contributed, together with the Wykehamist poet Thomas Warton and Winchester Catholic historian John Milner, to *Essays on Gothic Architecture*, first published in 1800. Perhaps the conversation of Aunt Bell and her friends touched on these interests as well as circling his many others, which included 'cathedral music, the drainage of the fens and driving turnpike roads through them' (T.R. Cocke: In 'James Bentham', ODNB).

After the death of her sister, Miss Williams apparently lived as a companion to 'Old Mrs Green, the Bishop's Widow', in the 'Dean of Salisbury's Prebendal House' (W241). She often appears in the letters of John Gordon to his stepson, who was at pains to unravel the will of PW(II), which was entailed with the obligation to contribute to her income. Hence there are references to 'a degree in chancery to pay your Aunts fortunes' and her 'shares of Ransome Moor [a small estate near Doddington]' (Letter 10), as well as 'money advanced to Aunt Bell', who is described as having had 'her 40 years tug at' the estate in Wales that the family still held, probably at Llanwnda, near Caernarfon (Letter 38). When Philip Williams's sisters wanted to sell some untenanted land, Gordon commented (Letter 39):

> Aunt Bell also was consulted on the subject. And she aukwardly enough has referrd the Girls (as I cannot help calling them) to Charles Cole (by the by, my pen has made his name as black as a coal, with less resentment on my part, than I might have shewn in another instance) which shews her to be more under the guidance of that worthy Relative, than I coud have wishd.

He is referring here to a nephew of Miss Williams, Charles Nalson Cole, a lawyer of the Middle Temple and the son of her sister Mary (b.1693), who in about 1720 had married the son of an Ely apothecary, the Revd Charles Cole, rector of North Crawley, Buckinghamshire: as John Gordon says, at this point in the letter his pen floods and he uses the accident to reveal the tensions in the family that Charles Nalson engendered.

More broadly, the Cole family also unwittingly set a trap for the genealogical researches of PW(VI) and Mrs Edwyn Jervoise, who consulted the manuscripts of the antiquary William Cole - and probably the Index of G.J. Gray published in 1912 - and at first concluded, incorrectly, that he was a member of the family. There was, indeed, a William Cole in the family tree of the Williams family, not the antiquary, but a son of Revd Charles Cole and Mary. The family researchers were encouraged in their views by that fact that Cole the antiquary often mentioned Charles Nalson Cole in his manuscripts. The confusion was heightened because the Cole MSS, now in the British Library (115 volumes amongst the Additional Manuscripts), contain references to PW(I) and his son, PW(II) – i.e. Philip Williams's father and grandfather, as well as his stepfather, Dr John Gordon. Eventually, the confusion was recognised, as Mrs Jervoise indicated in a note to her father about a visit to the British Museum to view the Cole manuscripts (W294):

I have just had the William Cole book, not our W.Cole but he mentions ours as his double namesake, son of Rev. Chas. Cole of N. Crawley.

Aunt Bell is painted in the record as 'stout and hearty' (Letter 13), a lady of beauty, a firm favourite of the cathedral close, but not easily impressed. After her death in 1789 a memorial was erected in Ely Cathedral by her lawyer nephew (W309-310; TNA/Prob11/1182/55). It had the same bogus Williams coat-of-arms (*see* Chapter 1) that tops the two memorials to Sarah and Philip Williams in Compton church. In one of the 115 large-format volumes of manuscripts of the antiquary Cole resides a ravishing 20-line verse sent to him in 1779 by a 'Sam Knight Esq' and written in 1737 by the author and politician Soame Jenyns (1704-1787). Described by Cole as 'of a finical and beauish turn', he was obviously infatuated with Heleonora Theabella, and wrote a panegyric in her praise. A few lines depict lover and loved (W241, citing BM/Add. MS 334498):

> There lives bright Nymph, so charming and Fair,
> My heart will scarce ever get out of her Snare.
> Her shape's so genteel, and so pretty her size,
> Such rosy red Lips, and such rolling black Eyes
> ...
> Her Lips move so sweetly, her Eyes do so shine,
> That I'm sure here Devotions will always Spoil mine.
> The Name of this Picture I need not to tell:
> Who sees it must know, 'tis dear Charming Miss Belle.

Whether Soame Jenyns ever wanted to take his devotions further as the object of his desire entered her 30's is not clear. If she ever saw his verses she must surely have regarded them with alarm, as he was a married man, albeit with a wife who was finally to desert him. Jenyns was apparently a most unattractive man, with broken teeth, but a dandyish mode of dressing and good conversation. He was the son of Sir Roger Jenyns, seated at Bottisham Hall, six miles east of Cambridge, and 'Receiver and Expenditor General' of the Bedford Level Corporation in London - the body that came to direct the drainage of part of the Fens - of which Miss Williams's nephew Charles Nalson Cole was 'the register'. Like Aunt Bell's brother, PW(II), Jenyns went up to St John's College, Cambridge, but left without a degree. He subsequently sat for the county for Cambridgeshire (*History of Parliament*, 1754-1790, 1964, pp. 217-21). In his Epistle to Lord Lovelace (1735), included in the four-volume collection of his works (1790), edited by Charles Nalson, he described Bottisham Hall as a place with:

Choice books, safe horses, wholesome liquor,
Clean girls, backgammon, and the vicar.

Was Aunt Bell one of these 'clean girls'? In the event, she never married, though in the summer of 1774 she appears to have been courted, as John Gordon tells his stepson (Letter 18):

> Aunt Bell shoud be with us – but the Faithfull Dean (with whom we took a Dinner last Wednesday) has smuggled her away to Cottenham and vows he will not part with her till _____he goes to London so you know as there is not likely to be any deficiency in the list of Maiden Williams, one woud be unwilling to throw any damp (more than what the prudence of sixty and the neighbourhood of the Fens may supply) upon such a little tender connection.

As mentioned above, John Gordon's daughter Anne, may have once been in love with Richard Beadon, junior dean of St John's College, Cambridge, also described as a 'faithful dean', but Aunt Bell was surely involved with another dean, ecclesiastical or academic.

Miss Williams was obviously popular with her nieces and nephews. In 1781 Philip Williams stayed with her at her house in Ely during one of his trips to the Fens (W351) and eight years later his sister Fanny had 'got well to Cambridge, proposed visiting Aunt Bell for a Day … and setting off the next morning for Fornham' (Letter 131). That such an apparently attractive woman as Aunt Bell could get through life well without marriage, and yet without apparently any occupation, is proof of the fact that in an age of male ascendancy women could still make firm decisions to go their own way, albeit within a family able to provide support. If she had been active with her pen, who knows what novels of life in the Fens in the late eighteenth century she might have written.

14. *'The happiness of being with you'*

A CENTRAL ISSUE which dominates the Letters is the separation for various periods that Sarah and Philip experienced between May 1784, when he took up his duties at Westminster as the Speaker's chaplain, and September 1787, when she died. He seems to have been comfortable in the London scene, though at the beginning of his office he expressed a whiff of homesickness (or was it for Sarah's benefit?) when he wrote (Letter 49):

> I would give something to exchange at this instant the beautiful prospect of the Thames, Surry hills, and Westminster Bridge, for the Itchin, Catharine Hill, and Black-bridge.

For her part, there are many passages that express feelings similar to the following (Letter 100):

> I am not at all relieved by your letter as you may guess; I had flattered myself that you would have been able to have said something decisive about that most desired event, your coming home, I am sensible that you cannot command events, but I cannot help looking up to you for relief in all my distresses and I need not tell you that this is one of the most afflicting kind, indeed I can hardly bear up against it, and if I knew of any wretched hovel where I could hide myself with my children in the country till you come home, I should be glad to do it, merely to avoid being asked by every person I meet when you can come home. If there is to be an adjournment for ten days, it may give you an opportunity of attending the [Winchester] College meeting, otherwise I cannot wish to see you again in the way you came at Easter, when you can stay I shall rejoice to have you, you know not half the love I have for you or half my misery.

On another occasion she expresses a rare touch of cynicism (Letter 107):

If by next Sunday you should not be pretty certain of the time of Parliament's rising, you had better write a civil letter to our Inky Head [Joseph Warton], desiring him to put off the meeting for a longer time, in case of accidents, the second of August is in three weeks you know, and by the time these Irish propositions have been handed from the Lord's to Commons, some fresh spectre may be raised for them to stare at.

She yearned to spend some time with him when he was in London and the Letters illustrate the sort of accommodation that she sought, as well as the difficulties faced by a couple with limited means. Bringing up a family in a quiet and settled place whilst the breadwinner goes off to the capital is a situation still endured by countless commuters who might prefer to live in a plum position in the former villages of Chelsea or Hampstead, but cannot afford it. More than 200 years ago, Sarah and Philip were facing a similar problem, compounded by the fact that he only needed to be in London when parliament sat, which was not entirely predictable.

The dates of Letters between them broadly reflect the timing of parliamentary sessions (*see* Appendix III), with the exception of 1786, when none survives and 1787 when none survives after 1 April The reason for these gaps are that in 1786, as already mentioned (*see* Chapter 9), Philip was ill, and after April 1787, as will be shown, Sarah was living in London. The possibility of reducing the burden of separation surfaced in the very first missive she wrote after Philip had taken up his post in May 1784 (Letter 50):

Papa is very good, and spends more time with me than I believe he can well spare, because he thinks that I am not quite comfortable. I have one thing to say to you upon that subject, which is, that you would omit no opportunity of getting information about the rents of houses and lodgings in town, in the different parts of it; and also the price of furniture, that is the rent of hire of furniture. You know our house at Winchester will in future stand us in £50 per annum; butcher's meat and bread are the same in London that they are with us, and we can easily dispense with luxuries, many articles such as tea and sugar will be cheaper. …. You will I am sure do me the justice to believe that I have as little inclination as you can have to involve you in expence, for in fact I should only injure my dear children and myself; but I look forward with horror to a three year banishment, and what with your engagements at Oxford, and other occurrences that may arrive, it will be little short of it. … I hope you will not be displeased at what I have said above, or mention it to any one; if I am disappointed and things turn out different from my wishes, I have a never failing resource in my religion, which will always prevent my fretting and repining to the prejudice of my health.

It was clear that with three young children, and carrying another, she already feels the loss of her husband's company; during the three years of life that remained to her, this overwhelming feeling of loss and desperation only escalated. Was Philip uncaring, hard-hearted or just plain lazy in not making some arrangements for her to live within meeting distance? Or was Sarah unrealistic and naïve, and did she ever really believe that something of this kind would work? He had board and lodging in the Speaker's House in Privy Garden, in the palace of Whitehall. He was so much part of the Cornwall family that on one occasion he surprised the Speaker's wife (Letter 108):

> Mrs C had forgot to lock the water-closet door, and seeing it a-jar, in I bolted, and catched her sitting upright as a dart, reading the news-paper.

His duties as chaplain to the House of Commons were extremely light, but, as his letters made plain, he spent much time dining with the great and the good – partly to fulfil his official role and partly to rub shoulders with those who might be able to grant him patronage. To expect him to follow that sort of life alongside a wife and children, in the centre of a city that was a midden of low life and awash with poverty stricken ruffians of all kinds was hardly realistic. Although the Speaker lived with his wife, they were much older, had a grown-up family and were far better heeled. To find suitable lodgings for a family and servants at a suitable price within a reasonable distance of Westminster was not easy. And what sort of life would it have been for a woman in the 'monstrous' city (White, 2012), who since childhood had lived in and around Winchester College and, as a result, had many friends and acquaintances in the area? Even so, suffering from the first taste of separation, she persisted (Letter 52):

> I am truly sorry that I have given you any uneasiness by what I said in my last letter; whatever I may suffer, in future, I will say nothing more of the matter; but as I am going to take leave of the subject, I will just tell you what my thoughts are upon it: that I am not very easy or comfortable without you is out of all dispute, but that I will gratify myself at any rate and at the expence of my poor children is a thing the farthest from my thoughts; we live up to the

full of our income at present and whilst we live in Winchester most continue to do so; now if I could have a small house that would just hold me and my children in the neighbourhood of London, within four or five miles, you could come to me every Saturday and stay 'till Monday; besides many other days that you would be wanted and as you would be so much from home, I could live in a very frugal manner and I daresay spend less than we do at present; in this case our house at Winchester might be sold, if we can get a purchaser, which would get rid of that incumbrance, and we should have Compton to return to, at the time we wanted it, and our furniture 'till such time might be deposited in the College; remember I want nothing to be done rashly, but I would wish you to enquire what the price of a small ready furnished house will be in one of the villages near London, that I may state the expense in my own mind – and so like your old antagonist I say fiat.

Only six weeks later, her desperation rings out (Letter 58):

There should seem by Dr B's letter [from Henry Bathurst?] to be a pressing call for your presence at Oxford, which I would by no means have you neglect... though it is a melancholy consideration to me that the little money you are to have should {be} spent in this manner, and which I could dispose of with so much satisfaction in lodgings in London in the winter; if you lose me out of it, I hope to God you will take care of the poor children.

During the Christmas holidays it seems that he suggested she should return with him to London and spend some time with an old friend, Miss Pyke, 'who much wishes it'. The implication is that he has found her in a state of deep depression and hopelessness (familiar to many young mothers) and wants to offer a solution (Letter 78):

Consider of it, and vary the scene, if only for a fortnight. If your appetite does not return, venture upon a little puke, and keep back one of those papers [ipecacuanha, a medicine] you are to send to Midhurst.

By return, she told him that the youngest child, Charles 'takes his weaning perfectly well and has no complaint but crossness', that her only health problem is 'a dreadful cold', which has lasted for ten days, but her 'spirits' are extremely low due to his absence, and are likely to remain so 'for some years'. This, of course, was an exaggeration, as she could expect him home during the recesses, but clearly it weighed heavily on her mind. Even so, she declined his suggestion (Letter 79):

> … I am much obliged to Miss Pyke and you for the scheme you have suggested, but it is better as it is, for that I can ever tear myself away from a place where you are, is more than I fear I could prevail upon myself to do…

This pattern of protest, suggestion, consideration and ultimately rejection of a proffered solution was recurrent. It would be harsh to dub Sarah a 'drama queen', but she evidently gained relief from pouring out her troubles, in an almost endless stream, and it is hardly surprising, therefore, that his responses were infrequent and inconclusive. It is clear that she was always trying to come up with a solution to 'her problem' but he, unwilling to risk anything, refused to take her seriously. Taking a family of four to London would have been a herculean task and she seems to have realised this. In April 1785, her sister Charlotte was about to take a trip to London to seek medical advice for her sickly daughter, Mary. She suggested that Sarah might like to accompany her, but she shied away (Letter 87), saying 'had it been any where but to London I would have gone with the greatest pleasure with her.' Again in June 1785, a month before parliament was to rise, Philip is still not certain what she wants to do for the next session and poses the question again, albeit curtly and in the final paragraph of a long letter packed with other matters (Letter 103):

> You have never told me what I shall do about lodgings next year.

Her reply is as specific as it could be, and must have daunted Philip. But it reeks with unreality (or 'vision', in her language) and even she sounds as if she does not expect it to happen (Letter 104):

> With regard to lodgings for next Winter, I can do nothing at this distance, but you must enquire the price of lodgings, in different places that are not very distant from you, one room to sleep in with a large bed and a tent bed would hold me and co., the two girls, myself and the maid, we must have the use of a kitchen, to have a scrag of mutton dressed in; this is all that I can say, for I look upon the scheme to be quite visionary and not {more} likely to take place next year that {it} did {th}is, we shall not be richer, and {t}herefore the impediments will not be fewer, if it has not been practicable for me to go this year, what will make it more so hereafter?

A letter written two years later indicates that at some time in 1786, the year during which Philip was ill, she did in fact spend some time in London, though it sounds as if it was a disaster, perhaps due to a miscarriage. But she is as unhappy as ever when he is away and is willing to have another try (Letter 118):

> ...with regard to my coming to London, I shall not do it before Easter, afterwards I must try it, because my situation of body [she is pregnant] will by that time be full enough for me, though from the experience I had last year, I don't promise myself much, except spending my money; my scheme of happiness has been cruelly destroyed and I have no resource from which I can expect relief...

Her next letter was written in a tone of hard-bitten misery edging on self-pity; she was obviously near the end of her tether and called herself 'not nice' and a 'feeble Governess' (Letter 119):

> You had better look at some lodgings for me, there is no occasion to trouble Miss Pyke with me and my miseries, I am not nice, any garret that is tolerably quiet, will do for me; my maid's room must be within mine or next to it, I should like best a house that has no other lodgers in it, quiet is all I aim at; every idea of comfort is out of the question, that is what in this wor{ld I} never expect to know again; I am in {all} respects very indifferent; God in his good{ness will} mend all, and take you and my children into his protection, if it is not permitted me to have the happiness of living with you and them...

A week later and the scheme was still alive: she talked of travelling up to London in 'the 'Dilly' – an abbreviation of 'Diligence', a type of coach – (Letter 125) with Letitia Mildmay, a daughter of Carew Mildmay and his wife of Shawford House, near Winchester, 'who is in distress for a chaperon ... as she takes no maid.' Sarah is happy to oblige, as 'they are all so very kind and friendly' (Letter 120). It is clear that the previous attempts to find suitable accommodation for her in London have failed and this time the plan is to take advantage of an offer from his friend Lovelace Bigg-Wither to stay with him in a house he is to rent. The two men are scouting for a suitable place, though there are problems (Letter 123):

> He prefers a situation north of Oxford road, and Mr M [a landlord] has sent him an account of what we looked at, which if

he closes with I am afraid you will be cramped, and if he does not
I fear he will not be able to get a larger house within his price,
which he does not chuse to extend beyond 5 guineas.

Sarah is, however, determined to go – amongst her reasons may even be a
hint that she wants to find out why he is getting nowhere in his search for
preferment (Letter 124):

> I shall go to London, and if I find the hurry and bustle of that
> place too much for me, I will either go into Sussex [probably to
> Midhurst to her father's] or come home ... you neither get
> preferment, or a promise of any; you know you have before said
> that we should never again be separated, [but] I have lived long
> enough to be sensible that much more is often said than is meant,
> and whilst matters can be adjusted to the satisfaction of all parties,
> with the sacrifice only of my happiness, it is a trifle that must be
> left out of the scale.

She had previously expressed doubts about his belief (or was it an
excuse?) that mingling with the great and good in London would bring its
rewards (Letter 105):

> How many months are there from the 21st of January [when he
> left to go up to Westminster] to I suppose the same day in
> August? More than four I doubt [not] – think of this and never be
> positive again, had you for once given up your opinion I should at
> this moment have had the happiness of being with you we should
> have been just as rich and I don't think your dignity would have
> suffered in the eyes of the world, because you lived with wife and
> family.

Overall, it is a tale of a woman who just could not cope with separation
from her husband, a man who was not making use of the opportunities
offered by his position in the capital, and of a city that was growing rich
quickly and getting less accessible to the middling sort. Besides, Philip did
not want his life at the centre of power, mixing with the great and the
good (all men, of course), to be complicated by a wife and children, as
recognised in an unpublished essay by Winchester College history teacher
G.H. Blore, himself a bachelor until retirement (Blakiston, 1974;
WCA/E10/14):

> She loved her husband and often found his absence intolerable,
> when life pressed hard on her, and he was amusing himself in

London. She would gladly have moved to London to be with him, but he constantly urged practical difficulties and evaded the question. No doubt a Speaker's chaplain found life in London easier as a bachelor. She would gladly have surrendered part of his preferment and lived more cheaply, if they could make a home together ... but Philip could not bear to descend from the rank which he had reached or to quit the company which he enjoyed.

***

SARAH'S MISERY when Philip was not with her is painful to read. Repeatedly and in similar terms she leaves him in no doubt that she was on the edge of some awful psychological – even psychiatric – abyss. Her missives are a thesaurus of woe (Letters 44-125 passim):

I feel that I cannot a second time endure to be separated from you… I wish I could send you a journal of myself that would give you half the pleasure that your's did me. My days are so much alike that, when I tell you I get up and breakfast at the usual time; work till dinner, dine with my children, and walk out with them in the evening, you have my whole history since your departure. … the happy hours I have spent with you, a sad contrast to those I now drag on. … I am very un{hap}py, and seeing no prospect of alteration … I am glad to find we are to meet again some time or other... the last time you said any thing upon the subject, which was a fortnight ago, you talked of Wednesday three weeks, you now talk of a fortnight more, which I fear will be three weeks at least … I wish I did not love you half so well as I do, I might then feel that peace and quiet, which at present I never know …the day you left me I could not go out of my own house, I felt so many achs of body and mind that I may set it down as the most wretched day I have yet known, but it is gone and may I never spend such another … I thought I should never have recovered your last visit…write more next time, I am very wretched at the idea of a mu{ch} longer separation … two more years of it! I shall never see the end of it I doubt... I should at this moment have had the happiness of being with you we should have been just as rich and I don't think your dignity would have suffered in the eyes of the world, because you lived with wife and family. … [the day of your return] will never come and I believe it will be better for you if it does not, you will meet one of the most wretched creatures… my spirit is harassed to death and I cannot fight up at all… I am very grumbling, and miserable, hardly able to crawl on, wretched, wretched days that will never end, my sole reward for doating upon {you} and my children. ...

Some husbands might have dismissed all this as the behaviour of 'a nagging wife', or much worse, but there is no evidence that Philip Williams ever took this line. She was obviously aware that she was a depressive and that he has a much more positive personality (W53):

> ...I should be much better and {happier a} woman if I could keep my uneasiness to my{self}, but as {ma}tters are at present, I am very un{hap}py, and seeing no prospect of alteration, I am not apprehensive without reason; I strive to get other ideas, and make a point of never refusing any engagement, whether agreeable or otherwise; hoping that it may be a means of giving another train to my thoughts, but it is just the same, the same object returns incessantly, and in the end I fear it may be too much for my constitution, good as it is; you may be sure I take all the care I can of myself; I have every reason to wish to live, and by no means think myself fit to die. You are of a happier constitution than I am, you love me with reason, and I love you without; but enough of a subject that must be irksome to you. I will do as well as I can and trust to providence for the rest...

Although the misery of separation was mostly hers, and Philip was much less affected, it did occasionally get to him, as in July 1785, when he admitted that 'never was a being more tired, and almost wearied of existence' (Letter 110) and 'every day produces a new report about the rising of parliament and the times of ... assembling again' and, frustrated by the uncertainty, he makes a clear statement of commitment and orders her 'not [to] Martha [moan] about it, or mention or think any more of it' (Letter 106; *see also* p. 114):

> London grows so insufferably stupid, and every body is running away except him who most wishes it, so that I shall have nothing and nobody to write about. As proof of it, I shall begin quarelling with you for your last paragraph. If I have any dignity it is derived from you, and if I have any pride, it is in exhibiting you to my acquaintance, and you know as well as I do, that I look forward with the utmost impatience to the time when my whole life and existence will be devoted to you and my family, and our domesticity be separated only by the sisters three.

What can be made of Sarah's litany of misery? Almost every letter includes at least one passage in which she talks of being wretched. It usually starts off with some statement to the effect that she can no longer tolerate his absence or that an assurance that parliament will soon be rising cannot be credited. Then she often makes a passionate statement of heart-breaking woe and rounds off by saying it doesn't matter if she survives or not, except that the children would suffer, and that he is her greatest love. As time passes, she puts more and more trust in God's providence.

It is clear that she had a personality that needed to unburden itself frequently. There is a submissive edge to her complaining, throwing herself on his charity in a way that may have heightened his sense of importance. So frequent was her misery that it is surprising that she did not drown herself in the Itchen, as Winchester pupils did from time to time, generally by accident. Was it her way of working off the frustration of being a captive, intelligent mother trapped by four children and a house to run (and a parish!), with a husband in London having a good time, but not climbing the clerical ladder? She is often at her wit's end, but although she is disarmingly frank she generally holds off from ranting and remains articulate and rational. Often her 'martha-ing', as she terms it, is a brief sentence or two dropped in between other less alarming items, but in one letter written after nearly eight years of marriage she attempts a more extended self-analysis (Letter 117):

> I thank God that my health is tolerably well, but in every other respect, I am a most wretched creature; the hours, days, and weeks that I spend, not in dulness, for that would be supportable, but {in re}solute misery; though there is no appare{nt explan}ation for the worse[ening] in my constitution as yet, depend upon it, that it will all be too much for me in the long run; I have no doubt but that if I live to be sensible of it, you will make me all the amends that you are capable of, for my sufferings; but I do not feel anything that prompts me to look so far forward and I cannot help lamenting some years passed in wretchedness that might have been otherwise disposed of, without injury to our finances and of course to our children. The only thing I can charge myself with in this unhappy business is the not being able to endure with more resignation a situation that is thought expedi{ent}..

She then tries to answer a question by resorting to scripture, the only time she does so in the Letters:

... am I to blame for doating upon the man whom I am bound to by every tie of affection and regard? No. I am to blame for not laying up to myself treasures where moth and rust doth not corrupt; Oh! put not your trust in Princes, nor in any child of man. I wish that the distracted state of my mind would permit me oftener to reflect upon the great comfort contained in these words; may this find you in good health and spirits and may the great God continue these blessings to my dearest life, the first joy I have on earth – from your's entirely SW.

In short, it seems as if she wishes she had been more independent and guarded better her own interests. For his part, Philip mostly seems not to take her misery too seriously. Indeed, in one letter (Letter 61) she herself gave him a way out: after admitting to having 'a most ungrateful heart, for all [God's] blessings', and saying that 'she hardly knows a happy moment' she says '... but she cannot help it, so take no notice of it.' She need not have said it; this was generally exactly what he did (Letters 63, 83 & 86):

I recieved [sic] my dear Sal's letter, which though I am impatient, I dread to see, when she talks so despondently of herself, but I trust without reason. ...Tuesday brought me your letter which always brings me some uneasiness, when you speak of yourself, and the more so, as it is not in my power to remedy it, or your own either, and yet as it proceeds only from your affection for me, I cannot but love you the better for it. ...I write this after a most pleasant ride, the day being one of the finest spring ones I ever was out in. ... I met Dr Warton upon the road, who I believe is travelling down [from London] with almost as heavy an heart as one that was coming up - but ... it will never happen again.

Yet, after this letter was written, at some time in April 1795, it did 'happen again'. In fact it went on for another two years, until an end came in sight when Philip wrote (Letter 123):

This day fortnight I shall be upon the road to you, and consider, my love, we shall meet to part no more.

This time it seems that she did go back with him to Westminster, though the inevitable absence of any more letters denies absolute proof. And within six months she was dead. A poignant entry in the Compton parish register for 1787 in her husband's hand reads: 'Sarah, wife of Rev. Phil. Williams (31) in child-bed. Sep 23' (HRO/1M76/PR1). But his life went on: two days later he is burying another, aged 73, and a month later he is officiating at the marriage of a namesake of his wife's father, Thomas Collins, and his bride Mary Elcock.

**

THREE DAYS after Sarah's death Philip Williams's stepfather Dr John Gordon sat down to that difficult task, a letter of condolence, which contained a rare show of piety (Letter 129):

> What can be said to a loss like thine? Common topics of human comfort woud be mockery! The Hand that gave the stroke can alone alleviate its force! May that Great Being give you the aid of his comfort! Though He may seem at present to have forgotten to be gracious, yet you have heretofore experienced the help of his goodness; or you might have left one still less able than yourself to have struggled with the weight of a similar calamity!

He then asked what he could do to help:

> Your Sisters, if that woud lessen it, will take their full share of your sorrow. Fanny had been kind enough to promise me her company at Lincoln this Autumn. But I take it for granted her attention will now be directed another way, if she finds she can be of any use. … If I offer no interposition on my own part, it is only because I really know not what to do.

Signing himself off as 'Your sincere and sympathizing Friend', he finishes with the sort of prayer he must have often meted out:

> May God keep you under his mercifull protection, and give you grace and strength to support the burthen his Providence has been pleased to lay upon you! And may you have a more powerful Advocate, and Comforter, than such a frail unworthy Sinner, as he who now presumes to offer up his feeble prayers for you…'.

Then, all condolence spent, he added a postscript about some business, ending with a quote (slightly wrong) from the Sermon on the Mount, Mathew 6:34:

> I have received a very friendly answer from the Master of [Christ's College, Cambridge] on the subject you mentiond with a wish, that I shoud write to him about [it]. And I was only waiting till I learnt, under what cover I might convey his letter to you for your

THE HAPPINESS OF BEING WITH YOU'

inspection. It is not an absolute engagement, but it is a favorable promise to remember the application. It may now keep till better times – sufficient for [unto] the day is the evil thereof.

It is easy to pick holes in John Gordon's response, but death in childbed was unfortunately a common occurrence, affecting 6-7% of married women (Vickery, 1998, p. 97). Philip Williams's friends Lovelace Bigg-Wither and Francis Mundy both lost wives after only a year of marriage. For the former, this evoked a letter from her brother-in-law and his cousin, William (later Sir William) Blackstone, celebrated for his *Commentaries on the Laws of England*, who offered 'consolation upon the footing of reason and religion', adding briskly (R.F. Bigg-Wither 1908, p. 48):

> I feel for you as a Friend, and a relation, and more especially as a husband; but I write to you as a man, and as a Christian... Providence has happily ordered it, that violent sensations are not lasting.

At the west end of north wall of the nave of All Saints Church, Compton, which Philip Williams served for 50 years, is a memorial to Sarah. It is topped with a coat-of-arms that the Williams family was not entitled to hold (*see* Chapter 1). Originally sited elsewhere in the building, it was placed in its present site when the church was extended in 1905. In a similar position in the old nave is memorial to him and their younger daughter, Charlotte. His is in English and hers in Latin, written by him:

H. S. E.
Faemina si quae alia omni
Praeconio major.

Quam flevere omnes: gravius tamen ipse superstes
Cui sociam dederat connubialis amor.
O foveas. orbaeque adsis. DEUS OPTIME. proli.
Ut MATREM referant moribus. ingenio.
Obiit SARAH WILLIAMS
Die Sept. 19. 1787
Anno aetat. 30.

At least two translations have been made, one in 1988 by the Winchester Group of the Hampshire Genealogical Society (Monumental Inscriptions, Compton, Church of All Saints, 1733-1990):

Here lies buried
A woman who far surpassed all common praise:
Bemoaned by all, yet most by one remaining.
To whose lot fell the love of such a wife.
Great God, the orphans in Thy Care sustaining Still
May her grace and worth through them find life.
SARAH WILLIAMS
who died in her 30th year
on the 19th day of September 1787.

and another for this volume by the classicist Roger Davies:

Here lies buried
A woman greater than any other
in every public celebration.
All wept for her: however, one survivor himself more deeply,
the man to whom love in marriage had given her as his partner.
Great god, may you cherish and be at the side of her bereaved
family,
so they may reflect their mother in their morals and character.
SARAH WILLIAMS
Died on September 19, 1787,
in her 30th year.

Philip Williams obviously worked at the epitaph, as there are two other
drafts which in translation contain similar sentiments, with the addition of
a lament that he, as a widower, may 'keep a sane mind, so that he may tell
his children of her life and talents' and an admonition to 'abstain from
vain complaints – hope and piety are more fitting for a disciple of Christ'
(W243-244). He also wrote a tribute in English which shows his feelings at
the time (W244):

Beneath this turf the sacred reliques rest
Of his whose form when animate possest
Whate'er could dignifie the human mind
Adorn the woman, or delight mankind –
And when the mournful writer of these lines
Within this grave his once-lov'd Sarah joins
May no rude hand their mingled dust remove
In death united as in earthly love.

15. *Three Daughters, Three Marriages*

DURING THE FOUR YEARS after the wedding of Philip Williams and Sarah Collins in 1779, the other two daughters of Thomas Collins, second master of Winchester College, were married. To the casual observer it might have seemed that three young women were plighting their troth to three promising young men. Yet the men and the styles of marriage they engendered could scarcely have been more different. First to walk up the aisle was Elizabeth Collins, who married Jeremiah Dyson – later marked out as 'apt to be tardy...where œconomy is concerned'. The wedding took place in St Swithun's church, the tiny chapel that still tops the Kingsgate, the southern entrance through the city walls of Winchester (*Alleg. Marr. Lic. Winch. 1689-1837*, Harleian Soc, I, 238). Then in 1783 it was the turn of Charlotte Collins and the Hon. George Richard St John – said to be 'variable in his motions'. They were married by licence in the seclusion of the rectory at Compton by Philip Williams. For an elderly schoolmaster it was a remarkable feat to have married off all three of his daughters on the eve of his retirement. But though Philip Williams had clearly married someone of a similar class, Dyson, and especially St John had married 'beneath themselves'.

St John was undoubtedly a nobleman, the son of Frederick St John, the 2nd viscount Bolingbroke and 3rd viscount St John, who in turn was the son of John St John, 2nd viscount St John, who was a half-brother of Henry St John 1st viscount Bolingbroke and 1st viscount St John, the tory grandee and statesman (his online ODNB entry runs to 24 pages). When George Richard matriculated at Christ Church, Oxford, in 1777 there was no doubt that he was registered as a nobleman; on the other hand, Jeremiah Dyson, who had gone to Eton as an oppidan (non-scholar), at first only managed recognition as a gentleman commoner, but in 1778 re-registered as a nobleman by paying 'additional caution money' (Judith Curthoys, pers. comm., 2008). Both young men had the same tutor, namely, John Randolph, who could have taught them a great deal if they had listened: at various times he held four different chairs at Oxford – in poetry, Greek, moral philosophy and divinity – and he followed his academic career with the bishoprics of Oxford, Bangor and, finally,

London. But, like many well connected young men, they left without a degree. They had, however, obviously become firm friends; even late in life Dyson appears as a trustee in a number of deeds involving St John.

For some reason, after Oxford both young men went to Winchester under the tutorship of Thomas Collins, presumably for a fee. The reason for this is not clear, but somebody judged that they needed to be 'kept on a rein' for some while. Of course, boys who were not scholarship material often attended Winchester College as commoners, more in the manner of a finishing school than a desire to acquire any real education. In particular, Warton's predecessor as head master, Dr John Burton, had been keen to surround himself with young noblemen: it brought in good money and did no harm in forging useful relationships. But extension of the system to 'postgraduates' (or more accurately, non-graduates) is not documented, though it may have happened with other young men. In essence, Thomas Collins was probably acting *in loco parentis*, for which there were good reasons.

Dyson was an orphan under the guardianship of an uncle: his mother had died at the young age of 34 the year after he went to Eton, and his father had died in 1776, two years after he matriculated at Christ Church College. St John still had both of his parents, but neither was in a position to offer him any support. His mother, Lady Diana Beauclerk (née Lady Diana Spencer) had been divorced by the 2nd viscount Bolingbroke in 1768 by act of parliament – only the 5th peer ever granted such a divorce – for adultery (euphemistically termed 'criminal conversation') with Topham Beauclerk, a salon intellectual and book collector. Over breakfast one day in May 1773, at the house of Henry Thrale, the brewer, Boswell attempted to defend Lady Diana's behaviour, saying that Bolingbroke 'had behaved brutally to her, and that she could not continue to live with him', to which Johnson gave a brutal reply (Womersely, 2008, p. 392):

> My dear Sir, never accustom your mind to mingle virtue and vice.
> The woman's a whore, and there's an end on't.

St John was nominally under the care of his father, nicknamed 'Bully'. But gambling and drink had taken their toll and turned him insane. When he finally died in 1787 in Paris, obituarists blamed his wife for destroying 'the noblest mind that man was ever endowed with'. More to the point, both parties were dissolute aristocrats and, to say the least, neither was suited to parenthood (Hicks, 2001).

Jeremiah Dyson was the eldest son of a namesake father who in 1748 at the age of 26 had purchased, for the extraordinary sum of £6000, 'the reversion of the appointment' to the clerkship of the House of Commons. According to a standard work on the clerkship, Dyson senior was much more than a clerk (Williams, 1954, p. 65):

> Jeremiah Dyson's birth was obscure, but he was not unknown, especially in the literary world, for he was already the friend and benefactor of [Mark] Akenside, doctor and poet, whom he had first known as a student at Leyden where he had become learned in the history of law.

It seems that he had enlightened, even radical views, as 'he never himself sold a place in the House and on his retirement the appointment passed on without fee to his successor' (Marsden, 1979, p. 41). He did well with his official clerkship of the House of Commons, and profited also from shepherding private bills through the Westminster machine. Subsequently, he was elected to parliament and died a relatively wealthy man. He acquired an estate at Stoke, on the outskirts of Guildford, Surrey, as well as land elsewhere 'formerly the estates of Sir William Stanhope [1626-1703]'. He also received a parliamentary pension of £1000 a year drawn on the Irish interest – albeit with much controversy – for his life and those of his three sons (P.D.G. Thomas, 'Jeremiah Dyson', ODNB). His will laid down that his estate was to be put in the trust of his brother-in-law, Samuel Dyson; Jeremiah senior had married his sister, Dorothy, and both men having the same surname may indicate a family link. In essence, the will required all his landed property to be sold and a trust fund set up for the benefit of Jeremiah Dyson junior, his two brothers and four sisters (TNA/Prob/11/1023). An unusual clause required 'several Burgages held of the Manor of Berealston [Devon]', which had been conveyed to him by the place's MP, Sir Francis Drake, to be given to Samuel Dyson on the condition that they were conveyed back to Sir Francis. The will set the parameters for his eldest son: he had to wait until 1778 when, at the age of 21 he would succeed. He was therefore dependant on the good will of Samuel Dyson, and, as it also it turned out, that of Sir Francis.

Jeremiah Dyson junior first appears in the Letters in 1780, when it is clear that he and his 'friend' St John are spending a good deal of time with Elizabeth and Charlotte Collins. Sarah Williams reports that Dyson 'made a good song upon the girls, for which he is in high favour' (Letter 25). A few months earlier Philip Williams had been collated to the rectorship of Compton, only two miles from Winchester, but he had no intention of living there, even though the parsonage house was relatively modern – built in about 1758 (White, 1859, p. 126). As it turned out, although he did not intend to serve the church himself, nor appoint a long-term curate, he had friends locally who would 'do the duty' when required (*see* Chapter 12). The parsonage house would therefore become vacant shortly, and, in the following January, Sarah enthusiastically reported (Letter 29):

> I am to inform you that you have a tenant for Compton in Mr. Dyson. We had a grand expedition thither on Wednesday and all parties returned so well pleased that there is no doubt of their taking it; Papa laments that there is so little scope for his genius, everything being so complete in the house, but he casts a longing eye towards the destruction of the wall at the end of the garden…

Thomas Collins was perhaps exercising the then current ideas of Capability Brown and itching to construct a ha-ha. It is clear that Jeremiah Dyson and Elizabeth Collins, with the consent of her father, had decided to get married and as soon as the departing rector – who was apparently still in residence – moved out matters could move on. By July they were wed and living at Compton. The parish registers show that whilst there they baptised four children, namely, Jeremiah in April 1782, George a year later, Henry in September 1784 and Francis in October the following year. Elizabeth also probably had a miscarriage in July 1783, when Sarah reported that 'Betsy has mispetred, which is what I can scarcely believe, as she was at the Ball on Thursday' (Letter 41).

The young couple seem quickly to have integrated into local society, the Mildmays of Shawford, the Ricketts of Twyford and the Newbolts. Dyson is clearly enjoying life on the proceeds of his inheritance. In particular, he has a close friend in the Revd John Monk Newbolt, nicknamed The Blade, and his father 'old Ricketts', a Winchester druggist, deemed a gentleman. They spent much time together in London and he and The Blade went together to the Montem celebrations at Eton (Letter 50). Elizabeth Dyson clearly has the support of maids in the house, they have a chaise and horses and a postilion. When a servant crisis left her alone with two young children and new-born Henry, Sarah sent one of her own stalwarts to assist, justifying herself to a worried husband by saying 'she would have been left without a creature if I had not spared Molly to her, which I could very well do not having a young child myself at present' (Letter 66).

Sarah Williams is clearly less than impressed by all the socialising. In one letter she wrote (Letter 61):

I dined at Mrs Mildmay's with all the Ricketts's, Mr Dyson and Mr
Newbolt, all the company except myself in very high spirits...

Although still in his twenties, Dyson took some responsibility for his
younger brothers, Henry and George, both of whom he, in the company
of one of the Ricketts, settled into King's College, Cambridge, in July 1784
(Letter 66). George became a lawyer and Henry vicar of Wexham,
Buckinghamshire, and rector of Baughurst, Hampshire, where he became
acquainted with the novelist Jane Austen. Staying in 1801 at Manydown,
the home of Lovelace Bigg-Wither, she told her sister of a visit to the
rectory (Le Faye, 1995, p.81):

> The house seemed to have all the comforts of little Children, dirt
> & litter. Mr Dyson as usual looked wild, & Mrs Dyson as usual
> looked big.

Henry is recalled by James-Edward Austen-Leigh, a nephew of the
novelist, as a hunting man with 'the most wooden and inexpressive
countenance imaginable' (Le Faye, 1995, p. 519).

As a young man, Jeremiah Dyson was clearly still under the supervision of
his uncle, Samuel Dyson, with whom Philip Williams, who was fifteen
years older, acted as an intermediary. In July 1784 he wrote (Letter 63):

> Dyson's Uncle called upon me yesterday... I was out, which I was
> sorry for; shall wait for the arrival of his shatter-brained nephew
> before I return his visit.

Running errands in the way that all local people did when they went up to
London was also expected, including ferrying funds to Sarah. Thus in one
letter she writes (Letter 69):

> I thank you for your seasonable supply by Mr Dyson, which I
> shall take good care of.

Philip Williams soon got together with Dyson's uncle (Letter 65):

> I paddled into the city, and called upon Sam Dyson, whom I have
> promised to dine with one day next week.

On the agenda, no doubt, was the feckless way in which Dyson was
spending money, including the 'Irish pension' inherited from his father,

and the need to mend matters. Some of the details emerged a few months later, as Sarah learned from her husband (Letter 73):

> I found a letter from Dyson, intimating his necessity of relinquishing Compton and his present idle way of life – that he is come up by way of getting the arrears of his Irish pension, £800, which will clear him and leave a neat £600 a year regularly paid ... he wishes me to decide for him about the future place of his residence – an hard task.

Clearly the business was on the minds of the couple: no doubt they felt responsible for helping the Dysons; they may have felt slightly jealous of his private income; and, like most of us, they probably enjoyed 'solving other people's problems'. Sarah replied at length in a hurried tone (W61):

> ... I cannot see that there is any reason for their leaving Compton at present, if he gets any thing, they must live in London, and they would then have to move again; why should they not sell their carriage and horses, and hire for the few times they want to go out, Betsy is in a way to have another child, which will necessarily confine her a great deal, and he can take his horse when he wants to go from home, they may live better at Compton upon 600£ (getting rid of all incumbrances), than we can at Winchester upon 500£ surely, they could not live cheaper at Midhurst [the home of Sarah's father, Thomas Collins], provisions are to the full as dear there as they are with us, he has nothing to do, but to say that he has no room for useless men, horses, and dogs, and he might then have every comfort as I think, that this life can give, we have done nothing but talk of this matter every time Betsy has come over, so that I think the first time I see him, he will say something upon the subject to me, and I shall certainly tell him what he must give up, to enable him to live within his income... to think that they should have frittered away such a sum of money, without any pursuit to justify it in the least; if they will enter heartily into the cause, I am not without hopes that they have it yet in their power to retrieve all...

Dyson did not help his cause when he subscribed a guinea for a ball in Winchester at The George. When Sarah told her sister she went into 'a rage, and declared she would have nothing to do with it' (Letter 75). Philip Williams drew up his own plan, which he felt unable to present face to face, preferring to write, as he told Sarah (Letter 76):

They have not spent so much as I thought they had, as great part of their furniture was not paid for in August 1782 - and therefore is to be included in that sum. Your ideas about the possibility of their remaining at Compton without a carriage will never do, and if they did, Bisset [a servant] and such idle fellows have already been too sensible of the sweets of living upon him, not to repeat the dose upon every opportunity. However you will have talked the matter over with them I imagine long before this time, and find out what plan they incline to, if they can be brought to think seriously of any.

However, Sarah shied away from the business, noting that the couple had developed a 'disposition rather to snap [at] each other ... which I never perceived before' (Letter 77). Meanwhile, Philip Williams had been in touch with Samuel Dyson, who reckoned that his nephew had debts of £1550. Philip observed (Letter 78):

I want to know more particulars about them, what are likely to embarrass him, and what not. Sam. Dyson declares his inability to assist him. What is your objection to Midhurst? at Compton they must not stay.

She replied (Letter 79):

Mr Dyson has been gone this week to Critchill [Moor Crichel, Dorset, where they were living], and was to have returned to night, he has not yet said a word to me upon the subject of their removal, though Betsy tells me that they are all harmony again and he has promised to pay his bills with his income instead of throwing it away upon nonsense…my objection to their going to Midhurst is the great expense attending their removal which is to be only temporary, and therefore when they do move, they had better go to their final home at once…they have heard from Mr Talbot that they cannot have Kensington, of which I never thought they had the smallest chance; I was to have gone to Compton to day but one of the horses is lame, which I was not sorry for, as James was so drunk the last time he drove them from my house that he went out of the road, and threw down one of the horses, and he has not had a word said to him upon the subject, he is one of the things I am glad they will be obliged to part with.

Later, she returned to the matter (Letters 81-2):

> What the Dysons intend to do I cannot guess, he told me the other day that he should wait for his uncle's answer, before he determined, but I am afraid they will linger on and do nothing, I say all that I can possibly think of to induce them to set about something for themselves; but I have been cassandra-ing for these three years, and at present I do not find that I am more attended to, however I will try again the next time we meet…
>
> I do talk to Betsy about them whenever I see her, her constant answer is that she spends nothing, and is ready to do whatever he desires, but when I tell her what particular things she must give up, she does not listen to me, and I have found out that you and I are more in earnest in the matter than they are, notwithstanding I hope you will assist him as much as lies in your power…

Gradually, Dyson realised that he must solve his financial problems, and even considered moving to Wales, which seems to have been a standard response to such matters (*see*, for example, Letter 125). Starting to take the matter seriously, Dyson obtained an offer of £40 'for a list of books which he means to part with upon leaving Compton' and discussed with St John the possibility of moving to Stockbridge, near the nobleman's fishing lodge at Leckford, which Philip Williams reckoned would 'be the ruin of both parties' (Letter 83). Dyson also went to see Thomas Collins in retirement at Midhurst, perhaps therefore still acting as if still *in loco parentis*, with a view to moving there, but nothing came of it. However, by the spring of 1785 there is expectation of a solution, which impelled Sarah to write in a generous spirit (Letter 85):

> I was greatly pleased with your account of Mr Dyson's affairs, in the first place that there are people in the world capable of such acts of friendship, and in the next that it should fall to the lot of one every way so deserving as is Mr D to meet with them; I flatter myself it will be an additional spur to him, to induce him to curtail every superfluous expence that he may trespass as short a time as possible upon the generosity of his friend; I hope you have instilled this idea with proper emphasis; no one has the principles of doing right more than he has, but he is apt to be tardy in the practice; especially where œconomy is concerned.

It seems that appropriate strings had been pulled at Westminster and, as emerged later, a friend of Dyson senior, the MP for Bere Alston, Devon, Sir Francis Henry Drake, was working to find 'a place' (a near-sinecure) for the young man in the House of Commons. Perhaps Philip Williams had been able to help in his role as the Speaker's chaplain. There were also other links that may have played a part: Sir Francis was a Wykehamist and his mother Anne, was a sister of Sir William Heathcote, 1st bt, of Hursley Park, near Winchester. Whatever transpired, it cannot have been the parliamentary performance of Sir Francis that played a part. *The Public Ledger* of 1779 noted that he was 'a silent, eccentric man, [who] always votes with the ministry'; during 30 years in the House there is no record of any speech he made. Clearly, Dyson had come to terms with a practical plan, namely, to move to London and work! One servant had already been dismissed from Compton and there was an 'immediate determination to part with James and the horses' (Letter 93), though 'one of [them] is good-for-nothing and the other is to be sold to the first purchaser' (Letter 100). For their part, Philip and Sarah were preparing to let their house in Kingsgate Street, Winchester, and move out to the rectory. But Sarah worried that there was a problem – and also displayed a certain disappointment that Philip Williams would himself not get any preferment until the end of his stint as the Speaker's chaplain (Letter 95):

> … we have some fears that he may have met with embarassments (which I pray to heaven to avert) to detain him, now they have it in their power to spend their present income, and pay their debts with the profits of the place, and I cannot but think they are in high luck however his time may be taken up; think only of their getting that at once, which will not fall to our lot till after four years, I will say slavery, for I cannot know a greater.

When it looked as if Sir Francis really might obtain a place for her brother-in-law, Sarah drooled over the details (W74):

> Dyson thinks he is certain of the place, which is 300 guinneas a year, he is to have four months clear to himself every year, and the attendance is only from 12 to half after two; very easy terms indeed! I wish I could as easily earn the same sum, I would begin learning to write a good hand immediately.

However, it was not all plain sailing (Letter 102):

Dyson would be very glad to settle his future plan, and to do it immediately, but Sir Francis Drake is such an oddity, that he does not think it would be wise to attack him again, and he is told that, the plan most be disposed of soon; the children at Compton are not very well, the eldest and youngest, one has worms and the other they think has an ague, but I hope there is no great deal the matter with either …

But eventually, in July 1785, came good news (Letter 105):

Mr Dyson received before I came away the welcome tidings of his appointment being confirmed by Sir Francis Drake, he will be in town in about ten days to take possession, he has a fortnight allowed him, before his attendance is required.

Philip Williams was equally relieved, (Letter 106):

I rejoice much in Dyson's success, and trust they are both now sufficiently convinced of the value of money, and the expences of an increasing family, as to make a right use of the blessings of providence, and go down upon their marrow-bones [knees] by way of returning thanks.

However, Dyson was still living beyond his means, staying in London before the job had started, not living 'for as little as a guinea a day' and going 'after an house in St James's place, [which] is going to take up £600 [annual rent]' (Letter 110). In the event, the couple finally settled for the village of Acton, Middlesex, where their son Charles was born in about 1788. Now subsumed by the metropolis, and once known as 'soapsuds island' for its laundries, it was then a village valued as a spa and a country retreat for the wealthy. Deeds involving St John show that the couple later (at least by 1809) lived at Twickenham, made fashionable by Hugh Walpole, Alexander Pope and others. Elizabeth Dyson died in 1795 at the age of 31, a year older than her sister Sarah and probably from the same cause, following the birth of Frances Sarah Dyson. A memorial in Stoke church, Guildford, describes her, rather starchily, as (Manning and Bray, 1804-1814, vol. I, p. 179):

A young but domestic Wife; an early, but exemplary, Mother of a numerous family.

In later life Dyson and his family moved out of town to New Grove, Petworth: by this stage, he had subordinates to carry on the business in London. And he had married a widow, Mary-Anne. Their daughter, Marianne Dyson, carried out an extensive correspondence with the daughter of the politician William Sturges-Bourne, a son of a Winchester prebendary, that is now part of the collection of the Hampshire Record Office (The Sturges-Bourne-Dyson Correspondence, HRO/9M55). It is clear from this source that the Dysons kept in close touch with the Sergeants of East Lavington, who were relatives of Thomas Collins.

Dyson, like his father, morphed into a servant of the House of Commons, but was not as successful, only rising, in 1814, to the deputy clerkship. However, he must have made a fair job of it, as he served under one of the most brilliant clerks ever known to the House, John Hatsell, who 'ruled … with a rod of iron …studied the [House of Commons] Journals as other men might study the Bible…[farmed]…(the considerable) fees and payments of his office…[and]…died a very wealthy man indeed' (Marsden, 1979, pp.42-3; who misnames him 'Henry Hatsell'; Williams, 1954, p. 280). He is best known for his 4-volume *Precedents of Proceedings in the House of Commons*, which he dedicated to Dyson senior. Philip Williams played cribbage with Hatsell (Letter 106), who more significantly is depicted in a famous picture by Anton Hickel in the collection of the National Portrait Gallery, *William Pitt Addressing the House of Commons on the French Declaration of War, 1793*.

An insight to the world of Jeremiah Dyson came in 1833, when a select parliamentary committee investigated the fees, salaries and other rewards of public servants. At a time when 'investigative journalism' was getting legs, detailed accounts of the proceedings in *The Times* unlocked the secrets of the 'large emoluments' that Dyson and others received as the clerk of various committees. Subsequent proceedings, such as that reported in *The Times* of 21 October 1835, noted that 'Mr Dyson is also employed largely as an agent for private business before the House, which engages the chief part of his time'. The searching eye of Reform, which rooted out corrupt practices and set up systems that endured to recent times (Marsden, 1979, pp. 117-119), might have been discomforting to Dyson, then in his mid-70s, but by the time this 'third report of the select committee' hit the press it was too late: the deputy clerk had died in September

***

THOMAS COLLINS was very unfortunate in the marriages of his three daughters. Both Sarah Williams and Elizabeth Dyson died in childbirth at a young age. By 1795 he was therefore left only with his youngest daughter, Charlotte, who had problems of a different kind. He might have drawn solace from Philip Williams, his widowed son-in-law, who was also involved with Charlotte – at the level of being a trustee in legal matters – but two years before the death of Elizabeth he had remarried and therefore had other matters to keep him busy. The picture of Collins drawn after his death (*see* Chapter 5) is of a broken-hearted old man.

There was no way, of course, he could have guarded against the dangers of childbirth for Sarah and Elizabeth (and he may have lost his own wife in the same way), but he must have many times regretted his agreement to the marriage of Charlotte to the Hon. George Richard St John, later the 3rd viscount Bolingbroke. (To avoid confusion, it should be noted that 'St John' in the Letters may refer to this arm of the family, or to a distantly related arm of a different suit, namely, the St Johns of Dogmersfield, Hampshire. George Richard St. John and Sir Henry Paulet St. John Mildmay of Dogmersfield, who married Jane Mildmay of Shawford, near Winchester, were 7th cousins ; Sonia St John, pers. comm.). Much of this chapter follows material published in the *Reports of the Friends of Lydiard Tregoz* (hereafter abbreviated to RFLT and available from Lydiard House & Park, near Swindon), with notable contributions by Canon Brian Carne.

In terms of the norms of the day, the marriage between Charlotte Collins and St John was very unusual. Any couple in their situation would have had to have made a secret engagement and then sought parental approval, to reach an acceptable settlement in terms of the bride's portion and the bridegroom's agreement with regard to a jointure in case of widowhood and even arrangements for any sons. As any reading of Jane Austen's novels shows, all this would normally have been discussed in the context of entailment of the St John estates (Gornall, 1967). Perhaps an analogy to St John and Charlotte Collins is Darcy and Elizabeth Bennett in *Pride and Prejudice,* when her sister Jane suspects her of marrying without true love (Chapter 59). She says, 'Oh, Lizzy! do anything rather than marry without affection. Are you quite sure that you feel what you ought to do?'

The real problem was the family setting in which the young man was ineluctably contained. The Hon. George Richard St John was the son and heir of Frederick St John, 2nd viscount Bolingbroke and 3rd viscount St John, who had married Lady Diana Spencer, a daughter of the 3rd duke of Marlborough and the Hon. Elizabeth Trevor. His parents' marriage was unhappy, largely due to Bolingbroke's infidelity and cruelty, which led in 1768 to divorce by act of parliament. The grounds were adultery by Lady Diana, who lived with Topham Beauclerk and had had two surviving illegitimate daughters, Elizabeth and Mary Day. Until her divorce, she had been lady of the bedchamber to Queen Charlotte.

The misbehaviour that Charlotte had to endure from her husband managed to cover the full spectrum, including financial wrecklessness, incest and perhaps even bigamy. By the time the young George Richard came to Winchester, the extramarital and highly-charged social behaviour of his parents must have been common knowledge and would have sounded alarm bells in the kindest of hearts. His father had been insane for six years before his death, in May 1787. From the very first mention of the Hon. George Richard St John, in the earliest surviving letter between Philip and Sarah, written in July 1780, there is a note of caution (Letter 25):

> We ... have seen Mr. St. John often, he being in constant attendant upon the Squigg, and quite the reverse of every thing we suspected him to be; we are exceedingly pleased with him, he has a vast share of diffidence and good humour.

She uses the unflattering nickname 'Squigg' for her sister Charlotte, a word that does not appear in the OED; even 'squiggle' is not noted until later, but perhaps the name referred to wavy hair or a tendency to giggle. (Current slang uses exactly the same word for 'a good-looking slut'; www.urbandictionary.com.) A few months later St John left the country and went to Bavaria for a long period, leaving 'poor Squigg... pretty well in health, but rather out of spirits' (Letter 29). In late February 1781 he left Winchester with his friend Dyson and travelled to Munich via Margate and Ostend. Sarah archly reports (Letter 32):

> There is a long tale belonging to this matter which I shall keep 'till we meet; it is sufficient for the present to say that nothing can have behaved better than he has done upon the occasion, and the Squigg though exceedingly hurt bears up better that I could have expected. I hope and firmly believe that nothing on his part will ever give her uneasiness.

It can only be imagined how a young man 'behaved' in a distant land during a long sojourn; and a month after his departure Charlotte fell ill.

She was so poorly that there was even talk of her seeking the advice of the physician to the Prince of Wales (and later to George III; Letter 35):

> Poor Squigg is very indifferent; Papa talks of sending her to Sir R[ichard] Jebb; she fainted away yesterday three times, but I have yet hopes that she will do without going to London.

Eventually, the young man returned, but nothing is known of the courtship until two years later, when both he and Charlotte were 21 years of age (by coincidence, their dates of birth were within a day of each other). In the previous May, St John had been elected a member of parliament for Cricklade, in which constituency his family had been seated for centuries at Lydiard House (RFLT, 34, pp 34-55). The young couple were married on 26 February 1783, in the parsonage house at Compton by the rector, Philip Williams, with Thomas Collins and Jeremiah Dyson as witnesses. It had all the signs of a shotgun marriage, but the record suggests otherwise. Also, as Charlotte did not live in the parish of Compton, and the ceremony was not performed in a church, as required by Hardwicke's Marriage Act of 1753 – named after Philip Yorke, the 1st earl of Hardwicke, and designed to prevent clandestine marriages – it required a licence. The entry in the parish register was very carefully worded, like the legal agreement it was:

> By special licence of his Grace the Archbishop of Canterbury the Hon. George Richard St. John (elder son of the Lord Viscount Bolingbroke) & Charlotte Collins second daughter of the Rev. Thomas Collins under-master of Winchester School were married in the Parsonage house between the hours of ten and eleven in the forenoon this twenty sixth day of February one thousand seven hundred and eighty three by me
>
> Philip Williams Rector of Compton
>
> This marriage now solemnised between us
> Geo: Richd St. John
> Charlotte Collins
> in the presence of us
> Thomas Collins
> J. Dyson

Within six months of the event Philip Williams wondered what was happening (Letter 42):

I wrote to Charlotte to day to inquire if she was alive, and if she did not mean to give life likewise to others in due time.

Eventually she did 'give life' to a child, George, baptised on 4 January 1784 at Moor Crichel, a small village where the couple were living in Dorset, near Blandford Forum. The date of the baptism is, of course, wholly consistent with a post-marriage conception. Sarah went to support her sister and wrote to her husband in Winchester (Letter 44):

Tell little Bess that her Aunt [Charlotte] St. John cannot part with the little boy yet...

Perhaps St John was renting Crichel House, built by fellow parliamentarian Sir Humphrey Sturt (ca 1725-1786), member for Dorset, who had inherited the estate in 1765 (H Colvin, 1995, 3 ed.). He certainly did not seem to be concerned about being so far from Westminster, and in any event in the 1784 general election, when he stood for Wells, he was defeated, along with all the other 'Fox's Martyrs'. Although a young man, he was clearly not interested in politics; a contemporary pamphlet records that he was 'not very remarkable for sage deliberations or for deep researches into the speculative points of politics' (Namier and Brooke, 1964, vol III, pp. 383-99). More to his taste were country pursuits, whilst the impending birth of his heir sent him temporarily back to the family seat at Lydiard Tregoze, though Sarah seems rather vague about the history (Letter 44):

Mr. St. John is at Lord Powis's for some days; he (Lord P.) has taken Lydiatt, a house that Mr. St {John} was about formerly.

This was a huge understatement as Lydiard Tregoze had been the seat of the St John family for centuries (it was sold in 1943 for £4,500, to Swindon Borough Council, together with 750 acres of land and is now open to the public; Carne, RFLT, 2001, No. 34, pp 34-55).

It is hardly surprising that St John sought amusement elsewhere, as Sarah admits that for her and Charlotte life in the depths of Dorset in the winter, with apparently limited funds, was dire (Letter 40):

We live like hermits here, never go out, or see any body; the coach horses are gone to be sold, but I have a fund of amusement in my friend Massinger [the playwright] ... there are some good things {in} him and many very coarse ones.

To this very day the marriage that St John entered into invites comment from his descendants, who find it difficult to understand why he married Charlotte Collins. One 'family myth' is that it was a morganatic marriage, but this does not stand up as his 'heir was his surviving son by Charlotte and no claims for legitimacy appear to have been made for the six children a second wife, "the baroness", bore him before their marriage in New York' (B. Carne, pers. comm.). Another version of events is that Thomas Collins lured a young man to marry a daughter devoid of fame or fortune (Sonia St John, pers. comm.). This certainly seems to be the line that St John himself put about. In a letter to the *New York Times* of 29 January 1877, 'Julia Lawrence of Washington' told the story of St John's marriages, as she believed them to be (RFLT, 6, p. 112):

> Lord Bolingbroke, when a youth, was placed with a private tutor, who aided his daughter, a woman much older than the young man, in her design to marry him. They succeeded in their plan, but he soon became disgusted with his wife, and on the death of his father, being his own master, and unrestrained by any principle, religious or moral, he left her with her father, and went on the Continent, where he became acquainted with Count Niemcewicz [a Polish nobleman] and many other celebrities.

This account, although clearly inaccurate – Charlotte was in fact exactly the same age as St John – probably gives the flavour of the story as St John related it. For her part, Charlotte seems to have been bowled over by the young man – who could refuse the attention of a peer-to-be? – especially a girl who was 'a mouse', as her sister called her (Letter 58). No doubt St John married without the slightest regard for his parents, neither of whom was in a state to offer advice, and presumably because he fancied a pretty young woman. If his father had been able to offer advice it might have been along the lines of that the earl of Pembroke gave to his only son when he learned that he was to marry a cousin, St John's half-sister, Elizabeth Beauclerk (Hicks, 2001, pp. 298-9):

> You know how much our affairs stand in need of at least thirty thousand pounds. I now fear them irretrievable for our time, at least; it would have been lucky for us had you found a thirty-thousand-pounder, as agreeable to you as Elizabeth.

However, St John was not the catch for Charlotte that he might have been. He was almost certainly saddled with the gambling debts of his father, who 'was largely responsible for starting the St John tradition of disposing of capital rather than living on income alone' (Anon, ND, *Lydiard Park and Church*, p. 4). This had already led in 1763 to the sale of the manor of Battersea where so many of the family had lived, including Henry 1st viscount Bolingbroke, and the same fate awaited Purley Park, Berkshire, in 1789. The beneficiary of the latter was Robert Mackreth, the owner of White's Club in the West End, a notorious gambling haunt. It was a fate common to many feckless aristocrats of the time, including Thomas Collins's patron, Sir John Shelley, whose estate at Michelgrove, Sussex, was similarly administered by 'Robert Mackreth Esquire a creditor by bond' (Letter 58).

Within a few months of the birth of his heir, having just given up his seat at Westminster for Wootton Bassett and failed to win Wells, St John was enjoying some of the finest trout fishing in the country, on the river Test in Hampshire, where he rented a cottage at Leckford, near Stockbridge (Letter 51). Although use of the dry fly – the quintessential method of fishing for trout – had not yet been invented (Hills, 1921, p. 114), the Test was already well known in sporting circles. Joseph Warton's favourite poet, Alexander Pope, portrayed a fisherman of the period in his long poem *Windsor Forest*:

> In genial spring, beneath the quiv'ring shade,
> Where cooling vapours breathe along the mead,
> The patient fisher takes his silent stand,
> Intent, his angle trembling in his hand...

It is a tempting to suggest that it was through Pope and headmaster Joseph Warton that St John came to Winchester College, as Pope was very close to the 1st viscount Bolingbroke and in Warton's *Essay on the Writings and Genius of Pope*, published in 1756, he refers to his sources as 'an intimate friend of POPE' and 'A PERSON of no small rank' (pp. 11 and 29). But this is pure speculation.

Sarah was rather scathing about her brother-in-law's sport, though pleased that he was only 'absent' in pursuit of trout and dismissive of a suggestion from her husband that he had been seen rallying support in London for the whig politician Charles Fox, who had been roundly defeated by Pitt in the country in the recent general election (Letter 51):

> Charlotte etc. happily disposed of at Leckford, from which place I believe Mr St John has not been absent an hour except in fishing since they first came; so that it certainly was not him who assisted

at Mr Fox's triumph. I wish it had been him, any thing is better than this trout-hunting.

'Pitt's triumph' might have been a better phrase, as Fox believed he had won the City of Westminster, and the Prince of Wales threw a great party to celebrate it, but a scrutiny of the vote was called and initially he had only the hollow victory of being returned for Orkney. He had to wait almost a year before he did eventually triumph and gained the prestigious seat (Hague, 2004, p. 190).

Fishing had its downsides, and might lead to medical treatment, as Sarah reported (Letter 58):

> Charlotte came to me Tuesday morn, and St John in the evening with a most dreadful hoarseness and fever, which he got in the old way by standing all day up to his knees in the river; by the help of Dr Littlehales he is got quite well, and was able to go to the last ball. He has made a hundred promises not to do so again, but I doubt whether he will keep them… Mrs Booth was here to make all Mr St John's broths and sago.

But renting in a small place like Leckford was apparently affordable (Letter 70):

> I have had a great desire to see Charlotte and her little boy, she has been so good to me in a hundred instances that I can tell you, that if it is possible I love her better than ever; they stay at Leckford till October, and if she could lie in there I believe they would spend the Winter there, they find the sweets of living in a small house in the difference of expence, which is very great.

Money was always to be a problem for St John. This was apparent from the day he married Charlotte, as most couples in their situation would have negotiated and signed a marriage settlement a day or so before the event, as Philip and Sarah Williams had done (W233). This was a pre-nuptial contract that made provision for the wife and her children if she should outlive her husband and was usually negotiated by her male relatives or an agent. Women whose families lacked property might expect no settlement, but its absence, if nothing else, should have signalled the dysfunctional nature of the marriage. Two years later Philip informs his wife that 'Dyson has been here [in London] and tells me something is to be done about Charlotte's settlement' (Letter 73). Sarah confirmed that something was in the wind, but delivered a dose of her characteristic caution (Letter 74):

> I had a letter last night from Charlotte, who says that Mr St John has sent her word that he certainly shall have it in his power to make a settlement upon her; I wish it may be so, but I am not too sanguine in this matter from the embarassed state of his father's affairs.

But she was mistaken: he settled £500 a year on the estate at Lydiard Tregoze, with his brother 'Frederick and his family having joined with him to do it' (Letter 79). Two months later a collective sigh of relief must have gone up when Philip reported that Richard Hollist, who was the family lawyer, 'has pronounced her settlement valid, so that there is an end to that part of your father's apprehensions' (Letter 90).

Although with regard to the settlement St John 'did the decent thing', he and Charlotte were not much in each other's company. Hence, in February 1785, he and his friend Dyson attended on their own a benefit performance for Sarah Siddons in London and dined near the theatre, though Philip thought himself 'too old for tavern dinners, at least with such young stuff' (Letter 73). Two months later it was Charlotte's turn to go up to town, where Philip sat with her for an hour in the morning and noted that she 'looks very well, and is in good spirits, and seeing his relations, which I am glad of, as the more she is known and seen, the more she must be liked' (Letter 88). The 'relations', visited at Marlborough House, included siblings of St John's father, namely, 'General [Henry] St John', and, Elizabeth Louisa, together with her husband Lord Bagot, and relatives of St John's mother, née Lady Diana Spencer. It can only be imagined how daunting it must have been for the schoolmaster's daughter to be taken to the huge pile in Pall Mall designed by Wren for Sarah Churchill, duchess of Marlborough, situated in the very heart of London, close to St James's Palace and Buckingham Palace.

Sarah sounds relieved to hear that her little sister is putting herself about in London (Letter 89):

> I have this moment your letter, and am glad to find you have seen so much of Charlotte, who is now where she ought to have been some time ago, I left Mr St John at Compton [with the Dysons] where he stays a short time and as soon as she comes home, they are to be at Leckford for the summer...

She might herself have accompanied Charlotte to London, where her 'poor little girl ... is to be taken ...for advice', but she declined (Letter 87).

In the Letters there are frequent mentions of a 'Miss Beauclerk', who was almost certainly Mary Day Beauclerk, a half-sister of St John, though in principle it could have been her sister Elizabeth. They were the daughters of St John's mother, Lady Diana Beauclerk, and her lover turned husband Topham Beauclerk, who were married immediately after St John's parents' divorce was finalised by parliament in March 1768. There is some uncertainty regarding the dates of birth of Elizabeth: the standard version is that she and Mary were both illegitimate twins, born on 20 August 1766 (*see*, for example, RFLT, No. 7, p.84), though Elizabeth may in fact have been born in March 1769, thereby making her legitimate (Hicks, 2001, pp. 182, 200). The Letters give some support to them not being twins, as there is a reference to 'the youngest Miss Beauclerck' (Letter 100), though this could of course still technically be the case, even for twins. The Letters show that in 1785 only two years after the St Johns had married, 'Miss Beauclerk' is assuming a large part in their life. Her parents cannot have had much interest in her, besides which Lady Diana had discovered that her second marriage was, in a different way, as bad as her first.

'One of the Miss Beauclercks [sic]' surfaces in April and May 1785, when Sarah Williams sent her husband news of the comings and goings of the family and the difficulties of arranging a visit to her father in Midhurst:

> Mr St John is grown fat and looks very well indeed, [and] is happy that Charlotte is going out so much... [he] is at present shooting, I don't know what, in the Isle of Portland and does not come home till Thursday when Charlotte leaves ...we have not been able to come to any determination about Midhurst... Mr St John ...is very variable in his motions...Charlotte has not got her chaise home, and what is worse, she has one of the Miss Beauclercks with her, which effectually puts it out of her power to go, and of course mine, for I should not chuse to be at the expence, and if I did I have no servant to go with me, so for the present there is an end of that business, and a great disappointment to all parties (Letters 89 & 95-7).

A month later Sarah 'went to Leckford [and]...had a most charming day... the youngest Miss Beauclerck [aged 16 or 18, depending on her true date of birth] is with Mrs St John, and a very pleasing, well behaved girl indeed and would be pretty if she had a colour ... Mrs St John ... is to keep Miss Beauclerck as long as she possibly can, and Miss B will never go away if she can help it… (Letters 100 & 104).

The upshot of a pretty young girl living in the vicinity of St John is not hard to imagine. The sordid details of a libertine's life are rarely very illuminating, but in this case they illustrate the canker that Philip and Sarah Williams, and their close relatives – especially Thomas Collins – had to endure for many years. Eventually, Mary Beauclerk fell pregnant by him, and the story entered the gossip machine, as Betsy Sheridan, the playwright's younger sister wrote in June 1789 (Le Fanu, 1960, pp. 176-7, cited in RFLT, 7, 82-85):

> We heard a most shocking story … .The present Lord Bolingbroke …has been married about six years to a very charming Woman. Miss B was invited to spend some time with her Brother and the consequence was a most infamous connection between them: So completely criminal that the Young Lady was with child: Lady Bolingbroke to prevent if possible the horrid story getting wind, went abroad with her and nursed her in her lying-in.

The lifestyle enjoyed by the ton at the time is exemplified by a riotous ball held in July 1785 by Lord Radnor at Radnor Castle, near Salisbury and attended by the Prince of Wales. Although Sarah 'exhorted the St Johns to go, as they are to meet many of their friends there, and it will be a splendid business' (Letter 105), she was clearly not comfortable with the 'Prince of Wales set'. As well as the St Johns they included Miss Arabella Ogle, who became the third wife of the Hon Edward Bouverie (1760-1824), son of the 1st earl of Radnor. The ceremony took place at Martyr Worthy, near Winchester, where her father, admiral Sir Chaloner Ogle, was seated, on 20 December following the ball – an odd month for a wedding. The Winchester prebendary John Mulso, in a letter to the naturalist Gilbert White, noted the family's approval and wrote that the wedding 'promises much happiness, as the young folks are affectionate and worthy' (Holt-White, 1907).

The ball was perhaps not a complete success, but those who went made the most of it, as Sarah described soon after the event (Letter 109):

> …[it] was not very full, owing to the London party's having fallen very short of the numbers that were expected; the preparations extremely splendid and elegant; the gentlemen did not rise from

dinner till eleven o'clock, and their situation is easily to be guessed; the Prince danced country dances first with Lady Bampfylde; then Mrs St John, Miss Beauclerck, and Miss Arabella Ogle; Charlotte got to bed with Miss Beauclerck about three o'clock, and the Prince and his associates made a great riot, and I believe did not get to bed all night; the next day there was a very fine breakfast, after which they went to the Race [at Salisbury]...

The outcome of St John's affair with Mary Beauclerk first surfaces in the Letters in March 1787, fours years after his marriage to Charlotte. Sarah has charge of the three St John children, who are being kept and being cared for by hired nurses in the rectory at Compton. As noted in Betsy Sheridan's Journal, Charlotte is in France, aware that her husband has tired of her, yet helping his lover, her sister-in-law, to give birth to their first child. Sarah's correspondence on the events 'transacting in a higher sphere' is restrained and matter of fact (Letter 122):

> ...I have been plagued to death this last week by Mrs St John's nurses, who have both behaved very ill and one to leave Compton on Saturday; they have drank nothing but strong beer and brandy, except when they had not money to buy it, and as long as the money would last, they went on very lovingly, but when that cementer failed and they got in debt they did nothing but quarrel, and one thing brought out another, till at last they came to an open feuding and proving before me; the consequence of which is the dissmission of both, and an entire change in the disposition of the children, who are to be consigned over to the care of Mrs G Cole where I am sure they will be taken care of, and for about half the expence; I have thought it adviseable to remove them from under the roof of old Cole for reasons that I will tell you hereafter, but there is wheel within wheel and so many intrigues in this little state, that it is quite an epitome of what is transacting in a higher sphere...

As usual, Philip Williams is less than energised by his sister-in-law's plight and the declining state of St John's father, the 2nd viscount Bolingbroke (Letter 123), who was said to be insane for the last six years of his life (*The Complete Peerage*, vol. XI, p. 333) and was to die aged 54 two months later (Letter 122):

> I had a letter from Charlotte this week, giving a good account of herself, but [she] is angry with you for not writing. I beg you will

do it the first moment you can spare, because it will be a great satisfaction to her; you are to direct à Madame St John, chez Monsieur Girardot Banquier, Rue Vivienne à Paris; they have had the same account of Lord B[olingbroke] that you mention which makes their future motions very uncertain, they remain for some time longer at St Pierre l'Aigle to wait the event…

St Pierre-Aigle is a village in Picardy, about 15 miles southeast of Compiègne and about 40 miles northeast of Paris. To the southwest is the small town of Villers Cotterêts, which at the time was possessed of an imposing château, as well as a charitable hospital and crops up as 'Villers Cotrez', together with the direction of 'Monsieur Giradot', in a letter written in March 1787 by Elizabeth Beauclerk (daughter of Bolingbroke's ex-wife Lady Diana Spencer) to Sarah Williams (W196). In the opposite direction lies the larger town of Soissons, which had been visited by Philip Williams two years earlier, though the reasons are obscure (Letter 85). The plan was probably to pass off the child as one of Charlotte and St John. Whilst all this was going on, Mary's twin sister Elizabeth was arranging to marry the earl of Pembroke's eldest son (W196), though Sarah thought her 'too good and too pleasing for the set she belongs to' (Letter 85) and elsewhere wrote (Letter 122):

> Miss [Elizabeth] Beauclerck's marriage is certain with Lord Herbert; they had Lord Pembroke's answer the day she wrote to me, and she thinks herself the happiest creature in the world as indeed she ought to be, for he bears a very good character; I am very glad of it, as I think she deserves her good-fortune, you would like the naive and open manner in which she mentions her marriage, I have inclosed a note to congratulate her upon it.

Elizabeth Beauclerk was gaining a father-in-law who had married an aunt, Lady Elizabeth Spencer, and had had at least two illegitimate children, including one from Kitty Hunter, which invited the stinging wit of Horace Walpole (*Correspondence*, 1820, vol. II, p. 344):

As Pembroke a horseman by most is accounted,
'Tis not strange that his lordship a Hunter has mounted.

The different fates of Mary and Elizabeth Beauclerk resonated with the sentiments of the time. The novels of writers such as Richardson, Fielding and Madame D'Arblay (Fanny Burney) are virtually all about innocent young girls who get robbed of their virtue and ruined in the process. After the birth of Mary and St John's second son the ménage à trois and the pretence of the children being Charlotte's could no longer be sustained and the couple went to live as 'Mr and Mrs Barton' in Paris, where they had two more sons, all born before 1793 (Carne, RFLT, No. 39, p.30).

But St John soon tired of Mary, too, and paid off her and the children with annuities. Then, in about May 1794, he moved on to this third partner, Baroness Isabella Antonia Marianne Charlotte Sophia von Hompesch-Bolheim, then aged about seventeen. Much later in her life she was described by Augustus John Foster as 'anything but handsome; a little square German with broken teeth, but they say very amiable' (Foster, 1898, pp. 239-40). She came from a family famed for being grand masters of the Knights Hospitallers, seated at Bolheim, near Düsseldorf. They even went through a form of (bigamous) marriage ceremony in Germany. They returned briefly to London, and then lived in obscurity in Wales, before sailing off for a new life in the United States, where they eventually set up in Elizabeth Town, New Jersey, in a grand home, Liberty Hall, as 'Mr and Mrs Belasise'. For her part, Mary Beauclerk was given an annuity by St John and retrieved her respectability in 1797, when she married Franz Raugraf von Jenison-Walworth Graf von Heidelberg, who was the son of Francis Jenison-Walworth, seated at Walworth, County Durham, and the grand chamberlain of the household of the king of Württemburg.

As St John careered through life, Philip Williams, and especially his friend Jeremiah Dyson, separately and together, were long involved with the peer as trustees in complex legal arrangements to support Charlotte, provide annuities for the Barton boys of Mary Beauclerk and other 'compensatory acts', as demonstrated by deeds under the guardianship of Swindon Borough Council, the present owners of Lydiard House, (Lyd 1993/289.1 to 289.5; RFLT, No. 34, pp.49-50), and also in the West Sussex Record Office at Chichester (Lavington MSS). None of the women that St John fell in love with brought any capital to the family estate and he was only able to continue his way of life by selling off farms and land (Carne, 2001, RFLT, 34, p. 34).

Even though Charlotte had lost the affections of her husband, after the death of his father the 2nd viscount Bolingbroke in 1787, she gained the title Viscountess Bolingbroke and lived with her children in the family mansion at Lydiard Tregoze. Her prime support for these long years was her father, with whom she spent a long time in Italy, at least between about November 1793 and June 1796, living mainly in Pisa, but also in Venice (Ingamells, 1997, p.102). There, amongst others, she met the physicist Sir Benjamin Thompson, Count Rumford, abroad for his health, who noted in a letter (Broadlands MSS, 29 November 1793, quoted by Ingamells, op. cit.):

> I found her with her father, a Lady who I did not know and three charming children. Poor thing how interesting she is in her present unfortunate situation. I felt quite grieved for her.

Charlotte's elder son, George, had long been sickly, described as 'dying by inches' and in 1803 he succumbed, causing her to write heartbrokenly to Philip Williams's daughters (W196C):

> …the separation from this belov'd object of my tender care for 19 years stings me to the heart … Providence supported me wonderfully in the last trials, I never felt my own debility, and had the resolution never to leave the dear angel 'till he had breathed his last – and I kiss'd his dear beautiful face every day 'till it was necessary to have his coffin soddered [soldered]…

Shortly afterwards, on 11 January 1804, at the Hot Wells, Bristol, where she had gone for health reasons, she herself died. Usually a summer resort, the Bristol waters were taken for diabetes, tuberculosis and other consumptive conditions, the custom being to drink a glass of water in the pump-room (built in 1695) and spend half an hour with the assembled company, entertained with music from the resident band (Shiercliff, 1789 etc). She stayed in a house 'beautiful beyond measure … every Ship that comes in or goes out of Bristol passes under our Windows' (W196B). It was at the top of the cliff, so she was 'spar'd the misery of seeing the unhappy Objects' at the foot of the cliff, near the hot wells. It was remarkably quiet, as 'the general rage for the Sea side has carried all away.' Here she grew weaker and poorer as she contemplated the idleness of her surviving teenage son Harry (W196A-C):

> We shall be fixtures here for this year at least – all my travelling money is gone off in five guinea fees to my Physicians…Phil [a lawyer, the eldest son of Philip and Sarah Williams] has most kindly offer'd to put him in the way of Mathematics & Algebra that He may not be quite at a loss when He goes to Oxford in Octr [actually postponed to the next term]. He has laid fallow so long & never looks in a book but by absolute force.

In the same year that she passed away, her only daughter Mary and her father Thomas Collins also both died. The hurt he felt at her fate is evident in the will he signed, which made clear that had he died first his estate was to be (WSRC/Lavington MSS/94):

>...for the sole and separate use and benefit of my daughter Charlotte Viscountess Bolingbroke to be by her taken received and disposed of according to her own will and discretion and independent of and not in any manner subject to the controul engagements or interference of George Richard Lord Bolingbroke...

As soon as St John heard the news of his wife's death, he married his German baroness in New York (this time properly) and the couple, with their 'seven lovely children' (in fact, one of them was probably a son by Mary Beauclerk, with the surname Barton; B. Carne, pers. comm.) returned to take possession of Lydiard House. St John lived another twenty years, but even after all this time his wife Isabella obviously felt insecure. In an unfinished letter written before 1822, when she was perhaps facing a similar issue to that Thomas Collins had faced with three unmarried daughters, she made an astonishing suggestion concerning her husband's friend Jeremiah Dyson (Carne, 2006, p. 36):

>...Dyson is the only Person to whose care I would trust my Children he alone comes up to my ideas of friendship...I wish much that you would find out if you see him whether in case of Accidents to you & me he would let the girls live in his family...I am not perhaps sufficiently acquainted with his [second] Wife...[but] with my Opinion of Dyson's Sense etc I feel sure he must have made a good Choice & at a time of life too when the passions are not so likely to blind our Judgements.

By this time, or shortly after, Dyson was living on the Petworth estate in Sussex, in a house called New Grove, where his wife Mary-Ann died in 1832 and he three years later. Even if a full draft of Isabella's letter was ever sent it is unlikely that that her daughters ever did live with the Dysons. One of them, Isabella, died in 1822 and the other, Antonia, four years later In between, in 1824 at Pisa, St John died and the baroness wrote 'all my earthly happiness destroyed' (Carne, 2006, pp.36-37). In the same year the estate at Lydiard Tregoze was visited by Cobbett, who wrote in his *Rural Rides* (1912, Everyman's Library, London, vol. ii, pp. 84-5):

It appears to have been a noble place ... but all, except the church, is in a state of irrepair and apparent neglect, if not abandonment.

Charlotte's hatchment still hangs in the church at Lydiard Tregoze and her coffin plate in the vault gives her age, accurately, as 44, meaning 'in her 44th year'. Brian Carne, on whose work so much of this story depends, points out that St John failed to build up the family fortunes in the traditional way – by marrying heiresses, but concludes (RFLT, No. 39, p. 45):

> He was a caring father to his many children, providing for them as best he could out of his disposable capital and income during his lifetime and by his will.

His mother, trying to rescue the situation, wrote of him: 'His is the noblest mind spoilt by an entire giving away to Passions, but the fond remains.' But an unknown correspondent, 'RJ', in about 1796, spelt out some home truths:

> The misfortune of your life has been that you have always given way not only to every passion but to every fancy you ever had and that you have never been used to resist the natural violence of your temper. I now see this disposition remains in full force and that you retain the same obstinacy and willfullness.

Is it likely that a man like this had been tricked by as unworldly a soul as Thomas Collins and his mouse-like daughter?

In April 1822, in a letter to his spinster daughter, Charlotte, Philip Williams added a tailpiece to the story, showing that the St John family was still able to surprise (W169):

> You know I suppose of Mrs St John's late trip to England, and after a stormy passage producing an 8th month's child at Dover, and proceeding to London 10 days afterwards. The occasion of her coming over, she concealed from her mother, but saw Lord Bolingbroke several times. Her husband could only attend her cross the water, for obvious reasons.

Arguably, the main purpose of sexual morality was – and still is – to protect women from exploitation and to ensure that men are responsible for their actions. In this respect, St John failed miserably as a husband and Charlotte and her father had to endure much heartbreak. The lives lived by St John and his kind were rich pickings for novelists. Plots are legend in which innocent young women are ensnared by heartless men, who go on to repeat the process with others. Perhaps Maria Edgeworth in her *Belinda*, first published in 1801, had men like St John in mind when she wrote of one of her female characters:

> ...[she] was carried off from a boarding-school when she was scarcely sixteen, by a wretch, who, after privately marrying her, would not own his marriage, stayed with her but two years, then went abroad, left his wife and infant, and has never been heard of since.

16. *Sally & After Sally – What Sort of Life Was it?*

THE EIGHTEENTH CENTURY was in many ways a good time to be a clergyman, especially for those of the middling sort, who might expect little in the way of inheritance. As the century progressed, more clerics had received a university education and incomes from tithes were growing, due to agricultural improvements and favourable exchanges or commutations made at enclosure (Walsh, Haydon and Taylor, 1993, pp. 6-7). As a result, they had edged closer to gentry and given suitable patronage – coupled with pluralism and non-residence – they could pursue an agreeable style of life. Not for them the need to be rooted in any particular place for long periods, as required by those with farms or small estates, nor to follow the crowd, as military men. Not for them the need to attend to workshops or clients, as required by artists, architects and skilled craftsmen. Within reason, some of them proved able to invent and reinvent themselves as they wished.

But was it a good time to be the wife of a clergyman? Certainly some of the benefits of the man could be shared by his wife – with a living often came a good house, as Sarah Williams enjoyed at the end of her life. There was always available a coterie of educated people, even minor gentry and aristocrats, who were willing to mix with clergymen's wives, especially in a place like Winchester. In the case of Sarah there was also some support to be found in the social life of Winchester College, even though chauvinism reigned – though few of its proponents were probably aware that it did so! As a clergyman's wife she could expect servants to help her with housework and childcare. Money was in relatively short supply, partly because Philip Williams ran a 'tight ship', but also because clerical stipends were modest, but the income was steady, without the concerns that might have ensued from being married to a man with a different profession or occupation. So, Sarah the wife could be regarded a relatively lucky, though the frequent absence of her husband, ostensibly in pursuit of patronage, bore down on her and often broke her spirits.

As for the clerics themselves, beyond whatever piety they might have, they could follow occupations that today embrace higher education and the creative industries. Hence the long line of ordained men who were naturalists, poets, polemicists, musicians, scientists, linguists – and much else. Philip Williams to some extent fitted the mould: he put his trust in education, moderate godliness, Christianity and the Classics, but his career as a classicist was half-hearted and gained him no credit. Nor was he an outstanding churchman and without good patronage he would have had a struggling sort of life. As it was, he benefited hugely from his links with the diocese of Winchester and Winchester College. Unlike many young Wykehamists he did not stay on at New College, Oxford, waiting for a living to come his way, but in 1769 returned to the school as a fellow and for much of his tenure acted as a yearly bursar. For almost a decade his preferments were relatively unprofitable, though help came from his step-father, Dr John Gordon, who made sure that he acquired a prebend at Lincoln and the living of Gosberton, Lincolnshire. Then in 1780, shortly after marrying Sarah Collins, a daughter of the second master of Winchester, he acquired the living of Compton from the bishop of Winchester, but for about six years was non-resident and continued to live near the school. It was almost certainly through Wiccamical contacts that he encountered his parliamentary patrons the Rt Hon.Charles Jenkinson and Speaker Cornwall and through the latter became chaplain to the House of Commons.

After the death of Sarah in 1787, he was appointed by royal assent to a prebend at Canterbury, which he later exchanged for one at Winchester, together with the living of Houghton. Edington's famous phrase of 1366, that 'Canterbury is the higher rack, but Winchester the better manger', was not strictly true in the eighteenth century, though there were many agriculturally productive estates in Hampshire and its environs, which gave succour to the see and Winchester College. But, like many widowers, Philip Williams must have felt bereft without Sarah (*see* Vickery, 2009). It was several years before in Kent he met his second wife, Helen Ward Fagg, who came to live at the rectory in Compton.

Historians have long argued about the virtues of the Church of England in the eighteenth century (Walsh, Haydon and Taylor, 1993, pp. 2-3). Was it 'a body of dutiful and conscientious men, trying to do their work according to the standards of the day', as concluded by Sykes, who was himself an Anglican clergyman (Sykes, 1934, p. 6)? Or was it more like Virgin's *The Church in the Age of Negligence* (Virgin, 1989)? Or was it somewhere in between? No single answer makes sense: it depends on the person and the time, but in the case of Philip Williams the suspicion is that he was closer to Virgin than Sykes.

Although Philip Williams never expressed it in his letters, he was only three generations from a humble Northern Welsh countryman – termed 'plebeian' in the Oxford record. His great-grandfather had made the first attempt to better himself, moving away from his humble birth to Oxford and returning home to serve as a country clergyman in Wales. His grandfather and father had progressively benefited from the opportunities opened up by education and climbed the academic ladder at Cambridge. They attached themselves to patrons, like the clergyman and polemicist Dr John Nalson and the minor gentry family of the Peytons of Doddington. They had all done well, but none had grasped any of the great prizes – such as a mastership of an Oxbridge college or a deanship, and they never had a chance of a bishopric. They were on the edge of gentry, but with little of the land that would have secured their position. Philip's mother inherited some small estates in the Fens, at a time when these lands were being greatly improved by drainage and new methods of agriculture. But none seemed more than a token of gentility, as today someone might own a few stocks and shares with no hope of ever making a fortune. In fact, as depicted by Philip's father-in-law, a man who seems to have been adept at getting his own way, the business of running such small estates was time-consuming, frustrating and ultimately unprofitable.

Philip Williams was unlucky to lose his father a young age, but it must have been commonplace: the habit of elderly clergymen marrying young women was well entrenched. Besides, even for men who married young, the chance of losing their wife in childbirth was relatively high, and then they might turn to another younger second wife. As a young clergyman, newly married in 1779, it is clear that Philip Williams was mildly ambitious. He had reason to be so: with a major work of scholarship on Polybius in hand, a fellowship of Winchester College, a family history of preferment and a stepfather in Cambridge with his ear to the East Anglian ecclesiastical wind, he could feel confident of the future. A year later he obtained a solid base, when the bishop of Winchester, Dr John Thomas, gave him the rectorship of Compton to add to that of Gosberton - and at various times he also enjoyed other livings, including the New College gift of Easington and Winchester College's Bradford Peverell – though he treated them lightly, as if it were beneath him to take much notice of such rural parishes. His wife Sarah clearly thought it not ridiculous to talk of a bishopric: many of their friends and acquaintances were modestly and even highly placed clerics and may have thought that a little patience would be rewarded by such great gifts.

Like many young churchmen, the road to betterment was paved with appointments to chaplaincies (Sykes, 1934, p. 162). After serving the politician, the Rt Hon. Charles Jenkinson, Speaker Charles Wolfran Cornwall appointed him chaplain to the House of Commons, when he must have believed that he had entered a fruitful arena for advancement; now mixing with the great and good in the full flow of a life in London, it was only a matter of time before the heavens rained manna. But all those long months away in Westminster did not seem to be bearing fruit. Sarah chided him with his lack of preferment, at the same time acting virtually as a surrogate rector of Compton. But after three years at Westminster he was getting nowhere and then disaster struck - twice, in less than two years. First, in September 1787, aged only 31, his wife died 'in child-bed' and was buried at Compton. What happened to the children at this time is not clear, though Sarah had employed a nursemaid. Then, sixteen months later Speaker Cornwall died in office, at his official house in Privy Garden, Whitehall. By this, Philip Williams lost a patron (he never found another) and subsequently gained a Canterbury prebend, but hereafter his main hope must have been his stepfather, John Gordon, who was, however, unable to deliver any further advancement.

In his late 40s, with four young children and a nowhere-near completed edition of Polybius, his life was set to assume a more modest tone. It is clear from comments of John Gordon that his stepson was for some while seriously depressed after the death of his wife, though the Compton registers and the bursars' account books at Winchester College show him doggedly doing his duty in central Hampshire. His prebend at Canterbury, when it finally came, took him to Kent from time to time and it was here that he somehow met his second wife, Helen Ward Fagg, daughter of Sir William Fagg, from a well-seated family with a pedigree peppered with baronets and clerics. Six years after the death of his first wife, and less than two years after the death of Sir William, he and Helen married. He had turned 50, she was in her mid-40s and the children were aged 9 to 13: by all accounts they took to her like a true mother, and family life proper resumed.

A few years later, when he exchanged his Canterbury prebend for one at Winchester, together with the rectorship of Houghton, he became more than ever firmly settled in the Hampshire capital, perhaps all ambition spent. He and his new wife took to a simple country existence at Compton, with him making regular forays into Winchester to perform his 'strict residence' in the cathedral close, make up the bursars' accounts or dine with his many male friends. But the couple were no stay-at-homes:

the Letters show them regularly travelling to Kent and elsewhere, with him – and to a lesser extent her – enjoying an extraordinarily rich social life with relatives and a wide spectrum of friends and acquaintances.

What kind of life was it? His ambitions were not fully realised (whose are?), but he never seemed to be short of funds, which allowed him, perhaps unwisely, to indulge his two spinster daughters and support his sons. His younger son Charles struggled, but found security eventually on the coat-tails of the earls of Chesterfield, which gave him a modest living at Gedling in Nottinghamshire. His wife, Charlotte Roberts, brought him into the orbit of Eton College, a winning rival of Winchester, but overall Charles's life seems to have been a struggle. There were signs of this from the beginning: his mother found him a problem child, difficult to breast-feed, throwing tantrums and generally being discontented (*see* p. 127). Philip Williams's greatest joy was undoubtedly seeing his elder, namesake son prosper and gain considerable distinction as a lawyer; as well as having a thriving private practice, he was for a time the Vinerian Professor of Common Law at Oxford and became King's Counsel and recorder of Winchester.

Taken together, the lives of the Williams family are strong on survival - most of them even thrived. They were the mildly struggling middling sort, not amongst the obviously most successful members of their class, certainly not aristocrats or landed people, but socially comfortable in the presence of them. Indeed, despite being formally, even well educated (especially, of course, the men), they relied for their well-being on the power of the establishment and paid little attention, as far as can be seen, to those intellectuals who in retrospect were ahead of their time. There is, for example, little evidence that they meshed much with local talents in the cathedral close, nor with the avant-garde family of Jonathan Shipley at nearby Twyford, though they did mix with the early abolitionist Beilby Porteus, master of St Cross Hospital 1776-1785. Nor did they seem to be aware of other contemporaries within a ride by carriage or horse who might have interested them – such men as James Harris of Salisbury, Gilbert White of Selborne, or William Gilpin of Boldre,.

As regards their reading tastes, the Letters give a better clue to Sarah's than his. She read literature and plays, such as *Don Quixote*, and the works of Shakespeare, Massinger and Ben Jonson. The most detailed example of his interests, apart from the proofs of his ill-fated edition of Polybius, is a a heavily annotated copy of Edmund Burke's Speech on American Taxation; the second edition of 1775 is still shelved in Winchester College

Fellows' Library (*see* Appendix IV). The Letters also show that Samuel Richardson's *Clarissa* circulated within the family, but there is no trace of such luminaries as Bentham, Blake, Mary Wollstonecraft, Hume, Gibbon, Paine, Frances Burney, Jane Austen (though they did hover on the edge of the Steventon coterie) nor even Hannah More. Undoubtedly the 'revolution', quiet or otherwise, presaged by some of these writers, especially Thomas Paine, spurred on by events in France, threatened the lives of the clerical classes and a softer style of 'reform' had to await the zeal of the Victorians. The Williamses were extremely well acquainted with the system of social advancement as it existed and operated it to the best advantage of themselves and their families. In this they were undoubtedly like the vast majority of the professional classes of late Georgian and Regency England. Those who fought and argued for change were regarded as aberrant, and only won their arguments slowly.

Philip Williams, like most Wykehamists, was undoubtedly a traditionalist, a tory and perhaps, as much as it mattered in the late 18th century, a crypto-Jacobite (but definitely not a Jacobin, as he showed when he cancelled his 'old review, which became too Jacobinical, and stupid, and irreligious to continue'; W140). He was one of the last in the Winchester district to wear a wig, when fashion favoured natural hair. He was steeped in the Classics, though unlike his stepfather he never flaunted his learning. We can probably agree with Winchester history don, G.H. Blore, that he 'was not a snob' (WCA/E10/14), but he was certainly not a reformer, nor one with any obvious passion for the poor. He might have been Johnsonian: his Winchester master, Joseph Warton, had been a great friend of the literary giant, at least until he fell out of favour, but unlike Johnson, Philip Williams gave scant charity to the poor and disadvantaged; his eye was on the main chance - obituaries and vacant livings were more frequently the subject of his letters than philanthropy or philosophy. And he had no talent for versifying, as the fragments of verse preserved in the Papers demonstrate. In contrast, his former master, who is still remembered for his literary criticism of Alexander Pope, and his brother Thomas, are firmly placed in the history of 18th century literature.

Although the Letters are disappointing on what Philip Williams read, he must surely have pored over Boswell's *Life of Doctor Johnson* first published in 1791, or the second edition two years later (references below are to the 2007 edition edited by David Womersely, who is, appropriately, the Thomas Warton Professor of English Literature at Oxford). Philip Williams might have recalled the visit of Dr Johnson to Winchester College in 1778 in the company of the young Charles Burney (Frances

Burney's brother), whom he had recommended to Joseph Warton (p. 722). He would certainly have found much of interest in the *Life* on his former master and on his brother Thomas's success in securing the great man an Oxford MA in 1755 (pp. 151-2). Less attractive might have been Johnson's comment on Lady Diana Beauclerk (*see* p. 258). Nor, in later years, when Philip Williams's son Charles was tutor to the son of the 5th earl of Chesterfield, could he have felt easy at reading Johnson's famous non-deferential letter to the 'failed patron' of his *Dictionary*, the 4th earl (p. 142). So much else might have caught his eye, including the Revd William Maxwell's report of a comment by Johnson (p. 323):

> He told me, that he had frequently been offered country preferment, if he would consent to take orders; but he could not leave the improved society of the capital, or consent to exchange the exhilarating joys and splendid decorations of publick life, for the obscurity, insipidity, and uniformity of remote situations.

Having tried London and settled for Winchester, did Philip Williams sometimes wonder what else might have been? Or was he, although country born like Johnson, and with many 'Lincolnshire friends' like Johnson, happy with his lot? Perhaps it is fitting to leave the final word to G.H. Blore, always elegant and humane, who in his unpublished essay on the Letters (WCA/E10/14) took pluralism for granted, yet made it an excuse for Sarah's long periods alone in Winchester. He balanced this shortcoming with other virtues, suggesting that Philip Williams 'was something more, a scholar, a man of the world, a favourite in society, a good man of business, with whom Wardens gladly took counsel.' He went on:

> He was equally at ease with men and women, clergy and laity, Londoners and country folk, a good judge of his fellows, one who did not intend to hide his light under a bushel; and while he pursued the path to preferment, from Winchester and Oxford to Lincoln and London, his home saw him but rarely. So his wife had to bring up her children, to manage a household and sometimes a parish also, almost unaided by her husband, to whom she remained dutiful and affectionate.

Of course, it is to this neglect of his role as father and husband that we owe the existence of the Letters that make this volume. His memorial inscription in Compton church also talks of 'an easy urbanity of manner, and social disposition of mind [that] render'd him a general favourite in the intercourse of society' and of 'various classical attainments and character of a scholar'. But sadly his scholarship, in the form of the projected new edition of the works of Polybius, was never published and his undoubted bonhomie might have fitted him better to another career.

Whatever else Philip Williams and his like were, it is clear with hindsight that they were engaged in both a class war and an intellectual struggle that pitted science, industry, enlightenment and institutional reform against a traditional system depending on complex human relationships within a hard-wired social structure. Not surprisingly, those who got advancement based entirely on where they came from and who they knew felt threatened by 'reform', in whatever guise it was presented. The horrors of the French Revolution, which demonstrated just how awful constitutional reform could be, gave succour to the anti-reformists, but it was the industrial revolution, and associated economic growth, coupled with labourers' riots, that finally changed the world that Philip Williams knew. Young Victorians were different from young Georgians; some of them wanted to make a better life for ordinary people, a concept that never seems to have entered the minds of the Williamses. Others wanted to bring about reforms that had long been in the air – to change parliament and other institutions to make them more representative of the people at large, though universal suffrage was, of course, a long way off. The cosy string-pulling that dominated the Georgian world has all but disappeared, though the networking and opportunism that they depended upon are alive and well. To send a letter, as many did, to people in power and, in essence, ask them for a job for life, is unthinkable in the early 21st century, but only blind idealists would believe that the human instincts that drove Philip Williams are not still at work.

His successor as rector of Compton certainly seemed to be of another mould. John Old Zillwood came from Dorchester and had served as chaplain to the county gaol and bridewell in Winchester. Even in this humble position he showed signs of welcoming the 'cursed spirit of reform', suggesting, for example, that inmates be given books and provided with schooling (HRO/92M95/F2/1/14). Within three years of his institution to Compton he had rebuilt the rectory and five years later, in 1838, opened the doors of All Saints School to the poor of the village. He stayed in post with a single living until his death in 1871, when his furniture, paintings and private library were put up for sale (HRO/1M76/PZ7). There are a substantial number of other records of the life of Philip Williams's successor, including his will, his sermons, and his letters to Sir Thomas Baring and others – but that is another story.

17. *The Williams Papers – Notes for Researchers*

HINDSIGHT SHOWS that the Enlightenment in Western Europe did much to create the modern world (Porter, 2000). Many believe that it still has a great deal to do, as a study such as this may demonstrate. Yet, like most research, it depended on some rather dry matters, which are the subject of this chapter.

The Williams Papers are preserved in the archives of Winchester College, Winchester, UK. They make more than 433 items (W1-433) and form the basis of this study of the family and friends of the Revd Philip Williams (1742-1830), and more generally the Georgian world they inhabited. Overall, they include a wide range of material, including late seventeenth century love letters, a large number of personal letters written mainly between 1780 and 1828 and scruffy jottings from genealogical research carried out mainly in the last century. A detailed synopsis of the papers is given below and a complete catalogue can be found in the archives of Winchester College.

The Papers were collected by family members over the years and passed down, probably via the line of Philip Williamses (*see* p. ix), until they came into the hands of the last of the direct line, Mrs Edwyn Jervoise (née Lettice Williams, 1886-1981). She was a daughter of PW(VI),(1852-1939), a great-grandson of Philip Williams and a master at Eton College, Windsor. The papers contain a letter from him of 1864, written to his mother from boarding school, recording the trials of a 12-year-old boy managing his budget (W212). In the 1930s Mrs Jervoise assisted her father, then in his late eighties, with genealogical researches he had started 30 years earlier. As a young master at Eton he had been particularly interested in the Welsh roots of the Williams family and corresponded with the genealogist and lord lieutenant of Flintshire, Hugh R. Hughes of Kimnel Park, Abergele, North Wales (*see* Chapter 1). PW(VI) and Mrs Jervoise researched many other aspects of the Williams family, showing that for more than 200 years preferment, nepotism, the old boy network, favouritism – call it what you will – flourished and kept it in relative comfort and security.

The sorties that Mrs Jervoise and her father undertook and the notes they made were rather random – not the work of professionals, but just people with an interest in their family history – though they probably captured much that might have been lost. Noteworthy is a pedigree starting in the early seventeenth century that was written on both sides of an opened-up large envelope, now in a fragile state (W418). As well presenting a family tree, albeit an extremely contorted one, the source includes information taken from a 'Family Bible', which has probably now been lost. As an example of how not to do research the envelope can scarcely be bettered, but it contains much detail that would otherwise have been very difficult to retrieve or even been lost.

It was recognised by Mrs Jervoise that many clues to the world of Philip Williams and his family were contained in the 31 letters to him from his stepfather Dr John Gordon, though they were treated with some levity. In one letter to her father written in 1932, she says:

> Here are old Gordon's letters which I am sending to you as I don't want to take them all round Wales with me! but I do want to have them to show you the bits about Compton's properties etc [she probably means 'Catlidge', where the Williams family had a small estate], which we can [do] at the end of the Tour.

In another letter, she referred to a paper published in the *Derbyshire Archaeological and Natural History Society's Journal* containing correspondence between Philip Williams and a schoolmate Francis Mundy. It was written by a relative of Mundy, the Revd W. G. Clark-Maxwell (W400a-f), of whom she wrote (W249i):

> This is what old Clark Maxwell says about the Gordons [presumably she means the Mundys]. Please keep this letter for me [it contained information from standard sources].

In her historical forays, Mrs Jervoise might have had a helping hand at home, since her husband, Edwyn (1884-1955), was an industrial archaeologist cum transport historian and wrote several authoritative books, such as *The Ancient Bridges of Wales and Western England*. And in the last few years of his life had letters on the choice of Christian names published in *The Times*. He and other members of the Jervoise family are commemorated in the parish church of Herriard, the small Hampshire village where it has been seated since the reign of James I.

After the death of her father in 1939, Mrs Jervoise presumably took charge of the Williams Papers until in 1953, perhaps following contacts with the Winchester history master G.H. Blore, she explored the possibility of giving the papers to Winchester College. This was greeted with enthusiasm by the Fellows' Librarian, J.M.G. Blakiston, who was a young friend of Blore (Blakiston, 1974), and recognised, in particular, the historical value of the Letters (W433). In 1968, following a meeting with the College Archivist , Peter Gwyn (WCA/P9/1/25), Mrs Jervoise began to hand over the papers to the College, starting with the letters between Philip and Sarah Williams (W5-93), transcripts of which form the basis of this volume and are available online at www.winchestercollege.org /archives. The material continued to be handed over in dribs and drabs until, by February 1976, all the items had been donated to the College. In May 1976, perhaps feeling bereft of all links with her Williams ancestors, she asked for the oldest items in the collection, two late seventeenth century love letters (W416-7), to be returned to her until her death. A note in the hand of Virginia Clanchy on the last page of the catalogue records that this was done, and another by Dr Roger Custance (Archivist 1976-2005) indicates that the items were returned in January 1982.

In addition to the Williams Papers, an eclectic collection of other items was donated by Mrs Jervoise, namely, two portraits of Philip Williams, a rather fine one of 1823 by George Sharples (*see* List of Illustrations) and another crude miniature of 1809 by George Hayter (later knighted), and a number of books: a New Testament in Greek, two editions of the poems of the Wykehamist William Collins, a copy of *The Countermine* (London, 4 ed., 1684) by John Nalson (Philip Williams's great-grandfather), an edition of Cicero and a nineteenth century book on public school cricket matches.

Historiography

The first known use of the Williams Letters, as mentioned elsewhere, appears to have been by Drew in his *Compton, near Winchester* (1939, passim, pp. 124-130), where he called Philip Williams 'the last and perhaps the most notable of the Compton pluralist rectors', adding:

> These letters, apart from being a mine of information on the doings of Winchester society and the general 'atmosphere' of the times, have a good deal to say on Compton affairs, and naturally throw much light on the characters of the writers. Philip appears as a good-natured man, full of ambition, essentially worldly-minded – in all these scores of long letters there is not a sentence

which suggests he was particularly interested in religion – delighting in the society of the great (yet no snob, for he was extremely popular with all classes in Compton), devoted in his own way to his young wife. Sally, who seems to walk straight out of the pages of Jane Austen, is a capable high-spirited girl, out for any fun which comes her way, perhaps a trifle neurotic, rather overwhelmed by a constant succession of babies, alive to her husband's faults but devoted to him all the same.

Two benefices [Compton and Gosberton; three counting the fellowship of Winchester College], however, were far from satisfying Mr. Williams. He had now been 16 years in Holy Orders, and so far no really highly-paid sine-cure had come his way. Clearly, if he was to share in the good things, he would have to bestir himself, and Philip, who did nothing by halves, set to work with a will. This was in fact the seed-time; the harvest was to come later.

Drew mentioned Philip Williams's prebend at Lincoln, which 'he held for 47 years without performing any duty there' and in May 1784 his appointment as chaplain to the Speaker of the House of Commons. In August the House moved 'an humble address praying the Crown to bestow preferment on their Chaplain', which was of course a formality, though Drew commented:

It says little for the gratitude of George III that Mr. Williams was kept waiting for five years before he was made a prebendary of Canterbury. This delay, however, did not discourage him [it was, in fact, normal]; the possibilities of London are great, and his naïve accounts of how he cultivated the acquaintance of those who had patronage to bestow makes very amusing reading.

Sarah Williams, he noted, did not approve, writing (Letter 47):

I had rather see my poor Phill a country curate his whole life with some feeling and humanity, than at the top of his profession in Westminster hall if it is to be purchased by the sacrifice of every amiable virtue and sentiment.

She was in fact responding to some 'shockingly indelicate and altogether unpardonable' expressions in a letter from an unidentified 'friend' of Philip – perhaps an MP – to an unidentified 'Mr D' concerning some business at Winchester College that had sent her father, the second master, into a 'state of anxiety'. Drew suggested that Philip 'replied to her homily in a tone of amused urbanity', though, since her letter is undated it is not clear to which reply he is referring. However, 'amused urbanity' was definitely not in short supply and, for example, in what seems to have been to be a response to Letter 102, he wrote (Letter 103):

> I recieved [sic] your letter, and love to be scolded and lectured by you.

Drew also emphasized the key role of Sally in running the church at Compton, when her rector husband, was absent for long periods:

> There was no curate at Compton at this time, and Sally kept the church going; it was she who arranged with neighbouring clergy to take the services and she spent each Sunday in Compton herself to see that all went well. One of the Heathcote family [probably Thomas] often officiated in this way to her satisfaction, but not every visiting clergyman created such a good impression; a rector from Winchester [William Mence] seemed to Mrs. Williams so 'bloated and puffed up' that she doubted if he would be able to get through his sermon [Letter 82]. Nor did Sally hesitate to stand up to her husband when she thought that Compton people were not getting a fair deal.

Drew noted that before they had taken up residence at Compton, which was in about 1786, the couple lived in Kingsgate Street, close to Winchester College, and let the rectory to their brother-in-law Jeremiah Dyson 'a young gentleman whose inability to live within his income was a constant source of indignation to the family.' But in 1787 the couple seemed to be facing a bright future:

> To his wife's great happiness the rector spent the summer in Compton, but Sally Williams' short life was nearing its close, and in November she died [a slip: actually it was on 19 September]. The rector returned to his work, the quest for benefices still went on, but his heart was in Compton churchyard and a reference to Sally [Sarah], written by him 30 years after her death, is difficult even now to read unmoved.

The 'reference to Sally' has not been identified.

The next use of the Letters seems to have been in 1951, when G.H. Blore, who taught history at Winchester College from 1901 to 1930 (and briefly during the 1939-45 war), published a paper on Winchester in the eighteenth century with the following footnote (HRO/12M73/Z62; WCA/E10/13):

> Of the letters which illustrate life in Winchester, too few survive, and those are all from the clerical circle [not strictly true]. Two Canons contribute – Edmund Pyle, who was in Winchester 1756-76, and John Mulso, 1770-93. The Warton letters, published in 1806 by John Wooll [in his *Biographical Memoirs of ...Warton*], were written to Joseph Warton; but the [Winchester] College library also owns manuscripts of letters which he himself wrote to his daughters in India and to others. Those of Sarah Williams, written 1780-87, are more full of Winchester news and gossip; and it was by the kindness of her descendant, Mrs. Edwin [or Edwyn] Jervoise, that I have been able to read them and make use of them.

Blore's paper was based on a talk, one of a series, given to pupils at Winchester College. It is clear that he had a particular interest in the letters and for some years had been making a study of Winchester in the eighteenth century. A picture of him as historian is given in a short memoir by Blakiston, who wrote (1974, pp.10-11):

> The first thing that struck you about George – after his tall figure, his bald head and his high high-pitched voice – was his insatiable appetite for knowledge. ...He had a special partiality for memoirs and letters; which was not unnatural, as the whole basis of his interests was towards the human individual, the details which revealed his quality or his oddity. 'What sort of man was so-and-so?' was a question he was constantly asking, perhaps too readily dismissing as dry and pedantic the preoccupations of another sort of mind [concerned] with the abstract and the general. ...Almost all his published work ... is of a biographical nature. ...With all his knowledge, Blore was not a great scholar. He was both too impatient and too modest.

After his retirement, Blore became the founding editor of and contributed to the *Winchester Cathedral Record*, and wrote a number of small works, such as *The Monuments of Winchester Cathedral*, (1935, 1949; revised 1983), *Some Wykehamists of the Eighteenth Century* (1944), and *Thomas Rennell, Dean of*

Winchester, 1805-1840 (1952). Amongst the items he left at his death in 1960 (WCA classmark E10) are several essays in draft written with a mind to publishing a book on Winchester in the eighteenth century, which was never completed.

Blore suggested Winchester College in the eighteenth century was so dominated by males that 'a scholar could go for months/weeks without seeing a woman's face' (WCA/E10/14), though perhaps this is taking the point too far, since head master Joseph Warton had numerous children and was married for virtually all the time he was at the school between 1755 and 1794. His first wife, who was 'universally liked and admired', according to the ODNB, died in 1792 and within the year he had remarried. Also, when Sarah's father, Thomas Collins, was recruited in 1766 as second master by Warton he too had children, three daughters, all of whom wed men they had met at the school. And when G.I. Huntingford was elected warden of the school in 1789 he moved into his lodgings with his widowed sister-in-law, Mrs Mary Huntingford, and her large family. Two years earlier, when his brother Thomas died suddenly, he had taken responsibility for her, with six children and another on the way. Both he and Thomas Collins were eventually faced with the need to 'marry off' several young ladies. Andrew Robinson in the ODNB entry for Huntingford comments:

> He was devoted to his brother's children: he sent four of his five nieces to school and married them into prominent families associated with Winchester College, and energetically supported his nephews' careers in the Church of England.

Thomas Collins was perhaps less successful: the marriage of Sarah and Philip must have looked good to observers, though his other two daughters had less conventional marriages, Elizabeth to a feckless young man and Charlotte to an unfaithful aristocrat (*see* Chapter 15). As Blore commented: 'In the eyes of the world it may have seemed that the three sisters had married well, but their happiness was short-lived.'

Also extant are the Blore's notebooks (WCA/E10/1-6) and an unpublished typescript, 'Who's Who for 18th Century: A Biographical Dictionary of Winchester and Neighbourhood' (HRO/9M91/W), which contains many references to F.W.C. Pepper, the Winchester City Librarian from 1921 to 1950, who presumably helped him in his quest. The 'Who's Who' is not dated but was compiled from his 'small notebooks about the year 1944'. Its provenance is revealed in the preface to *Some Wykehamists of the Eighteenth Century*, (Blore, 1944):

> For the last five years I have been studying the lives of our local celebrities in the 18th century – in City and County, in the School and in our Cathedral Close – and have been putting my material into book form. As it seemed unlikely that I should be able to publish anything on a large scale [amongst other things, there was an acute shortage of paper in the war years], I have separated and developed a single chapter which may interest some Wykehamists.

One of the essays he left is on Sarah and Philip Williams (WCA/E10/14); it is in draft, and is considered in detail elsewhere. It opens with the sentence:

> In the 18th and 19th century, College was a masculine (?monastic) preserve ... yet it is to a woman's pen that we owe our knowledge of some of the details of its life which otherwise would have been lost in oblivion.

This was from the pen of a man who had himself been at Winchester in the late nineteenth century and had spent all his time there as a teacher and a bachelor but had – like so many Oxbridge fellows leaving hallowed walls – on 'the eve of his retirement' married (Blakiston, 1974, p. 10). Other essays in draft include one on the diarist and letter-writer Melesina Trench (1768-1827), and several on Winchester church dignitaries, including Edmund Pyle, John Mulso, Jonathan Shipley, and Newton Ogle.

The next use of the Letters was probably by Winchester local historian Barbara Carpenter Turner, in her *History of the Royal Hampshire County Hospital* (1986, p. 46). She quoted excerpts to illustrate the lives of two Winchester physicians well known to the Williamses, namely, Dr John Makkitrick, whose painful demise is detailed by Sarah Williams (*see*, for example, Letters 56 and 61), and Dr John Littlehales, who often administered to the Williams family and is commemorated in the cathedral; he was also roundly chastised in verse by Philip Williams for giving a maid of Sarah Williams, Molly Strong, ineffective medicine (W249; *see* p. 132). A letter of 14 June 1803 (W197; *see* p. 131), phonetically spelled, written by Molly to Philip and Sarah's daughters, Elizabeth and Charlotte, many years after she had ceased serving the family, has been published in *The Wykehamist* (11 February 1970, p. 429).

Virginia Clanchy, who catalogued the Williams Papers, wrote two articles based on her work. The first, published only two years after Mrs Jervoise had donated all items to the College, and quoted above, sketched the history of the Williams family, the life and work of Philip Williams, his life with Sarah and the people he knew (Clanchy, 1970). Although she was aware of many of the background stories – the career of PW(II) at St John's College Cambridge, George III's meeting with Dr Johnson concerning Philip Williams's edition of Polybius (*see* Chapter 4), his friendship with Lovelace Bigg-Wither (*see* Chapter 3) and Francis Mundy, his chaplaincy at Westminster and much else – she does not mention the scandalous life of the Hon. George Richard Bolingbroke, husband of Sarah's sister Charlotte, perhaps because at the time such material was regarded as not suitable for a school publication (*see* Chapter 15). Commenting on the Letters in general, she called Sarah's 'charming and poignant' and Philip's 'matter-of-fact, almost terse but vivid and amusing'.

In the second of her articles she explored the links between the families of Philip Williams and Lovelace Bigg (later, Bigg-Wither) and the novelist Jane Austen, who often mentioned 'the Biggs' and was friendly with Lovelace's daughters, Alethea, Catherine and Elizabeth. Much of it concerns a period outside the scope of this volume, but since the Biggs were seated at Manydown House, in the north Hampshire parish of Wootton St Lawrence, where Philip Williams was a frequent visitor, close to Steventon, where Jane Austen's father was the rector, it was natural that the two families would meet and that the Letters might mention members of the Austen family. In the event, as Virginia Clanchy pointed out, Jane's father and her brother, James, do in fact appear (W95, 116), but not Jane. By the time she had published her first novel, *Sense and Sensibility*, in 1811, Sarah was long dead, Philip was aged 69, and it is hardly surprising that she was 'off his radar'. However, she knew the family well enough to send 'kind remembrances' to his daughter Charlotte in a letter written in February 1813 to her sister Cassandra; and with the writer's eye she had spotted that his other daughter Elizabeth was a problem (Le Faye, p.205):

> Only think of your having at last the honour of seeing that wonder of wonders her elder Sister!

At the time, there was little to recommend Jane the author to an elderly cleric: she was a demure writer in the provinces who had not had 'overnight success'. Besides, her works were probably too close to the truth for him and his spinster daughters. The present author would have been overjoyed to have found otherwise, as would Clanchy, who wrote (1976):

So little is known of Jane Austen as she appeared to her contemporaries that it is almost a tragedy that the Williams letters, written by people who knew her, and which have survived until today, should contain nothing at all about her. On the other hand, they do describe the actual society in which she lived[,] with its problems of illness, the frequent tragic deaths of young mothers, the difficulty of travel – especially for women, the disaster of poverty and disgrace through debts, and above all the incessant exchange of gossip and news through letters and endless visiting.

Another link between the worlds of the Williamses and the Austens mentioned by Clanchy is the renting in her widowhood by Mrs Elizabeth Heathcote (née Bigg) of the prebendal house that Philip Williams was granted in the close at Winchester in 1797. On the advice of Canon Frederick Bussby (later author of *Winchester Cathedral 1079-1979*, Southampton, 1979), she identified the house as No. 9, whereas later research has shown that it was in fact what is now No. 11 (No.12 before 1842, when it was renumbered), which stands in its own grounds behind high walls, near the southwest corner of the cathedral (Crook, 1984, pp. 119, 167; Le Faye, 1995, p. 587; Barrett, 1988, p. 19). Clanchy's article is illustrated with a print by G. F. Prosser of the Bigg-Wither seat, Manydown House (now demolished), a painting of Philip Williams aged 81 by George Sharples, and a pencil and colour wash of 1841 of his eldest son, sometime recorder of Winchester, PW(IV), by George Woodley. Clanchy thought that Philip junior's wedding to Jane Blachford was the subject of an acid comment of Jane Austen's in a letter to her niece, Mrs Anna Lefroy: 'I have never seen it in the Papers. And one may as well be single if the wedding is not to be in print', but later research has attached it to the wedding in February 1815 of a sister, Winifred, to the Revd John Mansfield, rector of Rowner, Hampshire, where Philip and Jane were married two years later in December (Le Faye, 1995, pp. 289 & 498).

In 1988 the Revd Philip L. S. Barrett, who had himself been instituted rector of Compton (jointly with Otterbourne) the previous year, wrote an article for the *Winchester Cathedral Record* based on a careful reading of the entire gamut of the Williams letters (W5-177), together with some background material from Drew's *Compton, near Winchester*. It was illustrated with the Sharples portrait and entitled 'Philip Williams – the acceptable face of pluralism' – a title which in some minds requires a question mark at the end, but the author was perhaps constrained by the need to be loyal to his living. He wrote:

> Pluralism was widely regarded as an abuse...in the [late] nineteenth century, but Williams' career shows how a man could be diligent in the performance of his duties and exercise an influence in many varied spheres, even though he held a combination of several different preferments.... [and] in these days of united benefices...one wonders whether [pluralism] may not have survived in a different form. Although Philip Williams undoubtedly enjoyed his varied posts, there is no evidence that he was at all slack. His parishioners were well cared for, even in his absence and he was careful to see that deputies were arranged when he was away. Besides other contemporary pluralists, such as the flamboyant George Pretyman [a protégé of Pitt], who also held canonries at Winchester and Lincoln, Philip Williams appears as a pillar of respectability and sobriety.

Perhaps Barrett can be excused a 'whitewash job' on a predecessor, but Sally might have smiled to have read the article whilst she was stuck in Winchester and the Speaker's chaplain was fancy free in London!

In fact it is clear that Philip Williams in his later years 'did the duty' at Compton, satisfied his residence in the Cathedral close, and discharged his duties as bursar of Winchester College (and later as treasurer to the dean and chapter), but did nothing at the other places where he held appointments, neither in Lincolnshire, at Gosberton and Lincoln, nor at Houghton, Hampshire (W231). Barrett's article is weighted towards the time after the death of Sally and if it had been focused more on his earlier years he might have reached other conclusions. It seems true, however, that in his later years, Philip Williams took a full part in the life of Compton and came to be regarded as a good pastor. The letters from this period (W94-177) are outside the scope of this volume, but for the moment Barrett's article, which cherry-picks effectively, is the only source which makes an extensive use of them.

The theatre historian Paul Ranger has used the letters of Sarah Williams in his studies of theatre in Winchester, and Hampshire in general, in the eighteenth century (Ranger, 1976, 1996), writing (Pickering and Woolgar, 2009, p. 63):

> Correspondence relating to a small theatre is very difficult to discover... the letters of Mrs Sarah Williams ...described the hullabaloo surrounding the building of Winchester's New Theatre in 1785 and the attempts of a solicitor to prevent it opening until an effigy of him was publicly burned.

The present author has written three articles based on the Letters concerned mainly with the Worthy villages to the north and east of Winchester. One concerned Dr Newton Ogle, dean of Winchester and canon of Durham, and his family link with the Ogles of Worthy Park, Martyr Worthy, where home theatricals of the play *Douglas*, by Church of Scotland minister John Home feature in Sarah Williams's letters (Shurlock, 2010). Another was on the Revd Sir Henry Rivers, rector of Martyr Worthy and a son of Sir Peter Rivers Gay, prebendary of Winchester 1766-1790, who features in the letters between Philip Williams and his daughters (Shurlock, 2011). And the third describes the social scene on Worthy Down during Winchester race week, when, as Sarah's letters vividly show, the otherwise sedate cathedral city, boosted by many visitors, was turned by local society into a seething bowl of entertainment, laced with danger (Shurlock, 2012).

As far as is known, the letters of Dr Gordon to Philip Williams have not been cited in any work, though in 1932 Mrs Edwyn Jervoise was contacted by Canon C. W. Foster, secretary of the Lincoln Record Society, to 'send some copies or extracts from the letters [of Dr John Gordon] containing the news and gossip about Lincoln etc.', though it is not known if anything became of this (W249o,p).

Archiving

The Williams Papers were all catalogued as they were donated to Winchester College, which accounts for the non-chronological order of the items in the catalogue. The cataloguer was Virginia A. Clanchy, Assistant Archivist, who was employed between 1967, just before Mrs Jervoise started to donate the papers, and 1976, just as the donation was completed (*The Wykehamist*, 7 July, 1979, p. 586). Two years after Mrs Jervoise had started to hand over all the papers to the College, Clanchy wrote (1970):

> It is surely unusual for a family with no fixed ancestral home to keep and cherish, over a period of almost 300 years, a collection of purely personal documents and letters. But this was done by succeeding generations of the Williams family until now, when at

last there is no one to carry on the trust. Many of the letters were written from the College and to the College they have now returned. It is the details of family life that they reveal which are of such interest today – the same problems, joys and sorrows but in a totally different world.

Each entry in the catalogue gives a date, if available, and a short description (not more than about 100 words), with points of general interest, highlighting those relevant to the history of Winchester College. Most of it was typed in one style, though the Introduction and the last two pages are in a different face. The piece numbers of the items assigned by Clanchy are written in pencil on the originals, as well as on the corresponding pages of Transcript A (*see* below). On some of the letters, in the hand of J.S. Drew, dates, and occasionally other notes, are written in pencil, e.g. on Letter 108, 'Saturday 16 July 1785'. These were the dates assigned to the letters in Transcript B (*see* below), though further research has meant that the present editor has not always followed them.

Brief details of the Williams Papers are included in Himsworth's *Winchester College Muniments*, vol. I (1976, pp. 236-238), previously called 'The Winchester Descriptive List', to which Peter Gwyn and John Harvey contributed. Virginia Clanchy also worked on the list (Gwyn, 1976) and was also involved in two exhibitions based on the material, one on Jane Austen and the Williams family (WCA/F5/247, F6/5/24; *see also* Clanchy, 1976) and another on Winchester College, 1679-1832, which was mounted in June 1971 (WCA/P9/3/2).

Synopsis

The oldest items in the Williams Papers are two love letters, one dated 13 October 1687, in a miniature script by Philip Williams's namesake grandfather, PW(I), to his future wife, Elizabeth Nalson, daughter of the Ely historian and polemicist Dr John Nalson (W349-352, 416-417). More than forty years ago they were reproduced in *The Wykehamist* (9 December 1970, p. 540). Also in the papers is a book of prayers written in the same script (W352A). Apart from these love letters, the earliest letter in the papers was that written in August 1725 by Thomas Peyton, in Florence, to Philip Williams's father (W1), whose father had himself been presented with the living of Doddington by the Peyton family. There is also an undated cover addressed to 'The Revd Mr Williams at St John's College Cambridge, Inghilterra', bearing a seal with the Peyton crest (W214).

Legal papers include prenuptial agreements of Philip Williams's maternal grandparents, Dr John Dighton and Elizabeth (née Janes), of 24 April 1718 and 19 May 1718, the other parties being Lady St John, widow, of the parish of St Margaret's Westminster, and Barbara Janes, (W217-218). There is a copy of an award of probate granted in September 1719 for PW(I)'s will of October 1715, and of April 1736 for his wife's will of March 1733 (W219-220). The papers also include a copy of the marriage articles of Philip Williams's father, PW(II), and his mother, Anne (née Dighton), dated 25 May 1741 (W221), and probate of 6 July 1749 granted for the estate of PW(II) (W222). There is a copy of an inscription from a church at March, near Ely, where PW(I) held the living of Doddington, extracted from the Cole MSS in the British Museum (BM Add MSS 5804), concerning a bequest to the poor made by PW(II) (W237), and a copy of an inscription from the tomb in the south choir aisle of Ely Cathedral of Elizabeth Williams, the wife of PW(I), and their daughter Alice (W310). The marriage settlements between Philip Williams and his first wife, Sarah Collins, dated 9 March 1779, and his second wife, Helen Ward Fagg, dated 26 February 1793, both survive (W223-224). The main purpose of the first was to secure for Sarah rights to 'fenn or Marsh Grounds' held by Philip's mother but due to revert to him at her death; it had, as additional parties, Sarah's father, Thomas Collins, Philip's friend, Lovelace Bigg[-Wither], and the family lawyer, Richard Hollist of the Middle Temple.

The papers include a total of 264 letters, of which 129 written up to 21 May 1789 form the basis for this volume, though others have been cited. In brief, there are two early letters of August 1760 and June 1762 to Philip Williams from his mother (one co-written with his stepfather, Dr John Gordon on the occasion of his marriage to her) and one from one of his sisters of September 1768 concerning their mother's illness (Letter 8). A series of 90 letters between Philip Williams and his wife Sarah, written between some date in 1780 and April 1787, form the hub of this volume (W5-93, including 50A). A long series of 31 letters to Philip Williams from his stepfather Dr John Gordon written between November 1767 and May 1789 – almost all before the death of Sarah in 1787 – have also been used in this study. Similarly, four long letters from Lovelace Bigg-Wither (then named plain Bigg), a friend, written between February 1765 and August 1768, and two later letters of November 1789 and February 1790, have been used (Letters 3-5, 7 and 132-33).

Eighty-eight letters from Philip Williams to one or both of his daughters, Charlotte and Elizabeth ('Betsy'), written between September 1795 and August 1828, have been read and transcribed, but not published here, as they fall outside the period of this volume (W94-178, including 123A, 123B, 135A). Similarly, six letters from Philip to his friend Francis N. C. Mundy (1739-1815), a Wykehamist and Derbyshire grandee, and a surviving cover signed 'E.W. Mundy', fall into the later period (W390-395, 216). The Mundy letters have been published in the *Derbyshire Archaeological and Natural History Society's Journal* (1932, pp.1-24), by a descendant, the Revd W. G. Clark-Maxwell, MA, FSA, with the help of Winchester College archivist Herbert Chitty (W232, 400a-f). Several letters on genealogical matters, written by Clark-Maxwell in the early 1930s to Philip Williams's namesake descendant, PW(VI) (1852-1939), and his daughter, Mrs Edwyn Jervoise (née Lettice Williams), are also in the papers (W396-399).

Although Philip Williams had verse published as a young man of 20 at Oxford (*see* Chapter 2), poetry was not his forte, though epitaphs by him for his wife, in both Latin and English, survive (W243-244), as well as lines added (not without ambiguity) to an undated tearsheet bearing a humorous poem, 'The Choice of a Wife by Cheese' (W245). Also, extant are humorous verses by him (W246-248), and a rare social comment in verse, in the voice of former nursemaid Molly Strong, who took issue with a local physician, Dr John Littlehales, for taking money from the family for ineffective medicine and other misdemeanours (W249). There is one letter of 14 February 1785 from Philip Williams's children (W195), written in the phonetic fashion of Molly Strong, whose letter of 14 June 1803 from Compton, Hampshire, to his two spinster daughters Elizabeth and Charlotte (published in *The Wykehamist* 11 February 1970, p. 429) must have brought back fond memories (W197).

It is interesting to find a cover dated 25 August 1812 from Gloucester, addressed to Charlotte Williams at Compton in the hand of G.I. Huntingford, when he was bishop of Gloucester and warden of Winchester College (W215). Also in the papers is a letter of 2 May 1793 to Philip Williams from his namesake eldest son, then a scholar at Winchester, giving details of new rules drawn up in the wake of the boys' rebellion in that year – 'between 1780 and 1830 there were at least eight [such] major disturbances' (Blakiston and Gwyn, 1971, p. 4; W178). He also kept the medal task in Latin by his younger son, Charles (1784-1866), entitled *Cassandra vaticinium*, a 131-line piece on the Greek prophetess written in 1802 and entered in the much-prized annual competition that took place between scholars (W242). Interestingly, 'cassandra-ing' was a word often used by his mother (*see*, for example, Letter 81). Later in life, in January 1820, under the terms of an 'Act to Promote the Residence of

Parochial Clergy...' of GIII:17 (explained and amended in GIII:21), Charles raised a mortgage of £826.11s.6d. from his brother to build a new parsonage house at Cubley, Derbyshire, where he had been presented with the living by the young earl of Chesterfield, as 'minor patron' (W225).

In June 1832 Dr [William] Webb, Master of Clare Hall, Cambridge, and brother-in-law of Philip Williams, wrote as a favour to his namesake son about fines levied at 'the court at Kirtling', about 12 miles east of Cambridge, which in 1832 he, the son, declared to be his as part of the landowning qualifications required to be a Hampshire Justice of the Peace (W199; HRO/Q27/3/313). Other estates declared were 'Catlidge' (apparently the name by which Kirtling was known between about 1500 and 1900; www.kirtlingandupend.org.uk) and 'Upend' a nearby village, which are both mentioned in the letters between John Gordon and his stepson. PW(IV) also cited lands in Compton and Houghton, in Hampshire, the livings of which had both been held by his father, as well as land in Llanwnda, Caernarvonshire (now in the unitary authority of Gwynedd), originally held by the Quellyn family, into which a sister of Philip Williams's grandfather had married (W270, 301, 306, 307, 333, 336). In the papers are photographs of portraits (*see* List of Illustrations) of Philip Williams (one by George Sharples, the other by George Hayter) and his elder son PW(IV) (by George Woodley) and a photograph of his second son Charles (W331, 331a, 331b, 420). The portraits were donated to Winchester College by Mrs Edwyn Jervoise and now hang in the Warden's Lodgings. Other photographs include one of a memorial inscription in Lincoln Cathedral of George Gordon (1763-1845), son of Dr John Gordon, and therefore a step-brother of Philip Williams (W335), and of the parsonage house in the village of Llanwnda (W336).

There are also undated notes on the family's estate of Catlidge, Cambridgeshire, written by an unnamed copyholder (though internal evidence excludes the Dobito and Bacon families) on behalf of his family, saying: 'in case we all die without Heirs [it will] go to the Gordon family – as does the Freehold' (W239). It was addressed to Clare Hall Lodge, Cambridge, to [Theodore] Gould, who had been admitted to the college in 1753 and in 1787 married Philip Williams's sister Anne (Letter 123). Other photos are of Mrs Havilland, mother of Agnes, the wife of PW(V), Charles Williams's son (W332); and of a memorial inscription of the Quellyn family (W333-334). Also preserved is a list of portraits, books etc in the possession of Mrs Beatrice Simeon, who had married Algernon B. Simeon (1847-1906), a grandson of PW(IV), (W234; Bigg-Wither, 1907, p.147).

The papers include a letter of 14 March 1787 (W196) to Philip Williams's first wife Sarah Collins, from Miss Elizabeth Beauclerk, daughter of Topham Beauclerk (2nd husband of Lady Diana Spencer, the mother of the Hon. George Richard St John, himself the husband of Sarah Williams's sister Charlotte and later 3rd viscount Bolingbroke) and a sister of Mary, who had an incestuous relationship with St John (*see* Chapter 15). A sad end to Charlotte's life is portrayed in three letters written between 22 April 1800 and 3 October 1803 from the St John seat at Lydiard Tregoze, Wiltshire, and the Hot Springs, Bristol, to Sarah's daughters, Elizabeth ('Betsy') and Charlotte (W196a-c).

A letter written in 4 February 1832 to Betsy, who suffered from a lifelong psychiatric disorder, by her younger sister Charlotte, a few days before her own death, demonstrates the cheerful tone that the latter was generally able to bring to life, even under adversity (W198). A few years after the death of her father, between 7 March 1832 and 25 October 1834, Betsy made notes about payments to be made in the event of her own death (W227-229). After the death of Charlotte she seems at first to have gone to live at Gedling, Nottinghamshire, where her brother Charles Williams was incumbent (W201), though a cover dated 10 years later shows that she was by then living at Bar End, Winchester (W226).

The papers include items relating to Philip Williams's aunt, Heleonora Theabella Williams ('Aunt Bell'), who died in 1789 (*see* Chapter 13), including copies of an inscription on her tomb in Ely Cathedral, erected to her memory by her nephew Charles Nalson Cole (W309-310), and a copy of 'ravishing' 20-line verse on her by Soame Jenyns (1704-1787) written in 1737. This resides in one of the 115 large format volumes of manuscripts (BM Add. MS 334498) of the antiquary William Cole (1714-1782), rector of Bletchley, now on the edge of Milton Keynes, Buckinghamshire, to whom it was sent by a 'Sam Knight Esq' in 1779 (W240-241).

The papers contain many notes and letters, of varying significance, which were mostly generated by PW(VI)'s efforts and are merely listed here. A key source is an opened-up envelope containing scribbled notes and a family tree based on the findings of Mrs Edwyn Jervoise and her father, PW(VI), on the Williams family history, probably researched in the 1930s (W418). A number of other miscellaneous items (W230-236) includes letters from Canon E.H. Firth in 1928 concerning the rectory of Houghton, Hampshire, once held by Philip Williams (W230-231); a letter of May 1932 from Herbert Chitty, Winchester College Archivist, answering a query about the Dyson family (W232); an undated article from the Compton Parish Magazine about Philip Williams and other clergy of the parish, almost certainly written by J.S. Drew (W233); various papers, letters and documents relating to genealogical research, carried out between about 1899 and 1904 by PW(VI) as a young man with the help of the Lord Lieutenant of Flintshire, H.R. Hughes (W250-308; *see also* Chapter 1); miscellaneous genealogical jottings and notes on: the Dyson family, Charles W. Cornwall, Charles Jenkinson 1st earl of Liverpool, and the Gordon family (W311-330, 337-348); two copies of a photograph of a memorial tablet to members of the Quellyn family, related to the Williams family (W333-334); trial pedigrees of members of the Williams family (W401, 418); various letters, printed matter and newspaper cuttings concerning and by R.S. Barter, Warden of Winchester College, also involving John L. Elliot, H.G. Merriman, Mrs Jane ('Janie') Merriman and Janet her daughter, David Williams, Warden of New College, Oxford, and Anna his daughter 1848-ca 1874 (W402a-413); book plates of a Philip Williams, probably PW (IV), reproduced in this volume (W414); a copy of the Long Roll of Winchester College for 1755, when Philip Williams was elected to a scholarship (W415); a letter written in 1938 from the rector of Doddington, March, Cambridgeshire, where PW(I) was incumbent, to Mr and Mrs [Edwyn] Jervoise, with information from the parish registers on the Williams family (W419); a photograph of a portrait, said to be of Lady Bolingbroke, née Charlotte Williams, by Romney, but probably misassigned (W421); a print of the poet William Collins, a Wykehamist, aged 14 (W422; the Fellows' Library of Winchester College holds a copy of *The Poetical Works of Mr William Collins*, with an inscription on the flyleaf recording that it was given by PW(IV) to his sister Charlotte, though the notion that the poet was related to Thomas Collins, Sarah Williams's father, has no foundation; genealogical jottings (W423-430); typed extracts concerning Philip Williams from both *A Country Gentleman of the Nineteenth Century*, by F. Awdry, Winchester, 1906, a memoir of Sir William Heathcote of Hursley Park, Hampshire (W431), and *Compton, near Winchester: Being an Enquiry into the History of a Hampshire Parish*, by J.S. Drew, Winchester, 1939 (W432a-c).

Transcription

The only extensive transcripts known to have been made from the Williams Paper are of the letters between Philip and Sarah Williams (W5-93). There exist three different transcripts, termed A, B and C, of which A and B both predate by about 75 or more years the third transcript, C, which was made for this volume, and is available online at www.winchester.org/archives. Major editorial style decisions used in making transcript C are given at the head of the Letters.

The main differences between the three different transcripts are:

1. A and C are complete, whereas B, although extensive, is not.

2. A and B both contain identically some misreadings that further research has allowed to be corrected in C (*see* examples below).

3. In B and C the letters are laid out in paragraphs, generally based on the correspondents' use of long dashes.

4. All transcripts follow the correspondents' spelling and capitalisation, but in C short forms have been expanded, such as 'ye' to 'the' and 'yt' to 'that'.

Transcript A bears the piece numbers assigned by Clanchy, as written in pencil on the originals. In addition, the originals and the pages of the transcript each bear other sequences of numbers, different from each other and from the sequence used in Transcript B (*see* below). No attempt has been made to analyse these additional number sequences.

Transcript A was donated as part of the Williams Papers and was probably typed, or commissioned, by Mrs Jervoise, or her father, PW(VI). The quality of the typing is not professional, though the hand-corrected transcripts are generally well done and only suffer from the fact that much of the research needed to interpret them had not been done. As well as the piece numbers of the catalogue, A bears notes, variously typed and handwritten, concerned with dates, such as 'No date' (in typescript) and (in handwriting) 'February 1785…probably the 5th'; the latter are in a hand that also appears on B and the dates accord with the dates assigned in B (which uses round brackets to indicate dates assigned by the transcriber).

Transcript B was typed to a professional quality and a copy is kept in the library of Winchester Cathedral (W57C/7). Its numbering system is totally different from that of the catalogue. All but a few of the letters between Philip and Sarah Williams were included in it, the exceptions, for no known reason, being WCA/M/PW 28, 45, 51 and 80 (Letters 57, 62, 94 *&* 112). It is prefaced by a short note on the career of Philip Williams, and the Williams family in general, including a family tree, together with a few extracts from other items in the Williams Papers. It contains a few explanatory footnotes which have generally proven to be accurate, and have been used in this study, such as, in Letter 41: 'Philip Williams was collated to the Prebend of Stow in Lindsey on Nov. 10, 1783, and installed at Lincoln Cathedral on the 15th of that month.' Some of the letters were not transcribed in full in B; for example, the attendees at the many parliamentary dinners that Philip Williams attended were not copied. Also, quite reasonably, long dashes in the originals were interpreted as paragraph breaks.

Although Transcript B is unsigned, it has been unequivocally identified by by a former librarian of Winchester Cathedral, John Hardacre (pers. comm.), as the work of the local historian and medievalist John Summers Drew – a most scholarly man – who spent much time in the library translating medieval Latin documents (Turnbull, 1992). He lived in the village of Compton, where Philip Williams was rector for nearly 50 years, and – in an age before the photocopier – almost certainly used A to prepare his own transcript, B, for his book, *Compton, near Winchester: Being an Enquiry into the History of a Hampshire Parish*, published locally in 1939. In the preface he acknowledged the help of 'Mrs Edwyn Jervoise' and in Chapter XI, 'The Eighteenth Century', there are several direct quotes from the Letters. Notebooks by Drew survive (HRO/116A/3-4), but appear to contain nothing on the Williams Papers. He is known to have collaborated with the Canterbury Cathedral Librarian, William Parry Blore (Turnbull, 1992), and probably also with his brother the, Winchester history master, George Henry Blore. Their father was headmaster of the King's School, Canterbury (Blakiston, 1974; Blakiston, In: Blore, 1983).

A convincing sign of a link between A and B is that there are a substantial number of misreadings of the originals in both, as shown below:

(The first number is the piece number in the Winchester College Catalogue and the second is the number assigned in Transcript B)

43/1: both miss out 'that is the rent of hire of furniture'.

18/49: both misread 'Keates' as 'Heats'.

20/54: both misspell 'exhilerated' and 'Wotten', though in A the former is corrected by hand.

56/32: both have 'blest' not 'blessed' and both add matter to make 'con...' into 'consult', whereas 'construct' makes more sense.

76/62: both have 'Downs' not 'Downes' and 'Thernot (?)' for 'Kernot', due to misreading the K.

93/84: both have 'difficient' for 'deficient' and 'matters' for 'matches'.

Most of these misreadings were passively transcribed Drew, though there are also instances where he made changes that suggest he also had access to the originals. The clear implication of this evidence is that A was made by, or at the request of, Mrs Jervoise or her father, probably at some time before the 1930s, and B was derived from it and a sight of the originals by Drew, with the permission of Mrs Jervoise. His purpose was not to transcribe the Letters in their own right, but rather to use them as a source for his book on the village where Philip Williams was rector for 50 years, *Compton, near Winchester: Being an Enquiry into the History of a Hampshire Parish*, published in Winchester in 1939.

18. *Bibliography*

THIS LIST includes sources cited in the text of this volume as well as in the footnotes to the letters hosted online at www.winchestercollege. org/archives.

Adams, HC, 1878, *Wykehamica, A History of Winchester College and Commoners*, Winchester, Oxford & London.

Anon, 1827, *A Concise Description of Bury Saint Edmund's and its Environs*, London.

—1900, *Historical Register of the University of Oxford*, Oxford.

—ND, *Lydiard Park and Church*, Swindon.

Arnold, FH, 1864, *Petworth: A Sketch of its History and Antiquities*, Petworth.

Ashley-Cooper, FS, 1924, *The Hambledon Cricket Chronicle, 1772-1796*, London.

Awdry, F, 1906, *A Country Gentleman of the Nineteenth Century: Being a Short Memoir of the Right Honourable Sir William Heathcote* [of Hursley, Hampshire, 5th baronet], Winchester.

Baker, T, 1869, *History of the College of St John the Evangelist, Cambridge*, Cambridge.

Ball, C, 1818, *An Historical Account of Winchester, with Descriptive Walks*, Winchester.

Barrett, P, 1988, Philip Williams – the acceptable face of pluralism, *Winchester Cathedral Record*, 57, 13-26.

Barrow, GWS, 1956, *Feudal Britain: the completion of the Medieval Kingdoms, 1066-1314*, London.

Bayley, J., 1830, *Summary of the Laws of Bills of Exchange*, 5ed., London.

Beales, D, 2011, Ch. 3. In: Linehan, P., ed., *St John's College, Cambridge: A History*, Woodbridge, Suffolk.

Bentham, J, 1812, 2 ed., *The History and Antiquities of the Conventual and Cathedral Church of Ely*, vol. II, Cambridge.

Beresford, J, ed., 1924-31, *The Diary of a Country Parson: The Reverend James Woodforde*, 4 vols, Oxford.

Bezzant Lowe, W, 1912, *The Heart of Northern Wales*, Llanfairfechan.

Bigg-Wither RF, 1907, *Materials for a History of the Wither Family*, Winchester.

Binnion, E, 1976, Great days of Hampshire's mail coaches, *Hampshire: The County Magazine*, December, 39-40.

[Blakiston], JMG and G[wyn], PJ, 1971, *Winchester College 1679-1832* (catalogue of an exhibition held in Memorial Buildings in June 1971).

Blakiston, JMG, 1962, Winchester College Library in the eighteenth and early nineteenth centuries, *The library: Transactions of the Bibliographical Society*, 5th series, vol. xvii, 23-45.

—1974, Canterbury and Winchester, George Henry Blore 1870-1960, *Canterbury Cathedral Chronicle*, pp. 9-14.

Bliss, A, 1983, ed., *A Dictionary of Foreign Words and Phrases*, London.

Blomefield, F, 1806, *An Essay... Norfolk [etc]*, vol. 5, London.

Blore GH, 1951. An archdeacon of the eighteenth century, *Winchester Cathedral Record*, 20, 19-22.

—[1944], 'Who's Who for 18th Century: A Biographical Dictionary of Winchester and Neighbourhood', HRO/9M91/W (typescript).

—1944, *Some Wykehamists of the Eighteenth Century*, Winchester.

—1952, *Thomas Rennell, Dean of Winchester, 1805-1840*, Winchester.

—1983, *The Monuments of Winchester Cathedral*, 2 ed., with a biographical foreword and notes by J M G Blakiston, Winchester.

—ND, Winchester in the 18th Century, pp. 1-7, HRO/12M73/Z62, [primary source unknown].

Blunt, R, 1923, *The Letters of Mrs Montagu [1762-1800]*, 2 vols., London.

Boaden, J, 1825, Memoirs of the Life of John Philip Kemble, London, quoted in a review in *The Philomathic Journal and Literary Review*, 1825, vol. II, 414.

Borgman, AS, 1928, *Thomas Shadwell: His Life and Comedies*, New York, reprinted 1969.

Boswell, J, 1786, *Journal of a Tour to the Hebrides with Samuel Johnson LL.D.*, London.

—1791, *The Life of Samuel Johnson*, by James Boswell, London, *see* Womersley, D, ed., 2008.

Bottomley, F, 1988, *The Franking System in the Post Office, 1652-1840*, Society of Postal Historians, London.

Brayne, M, 2008, *Harry Peckham's Tour*, Stroud, Gloucestershire.

Buckley, GB, 1935, *Fresh Light on Eighteenth Century Cricket*, Birmingham.

Burney, F, 1778, *Evelina, see* Doody.

Burke, E, 1775, *Speech of Edmund Burke, Esq. on American Taxation, April 19, 1774*, 2 ed., London.

Buxton, J and Williams P, 1979, *New College, Oxford, 1379-1979*, Oxford.

Campbell, JL, 1848, *The Lives of the Lords Chancellors and Keepers of the Great Seal of England*, vol. II, London.

Capp, B, 1979, *Astrology and the Popular Press, English Almanacs 1500-1800*, London.

Carne, B, 2001, The decline and fall of the St Johns of Lydiard Tregoze, *Reports of the Friends of Lydiard Tregoz* (Swindon), 34, 34-55.

—2006, George Richard (1761-1824), 3rd Viscount Bolingbroke and his families, *Reports of the Friends of Lydiard Tregoz*, (Swindon), 39, 29-46.

Carpenter Turner, B, 1978, *Hampshire Hogs*, vol. 2, Southampton.

—1986, *A History of the Royal Hampshire County Hospital*, Chichester.

—1992, *St John's Winchester Charity*, Chichester.

Carswell, J, and Drake, LA, 1965, eds., *The Political Journal of George Bubb Dodington*, Oxford.

Cash, AH, 2006, *John Wilkes: The Scandalous Father of Civil Liberty*, New Haven & London.

Cecil, GS and Reade C, 1908, *The House of Cornewall*, Hereford.

Charteris, E ed., 1907, *A Short Account of the Affairs of Scotland in the years 1744, 1745 and 1746*, by David Lord Elcho, Edinburgh.

Chitty, H, 1906, *Medal-Speaking at Winchester College, 1761-1815*, Winchester (reprinted from *The Wykehamist*, No. 438).

[Clanchy, VA], 1970, The Williams Letters, *The Wykehamist*, No. 1194, 9 December, 538-541.

Clanchy, VA, 1976, Jane Austen and the Williams family, *Hampshire: The County Magazine*, December, 56-58.

Clark-Maxwell, WG, 1932, Letters of a Derbyshire squire and poet in the early nineteenth century, *Derbyshire Archaeological and Natural History Society's Journal*, 1-24.

Colley, LH, 1977, The Loyal Brotherhood and the Cocoa Tree: The London organisation of the Tory party, 1727-60, *Historical Journal*, 20, 77-95.

Colvin, H, 1995, *A Biographical Dictionary of British Architects, 1600-1840*, 3ed., New Haven.

Cooper, JM, 1999, Leisure and society in Georgian Winchester, *Hampshire Studies (Proc Hampshire Fld Club Archaeol Soc)*, 54, 127-145.

Crook, J, 1984, *The Wainscot Book: The Houses of Winchester Cathedral Close and their Interior Decoration, 1660-1800*, Winchester.

Custance, R 1982, ed., *Winchester College Sixth-Centenary Essays*, Oxford.

Dawson, W, 2014, *A Porter's Daughter*, Winchester.

Donoghue, D, 2003, *Lady Godiva: a Literary History of the Legend*, Oxford.

Doody, M A, 1994, ed., *Evelina* by Frances Burney, 1778, Penguin Classics, London.

Drew, JS, 1939, *Compton, near Winchester: Being an Enquiry into the History of a Hampshire Parish*, Winchester.

Edgcumbe, R, 2000, *The Art of the Gold Chasers of Eighteenth Century London*, Oxford.

Edgeworth, M, 1820, *Belinda*, 2ed., London.

Ellis, A, 1956, *The Penny Universities: A History of the Coffee Houses*, London.

Eliot, S. 2013, ed., *The History of Oxford University Press*, 3 vols., Oxford.

Edmunds, J, 1996, *New College Brats: A History of the Life and Education of the Choristers of New College, Oxford*, Oxford.

Ewald, AC, 1904, *The Life and Times of Prince Charles Stuart*, London.

Facer, R, 2010, *Mary Bacon's World: A Farmer's Wife in Eighteenth-Century Hampshire*, Newbury.

Fearon, WA, 1924, *The Passing of Old Winchester*, Winchester.

Fielding, H, 1742, *Joseph Andrews*, Everyman's Library Edition, 1910.

Finn, P, Johnston, P, eds., 1999, *A History of the Worthy Villages*, Worthys Local History Group, Headbourne Worthy, Hampshire.

Finn, P, 2007, Worthy Down Racecourse, *Worthy History* (Headbourne Worthy, Hampshire), 11, 2-11.

—2009, The Turnpike Road through the Worthys, 1759-1845, (Headbourne Worthy, Hampshire), 3, 2-16.

Firth, JD'E, 1961, *Winchester College*, 2ed., Winchester.

Foster, V, 1898, ed., *The Two Duchesses: Georgiana Duchess of Devonshire, Elizabeth Duchess of Devonshire, Family Correspondence [etc]*, Glasgow & Dublin.

Franklin, MJ, 2011, *Orientalist Jones*, Oxford.

Furley, JS, 1909, *Chernocke House Annals 1859-1909*, Winchester.

Gascoigne, J, 1986, *Cambridge in the Age of Enlightenment: Science, Religion and Politics from the Restoration to the French Revolution*, Cambridge.

Gash, N, 1984, *Lord Liverpool: The Life and Political Career of Robert Banks Jenkinson, Second Earl of Liverpool, 1770-1828*, London.

Gibson, JSW, 1958, *Monumental Inscriptions in Sixty Hampshire Churches*, Basingstoke.

Gilpin, W, 1782, *Observations on the River Wye [etc]*, London.

Gordon, J, 1771, *The Causes and Consequences of Evil Speaking Against Government Considered*, Cambridge, reprinted 2005, Farmington Hills, Michigan.

Gornal, JFG, 1967, Marriage and property in Jane Austen's novels, *History Today* (reprinted as Occasional Paper, No.3, The Jane Austen, Hampshire Group), Winchester.

Graves, A, 1905, *The Royal Academy of Arts: Exhibitors 1769-1904*, vol. 3, London, reprinted 1970, Wakefield and Bath.

Gray, D, 1991, *Chaplain to Mr Speaker*, House of Commons Library Document No. 19, London.

Gray, T, 1775, *Journal in the Lakes*, (written as letters to Dr Thomas Wharton, 1769), London.

Gunn, JAW, 1983, *Beyond Liberty and Property: The Process of Self-Recognition in Eighteenth Century Thought*, Montreal.

Hague, W, 2004, *William Pitt the Younger*, London.

Halliday, FE, 1967, *Doctor Johnson and His World*, London.

Hampton, [J], 1756-61, *The General History of Polybius*, 5 vols., London.

Hargreaves-Maudsley, 1969, WN ed., *Woodforde at Oxford 1759-1776*, Oxford.

Hartshorne, A, 1905, ed., *Memoirs of a Royal Chaplain...Edmund Pyle [etc]*, London.

Hicks, C, 2001, *Improper Pursuits: The Scandalous Life of Lady Di Beauclerk*, London.

Hills, JW, 1921, *A History of Fly Fishing for Trout*, London (reprinted, Winchester, 1973).

Himsworth, S, 1976-1984, *Winchester College Muniments*, vols I-III, Chichester.

Holgate, CW, 1893, *Winchester Commoners, 1800-1835*, Salisbury

Holt-White, R, ed., 1907, *The Letters to Gilbert White from his Intimate Friend and Contemporary, the Rev. John Mulso*, [digitally reprinted by Cambridge University Press, 2011].

Hughes, D, 2001, ed., *Eighteenth Century Women Playwrights*, London.

Ingamells, J, 1997, *A Dictionary of British & Irish Travellers in Italy, 1701-1800*, New Haven & London.

James, TB, 1988, The population size of Winchester over 2,000 years: a survey, *Section Newsletters, Proc Hampshire Fld Club Archaeol Soc*, 9, 1-3.

Johnson, S, 1775, *Journey to the Western Isles*, London.

Karlsson, G, 2000, *Iceland's 1100 Years: History of a Marginal Society*, London.

Kaul, S, 1992, *Thomas Gray and Literary Authority: A Study in Ideology*, Stanford, California.

Kirby, TF, 1888, *Winchester Scholars*, Winchester.

—1892, *Annals of Winchester College*, London.

Kitchin, GW, 1895,*The Manor of Manydown, Hampshire*, Hampshire Record Society, Winchester and London.

Lavery, B, 2003, *The Ships of the Line, vol.1: The Development of the Battle Fleet 1650-1850*, London.

Lassell, R, 1670, *Voyage or a Complete Journey through Italy*, Paris.

Leach, AF, 1899, *A History of Winchester College*, London.

Lefanu, W, ed., 1960, *Betsy Sheridan's Journal*, London.

Le Faye, D, 1995, ed., *Jane Austen's Letters*, 3ed., Oxford.

Lefroy, H, and Turner, G, 2007, eds., *The Letters of Mrs Lefroy: Jane Austen's Beloved Friend*, Winchester.

Leigh, RA Austen, 1907, *Eton College Lists, 1678-1790*, London.

Leighton-Boyce, JAS, 1958, *Smiths the Bankers, 1658-1958*, London.

Levi P, ed., 1984, *Penguin Classic Edition of Samuel Johnson's Journey and James Boswell's Journal*, London.

Locke AA, 1912, *In Praise of Winchester: An Anthology in Prose and Verse*, London.

Lysons, D and S, 1810, *Magna Brittannia ...Cambridgeshire and the County Palatine of Chester*, vol. II, London.

Mack, RL, 2000, *Thomas Gray: A Life*, New Haven.

Macnalty, AS, 1965, ed., *Butterworths Medical Dictionary*, London.

Majendie, LA, 1878, *An Account of the de Majendie family, both French and English, From 1365 to the Present Century*, reprinted 2009, Whitefish, Montana.

Manning, O, Bray, W, 1804-1814, *The History and Antiquities of the County of Surrey*, London.

Marsden, P, 1979, *The Officers of the House of Commons*, London.

[Mayor, JEB], 1893, *Admissions to the College of St John the Evangelist in the University of Cambridge*, Parts I and II, January 1629/30 to 1715, Cambridge.

Meadley, GW, 1809, *Memoirs of William Paley D.D.*, part 4, Sunderland.

Molloy, J, 2009, 'Synthesising success', The Triple Helix, *Cambridge Eight-Hundredth Anniversary Edition*, London, 22.

Nichols, J, 1812, *Literary Anecdotes of the Eighteenth Century*, vol. 1, 2 ed., London.

Nichols J, and Bentley, S, 1815, *Literary Anecdotes of the Eighteenth Century*, London.

Nicolson, B, 1968, *Joseph Wright of Derby: Painter of Light*, vol. 1, London.

Nokes, D, 1997, *Jane Austen: A Life*, London.

Oldfield, J, 1993, Printers, Booksellers and Libraries in Hampshire, 1750-1800, *Hampshire Papers*, No. 3, Winchester.

Osborn, EFD, ed., 1890, *Political and Social Letters of a Lady of the Eighteenth Century*, London.

Page, W, ed., 1905-12, *A History of the County of Hampshire*, London.

Paley, W, 1785, *Principles of Moral and Political Philosophy*, London; reprinted, 2002, Indianapolis.

Pead, PJ, 2009, *Benjamin Jesty: Dorset's Vaccination Pioneer*, Chichester.

Pickering, K, Woolgar M, 2009, *Theatre Studies, Palgrave Foundation Series*, (companion website: www.palgrave.com/theatre: Ch. 8 Undertaking a research project), 63.

Porter, R, 2000, *Enlightenment: Britain and the Creation of the Modern World*, London.
—1994, *London: A Social History*, London.

Pugh, RB, Crittall, E, Crowley, DA, 1999, eds., *A History of Wiltshire: the Kinwardstone Hundred*, vol. 16, London.

Ranger, P, 1996, *The Georgian Playhouses of Hampshire, 1730-1830*, Hampshire Papers No. 10, Winchester.
—1976, The lost theatres of Winchester, 1620-1861, *Proc Hampshire Fld Club Archaeol Soc*, 31, 65-108.

Roach, JPC, 1959, ed. *A History of the County of Cambridge and the Isle of Ely*, vol. III, The City and University of Cambridge, London.

Robinson, H, 1948, *The British Post Office: A History*, New Haven.

Row, EF, 1913, *A History of Midhurst Grammar School*, Brighton.

Sheppard, FHW, 1908, *Survey of London, vol. 40, The Grosvenor Estate in Mayfair*, pt 2, London.

Shiercliff, 1789 [etc], *The Bristol and Hotwell Guide*, Bristol.

Shurlock, B, 2008, Francis Wykeham Swanton (1746-1823) of Worthy, Hampshire [etc], *Hampshire Studies*, 63, 58-75.

—1999, The farmlands and estates of the Worthys. In: Finn, P and Johnston, P, 1999, eds., *A History of the Worthy Villages*, Headbourne Worthy, Hampshire.

—2010, The admiral and the dean, *Worthy History* (Headbourne Worthy, Hampshire), 14, 10-16.

—2011, 'By the rivers of water': Rev. Sir Henry Rivers of Martyr Worthy and family, *Worthy History* (Headbourne Worthy, Hampshire), 15, 13-20.

—2012, A day at the races on Worthy Down, *Worthy History* (Headbourne Worthy, Hampshire), 16, 9-16.

South, M, 2013, Smith inoculation campaigns in eighteenth-century Southampton, Salisbury and Winchester, *The Local Historian*, 43, 122-137.

Squibb, GD, 1972, *Founder's Kin: Privilege and Pedigree*, Oxford.

Steedman, C, 2007, *Master and Servant: Love and Labour in the Industrial Age*, Cambridge.

Stevens, C, 1998, *Winchester Notions: The English Dialect of Winchester College*, London.

Stokes, FG ed., 1931, *The Ble[t]cheley Diary of the Rev. William Cole MA, FSA, 1765-67*, London.

Stone, GW, 1962, *The London Stage, 1660-1800*, part 4: 1747-1776, Carbondale, Illinois.

—1981, ed., *The Stage and the Page: London's 'Whole Show' in the Eighteenth-Century Theatre*, London.

Stray, CA, 2013, Ch. 10, 'Classics'. In: Eliot, S. ed. *The History of Oxford University Press*, vol. II: 1780 to 1896, Oxford.

Styles, J, Vickery A, 2006, eds., *Gender, Taste and Material Culture in Britain and North America, 1700-1830*, New Haven & London.

Sutherland, LS and Mitchell, LG, 1986, eds., *The History of the University of Oxford*, vol. V, The Eighteenth Century, Oxford.

Sykes, N, 1934, *Church and State in England in the Eighteenth Century*, Cambridge.

Tanner, J R, ed., *The Historical Register of the University of Cambridge …to 1910, 1917*, Cambridge.

Thomson, 2006, *Cambridge Introduction to the English Theatre, 1600-1900*, Cambridge.

Tod, G, 1812, *Plans, elevations and sections, of hot-houses, green-houses, and aquarium, conservatories, etc, recently built in different parts of England, for various noblemen and gentlemen*, London.

Tomlinson, H, 2000, Restoration to Reform, 1660-1832. In: Aylmer, G, and Tiller, J, eds., *Hereford Cathedral: A History*, London.

Torry, AF, 1888, *Founders and Benefactors of St John's College, Cambridge, with Notes Chiefly Biographical*, Cambridge [pers. comm., Fiona Colbert, St John's College].

Trollope, TA, 1887, *What I Remember*, 2 vols., London.

Turley, RV, 1975, ed., *Hampshire and Isle of Wight Bibliographies: Selected Nineteenth-Century Sources*, Winchester.

Turnbull, B, 1992, John Summers Drew (1879-1949): A neglected Hampshire Historian, *Proc Hampshire Fld Club Archaeol*, 48, 161-179.

Vesey, F, 1827, *Report of Cases Argued and Determined in the High Court of Chancery, 1789-1817*, vol. IX, 1803-1804, London.

Vickery, A, 1998, *The Gentleman's Daughter: Women's Lives in Georgian England*, New Haven & London.

—2009, *Behind Closed Doors: At Home in Georgian England*, New Haven &London.

Viveash, C and Lefroy, H, 2009, 'Lovers' Vows' in Winchester, *The Jane Austen Society Report for 2008*, Winchester, 106-113.

Warton, J, 1747, *Odes on Various Subjects*, London.

Walsh, J, Haydon, C, and Taylor, S, eds., 1993, *The Church of England c. 1689-1833: from Toleration to Tractarianism*, Cambridge.

Wareham, AF and Wright APM, 2002, *A History of the County of Cambridge and the Isle of Ely*, vol. 10, London.

Wheatley, HB, 1884, ed., *The Historical and Posthumous Memoirs of Sir Nathaniel William Wraxall, 1772-1784*, vol. I, 419, London.

White, J, 2012, *London in the Eighteenth Century: A Great and Monstrous Thing*, London

White, W, 1842, *A History, Gazetteer and Directory of Lincolnshire*, Sheffield.

—1859, *A History, Gazetteer and Directory of Hampshire*, Sheffield.

Williams, OC, 1954, *The Clerical Organization of the House of Commons, 1661-1850*, Oxford.

Winstanley RL, 1986, *The Ansford Diary of James Woodforde*, vol. 4, Winstanley RL, Jameson P, eds. *The Diary of James Woodforde*, 17 vols., The Parson Woodforde Society (www.parsonwoodforde.org.uk).

Womersley, D, ed., 2008, *The Life of Samuel Johnson*, by James Boswell, first published in 1791, London.

Wooll, J, 1806, *Biographical Memoirs of the Late Revd Joseph Warton, D.D.*, London.

Wordsworth, C, 1891, *Annals of My Early Life*, London.

Yorke PC, 1931, ed., *The Diary of John Baker, Barrister of the Middle Temple, Solicitor-General of the Leeward Island [etc]*, London.

19. *Abbreviations*

CCED Clergy of the Church of England Database
        (www.theclergydatabase.org.uk)
HRO   Hampshire Record Office, Winchester
NCA   New College, Oxford, Archives
OCEL Harvey, P., ed., *The Oxford Companion to English Literature*, 4ed.,
        Oxford, 1967
ODNB *Oxford Dictionary of English Biography*
OED   *Oxford English Dictionary.*
RFLT   *Reports of the Friends of Lydiard Tregoz,*
        (www.lydiardparkfriends.org.uk)
W   A short form of the classmark for the Williams Papers in
        Winchester College Archives, WCA/M/PW
WCA   Winchester College Archives
WCM   Winchester College Muniments (now termed WCA).
WSRO West Sussex Record Office, Chichester

Concordance of Letter Nos. & Piece Numbers from the Catalogue

This concordance is provided to enable cross-reference to be made between the Letter numbers used in this volume and the relevant piece numbers of the Winchester College Catalogue of the Williams Papers (classmark WCA/M/PW).

On the left-hand side of the table below is a list of all the Letters in order of the numbers used in this volume, which is chronological, together with the dates (written on the letter or assigned, often from internal evidence), the writer/recipient, and the the piece number.

On the right-hand side are listed the piece numbers in the order of the catalogue and the corresponding numbers of the Letters.

The concordance concerns only the letters on which this volume is based, which are available online at www.winchestercollege.org/archives and held, together with all the other Williams Papers, in Winchester College Archives (open to researchers only by appointment). All references in this volume to these other documents use a truncated citation, so, for example, W395 is an abbreviation for WCA/M/PW/395, where 395 is the piece number in the typescript catalogue of the papers.

Three letters have been imported, with permission, from other archives: Letter 14 from the Hampshire Record Office and Letters 16 and 21 from Oxford University Press.

Abbreviations for 'Writer-Recipient'
'AW', Mrs Anne Williams (later Mrs Gordon); 'PW', Revd Philip Williams, PW(III), 'SW', Mrs Sarah 'Sally' Williams (née Collins), 'JG', Revd Dr John Gordon', 'LBW', Mr Lovelace Bigg (later Bigg-Wither), 'SIS', PW's sisters, Miss Frances 'Fanny' Williams and Mrs Anne 'Nanny' Gould (née Williams), 'SF', Revd Dr Samuel Forster, Oxford University Press.

Winchester College Catalogue Pieces in the order of the Letters

Letters in the order of Winchester College Catalogue Pieces

Letter No.	Date	Winchester College Catalogue Piece No.	Writer-Recipient	Winchester College Catalogue Piece No.	Letter No.
1	18/08/1760	2	AW-PW	2	1
2	07/06/1762	3	AW-PW, JG-PW	3	2
3	29/11/1763	355	LBW-PW	4	8
4	23/02/1765	353	LBW-PW	5	42
5	25/07/1765	354	LBW-PW	6	48
6	19/11/1767	359	JG-PW	7	49
7	11/08/1768	356	LBW-PW	8	60
8	15/09/1768	4	SIS-PW	9	63
9	16/09/1768	360	JG-PW	10	65
10	28/12/1768	361	JG-PW	11	67
11	01/04/1769	363	JG-PW	12	73
12	13/05/1770	368	JG-PW	13	72
13	04/11/1770	362	JG-PW	14	80
14	26/08/1771[a]	Imported: 1	PW-LBW	15	76
15	29/12/1771	364	JG-PW	16	78
16	07/02/1773	Imported: 2	PW-SF	17	83
17	09/01/1774	365	JG-PW	18	86
18	26/06/1774	366	JG-PW	19	88
19	17/03/1775	367	JG-PW	20	90
20	22/09/1775	369	JG-PW	21	98
21	25/11/1777	Imported: 2	PW-SF	22	101
22	02/11/1778	370	JG-PW	23	103
23	[18/07/1780]	29	SW-PW	24	106
24	[22/07/1780]	31	SW-PW	25	108
25	[29/07/1780]	30	SW-PW	26	110
26	21/11/1780	372	JG-PW	27	123
27	[Nov/Dec 1780]	371	JG-PW	28	112
28	31/12/1780	373	JG-PW	29	23
29	[04/02/1781]	32	SW-PW	30	25
30	early 1781	33	SW-PW	31	24
31	[18/02/1781]	34	SW-PW	32	29
32	[23/02/1781]	35	SW-PW	33	30
33	[Feb/Mar 1781]	38	SW-PW	34	31
34	[05/03/1781]	36	SW-PW	35	32
35	[09/03/1781]	37	SW-PW	36	34
36	06/06/1781	374	JG-PW	37	35
37	14/01/1782	375	JG-PW	38	33
38	06/06/1782	376	JG-PW	39	41
39	08/05/[1783]	377	JG-PW	40	44
40	16/06/1783	378	JG-PW	41	46
41	27/07/[1783]	39	SW-PW	42	51
42	13/08/1783	5	PW-SW	43	50
43	09/09/1783	379	JG-PW	44	52
44	03/12/[1783]	40	SW-PW	45	57
45	16/12/1783	380	JG-PW	46	47

Letter No.	Date	Winchester College Catalogue Piece No.	Writer-Recipient	Winchester College Catalogue Piece No.	Letter No.
46	[22/12/1783]	41	SW-PW	47	53
47	May 1784	46	SW-PW	48	54
48	[15/05/1784]	6	PW-SW	49	55
49	16/05/1784	7	PW-SW	50A	61
50	[17/05/1784]	43	SW-PW	50	56
51	[24]/05/[1784]	42	SW-PW	51	62
52	31/05/[1784]	44	SW-PW	52	58
53	Jun 1784	47	SW-PW	53	64
54	Jun 1784	48	SW-PW	54	59
55	21/06/[1784]	49	SW-PW	55	66
56	[28/06/1784]	50	SW-PW	56	68
57	[before July 1784]	45	SW-PW	57	69
58	1/07/1784	52	SW-PW	58	70
59	22/07/[1784]	54	SW-PW	59	71
60	03/07/1784	8	PW-SW	60	74
61	[04/07/1784]	50A	SW-PW	61	75
62	[05/07/1784]	51	SW-PW	62	77
63	17/07/1784	9	PW-SW	63	79
64	[18/07/1784]	53	SW-PW	64	81
65	[24/07/1784]	10	PW-SW	65	82
66	[25/07/1784][b]	55	SW-PW	66	84
67	31/07/1784	11	PW-SW	67	87
68	[01/08/1784][c]	56	SW-PW	68	85
69	[09/08/1784]	57	SW-PW	69	89
70	[16/08/1784]	58	SW-PW	70	91
71	31/01/1785	59	SW-PW	71	92
72	Feb 1785	13	PW-SW	72	93
73	[05/02/1785]	12	PW-SW	73	95
74	[06/02/1785]	60	SW-PW	74	96
75	[13/02/1785]	61	SW-PW	75	97
76	[19/02/1785]	15	PW-SW	76	99
77	[20/02/1785]	62	SW-PW	77	100
78	[26/02/1785]	16	PW-SW	78	102
79	[27/02/1785]	63	SW-PW	79	104
80	[05/03/1785]	14	PW-SW	80	94
81	[06/03/1785][d]	64	SW-PW	81	105
82	[13/03/1785]	65	SW-PW	82	107
83	[19/03/1785]	17	PW-SW	83	109
84	[20/03/1785]	66	SW-PW	84	111
85	[Mar/Apr 1785]	68	SW-PW	85	115
86	[Apr 1785]	18	PW-SW	86	116
87	[Apr 1785]	67	SW-PW	87	117
88	[16/04/1785]	19	PW-SW	88	118
89	[17/04/1785]	69	SW-PW	89	119
90	[23/04/1785]	20	PW-SW	90	120
91	[24/04/1785][e]	70	SW-PW	91	122
92	[01/05/1785]	71	SW-PW	92	124
93	[08/05/1785]	72	SW-PW	93	125
94	May-June 1785[f]	80	SW-PW	353	4
95	[17/05/1785]	73	SW-PW	354	5

Letter No.	Date	Winchester College Catalogue Piece No.	Writer-Recipient	Winchester College Catalogue Piece No.	Letter No.
96	[22/05/1785]	74	SW-PW	355	3
97	[29/05/1785]	75	SW-PW	356	7
98	[04/06/1785]	21	PW-SW	357	132
99	[05/06/1785]	76	SW-PW	358	133
100	[12/06/1785]	77	SW-PW	359	6
101	[18/06/178]5	22	PW-SW	360	9
102	[19/06/1785]	78	SW-PW	361	10
103	25/06/1785	23	PW-SW	362	13
104	26/06/1785	79	SW-PW	363	11
105	03/07/1785	81	SW-PW	364	15
106	09/07/1785	24	PW-SW	365	17
107	10/07/[1785]	82	SW-PW	366	18
108	[16/07/1785]	25	PW-SW	367	19
109	[17/07/1785]	83	SW-PW	368	12
110	23/07/1785	26	PW-SW	369	20
111	[25/07/178]5	84	SW-PW	370	22
112	Jul 1785	28	PW-SW	371	27
113	02/04/1786	381	JG-PW	372	26
114	20/05/1786	382	JG-PW	373	28
115	04/02/1787	85	SW-PW	374	36
116	11/02/[1787]	86	SW-PW	375	37
117	[18/02/1787]	87	SW-PW	376	38
118	25/02/1787	88	SW-PW	377	39
119	[05/03/1787]	89	SW-PW	378	40
120	[11/03/1787]	90	SW-PW	379	43
121	15/03/1787	383	JG-PW	380	45
122	[18/03/1787]g	91	SW-PW	381	113
123	[23/03/1787]	27	PW-SW	382	114
124	[25/03/1787]	92	SW-PW	383	121
125	[01/04/1787]	93	SW-PW	384	126
126	16/05/1787	384	JG-PW	385	127
127	10/07/1787	385	JG-PW	386	128
128	22/09/1787	386	JG-PW	387	129
129	26/04/1788	387	JG-PW	388	130
130	12/06/1788	388	JG-PW	389	131
131	21/05/1789	389	JG-PW		
132	04/11/1789	357	LBW-PW		
133	25/02/1790	358	LBW-PW		

Footnotes: a. 26-29/08/1771; b.25-26/07/1784; c.1-2/08/1784; d.6-7/03/1785; e.24-25/04/1785; f. 08/05/1785 to 25/06/1785; g. 18-19/03/1787

Appendix II

Philip Williams's Appointments

Fellow, New College, Oxford	1760-1769
Editor, The Works of Polybius (OUP, unpublished)	1767-1804
Rector of Easington, Oxfordshire	1767-1773
Fellow of Winchester College[1]	1769-1819
Chaplain to the Rt Hon. Charles Jenkinson (later 1st earl of Liverpool)[2]	?1769-?
Vicar of Milborne Port, Dorset[3]	1770-?1778
Rector of Bradford Peverell, Dorset	1773-1781
Rector of Compton, Hampshire[4]	1780-1831
Rector of Gosberton, Lincolnshire[5]	1781-1830
Canon of Stow St Mary, Lincoln	1783-1831
Chaplain to the Speaker of the House of Commons	1784-1789
11th Canon of Canterbury	1789-1797
6th Canon of Winchester	1797-1831
Rector of Houghton, Hampshire[6]	1797-1830
Treasurer, Dean and Chapter, Winchester[7]	1805-1815

[1] *At various times he served as one of the two annual bursars (Himsworth, 1976, Vol. I, xli-lii).*

[2] *The source for this, the 'Andrews MSS', cited by Drew, J. S., [1935], in Transcript B of the Letters (Winchester Cathedral Library, W10/7) cannot be identified, and there is no entry for Philip Williams as a chaplain to Charles Jenkinson, Lord Liverpool, in the Register of Noblemen's Chaplains, Lambeth Palace Library (F5/1/13-14). Personal communication, R. Cosgrave, 2012.*

[3] *No cession record can be found, but by 1778 John Ballard was the incumbent.*

[4] *On 5 September 1828, John Pilkington was licensed curate on an annual stipend of £75 p.a. Previously he was curate at Oving, near Chichester.*

[5] *On 3 March 1806, John Calthrop was licensed curate on an annual stipend of £35 p.a. and on 2 March 1830 instituted rector, following Philip Williams's resignation.*

[6] *On 30 August 1828, John Smith was licensed curate on an annual stipend of £75 p.a.*

[7] *Drew, J. S., [1935], Transcript B of the Letters (Winchester Cathedral Library, W10/7).*

Appendix III

Dates of Parliamentary Sessions 1784-1790 and Corresponding Letters

Year(s)	Session dates[1]	Letters[2]	Comment
1784	18 May to 20 August	WCA/M/PW/ 6-11, 42-58	Philip Williams took office as chaplain to the Speaker in May, and gave a sermon on 16 August.[3,4]
1785	25 January to 2 August	WCA/M/PW/ 12-26, 28, 59-84	'...the address was given by the Rev Thomas Heathcote, who had officiated during the illness of Mr Williams'[3]
1786	24 January to 11 July	None	Philip Williams gave an address on 5 July[2,3]
1787	23 January to 30 May	WCA/M/PW/ 27, 85-93	Sarah Williams died on 19 September 1787
1787/88	15 November to 11 July	None	
1788/89	20 November to 11 August	None	On 2 January 1789, Speaker Cornwall died at Whitehall.
1790	21 January to 10 June	None	

[1]*Namier and Brooke, 1986, 1754-1790, vol. 1, p. 536.*
[2]*Piece numbers; for corresponding Letter numbers,* see *the Concordance (Appendix I).*
[3]*Gray, 1991, p. 68;*
[4]*Journal of the House of Commons, General Index XXXV-LV, 1774-1800, p. 416, citing volumes XL, 470 and XLII, 297; XLI, 155.*

Appendix IV

Phillip Williams on Edmund Burke's Speech of 1774 on American Taxation

Extracts from Philip Williams's critique of the Speech of Edmund Burke, Esq. on American Taxation, given on April 19, 1774, written in a copy of the 1775 edition of the text kept in the Fellows' Library, Winchester College (Shelf Mark BB12). Burke's text is shown below in Roman type and Philip Williams's handwritten comments in italics

p. 39: 'However the title of this Act of George the Second, notwithstanding the words of donation, considers it merely as a regulation of trade...'

So then parliament is at liberty to be as bountiful as it pleases in acts of donation, out of the goods of the Americans, provided it does not use terms of donation: or it may even use terms of donation in the preamble, or in the body of the act, provided the title of it be a title of regulation. So that the stamp act would have been good and constitutional, provided Mr Grenville had bethought himself to intitle it "an act to regulate the transfer of property into his majesties colonies and plantations in America".

p. 40: 'It was therefore in some measure with their consent...'

It was then with their consent that the commons – did what? gave and granted one should suppose, a duty to be levied on the colonists – No- says this gentleman though there was an act of donation – though there were the terms of donation; still it was no donation. For "it was an act of prohibition, not of revenue" – Should we suspect the accuracy of this hon. writer we are referred to?

p. 43: '...pains have been taken to inflame our minds... that in America the act of navigation neither is, or ever was, obeyed. But if you take the Colonies through, I affirm, that its authority never was disputed...'

What truth there is in this representation, the journals of the H. of Commons will inform us. From them we learn that so early as the year 1701 impediments were thrown in the way of the king's officers; combinations were formed against those who had the courage to execute the trusts reposed in them with fidelity; that the administration of justice was delayed, and the greatest unwillingness expressed to submit to any exercise of the supremacy of the mother country, and in particular to the acts of trade and navigation.

pp. 55-6: 'On the 15th of February, 1765, whilst the stamp-act was under deliberation, they refused with scorn even so much as to receive four petitions from ...respectable Colonies...'

Nothing is more common than to reject motions for receiving [sic] petitions against bills; more particularly when the principle of the bills has already been discussed: still more when the objections against them are drawn from topics which the house will not allow to be brought into question. It could hardly be expected that the house would allow the supreme authority of parliament or the extent of their power to be canvassed at their bar.

Yet what cannot a great genius effect? by force of the single word scornfully this rejection of petitions has been branded as inequitable and unparliamentary.

p. 51: '...this act was but a beginning of sorrows..

Thus appeared it to this orator; to me, to any one, who deigned to read the statute book, it must appear at the utmost but a continuation of sorrows.

p.67: '...[a] short current phrase, which the court leaders have given out to all their corps, in order to take away the credit of those who would prevent you from that frantic war you are going to wage upon your Colonies. Their cant is this; "All the disturbances in America have been created by the repeal of the Stamp Act".

No man ever meant to attribute a precedent disturbance to a subsequent measure. No man ever thought that the disturbances previous to the repeal of the stamp act were caused by that repeal. But many have thought and continue to think that the timid repeal of that act did cause all the disturbances that have succeeded [it].

pp.69-70: Citing a letter from the commander in chief General Gage of 4 November, in which he said 'unless the [stamp] act, from its own nature, enforce itself, nothing but a very considerable military force can do it.'

It appears from a letter to Mr Sec. Conway laid before the house and [cited] in the parliamentary debates "that when the Boston mob, raised first by the instigation of the principal inhabitants, allured by plunder, rose shortly after of their own accord; people then began to be terrified at the spirit they had raised: that each individual feared he might be the next victim to their rapacity; that the same fears spread through the other provinces; and that as much pains were then taken to prevent the insurrections of the people as before to excite them."

Upon this authority surely one may be allowed to believe that the disturbances caused by the stamp act were not of so dangerous a nature as the disturbances which have happened since the repeal of the stamp act.

pp.71-2: 'As to the fact of a strenuous opposition to the stamp act...I never heard a more languid debate in this House. No more than two or three gentlemen, as I remember, spoke against the act, and that with great reserve and remarkable temper.'

On the 18th of September a committee was appointed at Boston ["]to draw up and transmit to Mr Conway and Col. Barre, addresses of thanks for their patriotic speeches in parliament in favour of the rights and privileges of the colonists; and to desire correct copies thereof to be placed amongst their most precious archives."

I learn too from the same account "that they voted the pictures of these gentlemen to be placed in their town hall." This seems rather an extraordinary compliment than otherwise to be paid to speakers in so languid a debate "to orators who spoke with so great a reserve, and so remarkable a temper.["]

p. 75: [He argues that America was quiet after the repeal of the stamp act, and quotes from an address of 'the obnoxious Colony of Massachuset's Bay' to Governor Bernard]: "If it is not now in our power ... in so full a manner as will be expected, to shew our respectful gratitude to the Mother Country, or to make a dutiful and affectionate return to the indulgence of King and Parliament, it shall be no fault of ours; for this we intend, and hope we shall be able fully to effect." '

This is quoted as the genuine expression of their real sentiments, as originating from themselves. What then will be the feelings of the reader, when he learns that these pretended expressions of the Bostonians were expressions of their own: that they are only re-ecchoed back from the speech of the governour: that the assembly refused so much as to take into consideration the very measures to which these words had been applied by him: that the whole tenor of the address is perhaps one of the sourest, most sullen, most surly, that ever was presented to a governour.

Appendix V

Lovelace Bigg-Wither and the London stage

Two letters from Lovelace Bigg (hereafter called Bigg-Wither, as he was named later; *see* Chapter 3) to Philip Williams are mainly concerned with the London stage. In a self-conscious schoolboyish letter written in November 1763 (Letter 3), he parades a wide knowledge of the theatre, commenting on Elizabethan plays such as Shakespeare's *A Midsummer Night's Dream*, *Philaster or Love Lies Bleeding*, by Beaumont and Fletcher, first performed in about1606, and several Restoration dramas, including *Venice Preserved* by Thomas Otway (a Wykehamist) of 1682, *The Squire of Alsatia* by Thomas Shadwell (c1640-1692) of 1688, and *The Old Batchelor*, William Congreve's highly successful first play, which opened at Drury Lane Theatre, London, in 1693. He also mentions *The Beggar's Opera* by John Gay, first performed in 1728, *Miss in Her Teens*, a farce by David Garrick of 1747, and, most contemporaneously, *The Deuce is in Him* by George Colman, which had its first appearance at Drury Lane Theatre 4 November 1763, only a few weeks before the date assigned to the Letter.

Bigg-Wither is especially concerned with the performances of the actors and was obviously well acquainted with *The Rosciad*, Churchill's savage satire on the London stage, which had been published two years earlier and shot the author to instant fame. He was voyeuristically excited by 'bed and board' comment of the 'Fairy Queen' (presumably Titania [check]) in *Midsummer Night's Dream* and in the context of *The Squire of Alsatia* felt bound to mention 'stage morality'; by which he seems to mean the morality served up in plays about outlawed criminals who lived outside the walls of the City of London, in an area called 'Alsatia'. There is an element of 'young lads on the town' in his remarks – you can almost hear the giggles when the word 'firk' (with several meanings, well illustrated in the OED) is used on stage and obviously mistaken for another four-letter word. But even so Bigg-Wither tries to maintain a serious tone in the Letter, as you might expect between two young men whose whole friendship had been forged in a scholarly, environment.

The names of the actors he mentions, by surname only, can reliably be identified from those active at the time, all at the Drury Lane Theatre, namely, Thomas King, William O'Brien, Richard Yates and his wife Mary Ann Yates, Charles Holland, William Powell and Isabella Vincent. In the

1760s, the London stage and its two patent theatres offered a remarkable feast of theatre and opera that has been meticulously recorded (Stone, 1962). A notable event (in hindsight) took place on 6 June 1764 at Covent Garden, when a concert on harpsichord and organ was given by 'Miss and Master Mozart'. On 29 November 1763 Lovelace Bigg-Wither wrote to Philip Williams with detailed impressions of a several performances he had recently seen in a season that had started on 17 September. The previous season had witnessed some of the most serious riots ever, when the chandeliers at Drury Lane were ruined and the auditorium of Covent Garden severely damaged. The ringleader was a Thaddeus Fitzpatrick, who objected to abolition of the half-price entrance accorded after the third act of the main piece - and he won!

For his part, David Garrick at Drury Lane had abolished the 'loungers' who used to sit on the stage, from where they would heckle actors. When Bigg-Wither was writing the great actor/impresario was, however, out of the country and Drury Lane was in the hands of George Colman the Elder (ca 1732-1794), whilst the actor-singer-manager John Beard co-managed Covent Garden. During the 1763-4 season audiences were treated to no less than 472 performances, many in the traditional pattern of a main piece followed by an afterpiece or farce. Because the programme changed from day to day, and any given main piece was not generally played with the same afterpiece, the details given by Bigg-Wither can sometimes be attached to specific performances.

As he notes, in the 1763-4 season a newcomer to the stage in Beaumont and Fletcher's *Philaster* was William Powell (1735/6-1769), who had given up a career in a City counting-house to be coached by Garrick. He received 'prodigious applause' when he first appeared at Drury Lane on 8 October 1763. *Philaster* was one of the successes of the season and made about 18 performances. The production seen by Bigg-Wither was probably that of 21 November, when it was followed by the popular farce *The Deuce is in Him*, written by George Colman himself and first performed only a couple of weeks earlier. Bigg-Wither gives a lengthy account, generally accurate, though he misnames the apothecary Dr Prattle 'Mr Tattle'. David Garrick's farce *Miss in Her Teens*, first produced in 1747, appeared on 15 November at Covent Garden after *Comus*, with Miss Elizabeth Vincent in 'her second appearance [on] any stage'. Bigg-Wither suggests she was still in her teens, but if the Oxford DNB is correct she was in fact aged only 6 and was understandably watched over by her young mother, the singer Mrs Isabella Vincent (1734/5-1802). The performance of *Miss in Her Teens* seen by Bigg-Wither was probably that of 22 November, when it followed John Gay's *The Beggar's Opera*, with Polly played by Miss Charlotte Brent.

Bigg-Wither also gives his reactions to what is obviously some form of *A Midsummer's Night Dream*. During the season it was first produced as Shakespeare had intended, as a main piece, at Drury Lane on 23 November, and then three days later as an afterpiece, *The Fairy Tale*, when it followed a production of *The Jealous Wife*. The uncut play had been savaged by critics and the diarist William Hopkins noted that 'the performers first sung the audience to sleep, and then went to sleep themselves.' But the cut version was well received: 'Serious parts quite out. Went off well,' records the prompter. Colman had pulled the fat from the fire, virtually overnight, by accepting that his 'authentic production' was a light entertainment. In fact, *The Fairy Tale* became a popular afterpiece and was performed from time to time for several years. Bigg-Wither probably went to the first performance on 26 November, but 'after dinner', for the afterpiece only, as he offers no comment on *The Jealous Wife*.

Similarly, on 18 November, he might only have seen the second half of a programme that started with *Richard III*, followed by *The Squire of Alsatia*, with Miss Vincent playing Isabella, alongside her mother as Mrs Termagant. Billed as 'not acted these 10 years', it is said to have been 'the last important revival' of Thomas Shadwell's comic masterpiece (Borgman, 1928, p. 207). Other performances of the play that Bigg might have seen were on 24 November, when it was followed by Isaac Bickerstaffe's 'musical entertainment' *Thomas and Sally*, or *The Sailor's Return*, or on 28 November, with *Harlequin Sorcerer* as the afterpiece. *Venice Preserved* by Wykehamist Thomas Otway is also brought into the letter by Bigg-Wither when he mentions the character Belvidera. This was produced at Drury Lane on 22 and 24 November 1763 with Mrs Mary Ann Yates as Belvidera, but his choice of words suggests that he did not see it himself.

Bigg-Wither continued to have a strong interest in the stage, which he shared in correspondence with Philip Williams. In a missive written two years later (Letter 4), when he is starting out on a career as a lawyer (with little commitment, it seems), he writes: 'We men of business seldom find time enough to see a play.' But he then goes on to report what he has heard of *Maid of the Mill*, an opera by Isaac Bickerstaffe, with music by Samuel Arnold and others, which had just been premiered, opining that it has 'bad English words...set to good Italian tunes, that it is inferior to *Love in a Village*, and owes great part of its success to what some call the absurdities of [Edward 'Ned'] Shuter.' *Love in a Village* had been a great success and is now regarded as the first English comic opera. With music by Thomas Arne, and words by the Irish playwright Isaac Bickerstaffe (not to be confused with Jonathan Swift's pseudonym), it too relied much on Shuter when it opened at Covent Garden in 1762. Other works mentioned are *Pharnaces*, an opera on the life of the heroic Greek leader 'altered from the Italian' by Thomas Hull, the libretto of which was published in 1765, and *The Platonic* Wife by Elizabeth Griffith, one of the surprisingly numerous women playwrights of the eighteenth century (Hughes, 2001). It had first performed at the Drury Lane Theatre only a month before Letter 4 was written, but was harshly received by critics (Elizabeth Eger, 'Elizabeth Griffith', ODNB).

Appendix VI

Money values in the Late Eighteenth Century

In 1780-1790, a pound would buy goods to the value in 2005 of about £60, whilst a craftsman in the building trade in the same period would be paid about 5s. a day. By 1800 the buying power of money had approximately halved due to inflation, but the wage rate had fallen, to about 3s. a day. (Source: The National Archives, Currency Converter).

Index

Webb, Mrs William (née Anne Gould),
236
Webb, William, 236
Wellingore, Lincs., 238
Wells, James, 188
Wells, P & G, bookshop, 16
Wells, Somerset, 271, 273
West Indies, 149, 197, 217
Westcombe, Nicholas, 222
Westminster Election (1784), 170, 192,
274
Wetherell, Nathan, 25, 168
Wexham, Bucks., 261
Weyhill, Hants, 120
Weymouth, 3rd viscount, 54, 160-61
Wheeler, Dr Benjamin, 81-2
Whig politics, 5-7, 16, 97, 135, 153, 227-
9, 273
White, Gilbert, 120, 143, 277, 289
Whitehead, William, 19-20
White's Club, London, 273
Whitmore, Edward, 36, 38
Whitworth, County Durham, 225
Who's Who [in the] Eighteenth
Century: A Biographical Dictionary
of Winchester and Neighbourhood'
(Blore), 299-300
Wilkes, John, 16
William (manservant,1), 136, 185
William (manservant, 2), 136-7
*William Pitt Addressing the House of
Commons on the French Declaration of
War, 1793* (Hickel), 267
Williams family, *see* Genealogy
Williams Letters, xiv, 66, 84, 127, 103-4,
145, 162, 293-5, 304-13; *see also*
Online access
Williams Papers, xiv, 293-313
Williams, Anne, *see* Gould, Mrs
Theodore
Williams, Charles, 115, 125-7, 134, 216,
246, 307-9, [37]
Williams, Charlotte, 118, 124, 128, 131,
140, 255, 283, 301, 309
Williams, Daniel (fellow of Winchester),
24, 37, 43-5, 134, 161, 216
Williams, Daniel (of Llanpythid), 23
Williams, Daniel, 45
Williams, David, 310
Williams, Elizabeth ('Bess', 'Betsy',
'Crab'), 117-19, 131, 140, 175, 204,
300-1, 306-7, 309

Williams, Frances ('Fanny'), 8-9, 105,
232-3, 242, 254
Williams, Heleonora Theabella ('Aunt
Bell'), 3, 9, 226, 233-4, 239-42, 309
Williams, John, archbishop of York, 2
Williams, Lettice Mary, *see* Jervoise, Mrs
Edwyn
Williams, Mary, *see* Cole, Mrs Charles
Williams, Mrs, Anne, *see* Gordon, Mrs
John
Williams, Mrs Charles (née Charlotte
Roberts), v, 289
Williams, Mrs Daniel, 134
Williams, Mrs Philip (I), (née Elizabeth
Nalson), v, 305
Williams, Mrs Philip (III), (1) (née Sarah
Collins, 'Sally'), ix; absence of
husband, 172, 183, 243-53;
addresses to husband, 90, 110-11;
almanacs, 185, 188; ambitions for
husband, 158, 296; breast-feeding,
125-7, 289; card games, 200;
childbearing, 117, 122; children's
education , 117, 128-8, 218; church
attendance, 220; clergyman's wife,
285; coterie, 190-207, 221, 285;
cricket, 205; crime, 148; death, 186,
253-4; decoration of house, 187;
depression, 103, 109, 111-13,123,
200-1, 246, 250-3; domestic
finances 137-9, 142, 183-5, 244-5,
262, 265, 285; education, 90-91;
extreme weariness, 124-5; female
friend, 93; gardening, 143-4; gifts of
game, 142-3, 204; gynaecological
problems, 116; horses, 263, 265;
house in Kingsgate Street, 89-90,
142, 148, 205, 216, 265, 297;
housework, 200; indebtedness, 184;
iron oven, 188; knowledge of
Italian, 91; letter-writing, 103-4,
106-10; literary tastes, 92, 289;
living in London (plans), 61-2, 114,
121, 136-7, 244-8, 263, 266;
marriage settlement , 306; memorial
inscription (Compton), 255-6, [42];
miscarriages, 115, 144, 248; move
to Compton; on life in the country,
271, 273-4; on marriage, 113, 138,
203, 235-6, 238,279; on Pitt the
Younger, 199; on Reform, 171; on
sexual impropriety, 212-14; on 3rd

348